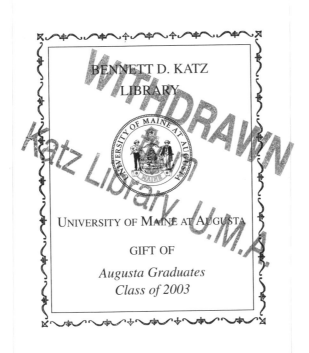

Family Romance, Family Secrets

Family Romance, Family Secrets

Case Notes from
an American Psychoanalysis,
1912

Elizabeth Lunbeck and Bennett Simon

Yale University Press

New Haven & London

Published with assistance from the Louis Stern Memorial Fund.

Set in Adobe Garamond type by The Composing Room of Michigan, Inc.,
Grand Rapids, Michigan. Printed in the United States of America by Sheridan
Books, Ann Arbor, Michigan.

Library of Congress Cataloging-in-Publication Data

Lunbeck, Elizabeth.
    Family romance, family secrets : case notes from an American
psychoanalysis. 1912 / Elizabeth Lunbeck and Bennett Simon.
        p.   cm.
    Includes bibliographical references (p.) and index.
    ISBN 0-300-09214-8
        1. Emerson, Louville Eugene—Notebooks, sketchbooks, etc.
    2. Psychoanalysis—Case studies.   3. Psychoanalysis—United States—
History—20th century   I. Simon, Bennett, 1933–   II. Title.

RC509.8 .L864   2003
616.89′17—dc21

                                                            200233164

A catalogue record for this book is available from the British Library. The paper in
this book meets the guidelines for permanence and durability of the Committee on
Production Guidelines for Book Longevity of the Council on Library Resources.

10   9   8   7   6   5   4   3   2   1

If these day-dreams are carefully examined, they are found to serve as the fulfillment of wishes and as a correction of actual life. They have two principal aims, an erotic and an ambitious one. . . . the child's imagination becomes engaged in the task of getting free from the parents of whom he now has a low opinion and of replacing them by others, who, as a rule, are of higher social standing. . . . It is, as a rule, precisely these neurotic children who were punished by their parents for sexual naughtiness and who now revenge themselves on their parents by means of phantasies of this kind.
Sigmund Freud, "Family Romances"

It is obvious that psychoanalysis is necessary for discovering the more intimate forms of family relationship. In a psychoanalysis all kinds of data come to light that remain otherwise entirely hidden.
L. E. Emerson, "The Psychopathology of the Family"

Contents

Acknowledgments

This book would never have come to fruition without the generosity, clinical insights, and hard work of many friends and colleagues. We wish to thank especially Christopher Bullock, Kenneth Levin, Eugene Taylor, and Russell Vasile, all of whom, in the context of a study group on the history of psychiatry and psychoanalysis, wrestled with the case, formulated interpretations of it, and prepared searching essays on it from which we have benefited greatly. Irene Briggin went over the case with an extraordinarily sensitive eye, offering us comments that prompted us to look at it afresh. Peter Brown, Axel Hoffer, and William McGuire read the entire manuscript; we are thankful for their informed and incisive commentaries. Lisa Herschbach and Julie Puckett assisted us in many ways in the early stages of this project, along the way offering us invaluable thoughts on the nature of the transactions between Emerson and his patient. Gladys Topkis of Yale University Press has been a source of encouragement and insight from the start. Gail Schmitt helped to prepare the final manuscript with care and efficiency. We thank them all.

We have presented portions of this material to various audiences, both singly and collaboratively, and have benefited from the responses and critiques of many listeners and readers. We are especially grateful to John Forrester and José Brunner for their astute comments at the Centennial Freud Conference in Jerusalem, December 2000, which forced us to rethink our interpretation of the case and, in the end, improved it immeasurably.

We would not have undertaken this project without the support and cooperation of Richard J. Wolfe, former curator of rare books and manuscripts at the Francis A. Countway Library of Medicine, Boston, which holds the Emerson Papers. Since then, both Jack Eckert and Thomas A. Horrocks have been unstinting in their assistance, in matters large and small. Eugene Taylor was instrumental in assembling Emerson's materials, for which all of us are in his debt. We have received generous financial support from several institutions; Simon and Russell Vasile from the Milton Fund, Harvard University; Simon from the Research Committee, Boston Psychoanalytic Society and Institute; Lunbeck, from Princeton University and from the National Library of Medicine, grant number RD1LM05934.

Note on the Text

Handwritten notes for sessions 1 through 12 and for sessions 80 through 292 are in Emerson Papers; handwritten notes for sessions 13 through 76 have not survived (we have notes in both forms for session 77), presumably discarded as Emerson typed them up (or had them typed). Despite the fact that handwritten notes for the initial twelve sessions exist, amounting to seventy-one pages, we have here transcribed the text of the typed notes for those sessions. We have done so largely because, early in the treatment (starting with session 6), Emerson began to experiment with a version of shorthand notation, which he later abandoned, that would have proved confusing in print. The typed and handwritten versions of these sessions have been compared, and discrepancies and omissions have been noted.

In preparing the text of Emerson's notes, which were written in haste, we have tried to balance the aims of readability on one hand and preserving the immediacy and flavor the written notes convey on the other. Abbreviations have been spelled out, and the occasional misspelling that had no bearing on meaning silently corrected. We have, for the most part, reproduced Emerson's punctuation and his use of dashes, semicolons, commas, and periods to record the rhythm and pacing of talk in the sessions, making corrections only in the interest of clarity.

First names of persons in the case have been retained, except for those of some members of Rachel's family, and surnames abbreviated (and, in the case of Rachel and her family, altered as well).

Chapter 1 Introduction

Rachel C., a twenty-two-year-old working woman, first saw the psychoanalyst Louville Eugene Emerson on 24 January 1912. A tall, muscular woman with, Emerson would later write, "a small, pretty and innocent face, like that of a young girl," Rachel told in this preliminary interview of her history of vomiting—for six months she had been unable to keep down either food or water—and of experiencing the return, after several years' respite, of convulsions so severe "it took several men to hold her." Rachel lived at home with her father and younger brother in a town north of Boston. She told Emerson she had been greatly shocked several years earlier, when her mother, with whom she was "absolutely bound up," had died suddenly and unexpectedly.[1] Referred to Emerson by the Harvard neurologist James Jackson Putnam,[2] she was, at the moment, terrified by her symptoms. She had broken her hands twice in falls sustained in the midst of convulsions, which interfered with her ability to work, and her body was constantly covered with bruises.

Thus began the psychoanalytic treatment that is the subject of this book. Two hundred and ninety-one sessions followed this first one, all but twenty-three of them within just over two years from the treatment's start. Emerson saw approximately 220 patients in the period from 1911 through 1917, some for a single session, some for extended psychoanalytic treatments. Although he kept notes on all of them, the notes he kept in this case are more voluminous and more worked over than any of his others. No other case engaged his attentions to the degree that this, his specimen case, did.[3] He saw Rachel regularly, sometimes as often as five days a week, and he published an extended account of his treatment of her. This was, in addition, the case that his medical colleagues targeted for censure. In April 1913, with Rachel hospitalized on account of multiple hysterical symptoms, Emerson was called upon to defend not only his treatment of her but also psychoanalysis as a science and a practice, before a suspicious and critical audience of psychiatrists.

Psychoanalysis was a relatively young specialty in 1912. Although by that date Freud had been treating patients with psychoanalytic methods for two decades and had published numerous papers as well as *The Interpretation of Dreams* (1900), in the United States relatively little was known of him and his work through the early years of the new century.[4] Historians customarily date the earliest evidence of American awareness of psychoanalysis to around 1906, when reports of the works of Freud and Jung began to appear in the professional literature. In 1905, for example, writing in the *Psychological Bulletin,* the psychiatrist Adolf Meyer lauded Jung's association test—of which Emerson, in his treatment of Rachel, would make use—and referred to Freud's "analysis" and work in interpreting dreams.[5] The following year, he reported on several of Freud's publications, including his treatment of Dora, and recommended in especially strong terms his *Three Essays on the Theory of Sexuality.*[6] The same year, the Boston psychopathologist Morton Prince[7] founded the *Journal of Abnormal Psychology,* which he intended as a vehicle to serve neurologists, psychiatrists, and psychologists interested in psychopathology and psychoanalysis. The first issue featured an article by Putnam reporting on three cases of hysteria he had treated by "Freud's method of psychoanalysis"[8]—an article Ernest Jones would later cite as the first on psychoanalysis to appear in English.[9] Prince and Putnam were leaders of the so-called Boston school of psychotherapy, a group encompassing the city's most eminent psychologists, philosophers, psychiatrists, and neurologists that, in the years from 1890 through 1909, developed and popularized a sophisticated and scientific psychotherapeutic practice.[10] A number of these men—Putnam, William James,[11] Hugo Münsterberg, G. Stanley Hall, E. B. Holt, and, on at least one occasion, the ubiquitous Jones—began, in 1906, to gather weekly at Prince's home to discuss psychoanalysis, with several of them soon thereafter identifying themselves as psychoanalysts.[12]

Not until Freud's American visit to Clark University in Worcester, Massachusetts, in September 1909, however, was psychoanalysis known outside the ranks of these relatively few specialists. Freud lectured at Clark to a warmly receptive audience of specialists and lay people, presenting a simplified and optimistic version of psychoanalysis well suited to the tastes and capacities of his American audience.[13] In five consecutive mornings of lectures, Freud presented his findings on hysteria and the talking cure, on free association and the analysis of dreams, on childhood sexuality, and on the dangers of sexual repression. Freud spoke at what his host G. Stanley Hall called a "psychological moment" in the United States.[14] The lectures, soon published and widely disseminated, both launched psychoanalysis into the popular realm of social commentary and quickened its professional reception. Within the space of two years, a number of prominent neurologists and psychiatrists were identifying themselves as psychoanalysts, passionately committed to "the cause." In 1911, both the New York Psychoanalytic Society and the American Psychoanalytic Association, with Putnam its president and Jones secretary, were founded.[15] A Boston Psychoanalytic Society followed in 1914; Putnam was once again president, Emerson a member.[16]

Emerson was thirty-nine in 1912, a man with a checkered vocational and professional past who followed a somewhat singular—nontherapeutic and nonmedical—path to psychoanalysis.[17] A native of Maine, he studied engineering at the Massachusetts Institute of Technology, leaving in 1896 before securing a degree to work at the Smithsonian Institution. After several years more of scientific and technical work, he enrolled as a graduate student in philosophy at Harvard in 1903,[18] studying with William James and Josiah Royce, among others, and earning the Ph.D. for a dissertation in experimental psychology in 1907.[19] After a year's sojourn in Europe, he assumed a temporary teaching position at the University of Michigan. There he first began to work as a clinician, seeing patients at the new Psychopathic Hospital in Ann Arbor.[20] He also began to read widely in the psychotherapeutic literature, drawn especially to the writings of Freud and Jung.[21] In 1911, dissatisfied with the "college laboratory psychology" he was teaching, he wrote to Putnam, inquiring about opportunities to return to Boston to study and teach psychoanalysis. He was particularly interested in questions of its "ethical and philosophical import," questions regarding which laboratory psychology, "so remote from actual life," offered little scope.[22] Within several months, Putnam was able to secure some private funds to appoint Emerson to a half-time position in the Department of Neurology at the Massachusetts General Hospital.[23] In 1911, Emerson moved to Boston and, in a makeshift office, jerry-rigged with two chairs and a screen on a third-floor landing, resumed the practice of psychoanalysis upon which he had embarked in Michigan.[24] More regular appointments at the hospital followed, where he eventually graduated to occupying a large private office. In 1912, he was also appointed to the staff of the new Boston Psychopathic Hospital, where he treated, with psychoanalytic methods, a number of cases of hysteria while at the same time tangling repeatedly with the hospital director, E. E. Southard,[25] over the scientific and philosophical validity of psychoanalysis.

Emerson returned to Boston as Putnam's protégé. Putnam's philosophical idealism as well as his—to Freud's mind, characteristically American—moralism would strongly frame Emerson's readings of psychoanalysis over the course of the years during which he was an active practitioner and contributor to the psychoanalytic literature. By 1914, six published analytic papers to his credit, Emerson was exhibiting a sure and thorough grasp of the Freudian corpus, citing recently translated works, such as *The Interpretation of Dreams* and *Selected Papers on Hysteria*,[26] as well as a range of less well known papers by Freud, Jones, Sándor Ferenczi, and others in the original German. He was as enthusiastic a reader as any of his colleagues in the emerging literature, abstracting numerous German papers for the *Psychoanalytic Review* and making notes for his own use of particularly significant publications.[27] He published a further eight analytic papers before the decade was out. Six of his twelve early papers were case reports, with substantial case material presented in two others, marking him as an important contributor to the store of early published cases.[28] Emerson identified himself and was thought of by others as a Freudian. Although to some this designation signified only that he was a psychotherapist, to others it carried more precise meaning. The psychologist William McDougall, for example, wrote Emerson asking if he would analyze some of his dreams "on Freudian lines," adding that neither Jung's analysis of his dreams nor that of another local psychoanalyst had yielded the "Freudian result" he was hopeful Emerson would be able to give him.[29]

From the perspective of Emerson's early-articulated allegiance to the primacy of ethics and his almost filial devotion to Putnam, it is hardly surprising that he consistently objected, in a Putnamesque vein, to what he interpreted as Freud's indifference to ethical and moral questions. The bonds of sympathy and obligation between Putnam and Emerson were strong. They referred cases to one another, and at times discussed their progress. When Emerson started seeing patients privately, he did so in Putnam's office, in his home on Marlborough Street. Emerson stood in for Putnam when the latter could not be present to run the psychoanalytic discussion group that met monthly at his home.[30] Emerson and Putnam analyzed each other's dreams, and in 1912, having just read Freud's paper, "Recommendations to Physicians Practicing Psycho-analysis," in which the analytic examination of the analyst's own personality "in the form of a self-analysis" was recommended, Putnam queried Emerson as to whether "we might make some arrangement this summer to practise on each other."[31] Long before Putnam's death in 1918, Emerson was being groomed as his successor. "You seem to be the bearer of his mantle," McDougall wrote to Emerson.[32] Indeed, upon Putnam's death, Emerson inherited not only his moral idealism but also his patient notes.

What is of perhaps more interest than the sources and extent of Emerson's objections to Freud's amoralism—for Emerson declared these publicly—are the less obvious ways in which the exigencies and demands of psychoanalytic practice shaped his understandings of psychoanalytic concepts and technique. The difficulties Emerson encountered in trying to put into practice a technique that Freud had not explained, except in passing, since the publication of *Studies on Hysteria* in 1895,[33] should not be underestimated. Even with the publication of Freud's major papers on technique, from 1911 through 1914, specific guidelines for carrying out analytic treatments evolved slowly both in Europe and the United States. Few practitioners were well versed in Freud's work and experienced in treating more than a few patients. There were no formal structures for supervision or review of ongoing psychoanalytic cases, and no consensus existed on such technical questions as the expected length of treatment, the nature of the transference, and the necessity for supervision. Freud's papers, moreover, did not offer the systematic exposition of technique that a man like Emerson, who was on his own clinically, self-taught and without the benefit of a personal analysis, might have wanted.[34]

Emerson devoured Freud's papers on technique as they appeared, making notes to himself on Freud's recommendations and comparing them to his own practices. Consider, for example, the single issue of length of treatment. When Emerson embarked on his treatment of Rachel, it is likely he expected it would be of short duration. Indeed, within five months of the first session, he was considering her to be completely recovered.[35] His contemporary Isador Coriat was analyzing patients for periods anywhere from one month to, in severe cases, four to six months.[36] Freud treated his early cases relatively quickly; his analysis of Dora lasted three months, of the Rat Man one year.[37] Yet he offered little explicit advice to novice practitioners on this and other questions, specifying in 1904, for example, the rather elastic period of from six months to three years as that necessary to treat severe cases.[38] In 1913, in the fourth of his technique papers to be published, Freud was emphasizing the slowness of analytic work, writing that psychoanalysis was "always a matter of long periods of time . . . of longer periods than the patient expects."[39] Emerson made notes on this paper for his own use, emphasizing Freud's contention that "the question as to how long the treatment should last is unanswerable" and highlighting Freud's words on the frustrations lengthy treatment engendered: "it's natural to desire to shorten an analytic cure, but one cannot get rid of this, that, or the other symptom alone." These notes were made at least a year into his treatment of Rachel, which by that point was possibly seeming interminable to him.

In the years coincident with Emerson's treatment of Rachel, Freud was not only for the first time providing technical recommendations on the practice of psychoanalysis, but he was also beginning to profoundly modify and complicate his views, publishing, for example, his landmark papers "On Narcissism: An Introduction" and "Instincts and Their Vicissitudes."[40] Emerson read and attempted to assimilate both, within two years publishing a paper in which he limned the erotic lives of a range of narcissistic characters and abstracting the latter paper—the title of which he rendered as "Impulses and Their Mutations"—for the *Psychoanalytic Review*. Emerson accepted much of what he read in the emerging psychoanalytic literature, whether by Freud or others. He assented without apparent qualms to the major tenets of Freud's sexual theories, manifesting little of the prohibiting moralism that Freud found so *echt*—and lamentably—American in Putnam.[41] Emerson's reputation, both locally and, in some circles, nationally, was as an expert in difficult cases, particularly those of a sexual nature. His Psychopathic Hospital colleague Martin Peck, who was attempting to treat some of his own patients psychoanalytically in those years, wrote Emerson several times seeking advice on the sexual eccentricities of various of his relatives and patients. Emerson was, as well, attuned to issues of domestic violence, and he evaluated a number of men remanded by the courts for violence toward their wives. By 1912, his work was well enough known that the chairman of the National Conference of Charities and Correction, an organization of social workers, could single him out as an expert "in regard to sex matters" and ask him to make a presentation before the group "that would take us into the very heart of what [he was] doing."[42] Evidence of Emerson's position within the mainstream of psychoanalysis, whether American or European, can be seen in several of his papers. In 1913–14, in a pioneering account of his treatment of a case of hysterical self-mutilation, he wrote insightfully and straight-forwardly of the perverse pleasures of masochism.[43] His 1916–17 study of "Some Psychoanalytic Studies of Character" featured a gallery of perverse types right from the pages of Freud's "A Special Type of Choice of Object Made by Men."[44] And, in 1918, anticipating Karl Abraham's reference to a patient who hallucinated a very big penis whenever she saw a man,[45] Emerson published a case study of a woman plagued by her habit of fascinatedly looking at men's "abdominal region"[46]—without, significantly, once mentioning the penis in print.

As this suggests, for all of Emerson's devotedly faithful and often-sophisti-cated Freudianism, there were significant limits to his apprehension and un-derstanding of psychoanalysis. In his treatment of Rachel, he encountered dif-ficulties he could not fully master centered around two issues in particular: around free association, which Freud in 1912 termed the "fundamental rule" of psychoanalysis,[47] and around the transference. Both are now recognized, of course, as the sine qua non of psychoanalysis, but neither was fully conceptual-ized at the point at which Emerson embarked on his analysis of Rachel. In the Clark Lectures, Freud invoked free association as but one of three possible ways of accessing the unconscious, the interpretation of dreams and of parapraxes being the other two.[48] Still, it is significant that Emerson, who was familiar with Freud's lectures, proposed neither dreams nor parapraxes but, rather, "in-sistent, vigorous urging the patient on when he stops" as an alternative to free association.[49] With respect to the transference, it is worth pointing out that Freud only offered a general exposition on the issue in his 1912 paper, "The Dy-namics of Transference,"[50] and that his understanding of it was at this point neither consistent nor clear.[51] Emerson's difficulties with the transference likely speeded what may appear in retrospect to have been his retreat from the confu-sions and frustrations of actual practice with a very difficult and traumatized patient to the familiar grounds of ethical exhortations and Putnamesque "dis-interested love." In the commentaries that precede each of the three parts of the case, we discuss these difficulties in some detail, tracking them as they emerge in the course of the treatment and situating them in relation to Emerson's read-ings of the psychoanalytic literature.

Emerson, like many of those Americans who practiced psychoanalysis—ex-cepting, that is, the large body of medical, psychological, and other opinion that was hostile to it—believed in its efficacy. The American reception of psy-choanalysis was exuberant and optimistic, and American analysts, treating in-dividual cases, expected to do so successfully. Emerson's record underwrote his high expectations in this case. In 1911, for example, in the course of a month, he had "cured" a case of hysterical conversion with multiple contractures in a nineteen-year-old girl.[52] The analysis of the hysterical self-mutilator that he published in 1913–14 likewise lasted but a month.[53] By around 1915, cautionary notes regarding the efficacy of psychoanalysis were creeping into the American literature, as was a sense that certain kinds of cases—in particular, those featuring an excess of narcissism—were unsuitable for treatment. Emerson began to voice similar doubts as the treatment of Rachel continued, and as it became clear that she was not getting better but in fact worse. In 1921, the American Psychoanalytic Association devoted its annual meeting to the topic of failures in psychoanalysis. It is noteworthy that in this context a history of severe trauma or abuse—which figures centrally in Rachel's case—was not included among the contraindications for psychoanalytic treatment.[54]

This case offers a privileged view on the practice of psychoanalysis at a time when the parameters of such practice were relatively fluid and when no consensual definition of a psychoanalyst had crystallized. To the best of our knowledge, there are no comparably detailed, daily psychoanalytic notes preserved from the beginnings of Freud's practice until the 1920s, and few enough even from that decade.[55] As such, this material represents a unique resource for the history of psychoanalysis in the first decades of the twentieth century. It offers the opportunity to examine, at the level of day-to-day practice, how Freud was interpreted at a distance, and to track the oscillations of hopefulness and despair, exhilaration and frustration experienced by one enthusiastic proponent of his new technique. It offers as well a particularistic account of one early analyst's embrace—smoothed by his philosophical idealism, prompted by the difficulties of practice—of a reformist, violineliorative version of psychoanalysis, the fate Freud most feared psychoanalysis would meet in American hands.

The case offers a window not only into the practice of psychoanalysis in the early years of the century but also into the rich inner life and day-to-day travails of a young woman of modest means who was, in some respects, quite ordinary. Rachel's inner life, despite her impoverished emotional and material circumstances, was as complex as anyone's. There is a good deal in the notes reproduced here concerning her dreams, wishes, aspirations, and fears; her readings and reactions thereto; her conflicts over sexual desire; her juggling the many duties of womanhood; and her almost heroic quest to make a place for herself in the world. The notes convey a full sense of the forces with which she was contending, both in the closed world of her immediate family and in her relations with the wider world beyond it. The incidental details of the case show her ne-gotiating the burdens of gender expectations, for example, dutifully supporting her father and brother, or working to pay her brother's medical bills at a time when she was plagued by disabling symptoms. The specifics of her relation-ships with her male psychoanalyst, with male and female physicians, and with female nurses and social workers weave a rich tapestry of contemporary gender relations, roles, and expectations. In all, the case notes supplement existing autobiographical, biographical, and historical sources on the lives of poor and working-class young women, documenting with a novelistic specificity the un-folding of the intimate contents of one woman's complex inner life.

Emerson was certain, within a month of embarking on this case, that sexual trauma lay at its center. Rachel's struggles over sexuality and desire were no doubt intensified by the traumas of which she told Emerson, but they were by no means singular. Rachel came of age in a culture in which sexual expression was the prerogative of men, in which a woman who admitted to or, worse, acted on, her desires was thought of as no better than a prostitute. Many women experienced conflicts similar—though perhaps not as disabling—to Rachel's in the sphere of sexuality. Emerson was, perforce, something of an ex-pert on the issue, for many of the young women he treated told tales of abuse at the hands of fathers, brothers, and uncles as well as of men in general. Practic-ing at a time when many professionals routinely assumed that hysterics lied and that rape was medically and legally a near-impossibility, Emerson distinguished himself from many of his medical colleagues by the trust he placed in the sto-ries his patients told.[56] Indeed, he expected to uncover memories of sexual trauma when confronted with hysterical symptoms. In the day-to-day work of analysis, he appears to have been relatively untroubled by the possibility—which his colleagues assumed was a certainty—that what he was hearing was not entirely true. Yet, in a less clinical than philosophical register, he could bluntly assert that "all hysterics tell untruths; some hysterics lie." He held it was up to the analyst to discriminate truth from lies, while admitting it was difficult to do so.[57] Philosophically he styled himself a pragmatist, holding truth a "functional affair," neither final nor absolute, always representing a compro-mise. Truth, he maintained, "means the agreement of our ideas with reality," which was not to be opposed to unreality but considered as "a matter of imme-diate experience."[58] What he called the "subjective truth" of the hysteric's ac-count, which the analyst could glean from her "manner and attitude," was thus to his mind of greater psychological consequence than any impossible-to-cor-roborate "objective truth."[59] That her symptoms waxed and waned in concert with the narratives of sexual assault and trauma she painfully patched together in analysis was evidence enough for him of her essential truthfulness. "The patient herself fully believed what she said," he wrote of another of his hysterical young women. So, too, did he.[60]

The material gathered here also offers the opportunity to examine the relationship between a clinician's daily notes and published account of a case. There are few, if any, comparable instances where both survive, with the exception, of course, of Freud's notes documenting his treatment of the Rat Man.[61] Freud advised analysts not to take notes during sessions, writing up his own more or less regularly on "the evening of the day of treatment."[62] But, if aware of this advice, Emerson ignored it, taking notes on 8 1/2 by 5 1/2 inch sheets of paper during sessions.[63] Through session 80 he had someone prepare (or more likely typed himself) a typewritten copy of the handwritten notes. The typed notes essentially mirror the handwritten ones; they were made on the same size and type of paper and were only lightly amended—largely, it appears, for purposes of clarification. In July 1912, at a moment when it appeared his patient had been cured, Emerson put the finishing touches on a 107-page paper, a detailed session-by-session account of the case, supplemented by, in his words, "a more schematic survey" and "abstract scientific analysis" of it. In this "Detailed Account,"[64] the words, phrases, and sentence fragments of the typed notes were transformed into finished sentences, and his own presence, whether as active questioner or silent interpreter, was more fully documented. In addition, the material within each session was compressed and rearranged, with superfluous bits excised and a linear narrative structure imposed. In 1912, Emerson started preparing yet a third iteration of the case, which he published in three installments, even as it was unfolding, in the *Journal of Abnormal Psychology*.[65] In this rendition, the capaciousness of the freely transcribed notes was subordinated to what Emerson likely felt were the narrative demands of the case history. He strove for narrative coherence and closure throughout, presenting successive accounts of memories recovered, repressions overcome, and symptoms cured. The relative anarchy and formlessness characteristic of the way in which the material originally emerged in the clinical encounter of analyst and patient were largely lost. Writing up his treatment of Dora, Freud marveled that others could produce "such smooth and precise histories in cases of hysteria,"[66] and went on to write a case history that has been hailed as a masterpiece of modernist literature. Freud's *Dora* is, as Philip Rieff has observed, organized "along multiple analytic perspectives," a brilliant piece of writing that captures the complexity of the neurosis whose story it charts.[67] "The patients' inability to give an ordered history of their life in so far as it coincides with the history of their illness," Freud noted, possessed "great theoretical significance."[68] Emerson's account of Rachel, if not precisely the smooth and precise sort that Freud rejected, neither aspired to nor realized the narrative complexity of *Dora*. It was organized straightforwardly, charting the emergence of a symptom, the interpretive attack on it, the epiphanic moment of revelation, when as its meaning became clear it disappeared—only to chart, with another newly emerged symptom, the same course.

Chapter 2 On Reading
Psychoanalytic Case Notes

The author of a psychoanalytic case report navigates between conveying the actual complexity of the way in which the patient's story unfolds and the need to fashion a coherent narrative for the reader.[1] In *Studies on Hysteria,* published in 1895, Freud wrote that it still struck him "as strange that the case histories I write should read like short stories and that, as one might say, they lack the serious stamp of science."[2] Stories they were, but ones in which the "intimate connection between the story of the patient's sufferings and the symptoms of his illness" that he was to discover in the case of Dora was not, perforce, represented.[3] As Stephanie Kiceluk has noted, Freud narrated his accounts of Anna O., Elisabeth von R., and Emmy von N. largely along straightforwardly linear and chronological lines, connected by a theme, supplementing this in places with a more complex zigzag-like narrative line that, in attempting to capture the overdetermined nature of symptoms, oscillated between surface event and the deep layers of the psyche.[4] Freud struggled in the final pages of the *Studies* with the difficulties of trying to represent in narrative form what had "never yet been represented," the nature of the neurosis.[5] By the time he was analyzing Dora, he had abandoned the more ordered technique he had formerly followed of aiming to clear up one symptom after another and was instead letting the patient "choose the subject of the day's work," starting out "from whatever surface his unconscious happens to be presenting to his notice at the moment."[6] This new technique, honoring the "fundamental rule," which meant that the patient's story emerged piecemeal, in fragmented and disconnected form, with past and present interwoven and converging, called for new narrative strategies. "If I were to begin by giving a full and consistent case history," Freud wrote in *Dora*, "it would place the reader in a very different situation from that of the medical observer."[7] Coherence would have to be achieved by novel means, more akin to those employed by writers of fiction than standard medical reports.

Case notes, raw and unedited, are likely to be even more difficult to follow than the shaped, selected, and organized material that appears in the published case reports. Sequences and reasoning that are clear to the analyst and patient may not be so in the notes. Emotional currents in the analytic encounter shape the flow of thoughts, memories, and what may appear to the reader to be diversions in ways that the written notes can neither capture nor convey. Affects in the room anchor the attention of the two participants, allowing them to follow the emerging story in all its complexity in a way that the reader of the transcripts may not be able to do. Readers or viewers of exact reproductions of sessions, tape-recorded and transcribed or videotaped, must work hard to sustain focus and attention in ways that analyst and patient have little need to.

The operation of modes of defense mean that the patient's discourse rarely follows neat, sequential patterns. Repression, isolation of affect, and, at times, conscious withholding of material that is too painful or embarrassing or felt to be potentially offensive to the analyst—all affect the manner in which the patient's story unfolds. These modes of defense work both ways. Everyday observation in clinical analytic work shows that the analyst's memory and selection of what to record are subject to unconscious and, at times, conscious, forces similar to those affecting the patient. On occasions when clinicians have the opportunity to compare their notes—or, even more dramatically, recollections of a session—with transcripts of sessions, it becomes clear how much is left out of both written notes and memory. In addition, in this case and many others, the length of what the analyst records and the detail in which he or she records it may vary from session to session, inexplicably to the reader. Thus, an intense and meaningful engagement may be taking place in the consulting room, but the reader of the case notes may not be able to grasp its depths.

Emerson's notes in this case, as is likely true for the vast majority of cases in which the analyst takes notes during a session or soon afterward, are sketchy and elliptical, intended more as aide-mémoire for his personal use than as a full account of the case. The bulk of what appears in them consists in what the patient said, with the analyst's comments reported unevenly. Taking stenographic notes is difficult work. For many analysts, too much attention to recording makes listening, engaging, and responding all the more difficult.[8] In addition, in the course of an analysis, shared points of reference typically emerge, with respect to both the patient's narrative and to the common history of their work together, and these are likely to be recorded by the analyst elliptically and briefly.

The reader can, however, become accustomed and attuned to the psychoanalytic dialogue even by way of the select and attenuated version of it presented in the analyst's notes. Several factors make this possible. First, readers gradually get to know the various participants in the case, and develop a sense for their various styles and rhythms. Second, as the case progresses, readers can find themselves entering the experiential world of the patient and, perhaps, developing feelings and attitudes about her, which enables a sense of connection between reader and patient, as well as between reader and the dialogue between patient and analyst. Third, in this case especially, moments of revelation, tension, and drama, and of exacerbation and remission of symptoms, draw readers into the unfolding narrative. Unraveling the mysteries around the many "whodun-its" and "did it really happen or not" encourage readers' persistence. Readers may experience relief and clarity as the patient improves, and may understand something of how and why she does. Correspondingly, they may experience frustration, anger, perplexity, and regret when she fails to improve or even gets worse. As partisans and critics, readers may be engaged by both positive and negative feelings about the process and one or both of the participants. Finally, there is a redundancy in the analytic process that the notes capture. Not only are facts repeated over time, but types of interchanges are also repeated, and incremental new elaborations or turnings of material already presented are made. This redundancy allows both analyst and patient to functionally remember a good deal without at any one time remembering everything.

Part I "Girls imagine a lot that don't happen"

Chapter 3 Commentary: 24 January–10 May 1912, Sessions 1–80

Consisting of 80 sessions, covering the three-and-one-half month period from 24 January through 10 May 1912, this first part of the treatment formed, to Emerson's mind, a satisfyingly interpretable whole. He determined at the outset that several repressed traumata lay at the root of his patient's hysteria and saw it as the task of analysis to bring them fully back to memory. This he and Rachel attempted to do, in a fitful process marked on the one hand by her fierce resistance and deteriorating condition and on the other by what he characterized as his intense psychic work and mounting frustration. Throughout they fought her resistance, and each other, and one after another long-repressed traumatic scene of assault, rape, and seduction from Rachel's past was pieced together. By the end of session 80, Rachel was apparently cured of the paralysis of her legs for which she had been hospitalized one month into the analysis, and in his unpublished "Detailed Account," Emerson could venture a persuasive and even elegant interpretation of the case.

This segment of the treatment is the best documented of its several parts, with four iterations extant: Emerson's handwritten notes, his typed notes, the "Detailed Account," and the account he published, in three installments in the *Journal of Abnormal Psychology.* The handwritten notes (Figure 1), from which the bulk of the text in this book has been transcribed, span the entire case.[1] The typed notes, which largely mirror the handwritten ones, span roughly one-third of it; the last ones Emerson prepared are from session 80. The "Detailed Account" comes to a close as this first segment of the treatment ended. It offers an invaluable gloss on the handwritten and typed notes, for in it Emerson supplemented Rachel's words, which make up the bulk of the handwritten notes, with his own, thus registering his own presence in the consulting room. The published version of the case ends with session 185, which coincides with the end of Part 2 in this book; the first installment of the journal article chronicles that portion of the treatment.[2] In it Emerson spoke with yet another voice, hurrying through the complex narrative and striving for closure, presenting successive accounts of memories recovered, repressions overcome, and symptoms cured. We thus have the benefit of multiple perspectives on this portion of the case.

SEX AND SECRETS

Emerson's notes began tersely, more modernist novel than grand epic: "Food and water wouldn't stay down. Comes up. Isn't vomiting. This commenced about six months ago" (session 1). In short order, he learned from Rachel that she had been suffering from convulsions, nausea, and daze-like "spells." She had been chased by men on two different occasions: the first when she was seven or eight, the second when she was fourteen. Her mother had been dead two years, she told Emerson, and her father, against whom she felt strongly, had been unfaithful to the mother. Much of the time she felt as though a cloud—which she associated with a "blue feeling" portending awful events (session 2)—were hanging over her; within several sessions, she associated the cloud with her mother, whom she saw standing in it "so condemning" (session 13). This much Rachel knew.

Rachel appears to have engaged quickly and unreservedly in the analysis, accepting its premises and Emerson's modus operandi from the start such that free associations, dreams, visualizations, and even the resistances that would so frustrate him began to emerge early on. The conflicts about telling and not telling, as well as her difficulties in being able to recall and articulate things of which she had some awareness but not the means to fully piece together and express, came up immediately. Emerson, too, appears to have plunged in directly,

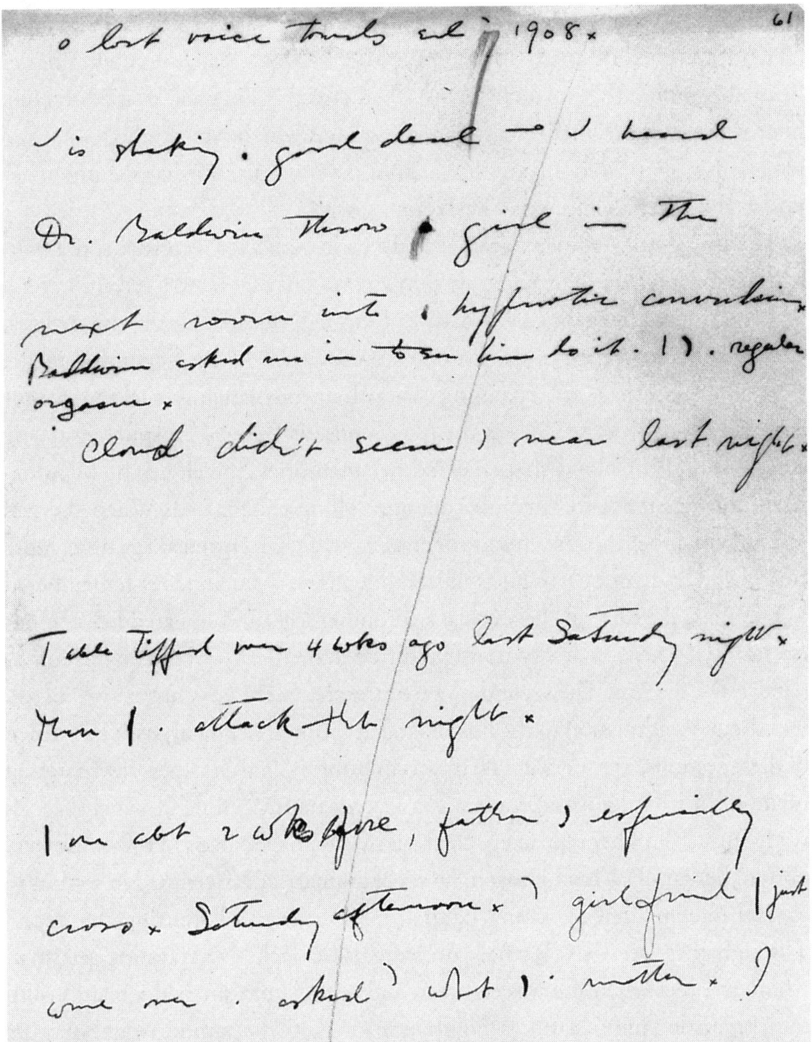

Figure 1. A sample of Emerson's handwritten case notes for 13 February 1912 (session 10). Note his shorthand, which he later abandoned. Reproduced, with permission, from the Boston Medical Library in the Francis A. Countway Library of Medicine.

anticipating Freud's warning—made in his paper, "On Beginning the Treatment," published in 1913[3]—that, in Emerson's words, "too long preliminaries before beginning the real analysis has a bad effect."[4] Emerson termed the first hour with Rachel a "preliminary interview," but whether or not he took a systematic history or told her anything about psychoanalysis, what she might expect and what was expected of her, is unknown.

The struggle of—and between—analyst and patient to reconstruct the traumatic incidents that she could only dimly recall but that he was certain were to be found forms the main narrative thread through this first part of the analysis, which falls into three phases. Emerson spent much of the beginning of the treatment (sessions 1–16), spanning a month during which Rachel came regularly, almost daily, to see him at the Massachusetts General Hospital, in trying to get behind the cloud that shielded her memories; the cloud, he hypothesized, her resistance to remembering and telling concretized. When she was able to remember the first episode of chasing, which occurred at age nine, more clearly and to describe it as an assault, if not a rape—a man (later remembered as men) attacked her in the woods, tied up her legs, and fingered her genitals (session 15)—her somatic symptoms shifted dramatically, from convulsions to paralysis of the legs. The second phase of the treatment (sessions 17–59) began with Rachel's admission to the hospital on account of the paralysis. The burden of these sessions, as Emerson saw it, was to bring to consciousness the repressed memory of what he was certain was a second trauma, hints of which had already surfaced, of her rape at age thirteen by a man who lived in the house next door to her family. "Yes, I know it," Rachel dramatically exclaimed in session 59 as "she remembered his doing it, then leaving her, and shutting the door." Through these sessions, Rachel's deceased lover Jack[5]—a traveling salesman whom she met when she was eighteen and with whom she had a relationship that Emerson summed up as highly erotic—and the raping neighbor were merged in her mind, the scenes of Jack's seduction of her and of the rape indistinguishable. The final phase of this segment (sessions 60–80) was marked by the patient's consolidating and partitioning the memories that had surfaced and by her recovery to the point where she could be discharged from the hospital. A pattern took shape in which as one trauma appeared to have been resolved, another was elicited. But clarity of memory proved elusive—through much of the second and third phases of this part of the treatment, Rachel tried, with little success, to distinguish among the assaults that had merged into one frightening and overwhelming whole in her mind.

From the start, Emerson attempted to chart the intricate network of secrets, betrayals, prohibitions, and illicit desires that was Rachel's family. Emerson decided early on that the father was a sadist, a man who routinely teased and tormented his daughter, who for her part was certain he spent money she judged was properly the family's on secret lovers, at least one of whom he brought home with the expectation Rachel would serve her dinner. The mother, whom Rachel both feared and worshipped, was in Emerson's estimation an incredible coward who did nothing to protect Rachel from the father's cruelty and who not only repudiated her account of the rape by the neighbor but actively coerced and threatened her into suppressing all memory of it. Rachel likely empathized with mother and identified with the father in trying to protect the former from knowledge of the latter's affairs, doing with the secret knowledge what the father did, concealing it from the mother lest it "wreck her life."[6] Rachel, who appeared to feel her mother's disgrace as if it were her own (session 28), was devastated when she later learned that the mother had known of the affairs all along and, further, by way of a deathbed confession accompanied with dire prohibitions against telling, that she had had an affair of her own. With their secret complicity, the parents had encouraged Rachel in her casting of them as victim and victimizer; when the truth of the situation was revealed, all of her energetic psychic maneuvering to protect the mother and unilaterally condemn the father was retrospectively rendered unnecessary—her parents were not at all the people she had assumed them to be. These were the same parents who, while complicit in their own infidelities, refused her any sexual knowledge and who relentlessly warned her against Jack on the grounds of his reputed bad character. Bending to her parents' wishes, she had sent him on his way, only to have him die three weeks later. The project of uncovering the eroticism around Jack that she could, for a long period, recall only as one more in a series of assaults was entered on midway through this part of the analysis and not resolved until near the end of the treatment five years later.

Emerson realized early on that sexual knowledge was especially fraught for Rachel. She had first learned of sex—which she referred to as "badness between man and wife" (session 5)—in a context marked by mystery, hypocrisy, and jealousy. The mechanics of sex so shocked her she "hardly spoke to her mother for a year" (session 5); the knowledge, she told Emerson, "used to make the shivers go over me" (session 7). She left school at age fifteen, weak and faint, after listening to a girl there tell "smutty stories" about a married woman whom men paid for sexual favors (session 6). She at once twigged her father's philandering, which turned her against not only him but also the mother—for the latter's duplicity in not leaving him (sessions 7, 21). As Emerson and Rachel homed in on the first of the traumas she was able to remember, they broached the question of her own sexual character. "I keep thinking I am not a good girl," she plaintively told Emerson (session 13).

Emerson saw it as among the tasks of analysis to enlighten Rachel regarding the facts of sex and to free her from guilt about it. He told her about her sexual constitution (session 47) and about the "sex running through everything" (session 15). He used visual aids, showing her anatomical drawings (sessions 52, 53). And, following what he explained was Ferenczi's lead, he used obscene sexual slang—"'trunk', 'fuck', 'cunt'"—as if to underscore his precept that "virtue consists in virtuous acts, and not in barren purity of thought."[7] Unlike the mother, who had blamed Rachel for the behavior of one of her boyfriends, repeatedly telling her "that Harry[8] wouldn't do as he did if I hadn't encouraged him in some way" (session 24), Emerson offered Rachel a Freudian "absolution after the confession"[9]: "I made her responsibility in the whole matter seem as little as possible," he wrote as she was in the midst of remembering the first of the traumas that would surface in this segment of the treatment (session 15). Rachel wavered between seeing sex as an aggressive act men inflicted on women and as a compromising act women incited men to perform. She could barely conceive of consensual sex; that a "good" woman or girl might actively desire sex was beyond her conscious imagining.

Even as Rachel was fiercely repressing and then producing memories of traumas inflicted on her, Emerson introduced the thread of her own desire into the unfolding drama. Later in the treatment, he would hypothesize that the root of her conflicts lay in her "sexual cravings,"[10] but for the moment, his characterization was less pointed. If, at the outset, he was envisioning Rachel as the pawn in webs of deceit spun by selfish, duplicitous adults—her mother, her father, the neighbor, the lover Jack—at some point in this segment of the treatment he realized that the key to understanding the case did not lie in casting her simply as hapless victim. He noted that she had defied her parents' prohibitions against seeing Jack; indeed, in session 9 she admitted that she might not have gone with him had her father not forbidden her to. He noted, also, that Rachel had had her revenge on the father. Long suspicious of him, at age sixteen she had followed him to the scene of a secret assignation in Boston, thereby proving to her satisfaction he was an adulterer (session 3). Perhaps identifying with the father, so distrusted and hated by his daughter, Emerson initially discounted her suspicions.[11] Yet it is possible Emerson saw in this rather remarkable incident, recounted at the very beginning of the treatment, evidence of the ferocity of character that he found immensely frustrating but that he would later summon up as he encouraged her to explore the depths of her own desires.

These desires—intense, incestuous, masturbatory, adulterous—would in the end prove more difficult for Rachel to accept than anything others did to her, for they, unlike the assaults, generated conflict.[12] The case at this juncture looks uncannily like that of Freud's *Dora*, in the second half of which, as John Forrester has pointed out, Freud shows Dora "how her own desires are reflected point by point in the desires and actions of others: 'Dora's reproaches against her father had a "lining" or "backing" [*doubliert*] of self-reproaches of this kind with a corresponding content in every case.' "[13] If Emerson's account lacks the parsimonious elegance of Freud's, with which it is likely he was familiar, he did eventually come to implicitly pose the same question to Rachel that Freud asked of Dora: "Where are *you* in all this mess?"[14]

Emerson was not yet ready to put the question so directly. But twenty or so hours into the treatment, he was seeing her as desiring subject, referring in his notes to the inner conflicts set up by her "cravings." Furthermore, he confronted her with this, telling her that her convulsions were "really intensified orgasms, symbolizing an imagined coitus with Jack" (session 24, n. 126).[15] Rachel was struggling at this point as she was confronting the question of her complicity in what she at first recalled as an attack by Jack. Having already merged together the men who assaulted her in the woods and the raping neighbor, she brought Jack into the confused picture, such that all three scenes appeared as one: "Woods—neighbor—mother—Jack." She then told Emerson of seeing Jack ask the mother's permission to take her into the woods (session 19), a revelation that startled Emerson, who immediately suspected that she was telling him she had been tempted by Jack and had fallen. Three days later she confirmed his suspicions, admitting she had probably "yielded to Jack" (session 22). Through several more sessions, she oscillated between on the one hand admitting to secretly thinking of him all the time—"I have a wish I could have him," she told Emerson (session 29)—and on the other recalling encounters with him that were indistinguishable from the rape by the neighbor. She dreamed of marriage to Jack as a scene of sexual assault one night, and as an occasion for endless—and, in Emerson's interpretation, pleasurable—intercourse the next (sessions 32, 33). She dreamed of living with him in secret and finding happiness in doing so (session 55). And, in a dream peopled by hectoring doctors and nurses that was manifestly about the treatment but surely about Jack as well, she drowned—in the dream she later lived—as she was buffeted about by waves while being repeatedly asked if she had given her consent (session 32). Her hand was clenched shut through this segment, holding the secret of her desire, which Emerson hypothesized she had hidden, even from herself.[16]

In these desires, he suggested, were to be found the keys to her hysterical symptomology. Only after Jack died did Rachel allow herself fully to experience the eroticism of their relationship, dreaming of sex with him with an intensity Emerson judged abnormal, of having the quality of hysterical fantasies. Unconsciously merged with memories of the two actual assaults, with memories of "the man in the woods"[17] and the raping neighbor, "the man in the room," and thus exciting repressed memories, the fantasy of sex with Jack became the occasion for what externally looked like a convulsion, Emerson wrote, but was internally "an intense sexual reflex, or orgasm" in which, in an "orgy of abandonment . . . arms and legs and body all enter into a perfect frenzy of reflex activity, . . . a perfect riot of self-satisfying activity."[18]

Emerson wrote this for himself. In print he was more guarded and circumspect, allowing only that the convulsions satisfied "the overwhelming desire for sexual satisfaction" and quoting Freud to similar effect: "The hysterical symptom serves as a sexual gratification."[19] Indeed, Emerson systematically censored himself—or was censored by Morton Prince—in publishing the case, systematically leaving out sexually explicit details of the various assaults and rapes that he recorded in the daily case notes and highlighted in the never published "Detailed Account." Writing of the psychoanalyst's necessary self-control and "absolute self-possession" while entering into "the most intimate psychical relations possible" with another, Emerson sounded a lament that was at the same time an admonition, as if in the service of Freud's attempts in the case of Dora to underline the scientificity of psychoanalysis: while scientists in other fields could "conquer their own feelings by being impersonal," in analytic treatment, where the "*personal* and *scientific* points of view" were inextricably mixed, this was impossible.[20] Emerson's position here was that the analyst may hope to be scientific but will inevitably fail. The Freud of *Dora,* by contrast, maintained the analyst could be scientific *despite* the secret, messy, and feminine stuff with which he dealt daily. Emerson held that the psychoanalyst could not allow himself to appear to have been seduced into endless intimate—and feminizing—talk about sex, seduced by patients skilled in the arts of "concealment, artful dissimulation, and cunning falsification."[21] Negotiating the divide between the necessarily secret nature of the case notes and the public, scientific quality of the published case was no doubt difficult for Emerson, as indeed it had been for Freud.

The same difficulty would surface in Emerson's tense relations with Psychopathic Hospital director E. E. Southard. Southard, on the one hand, admonished Emerson that a good many members of the hospital staff were offended by his language, "hardly used to the expressions of frankness which prevail in certain psychoanalysts."[22] On the other, he chastised Emerson for employing "euphemisms and circumlocutions" in print. His contradictory hectoring aside, Southard homed right in on the conflict generated by the secret science of psychoanalysis. He suggested to Emerson that "so far as possible you contribute notes of your interviews with patients to the records," anticipating Emerson's objection that the data "are too intimate for committing to the records." This might well be, Southard allowed, but why, then, could Emerson present the hospital stenographer with "a huge mass of the most intimate details about the cases"? He continued, "There is evidently no principle in your mind which prevents this detailing of facts for other people's scrutiny."[23]

Emerson did not resolve this difficulty. Rather, he enacted it in his keeping of a notebook, to which he referred several times. In this notebook, which has not survived, he apparently recorded detailed information concerning the rape as well as charting the ebb and flow of Rachel's sexual sensations (sessions 71, 72, 74, 80).[24] It is possible Emerson felt this material simply too intimate to insert into the flow of his own case notes; it is also possible he was attempting to dilute some of the libidinal charge associated with it by assuming for himself the guise of the laboratory scientist recording his data. The "secret" notebook was thus defense both against the charge of seduction and against seduction itself, private testimony to his analytic self-possession. In keeping such a notebook, Emerson not only replicated within the already secret space of the treatment the divide between intimate secrets and public knowledge that characterized the relationship between the case notes and the published case, but he also replicated it at the level of writing, mirroring Rachel's defensive structure in cordoning off the most sexually charged material from his faithful record of the case.

PARTY TO ANALYSIS

Summing up this portion of the treatment, Emerson wrote that just as Rachel "had been overcome by a man with evil intent, I overcame her, but with a good purpose." He admitted to blundering in his attempt to force matters by putting his hands over the patient's eyes; as some of her dreams showed, he wrote, "I stood, symbolically, for the man who assaulted her, and therefore aroused unconscious resistances which took a longer time to overcome."[25] Emerson here acknowledged that in the treatment he and Rachel were reenacting the traumas that precipitated her illness, and then worried the issue by first excusing himself on therapeutic grounds—he had harbored good intentions—before narrowing it to a single, though often repeated, gesture.

Tolerance was soon enough displaced by irritation. Frustrated, no doubt, by his inability to stanch the patient's worsening condition, Emerson rehearsed a litany of complaints in the published version of the case. The patient was not very intelligent, "of an extremely sluggish mentality,"[26] despite which he gave her William James to read (session 55). Her answers to questions were always, at first, superficial. She presented him with a "maze of equivocation," distracting his attention from the present conflict. She subtly concealed and often insisted, when asked to free associate, that there was nothing at all in her mind. Most irritating was her "impossible-to-be-exaggerated resistance." One expected resistance, "but such resistance!" It was almost unintelligible. The work of analysis was in this case, Emerson wrote, "more like drilling into rock and blasting than any intellectual endeavor." Had the patient "put forth a tithe of the mental effort necessary to the repressions to more useful work she might have amounted to a great deal."[27]

Harsh words from one who enjoined analysts to maintain "completely conscious self-control and self-possession." Emerson mentioned the countertransference—which he defined as "reaction feeling of the analyst"—but once in his writing, only to shy from examining it.[28] But his repeated expressions of irritation (he mentioned the word "irritating" three times in one paragraph) with Rachel suggest that the treatment conformed less to his stated model of the impersonal and self-restrained analyst leading the diabolically dissembling patient to insight than to a pitched battle pitting "the analyst's will-to-know" against "the patient's will-not-to-know."[29]

Committed to the project of recalling and retrieving in the service of therapeusis, Emerson saw resistance as a barrier to be broken through and penetrated, an obstacle that needlessly frustrated his will-to-know and his desire to cure. Rachel was as committed to concealing as Emerson was to revealing, raised as she was in a family knitted together by secret complicities and dire prohibitions against telling. The two were bound to clash. When Rachel could not recall, or could only recall fragmentarily, Emerson pushed her on, trying to overcome her resistance any way he could: he encouraged and exhorted her, reproached her and occasionally even threatened her in order to get her to recall.[30] He appears at times not to have realized that her inability to tell was not fully under her control: "You can tell if you will," he declared (session 12, n. 57). She told him variously that she kept "thinking I hadn't ought to tell things to anybody" (session 11), that if she knew she would tell (session 17) and that "it would be as much as my life to tell it" (session 19), and reminded him constantly of the promises she has made—to her mother, to the men in the woods, to the rapist—not to tell. Yet Emerson devoted little attention to the impact of his insistence, his pushing and prodding, on the waxing and waning of the patient's symptoms. He reflected on the issue only in the context of his technique of urging her to keep her eyes closed and the failure of his urging, which led him to put his hands over her eyes, "forcibly" holding them shut, in an attempt to get her to visualize.[31] Losing his patience, he stood behind her and demanded "that she tell me what she saw."[32] The first time he used this technique, she complied by giving him the information he sought, only to suffer a convulsive attack, after which she threatened to break off the treatment and commit suicide (session 14, n. 72). Emerson later abandoned the technique, which he borrowed from Freud, who had stopped using it by 1896.[33]

Emerson saw every retrieval, however painful and traumatic to the patient, as a step forward. He was clearly satisfied when a memory was recalled or elaborated, and he repeatedly announced—at times to the patient, at times to himself—that he, or he and she, had gotten to the bottom of it and that her distress would be soon relieved. That material continued to emerge, at whatever cost to Rachel, only encouraged him to push harder and to penetrate more deeply. He discounted any ambivalence or apprehensions on Rachel's part. For example, early in the treatment, in the midst of all his hectoring, Rachel reported that she had dreamed the night before that "she was in here again"—that is, in the consulting room—and that he "was trying to find out things." She also told him she had had a convulsion the morning previous to the dream, while reading page 159 of a novel, *Eagle Blood*.[34] The book had hypnotism in it, she said; "a woman makes a man do anything she wanted." She continued: "It seemed all the time as if I was afraid you would ask me something, but I couldn't think what it was." Later in the same session, she had a momentary thought that he was a hypnotist (session 9).

Rachel may have been using the novel to frame her understanding of the analysis, seeing in its different voices different dimensions of herself. Just prior to page 159, the novel's heroine, Miss Grush, persuades her suitor, Hugh, to go with her to a séance conducted by the Parisian medium Madame Grocroft. Hugh agrees to go—reflected in Rachel's "a woman makes a man do anything she wanted"—but not before expressing a good deal of skepticism regarding mediums and other soothsayers. "They're all humbugs," he proclaims. "The whole thing's a fraud, and it's the cruelest sort of imposition, because the victims are generally sorrowing women." Arriving at the séance, the two are greeted by the Madame Grocroft, who, upon learning that Hugh is a doubter, exclaims, "Ah, faith! faith! we are nothing without faith. . . . if this seeker for light will only have faith to see, who can tell what blessed message may come forth to him from the spirits who surround us."[35]

Rachel's convulsive attack while reading the novel suggests it may have provided her a means to express her resistance to and ambivalence about the treatment. Identifying with Hugh, she may have been expressing a wish that the treatment was fraudulent, all humbug, and thus rightly to be resisted. She may also have been expressing a worry that it really was a fraud, and that Emerson was leading her on in promising her, one of the sorrowing women, he could help. Was she making Emerson do anything she wanted, as she controlled the production of material for analysis? Or was the equation of control reversed, with Emerson making her do anything he wanted, hypnotizing her as he engaged her in a treatment about which she was skeptical and asking questions that she admitted to fearing? Did she have to believe in the treatment—have faith in it—for it to work? Rachel ended this long session (session 9) telling Emerson that "a gentleman asked her to go to a party," but she wouldn't go: "If I want to go any place I'd rather go with girls." If Emerson is the gentleman, and analysis the party, Rachel was saying she had rather not go.[36]

TRAUMATIC REENACTMENTS

Emerson probed, Rachel resisted but finally yielded. The pattern was repeated again and again. In session 15, for example, a day after she remembered the first details of the assault by the neighbor, elicited as she "twisted and turned and writhed terribly,"[37] Rachel released Emerson from his promise not to question her further and, he wrote, "let me probe deeper." He put his hands over her eyes and, through great distress, she told him details of being raped in the woods at age nine—the man had called another and the two had "hurt her 'stomach' awfully," and then threatened her not to tell. She then quickly segued into telling of the man in the room—the neighbor—holding her by the throat while she struggled terribly (the incident had not yet assumed shape as a rape—"she doesn't know whether he succeeded or not"). Emerson was sure he had gotten to "the bottom of her trouble" and told her so, predicting she would have no more attacks. Rachel, for her part, had violated the promise she had made to her mother not to tell and felt "as though she couldn't live." She came back three days later telling of having had two convulsions, from one of which she emerged with a hand that remained clenched for a day, and of having been in a long daze that was likely a dissociative episode; her legs were weak and she could hardly climb the stairs. Emerson, aware "that we had not got to the bottom of her trouble," again put his hands over her eyes, and she recounted more details of the first assault, but this did not, he wrote, relieve her. "She wanted me to let her go home, but I felt that if she did, it would only be to have more convulsions and that it would be better to get to the bottom of the thing at once, if possible, and have it over with." He insisted she tell more; she resisted, again "twisting, turning and writhing in her chair." It appeared she was going to have a convulsive attack, but, Emerson noted, he persisted and "suddenly it passed." She told him that suddenly it went from her head to her legs, and she found herself paralyzed, unable to walk, her legs "limp, flexible, and utterly powerless," her left hand clenched shut.[38]

Rachel was at this point admitted to the Massachusetts General Hospital where she would remain for two and one-half months, until the end of this segment of the analysis. Ensconced therein, she began to sleep well, better than she had for a long while, as if the environment provided her some succor despite her dire physical condition. Unable to walk, Rachel was, however, powerless, a captive to the treatment, and both she and Emerson were well aware of this. Yet he presented himself as not particularly perturbed by the onset of the paralysis, for, he noted both privately and in print, it as much as ensured her compliance in the project of uncovering the repressed traumas that he was certain the cloud concealed. Having rendered her—by means of his unwanted probing, and in his disallowing of her chosen symptom—as utterly helpless as the men who assaulted her, Emerson allowed that he had perhaps been mistaken in putting his hands over her eyes but that the "practical result" was that he had gotten by "the first great resistance" and had as well "secured more of a lever to give power to my urgent arguments." She didn't mind the convulsions, he wrote, but she hated being paralyzed. Thus, as he saw it, she tried "more heartily to enter into co-operation with my attempts to discover hidden complexes and to analyze them," promising Emerson she would look into "the depths of her mind" in order to get back the use of her legs.[39]

Emerson prevailed in this skirmish. His equability in its immediate wake may have covered confusion and even unsettledness; he had, after all, induced a serious paralysis, testimony to the power of the treatment if nothing else. His language of a year later, however, sounded the phallic themes of penetration—

with his new lever—and control. He knew that the transference had really taken effect, that she would respond to his desires; she now had motive power sufficient to give up her convulsions. Yet, if the convulsions were her sexual activity, self-inflicted punishments that satisfied "the overwhelming desire for sexual satisfaction,"[40] was he not acting the part of the prohibiting mother in so forcefully disallowing them, in paralyzing her pleasure? Indeed, it appears that genital anesthesia set in at this point as a concomitant of the paralysis, the undoing of which was the burden of the secret notebook. Was Rachel meeting his unwanted penetration with frigidity?[41]

The physician's power over the hysteric's body was made amply clear to Rachel in a remarkable scene early in the analysis. Interrupting a session, the doctor in the next room, Henry Baldwin,[42] invited Emerson in to watch him throw a young woman into a hypnotic convulsion. Emerson returned to Rachel, noted that she had overheard the whole incident and was "shaking a good deal," and then wrote in the case notes, "It looked like a regular orgasm" (session 10).[43] Although it is unclear whether or not he shared this interpretation with Rachel, it is likely she grasped there was some connection, at least in Emerson's mind, between convulsions and sexual activity. Further, witnessing this scene may have emboldened Emerson, giving him a taste of the analyst's power. Three weeks later, after Rachel had stopped having convulsions, he made the equivalence between convulsions and orgasms explicit for her (session 24, n. 126). Throughout, he didn't shy from confronting the issue of Rachel's sexual sensations. She told him the convulsions started shortly after Jack died, and he told her they were symptomatic expressions of her unconscious, dream-like desires for him.[44] Together Emerson and Rachel discussed the relation between "thrills"—common slang for orgasm—and thoughts (session 71), with Emerson speculating on how her capacity for "thrills" was related to thinking of Jack (session 72). Emerson recorded "a slight orgasm" (session 60)—whether this was his observation or her report is not clear—and "shudders" (sessions 73, 74), and noted the return of somatic feeling in her genitals as evidence "the abnormal anesthesia there is passing away" (session 63, n. 209). In the context of her finally fully recounting the rape by the neighbor and its aftermath, with the help of Emerson's interpretation that she had transferred her mother's prohibiting of Jack to her own prohibiting of her desire for the boyfriend (session 73), Rachel was once again able to experience sexual sensations and satisfaction. Her paralysis was relieved, it appeared; at this moment that she no longer needed the illness to protect her virtue.[45]

In the hospital, it was not only Emerson who was superintending Rachel's body. Indeed, her body and its peculiar ailments became common currency among the staff—physicians, nurses, social workers. Nurses recorded her nocturnal outbursts, social workers speculated on the root causes of her hysterical symptoms, and, most striking, hospital physicians engaged in a concerted campaign to open her clenched hand—the hand, Emerson later told her, a substitute for the genitals (session 52). First Baldwin successfully tried to force it open, using a wedge (session 19), aided by another doctor and a nurse. A Dr. Jennings,[46] skeptical of the reality of her illness, also expressed a desire to open it (session 21) and, later, to splint it (session 28); he succeeded in opening her hand only by stuffing a wad into it, which she reported to Emerson hurt her terribly (session 30). Other physicians were spectators at these various scenes but did nothing to stop them. Rachel dreamed in this context of Emerson failing her, of his having said he could do no more for her and, in a repetition of the scene wherein the mother handed her over to the neighbor who raped her, of his telling her "that the other doctors could now do what they pleased" (session 22). Later she dreamed of withholding consent and of being pleased "she hadn't given in to the doctors" (session 32).

Emerson's expressed position on the hospital as a site for psychoanalytic treatment was wholly positive, organized around the relief of responsibility and the proximity of expert advice. As he remarked in his 1913–14 paper "Psychoanalysis and Hospitals," the hospitalization of a difficult patient freed the psychoanalyst of medical responsibility for the case such that he could focus on the more purely psychological issues involved. It is not clear what he felt about these physicians' efforts to pry open Rachel's hand, nor is it clear whether he saw in them yet another reenactment, in addition to his own, of the various traumas she had experienced. Yet his invocation, in the same paper, of Freud's "Wilde Psychoanalyse" as "of the highest importance," in a context unrelated to what Freud actually wrote, hints at feelings he couldn't express directly. Freud's paper, published in 1910, opens with the case of a divorced middle-aged woman, suffering from anxiety states, reporting to him what another physician had told her—that lack of sexual satisfaction was the cause of her anxiety, that she would have to either return to her husband, take a lover, or satisfy herself, and that Freud would bear him out on this. Freud, while allowing that the woman's account might have been distorted, launched an attack on the sort of loose and wild theorizing the second physician's advice exemplified. He castigated the physician for construing sexuality too narrowly and for ignoring the phenomenon of resistance and then detailed the technical errors in the other physician's advice, holding that attempts to tell the patient "the secrets which have been discovered by the physician" were objectionable. Freud's paper spoke directly to Emerson's position treating his patient in the hospital. Others with little knowledge of psychoanalysis were brusquely telling his patient what was wrong with her, telling her—by the time he delivered the paper—that what she needed, like Freud's hysterical patient, was more sex. Like the woman's other physician, they were leaving no room for psychoanalytic treatment as a remedy for her symptoms—which, in the end, proved the only means to opening Rachel's hand and keeping it open.[47]

THE ANALYTIC BREAST

The pattern noted above, of Emerson's probing and Rachel's resisting before finally yielding, structured the last half of this segment of the treatment. His patient hospitalized with paralysis, Emerson turned immediately to penetrating the secret he was certain contained the key to her real troubles. However much Emerson stressed the therapeutic opportunities opened by Rachel's confinement, he could not fully moderate his disappointment in what he continually interpreted as her lack of effort. Discouraged from the start (session 16, n. 92), he was, by his own telling, impatient, insistent, stern, and scolding. She admitted to being afraid she yielded to Jack. "Can you not be brave, and face it?" he asked.[48] To get back the use of her feet she said she would try, acknowledging the motive power he ascribed to the paralysis. But try as she might, she could not give him as much as he wanted. "Got nothing," "no tangible results," "got nothing more," "could get nothing that was not forced out of her"—scattered through Emerson's notes is evidence of the frustration of his fiercely penetrating resolve. When she feared her throat would be paralyzed, he forced a pencil into her clenched hand, telling her the hand knew what she could not say (session 21). After she was able to recall the raping neighbor throwing her to the floor, he assumed control over her posture during the sessions, cranking the wheelchair to which she was confined such that she was lying down.[49] Shortly after this he made note of the concern she'd had, as she lay on the floor in the immediate aftermath of the rape, about whether "she would ever walk again"—a concern that her current paralysis no doubt reawakened (session 42). Later she was unable to lie down, even at night, so palpable was the feeling of a man on top of her (session 50).

Rachel could at times identify with Emerson's frustration, deriding herself for being as foolish and withholding as he told her she was. But what is more striking is that she identified him with the rapist, fusing the two as he drilled away at her resistance, and that this did not give him pause but, rather, encouraged him to push harder. Two days after her hand dramatically unclenched as she recalled the scene of the rape, Emerson, as an experiment, had her lie on the floor in his office. "Got nothing," he tersely wrote (session 61). That night she dreamed of being on the floor in his office. "It seemed as if the man was there and you were there and you kept saying you haven't told me this and you haven't told me that, until you do you can't get up," she reported (session 62). Although Emerson clearly realized the importance of this dream, noting that he interpreted it "into its elemental significance" (session 63), in the published version of the case these sessions were excised. "We got nowhere," was all he wrote.[50] Indeed, Emerson's complaints along this line had been escalating, and would do so until the remission of her paralysis. "The next week showed no apparent advance,"[51] he wrote, or, "nothing of significance was either learned or done today."[52] "Wednesday, Thursday, and Friday showed no advance,"[53] he summed up sessions in which she reported a number of significant dreams, including one in which he was provoked by her refusal to tell (session 66).

Emerson was so committed to an archeological-cum-geological model of the psychoanalytic process that he discounted material produced by the patient that did not lead him directly to the buried gems he sought. For example, despite what might appear to have been an abundant flow of material, Emerson complained repeatedly that Rachel did not easily free associate, which he saw as a concomitant of her limited intelligence in combination with her fierce resistances. To his mind, the regular flow of a session was not "free association"; rather, free association was what followed from his explicit instructions to her—"now, free associate." The process, he complained, "seems so aimless, so endless, so utterly without form and void." It was, he maintained in the published account of the case, "a great mistake to imagine that 'free association' is the essence of psychoanalysis," despite what he allowed were its advantages, the way it revealed unexpected relations and connections. His admission that in free association "the temptation to take things in one's own hands and direct the mental processes is almost overpowering" suggests it was as much what the analyst's surrender stirred in him as it was the impenetrability of the patient's resistances that made the technique so problematic. One had to "overcome a good many tendencies" in oneself in granting the patient free rein to associate. "Thus, there is a conflict in the analyzer's own breast between his desire to direct and his willingness to listen," Emerson wrote, his invocation of the analytic breast suggesting that the abnegation of control that free association demanded of the analyst was, for him, intolerably feminizing.[54] Not for him the maternal analyst, and no playing "the tender mother role" that Freud would later see Ferenczi playing and that Freud himself had assumed vis-à-vis Dora, despite what Forrester has noted was his "disinclination to play the woman's part."[55] Rather, the most essential thing in an analysis, Emerson held, was the analyst's "insistent, vigorous urging the patient on."[56]

Emerson's position on the transference, which he conceived of in almost completely positive terms—and thus, as in Rachel's reading of *Eagle Blood*, as akin to hypnosis—masked a similar conflict between his casting of the analyst on the one hand as miner, digging, blasting, and drilling to reach the patient's repressed complexes and, on the other, as an endlessly attentive and sympathetic maternal figure, the perfect listener.[57] He could write of the transference as a force he called on to supplement his prodding and scolding, explaining that once it was established that his desires had acquired "a motive power in her mind," she would respond to his entreaties to reveal ever more by letting down a little "the bars of her repression."[58] Her affection for him, that is, would lead her to take on his desires as her own. This conception of the positive transference as part of the miner's armamentarium all but overshadowed other possible interpretations of it, even though there was material in the analysis from which he might have arrived at a more nuanced interpretation. For example, Rachel reported having woken from a dream in which she had posed a simple question "hearing herself say she didn't see why it couldn't be answered without going through all those questions." Emerson noted: "I was in it" (session 42). Several days later she dreamed she "had something to tell; but couldn't do it," following which Emerson and another doctor "accused her of different things, and she said, I won't tell anybody" but then went home and told her mother. Later in this session, she told Emerson she had the thought she "was lying down, peaceful," adding she "thought if you were here I could tell you." Emerson uncharacteristically allowed "her to speak or not as she chose" (session 45). Rachel ambivalently cast Emerson as the good mother—the one to whom she could tell what was on her mind—one moment, the hectoring mother the next. In another dream "her mother scolded her and she cried and cried, then her mother told her," just as Emerson typically did after scolding and upbraiding her, "that she didn't mean anything but did it for her own good." Later in the same session he noted he was impatient with her (session 44).

Maternal concerns and themes run through the middle of this block of sessions, in which Rachel dreamed repeatedly of Emerson and of her mother. Her dream of happily walking in the woods with her mother is significant in that "the woods" was her shorthand for the first traumatic scene (session 51). Her dream of "the room and you," referring to Emerson, is similarly significant, "the room" in every other context serving as shorthand for the second traumatic scene, the rape by the neighbor. Both dreams suggest she was attempting to master the traumas by unconsciously associating them with the comfort and succor she hoped to get from the good mother-analyst; later, she dreamed she was sleeping with her mother, "begging her to help me" (session 53). She dreamed she helped her sick mother walk, taking her "in her arms and walk[ing] around the room with her" as perhaps she wished Emerson would do for her (session 43). As she focused more intently on Jack, however, and as Emerson pressed more sexual material on her, showing her schematic diagrams of the female sexual anatomy, the mother of her dreams—perhaps merged with the prodding analyst—turned critical and insistent (sessions 56, 57). Consider, for example, Emerson's interpretation of a dream Rachel reported in which the "mother was trying to make her do things but couldn't and said she would have to send her to me but she didn't see how it was a mother couldn't make her do more than a doctor." Provoked with the mother, she refused to do anything and, in the dream, went off by herself, which was, Emerson must have realized, precisely what she was doing with him (session 57). Yet, he wrote, "here we can see an almost complete Übertragung or transference of her affections from her mother to me," (session 57, n. 190) in this instance as in others equating transference solely with affection. Whereas Freud, in 1912, saw transference largely as resistance, Emerson saw it as a weapon to be used against resistance.[59] There was little room in Emerson's rudimentary conception of the transference for the sort of ambivalence about him and the treatment expressed in Rachel's dream. Emerson could appreciate the significance of Rachel's expressions of her desires and wishes and could instruct her such that she could say, after telling of a dream in which she arranged for the release of the raping neighbor from jail, "I seemed to be having a conflict in my wishes" (session 69). He appears by contrast to have been unable to comprehend the mix of reluctance, anger, desire, and wishes to please that constituted her transference to him.

NEGATIVE TRANSFERENCES

Emerson saw the negative transference not as integral to the work of analysis but as an interference with it. And he saw the patient's attachment to her mother—or mother-image, as he put it, borrowing from Jung by way of Freud—and hate for her father as hindrances to the development of the transference, not as templates that were constitutive of it. "Always it is the vision of her mother that stands between her and the knowledge she is seeking," Emerson noted (session 22). Locked in even fiercer battle with the dead mother than was Rachel herself, here as elsewhere he angrily blamed the mother for all but successfully "opposing every step of advance."[60] Emerson took on as his own the manifest story Rachel told, of the mother as hindrance to knowledge and sexual pleasure. But her stance was more ambivalent, and he seems to have missed this, as his remarkably callous dismissal of her maternal longings— "luckily, for the success of the treatment, her mother has been dead several years"—suggests.[61] It is possible Rachel unconsciously summoned up the prohibiting mother-in-the-cloud as counter to Emerson's insistent prodding, as the only means she had to control the pace and the content of her revelations. Further, not only did she admit to worshipping the mother (session 22), but, through a number of sessions, she fused the mother with Jack, about whom she several times expressed a double wish—either that she could have never even known him on the one hand or that she could have had him completely on the other. Her desires for the mother were likewise conflicted. Emerson, however, saw the mother only as an obstacle, not as object of desire, an opponent of the analysis who prevented a proper transference from developing.[62]

The transference did develop, but, again, in a form Emerson was not prepared to recognize as properly—that is, uniformly positive—transferential. Rachel's wish for a father like Emerson was to his mind indicative of "the progress of the Übertragung, or transference of her affections to me" (session 20, n. 105); conversely, her hate for her father, he held, "actively interfered with the transference."[63] Yet transferential currents were thick in a number of sessions during which, as she questioned the authenticity of the story she had been told of her origins, Rachel imaginatively reconstructed a family for herself. If her mother was an adulterer like her father, was it that she wasn't really her father's daughter? Her mother hadn't wanted her, had tried to abort her; was that because she was illegitimate? Where indeed was her mother's marriage certificate, she wondered as she turned over the possibility her family was legally a fraud. Her "real" family a possible fiction, Rachel invited Emerson to join her in forming a new one. Casting him as parent, she dreamed of his wife visiting her on the ward (session 28); and, in the dream that preceded her explicitly characterizing him as father, she dreamed of finding a baby and being of two minds about whether she wanted it or not (session 20). Later she dreamed two nights running that Emerson had betrayed her by telling another doctor—who she was sure would tell her father—of the rape (sessions 32, 33), a dream that may have been expressive of her struggle over whether or not Emerson would be faithful to her in a way her parents were not.

The dream may have touched a countertransferential nerve in Emerson. Rachel told Emerson she had deliberately tried to "tantalize" the other doctor in both dreams, sneering at him in the dream as she asked him whether there was anything else he wanted to know. Emerson changed the "tantalize" of the case notes—Rachel's word—to "irritate" in the "Detailed Account," suggesting that he was not immune to "the problems of jealousy and hate" that her playing "one physician against the other" raised. Was he alone to be tantalized by her? Or was it that he found her bringing the other doctor into the picture irritating? Emerson's only comments on the "Gegenübertragung"—"the reaction feeling of the analyst"—cast it as along the lines of "the famous problem of the three bodies," assuming the presence of a third party. "Reports of the patient as to what the other analysts may have said" were especially problematic, in this construction drawing another into the equation as a way of possibly deflecting the intensity of his own reactions. Patient reports, he maintained, "create currents and counter currents so complex and interfering as to render their analysis and control quite hopeless."[64] It is clear that Emerson's own analytic equanimity was unsettled by all the talk of new family alliances and that he mimicked some of the fluidity of identifications Rachel displayed. While for the most part he identified with Rachel against the prohibiting mother, in the immediate wake of her expressing her desire for him as father, he identified with the father against the silent, sneering daughter, faulting her in uncharacteristically arch language for the sullen set she displayed "against the author of her being" (session 20, n. 107).

Yet however much Emerson self-consciously abjured the model of the analyst as perfect mother, there is evidence to suggest that in the privacy of the consulting room he could play—but not acknowledge he was playing—the part. Rachel does appear to have identified with Emerson in his quest to uncover the hidden parts of her past, and by the end of this segment of the analysis, she was fighting herself as much as she was fighting him. On one occasion, associating about Jack and the rapist, she wondered "if we got that if there were anything else we would have to get," with the "we" suggesting that the project of retrieval was not Emerson's alone (session 42). Later she dreamed she would kill herself if she couldn't find out what it was that was the matter with her (session 68), and it is clear by this point that the desire to walk once again was hers as well as his, appearing intermittently in dreams (session 59). There are also hints of a more maternal-cum-erotic stream in the transference, of which Emerson made no note. Unlike the withholding real mother, Emerson was a font of sexual knowledge for Rachel. And unlike the skeptical real mother, Emerson believed in her stories of having been abused, acting the detective's part in unearthing every detail. "I wish you would start asking me," she said to Emerson in the midst of one session, after which he put his hands over her eyes. She then recalled not only more of the rape but also a dream of pleasurable sex with Jack, suggesting that she may have experienced the laying-on-of-hands as an intimate, not always unwanted, gesture (session 33). Three weeks later, she dreamed first of being "awfully happy" walking in the woods with her mother, and then of being "in bed without any pillows under her head." In the dream, Emerson, at last, came and tucked some pillows under her head, sensing and then relieving her discomfort (session 51). Learning that both parents had long forbidden her to cry and had punished her for it, Emerson the indulgent mother told her she should cry whenever she wanted to and informed the nurses and hospital physicians of the necessity of her being allowed this emotional release (session 68). Shortly thereafter, two nights before her release from the hospital, she dreamed she was playing with Emerson's children (session 79).

Emerson mentioned in passing that sexual attraction was part of the positive transference. But whatever libidinal currents may have flowed between him and Rachel went unremarked upon in print. Emerson was no doubt familiar with the vision of psychoanalysis as a scene in which analyst and patient traded in disgusting sexual details. The scene would be invoked by a Psychopathic Hospital psychiatrist who, after hearing Emerson present Rachel's case at a hospital conference, compared psychoanalysis to vivisection and said it was all "too much for me to discuss."[65] Rachel's father would invoke it as well, accusing Emerson of taking sexual advantage of his daughter (session 197). Even the young Karl Menninger found "something a little fishy" in Emerson's—and the psychoanalyst's—focus on childhood sexuality.[66] It is not surprising, then, that Emerson should have preemptively distanced himself from these anticipated accusations of wrongdoing, ensconced as he was in a private room with a young woman talking endlessly of sex. He could better envision psychoanalysis as a manly geologist's endeavor than as a scene of mutual seduction.

Emerson felt a good deal had been accomplished by the end of this segment of the treatment. The paralysis for which Rachel had been hospitalized for over two months lifted as she was able to remember the details of the mother's betrayal around the rape by the neighbor, which came in a rush in sessions 74 and 75. Emerson wrote that upon discharge from the hospital, Rachel was "very well, and has sent in her application papers for admittance to a training school for nurses. To be a nurse had always been her ambition, she said, but she had been prevented before, both by her illness and the absolute prohibition of her parents."[67] One year later, he was more guarded in his assessment, hinting that it was more Rachel's decision than his that she would go home. "I want to say that in any work I had urged a certain level and if the patient insists on going home it seems advisable to let her do so," he told his Psychopathic Hospital colleagues, adding, "trusting that if I had reached the bottom of things that she will then be all right; fearing if I have not she will then have further symptoms" (Staff Meeting; following session 175). She did, writing him within a month of vomiting and telling him she occasionally fell down.

Readers of the first installment of the published account of the case, which appeared in early 1913, might have thought Rachel fully recovered had it not been for the intervention of Morton Prince, editor of the *Journal of Abnormal Psychology.* "She continued to gain," Emerson originally wrote in summing up the case, "and was discharged from the hospital May 11, apparently cured." This was one optimistic closure too many for Prince. He instructed Emerson to underscore—italicize—the "apparently" and to add another sentence to indicate that "there were at work other complexes which remained to be discovered" lest readers be misled and Emerson find himself in "a false position."[68]

Chapter 4 Text: Sessions 1–80: 24 January–10 May 1912

Rachel C., 22.
Food and water wouldn't stay down. Comes up. Isn't vomiting. This commenced about six months ago.
At her mother's death, "it came over me that I had to get better and I started gaining right off."[1] (She was at Adams Nervine[2] and didn't know mother was sick till told of her death.)

It's like a cloud—A blue feeling hanging over me. This cloud feeling came on in the summer. I didn't want to go to any place; things I used to like to do, I didn't want to do—I feel like sleeping all the time, yet when I go to bed I can't sleep.
It was before the fourth of July. She and a number of other girls went to the field to see the fire-works. She ate some pop-corn and threw it

up. This passed off, and wasn't serious till Fall. This wasn't the very first time?[3]
"I can't remember." The blue feeling came on about this time.

Dreamed last night—troubled—it seemed to be some place I didn't want to
be there. I was trembling all over—I often do that. I went to bed about 11—
couldn't sleep—got up at 1—went down stairs—back at 4.

I sometimes have the feeling I am walking down in space, everything becomes
blurred, I can't seem to bring myself to where I am.

A week ago last Saturday the last "spell like"—I can't seem to keep my head
about me—I go off, dazed—I don't know anything.

The first one came on when she was 18 or 19 in a friend's house one Sunday
night.[4]

She was in Telephone Company, Winchester. Service men. "Bad test." Chief
operator—She was terrible—scolds.

Mother dead 3 years this coming March.[5]

Went to friend's house right from the office.

I never do cry to my knowledge, I haven't for years, I sometimes wish I could.

When I was in the Company I was always dreading it—bad tests, being discharged, scolded.

I was nervous before that, at school I was nervous—"My imagination was big."
In 7th grade about 11, was taken down with St. Vitus Dance.[6] I was in bed
some months; they said I was out of my head. After that I remember trying to
do things and couldn't, shaking.

Were you ever frightened as a little girl?

"Yes." How? "I've had men chase me; fire; like everybody else."

One time I was alone. With others, once, he grabbed her from behind. Others
stoned him. He vowed he'd get me. (About 7). He was the one who chased me
again when I was about 14. (In Worcester—cars—followed.)

SESSION 3: MONDAY, 29 JANUARY 1912

Friday night dreamed of her pastor and choir coming to her house on business. While there her father passed through the room without speaking which
humiliated her much. I was worked up in the dream because I was rushing on
some sewing and the house was very littered.

Had to go to grocery in Woburn—Father refused—Had a dress to fit when
she came home.

Saturday night dreamed she was coming in here with her brother. Left him
here. When she got home heard that he was dead. As I heard it I looked out of

the window and seemed to see mother coming down the street. She was old and bent. I told her and she said if he ever was dead she'd bring him to life. She asked me if father was any better than he was, I said no.[7]

Sees her mother sometimes in the day.

Always felt badly towards father. Was punished for not going to him. It wasn't like being stubborn, hate, fear exactly.

[Age] 16 knew—I followed him one night. Two years ago followed him to Boston—Postal—meet at square.[8]

Wouldn't go to him as a child. Remembers 5, mother tells her it was so at 3.[9]

Was 19 when fainted.

SESSION 4: TUESDAY, 30 JANUARY 1912

Medicine closet—2 weeks ago. (Thinking of suicide.)[10]

He accused me of killing mother—worry etc.

Rings on her fingers.

About a year ago her first fear of insanity.

Was at Adams Nervine from January to May 1, 1909. (1910)[11]

Mother died March 1, 1909. (1910)[12]

Born July 25, 1889.

SESSION 5: FRIDAY, 2 FEBRUARY 1912

Didn't sleep last night more than an hour.

Life—live—wish it wasn't so—(Wish what wasn't so?) to live—wish there was no such thing as life (is that on account of your father?) I suppose so, I never used to feel so—About a year ago. This was the time when the young man wanted to go with her.

Had another spell Wednesday night, at 6:30. Father at home. Seemed to realize she was going to have it. Went up stairs—Found herself on the bed where her father put her—Father got a girl friend to come and put her to bed. Slept well. Had just got her dishes done. It seemed as though all her blood had rushed into her head. Her brother remarked how red she looked. It was about 5 or 10 minutes after that. She felt a terrible headache. While washing dishes was thinking of going to church, to Wednesday night meeting. Father wanted her to go with him. I didn't feel as though I wouldn't go, I was thinking whether I would go or not. He asked to go during supper. I didn't really want to go, but I thought, if I can get ready I will.[13]

Feels as though a cloud hangs over her all the time, as though some awful news were coming, something awful going to happen.

Cloud[14]—gloomy feeling—wish I could tell what it was—wishing you wouldn't have me keep my eyes shut—keep thinking to keep them closed instead of thinking of anything else.

Childhood—my own—when I'm home with mother.

Went to kindergarten at 4 1/2—liked it. Half year in Brightwood.

Born in Worcester, went to Waukegan, Illinois, when 6 months old. Came to Brightwood when 4 1/2, to Winchester when 5 1/2, there ever since.

Mother said she was irritable as a child. If anyone spoke crossly she was stubborn, but if pleasantly spoken to could be gotten to do anything.

The strong feeling against her father seemed to come first in Brightwood.

Brightwood—our living there—house—Lived in a flat—played with the two children down stairs—girls.

Brother born just before we left Waukegan. 4 years younger. Doesn't remember ever taking care of brother. "Mama said I never wanted children."[15]

I know I used to dread having Sunday come because I had to go to walk with father, and brother in a go-cart. I know he used to plague me all the time. If we met a dog or a cat on the street he'd plague that animal knowing it would plague me. He'd pull my hair, he'd make believe throw brother out of the carriage, and laugh when he'd do it, but I wouldn't know whether he would do it or not. He'd make believe he was going to hurt mama—as if he were going to strike her—he'd be laughing, and mama would be laughing too, but I was afraid he would.

Did he ever strike your mother? Yes, I saw him once when I was 15 or 16. They were disputing—slapped her across her back. I know she was cross, but what she said I don't know. I couldn't believe it for a minute, I felt awfully bad. I told him he ought to be ashamed of himself, he told me to mind my own business.

I think it was right after that that I grew suspicious. I didn't know anything about badness between man and wife, but when I found it out I surmised where his money went to.

Girls let it out.[16] Was living at home, helping her mother.

Sex knowledge shocked her. When she first heard this she hardly spoke to her mother for a year. She said I ought not to feel that way that was the way people did. I blurted it out to her one day and after that I got over it. Was about 16 or 17.[17]

When she had St. Vitus Dance her father mocked her.

SESSION 6: MONDAY, 5 FEBRUARY 1912

Dreamed last night she was with mother talking. Sewing together. (Slept very little.) It seemed as if she had been off quite a while and come back. Was telling her how cross papa was; about brother; about house; about brother's toe, etc.

Up to about 15 thought father-mother relation purely spiritual. A girl was who always telling smutty stories, during sloyd,[18] said, "do you know that woman?" She goes around with another man.[19] (She was married.) I suppose my face betrayed my innocence because the other girls turned away their heads. She went on to tell her that men gave women money for that and I knew that money was missing in the house and it flashed right on me that was what it was.

Between 12 and 13 she and a friend who lived next door used to go and look for babies in the back of the family doctor's buggy. He said he brought babies. About a month after the revelation followed father.

A few months after this her mother asked her what made her so cold, etc.[20] She said Violet's mother was the same.

Wouldn't go out with her mother. "I just felt I didn't want her around with me." Mother was very much hurt. "I just wanted to die right off, it seemed as though I didn't want to live. I suppose I was afraid to live." It seemed as though everything was a mystery, and I didn't know anything. And then it came so sudden it frightened me.

Father was always surly and snappy to mother.

Doctors said it was studying that gave her St. Vitus Dance.

Broke her collar bone 3 times, shoulder blade once, ankle once, and 2 fingers. Had to walk 7 miles with broken collar bone. 11 A.M. Set 7 P.M. Picnic.

1) Stairs about [age] 8. 2) off bed fooling with brother. 9. 3) just before St. Vitus. 4) off couch, fooling with brother. Just over collar bone break. 2 days before Christmas. Mother—money—Brother. 5) Going down steps out doors, tripped. About 13. 6) Fell in kitchen. Just after St. Vitus. Really had it then. Was carrying some dishes, fell over box couch, broke 3rd. finger of each hand. Had scarlet fever when 4. Mastoid[21] on left side. Measles, mumps, pneumonia.

Two years before St. Vitus would faint frequently. Sometimes at a fright— Lamp tipped over. When she got especially nervous just before St. Vitus would faint away at nothing.

St. Vitus lasted a full year.

Was going with a friend[22] when first attack occurred. Was at his house at time. Had been going with him since 15 1/2 (February 1). It was Sunday night, he came to the office to take me home to his house to supper.

Gave him up about a year ago last October.

He came to live in the other half of double house in which she lived. Suspected his character then now she knew. Father told her some things.[23] Told her to look out for him. A girl acquaintance, who had a rather bad name, who had been drinking enough to be talkative, came out with her one day from Boston, and told her Henry had been in a bad house, she had seen him, she didn't think she would go with a boy like that.

Smoker, etc. Money—electrician.

Woman came out with her last July or August. She wrote him in October 1910.

Still goes to see his sister, mother, and invalid father. They still live next door.

He told brother he wasn't good enough for me—They work in the same shop.[24]

Started coming in to M.G.H. October 1908.

Jack died Nov. 1907. First attack Spring of 1908.

With her own doctor in Winchester all Summer—sent to Dr. Waterman.[25]

St. Vitus, fall of 1900.[26]

Discovered father in the Spring of 1904, just after she started going with Henry. Started with him in February.[27]

Always thought he was true till after she returned from the Nervine.

In telephone employ a year March 1907 to March 1908.

Feels a burden, a cloud, something going to break. Feels it all the time now. Ever since last night feels it stronger. To-day feels like a veil was coming right down.

Chief operator always picked on her, did her work under constant fear.

Veil[28]—cloud over me—everything ends in—what you ask me—wishing it wouldn't come—seems as if the cloud, or whatever it is keeps creeping nearer all the time.

Child—what you were saying about a child or baby being beautiful—everything you said about it.

Father—my own—wish he was good—cross things he says—what he said to make me feel bad—he wished I'd go away—said that last night—came down and found I hadn't gone to bed—wanted peace.

He found out that I was coming in here. He said if I'd eat, go to bed, etc., that the folks didn't know anything in here. Company in last night, he threw slurs at her, etc. He was never that way before, because when people came in he was more than pleasant. He asked her if she was coming in to-day.

SESSION 7: TUESDAY, 6 FEBRUARY 1912

Had an attack last night about 5:30, which lasted about 3/4 hour. Knew for a second before the attack that it was coming. Everything went dark. Was sick in the afternoon; threw off a lot of green slime[29]; couldn't eat any supper. Didn't the nausea come from having to sit at table with father?[30] Has felt that way.[31]

It seemed as if something were thrown over my head. I couldn't see anything. It seemed as if something had gone the other day but now it seems just the same.

It seemed wrong for her mother to go on living with her father after she discovered he went with other women. It seemed for a time as though under no circumstances should they live together.

Love—to love one another—I don't know what to do—thinking what love was—more often it isn't what they claim it is—I was thinking about the friends I'd been with.

One fellow died, I was going with Henry for a while, broke up with him for a while and went with this other fellow. I was about 17. Felt pretty badly about his death. Henry was jealous.[32]

Started to leave father when he hit her; might have thought of it before.[33]

First knowledge about sex "used to make the shivers go over me." Mother spoke of her loss of appetite. Doesn't remember that she was nauseated.

The time when father hit mother was the worst. It made me awfully mad, hurt, ashamed to go out. I was afraid people would know.[34]

Menses began at 17.

Dreamed she was coming in here.[35] As soon as she got here I told her what the matter was. Saw Dr. Waterman and some other doctors. I was talking with the other doctors. She said, "It seemed as if I were lying down."

Couch—laying down on a couch—brings back last night's dream—I can't put my thought to it.

When I asked her about marriage, she said, "I just feel I don't want to and I can't."

I don't know what the cause is but I can imagine different things.

She was about 7 or 8 when she was punished by her mother for not going to her father. She slapped her.

SESSION 8: WEDNESDAY, 7 FEBRUARY 1912

Slept in a high-back rocker, dozing for a half hour at a time. If she lies down she feels like jumping up and screaming.

This morning I gave her the association test, using Jung's list.[36]

During the test there were a good many disturbances, such as, baby crying, people talking, etc.

Many of the answers were given as though "Why of course you ought to know what that means, what a silly question."

I couldn't think about anything, only the word you asked.

99)[37] A picture of a woman papa brought home with him. Then thought of the reverse, a good woman.

Thinking of trouble about all the time. Things that worry me. The way father does; fault finding; these spells. Wishing all the time she could be happy.

Really does read a great deal. Crisis, St. Elmo, Beulah, by Lady Augusta Evans.[38]

Often reads two books in a day, Sundays. I read it, that's all there is to it. I read it for the time being.

I did try to fight it out by myself.

Last night she dreamed she was in the hospital and that I was trying to make her tell something she wouldn't and couldn't tell.

SESSION 9: MONDAY, 12 FEBRUARY 1912

Had an attack yesterday morning at 10. Father and brother home.

Thinking of here—wondering whether I'd ever stop having these spells—yesterday—work—around the house—company, was tired, wished they would go home.

Has a dazed feeling, as if her feet were not on the floor. Has these feelings with spells.

Couldn't speak till 11 last night, and was afraid she was going to lose her voice again. First lost her voice when the spells started.[39]

Grandfather died 4 1/2 years ago, November. Mother left her to take care of things.

This was the time she began to be worried.[40]

I didn't go with him openly, mother didn't want me to go with him, she didn't think he was a good fellow. She knew I met him at times on the street (Father had forbidden me to bring him to the house), but she didn't know how much.

I only went with him about 6 or 8 weeks. It was about 3 weeks later that he died. Both were jealous. It broke me up for quite a while.

I don't think he would have been all right if the girl hadn't been all right.[41] Full of fun, had a good time with him.

All this was going on when she was supplying at different telephone places.

He fascinated me when I was with him. I looked for him but once he was out of sight. I didn't feel the same.

I had one dream I always remembered. I went to the theater with him. When we came home, Henry met us. They had a fight and I ran home. Henry came in later with a revolver and I woke up with a scream.

I went to the theater a day or two before I broke up with Henry.[42]

I was always on the watch because they said he was not a good fellow.

Met him sometimes every night.

He was a Drummer.[43]

I don't think I would have gone with him at all if father hadn't forbidden it. Tried to see how far I could go and not have father know.

He kissed her once when he was going away to New York, but he hugged her about every night he was with her.

I don't remember thinking about it.

Mother said he was not a good fellow because he was so affectionate; i.e., talked, etc.[44]

I kind of felt it was deceit, in a way, but I couldn't help but like him.

She said she lied at home, sometimes, about him.[45]

What made you throw him over?

He was there to supper. She wouldn't make him what he wanted. He refused to play with her as a partner. She saw him cheat, etc.[46]

Mama was in Beverly at Grandfather's funeral; papa was away; sent word the house was clear (Wednesday).

He died in December. Attacks in March, 1908.

Dreamed last night she was in here again.[47] I was trying to find out things. Dropped asleep reading a book with Hypnotism in it.[48] A woman makes a man do anything she wanted. It seemed all the time as if I was afraid you would ask me something, but I couldn't think what it was, when I woke up.

The cloud came on first after that awful blue feeling 4 July 1911.

Papa was extra cross.

Went with this woman. He had brought her home before this, in the Spring. That night I met a fellow, went with him a short time.

It was hard to give Henry up, she had been with him so long. I thought of it off and on then I put it out of my mind. (About running away.) Brother held her.

When did you make the final decision? Sept. 1911. She first seriously thought of going in July.

Brother did want to go too, to uncle's in New Hampshire. She had very little sewing and didn't know how they could earn enough to support themselves. She was going to aunt's in Pawtucket. Mother's aunt, her great aunt. She had a baby when she was 15. We call her Auntie Eva. Asked questions about different ages. Found it out about a year after discovered father. Aunt Nettie.

Spells started again about 5 weeks ago. About 6 or 8 weeks before that had fazed feelings. It was then she went to the medicine closet hunting. Had the fazed feelings a little before Christmas. Made up her mind to stay in October. Felt a relief in making up her mind but all the time wished it was different. Was reading Eagle Blood yesterday morning when she had the attack. page 159. Thought I was a hypnotist, for a moment.

Lie—happy—must be happy to love—what you are going to ask me next—about those spells and what brings them on—everything—about going home tonight going away—saying I would go away—

A gentleman asked her to go to a party with him, she promised, but won't go. If I want to go any place I'd rather go with girls.

SESSION 10: TUESDAY, 13 FEBRUARY 1912

3)[49] Dreamed the old dream. It seemed as if I were running away from somebody or something. I would stumble and get up and stumble; but it didn't seem as if anybody were after me.

I have not had it for a long time but I used to have it often. First spells. She was 7 or 8 when first chased, about 14 next.

Mother once told me she wished she had never married. She was about 17. She understood that it was sexual intercourse that her mother objected to. That was about the time she went with Jack. She said she was happy till she came to Winchester.

1) She also dreamed last night that she was married to that Jack.

2) Dreamed she was taking cornet lessons from her girl friend's brother and was getting along fine.

He was at her house that evening and said, I wish you had a cornet Rachel, etc. He was playing a wedding march.

4) It seemed as if I went for the milk and met Henry.

Didn't like to play with other children at school.

Brother liked dolls.

She liked to slide; but doesn't care for skating.

Met Henry in school.

First lost her voice towards the end of 1908.

(She is shaking a good deal because she heard Dr. Baldwin throw a girl in the next room into a hypnotic convulsion. Baldwin asked me in to see him do it. It looked like a regular orgasm.)

The cloud didn't seem so near last night.

Table tipped over 4 weeks ago last Saturday night. Then had an attack that night. Had one about two weeks before, father was especially cross. Saturday afternoon. Her girl friend had just come over and asked her what was the matter. I started to tell her and that was all. The other attack came on about 10 minutes after the lamp tipped over. Some such thought as wishing it had been on me. I knew it was wicked and that I hadn't ought to think that. Tried to put the thought out of her mind but couldn't. Father and brother were fooling. The thought that is so strong is a desire for death.

She does have a dream that she cannot remember but when she wakes she feels sick and is shaking all over. The last time she had it was last Thursday night; attack was Sunday.

SESSION 11: WEDNESDAY, 14 FEBRUARY 1912

Vomited yesterday when she tried to eat.

1) Dreamed she was at a banquet. It seemed as if she were cutting thousands of loaves of bread. It seemed like two places mixed: hall we have banquets in and own house.

2) Dreamed brother was dying and she was tending him.

3) Dreamed something, but what, she cannot say. She felt very badly troubled.

Banquet—the dream—eating—wishing I could eat.

Loaf. bread—cutting—

Cut—cut, get cut—I hate to think of cut.

I was thinking where we were last night and the time we had. At an entertainment, with some girls, dancing. We came home, sat up a while, sewed, started to read, fell asleep in her chair.

Brother—my own brother—hope his foot will get well, I often wonder what kind of a boy he'll be good, think of other girl's brothers—the other fellow—Henry—Jack—I keep thinking I hadn't ought to tell things to anybody.

The last time she had the anxiety dream was last Thursday. (The day I couldn't come.)

It seemed as if something awful had happened to her. It seemed as if she were alone. Had this dream 5 or 6 times. First time about when stomach was so bad, about last October when she began to throw up everything easily. Just after that time she made up her mind to stay. The first time she was at her aunts. Adopted son—separated—wife in Worcester—living with another woman in Pawtucket.

He sneered at her for going to church—discussion with aunt in morning. Bert—Emma. Started talking about church again. She didn't believe in the resurrection or the hereafter. Argued with her but she always brought up some argument that would overthrow mine.

The next time she had the anxiety dream was soon after she came home. One time she woke up and screamed, about a week before the last one. It was after she began coming in here to see me.

Whenever she smells smoke and can not locate it, it makes her sick to her stomach.

"Cloud" came a little after first dream.

Awfully gloomy feeling came on after return from Pawtucket. (Was ten days there). Had it about 2 months before the attack.

Had the dazed feeling come on about January 1, too.

Went to the medicine closet last about 2 weeks ago. She said to herself when she came home from Adams[50] if they came on again she would kill herself.[51]

Second series of attacks January 6–20 February ? 5, 11.[52]

St. Vitus at school couldn't write.

Mother said when she was out of her head[53] she tried to kill herself; called for scissors, dagger, paper-cutter.

Father whipped her once when she was about 5.

SESSION 12: THURSDAY, 15 FEBRUARY 1912

Had that awful dream.

1) It seemed as if she were in bed and mother was trying to put her to sleep. It seemed as if somebody came in the room just as I was going to sleep but I did not seem to be bothered.

2) It seemed as if she were in a house. It was a place she felt she ought not to be. Very few women mostly men. I thought I would stay anyway. They were dancing and having a good time. It seemed as if I were dancing myself.

3) I had just dropped asleep, hadn't been asleep more than 5 minutes. Wakened with that terrible feeling as before.[54]

Dance—dancing—what they did—wanting to learn before I did—dancing I have seen at theaters—what I seemed to see in the dream last night—how the men were carrying on and it didn't seem nice—hugging and kissing-spieling[55]—girls kicking their legs up—telling horrid jokes—laughing vulgar—drinking.

I wonder whether I'll ever be that way or not.

(After a long wait) I can't tell everything that goes through.[56] I can't put them in words, I'd tell them if I could.[57]

I can't, it just seems as if my throat were all closed up.[58] They just go through my mind but I just cannot speak them.

It seems as if that dream were right back.

It seems as if I know, yet I can't speak it.

We found that the dream was partly of her mother.[59]

She stood and was telling her not to tell or remember something. That was what her mother did when she tried to get her to tell her. Her mother stood in front of the cloud and kept it from coming nearer so she could see behind it and tell what it concealed.

Three or four times we tried to get by that cloud and each time her mother stood in the way. Once she saw her pointing her finger at her. Her emotion was tremendous.

SESSION 13: FRIDAY, 16 FEBRUARY 1912

Yesterday had an attack—about 6.

Awake all night till 5. Slept half hour. No dream.

Associations.[60]

Mother—my own mother I keep thinking she wouldn't tell me anything not to tell—I keep thinking back over my life to see if there is anything she could have meant.

Tell—speak—I wish I could tell—it seems as if something kept going over me but I can't tell what it is—a thought and feeling both.[61]

Bed—sleep—I only got that feeling and thought flashed.

Sleep—I wish I could—it seems as if I could sleep it would come to me.[62]

I didn't get anything, only those old thoughts.[63]

I keep thinking I am not a good girl. (Because of something that happened to her.)

It was as if a screen were opened for a moment; as if I did see it for a moment but couldn't. If I could only make myself but I can't.[64]

I didn't think there was but it seems that way.

It seems as if my mother were standing in front of something looking down at me in scorn.[65]

I don't know.

Some boy assault you? It couldn't be; it can't be.

In that cloud she[66] stands so condemning—like that something must be.

It seems as if I might have been insulted,[67] I don't know.

SESSION 14: MONDAY, 19 FEBRUARY 1912

She had 3 attacks Saturday. Slept splendidly Saturday night. Felt well all day Sunday. She is much relaxed. Dreamed last night that she was off in the woods with a child. She seemed to be lost, and was running away from something. It was winter, snow on the ground. It seemed some way as if we had to get down in the snow to hide. I had to cover the child and the child had to cover me. It seemed as if we were hiding.

In another dream it seemed as if somebody were trying to take my ring off.[68]

Associations.

Woods walking in the woods picnics we have had dream it seemed just as I told you it didn't seem anything more

SNOW winter sleighing dream of snow how cross papa was this morning a note I got yesterday and a letter I wrote last night

Mother the way she comes before me sometimes hoping I wouldn't have any more spells wishing I could know what was the trouble wishing the cloud seemed as far away as it did yesterday, it seems nearer today it seems as if that feeling comes over me and I try to drive it away I kind of hoped it would come and yet I didn't what a girl said I said in my sleep I shan't, I won't, I can't, and once in a while I would holler out, 6 months (Saturday night) I also called, mother.

HIDE keep something it seems as if there were something I mustn't tell it seems as if there were something there but I couldn't tell it something seemed to flash over me and said, don't tell

You suspect that? Well, the dreams all seem to point that way.[69]

Oh, I never can do it. It seems a perfect blank and I have not got the courage to look. It seems as if I did that the cloud would come.[70]

Had another dream last night. I thought I had a good cry. It seemed as if I were crying about something and I didn't know what it was. It seemed as if I mustn't cry.

I dreamed about Henry. She cut him.

It seems more like a promise, as if my mother were over me.

I put my hands over her eyes.[71]

She sees a man. She sees herself. She is about 8 or 9.

She finally recalled that it was a neighbor. She was about 13. She had a slight attack, was rigid, eyes closed, etc.[72] I didn't leave her till she had promised to come back tomorrow, which was about 3 p.m.[73]

SESSION 15: TUESDAY, 20 FEBRUARY 1912

Did not sleep all night. Had no attack. Ate nothing.

I told her about sex running through everything.[74] I made her responsibility in the whole matter seem as little as possible. While she acknowledged it all it did not seem as though she were wholly relieved. She still felt the cloud. She relieved me from my promise[75] and let me probe deeper. I put my hands over her eyes.

She saw the room again. After a while she saw woods. Her mind went from woods to room. In the woods she was about 9. She was running. She stumbled. She got up and ran on. She kept stumbling, and getting up, and running. At last a man caught her just as she stumbled.[76] He undressed her. He tied her feet. He put something over her mouth. He called to another man, who came. They hurt her "stomach" awfully. They threatened her if she ever told. She got dressed somehow and got home.

In the room she saw the man again.[77] He had hold of her head. He threw her down. He had her by the throat. She struggled terribly. She doesn't know whether he succeeded or not.

She writhed terribly.[78] But she didn't stiffen as she did yesterday.[79]

She feels as though she had promised not to tell. It seems as though she couldn't live.[80] She is coming back Friday.

SESSION 16: FRIDAY, 23 FEBRUARY 1912

Had an attack Wednesday night at a friend's house.[81] Felt badly all day. Unable to sleep Tuesday night except a little in her chair. Was in a dazed state a good deal Wednesday. Couldn't tell what she was thinking of. Had another attack yesterday at 4:30. Knew for a couple of seconds its onset. Walked through the house from the kitchen to the parlor. Had the horrid old dream, that night, waking up and shaking. Last night had a confusing dream; lot of people in it, girl friends, brother. Dreamed Tuesday night that she was happy.

When she came out of the attack Wednesday her left hand was clenched; couldn't get it open till 10 Thursday morning. Has trouble walking up stairs; knees feel weak.[82]

I put my hands over eyes again. She told me more about the assault in the woods.[83] One man held her while the other partly undressed and assaulted her. Then both men fingered her genitals.[84]

But there was still a cloud.[85] In searching for that, she said that suddenly it went from her head to her legs. She was unable to walk, and her left hand was clenched. She was admitted to the Hospital for over night.[86]

She saw Jack in the cloud. Mother.[87]

SESSION 17: SATURDAY, 24 FEBRUARY 1912

Slept better last night than at any time, for a long while.

Reproduced many scenes with Jack[88]: Straw Ride; Fight with Henry[89]; "Rae isn't like you, she is innocent."[90] "Threw a pack of cards in her face." Mother wanted her. Came one night after father went to bed.

"I'm afraid he'll find out and I don't want to tell."[91]

"If I knew I'd tell."

"It can't be so."

"I wouldn't if I could walk."

"I was just thinking if mama had told me things how much better it would have been."

I put my hands over her eyes.[92] Saw Jack (looking all right); mama (looking scornful); papa (laughing).

She said yesterday that she wished Jack were living and then all this would never have happened. He would have asked her to marry him. She couldn't get Jack off her mind.

Dr. Lee admits her to the Medical Ward. #16.

SESSION 18: MONDAY, 26 FEBRUARY 1912

Slept well Saturday night and last night.

Dreamed of mother. Seemed as if she went some place in the afternoon, didn't want to go and was troubled. Saturday night dreamed of girls at home. Doing something but can't tell what. Also dreamt of Jack but can't remember.

After the assault never went through the woods again till she had left school.[93] Has no recollection of ever telling mother or anybody else about it. Has a vague feeling that she told her mother about the neighbor assaulting her when she was 13.[94]

A common phrase of her mother's was "Girls imagine a lot that don't happen."

Girl, at school, told her about man and woman when she was 15.[95] At the time she grew weak and felt faint, and the girls grabbed her. She stopped at a friend's house before she went home. Never went back to school. Knees have troubled her ever since she left school. Felt "rolling."[96] I don't think I ever thought of it except I felt awfully whenever I saw the man.

SESSION 19: TUESDAY, 27 FEBRUARY 1912

Dr. Baldwin tried to open her hand by force, last night, just after supper. He put a wedge in and did succeed in getting it open while he held it by sheer strength (it took another doctor and a nurse to get it open), but it closed up again immediately as soon as it was released. The wedge was left in and one of the interns tried to take it out but could not. During sleep, however, her hand relaxed enough for her to get it out herself, though she has no recollection of doing it. Her hand and arm was in such pain all night that she was hardly able to sleep at all. She dreamed at one time that her hand was being amputated. He took her mother's ring off, saying that it was likely to hurt her.

Went with Jack 2 months. Told him not to come to see her any more. He died in less than a month.

Put my hands over her eyes.[97]

Jack, mother, warning she gave me, I thought she was not right, different times I've been with him, how people talked about him.

Woods—neighbor—mother—Jack.[98]

It seems as[99] if I ever knew I'd never have any peace.

Cries some. She always said she'd come back. (mother)[100]

Told Jack in October not to come back. He died in November. Convulsions March.

Always sees mother when she lies down.

Jack kneels.

It seems as if Jack, mother, father, and she were in it. (cloud)

It seems as if I told it, it would be as much as my life to tell it.

She said that Jack and the neighbor seemed fused at one time. She sees the room[101] at another.

She goes through the scene in the woods again, but not so vividly. She sees the men on top of her.[102]

She seems to be sick and Jack is kneeling and holding her hands.

Her mother always stands in front of the cloud, and keeps it away. She fears lest her mother return to haunt her if she tells.

She says that it seems like her very life and if she tells she will never have any more peace.

Her mother forbids her to tell.

Jack seems to be asking mother if he may take me to the woods, and I am afraid to look for I know something awful will happen.[103]

SESSION 20: WEDNESDAY, 28 FEBRUARY 1912

Slept well. Letter from father.

1) Dreamed that father was keeping her here.

2) Seemed to be in some place; was trying to pay her board but they wouldn't let her.

3) Seemed as if I was in some place and I found a baby. It was lying down; I wanted to pick it up, but felt like slapping it, as if I wanted to and didn't want to take it.[104]

Woke up mad.

I was thinking I wished I had a father like you.[105]

Mother didn't want her when she was born. She wanted her first child, a sister who died, but was angry with her father for impregnating her. She did everything she could to prevent her birth, like running up and down stairs, etc. She doesn't know that she did anything else to cause an abortion.

Rachel never told her mother anything.[106] Even to get her school reports her mother had to go to the teacher. She was supposed to be a stubborn child. She didn't care for children; liked to be alone. This partially explains her attitude towards her father.[107]

Dr. Putnam[108] never found out the meaning of the "stumbling" dream.

Her mother told her once that she wished she had never married.

Whatever it is concealed behind the cloud it seems as though her mother held the key.

Her mother died of a shock; blood vessel burst in her brain, she said.

SESSION 21: THURSDAY, 29 FEBRUARY 1912

Dr. Jennings wanted to open her hand.

Waked up hearing herself holler, "Let me tell it."

I put my hands over her eyes.

Harry[109]: at Jack's house. He first began to pester her when she worked in the store in Woburn. 3 years. She was introduced to him just before she got rid of Jack. He used to follow her on the cars[110]; gave her candy; had dinners sent in to her at the store; sent her fruit; would take her wheel[111] from the back of the store so she would have to walk home; sent ice cream to the store.[112]

Had my hands off her eyes while she told me the above. Put my hands over eyes again. Writhed terribly.

Mother seemed to have her by the throat.

When a man in the next room said "syphilis" she thought of her mother. (Dr. Spooner was giving 606.[113])

Yesterday when in a sort of day dream it would seem as if her hands were open. While I had my hands over her eyes the second time, she said it felt as if her throat were going to be paralyzed. Not daring to force her further lest she indeed lose her voice, I gave her paper and pencil and said that she could write it, that her hand knew, and she need not know. I put the pencil in her right hand first, but not feeling any inclination to write, I said that of course it was her left hand that knew and managed to stick just the end of the pencil in the little finger. She said that she couldn't write with her left hand, but did begin her name. Then I put my hands over her eyes, told her I was not going to press, and awaited developments. When she got to the place where I have made a check, it suddenly occurred to me that she was trying to write "Adultery". At no time did I give her the slightest inkling of what I thought. I held my hands over her eyes about an hour while she wrote. It was while she was writing that she shuddered slightly and on asking what she thought of she said she thought of her mother. I had heard the word "syphilis" the moment before. During this time she was peaceful. I sent her back to the ward without telling her anything. I told of the morning's progress to Miss Burleigh,[114] and showed her the writing.

It may be that when she found out what her father was doing she told her mother he was an adulterer and that she ought not to have anything more to do with him. Then it was, perhaps, that her mother turned on her and told her never to tell anybody else, that it wasn't true anyway, and if she ever told anybody she would come back from her grave and haunt her.

It may be that she thought her mother an adulterer for not making any fuss. It may be that she thought her mother an adulterer anyway, for other reasons.

It is certain that she knew that there was adultery going on.

Perhaps the whole pathogenic nucleus centers around the conception of adultery.

SESSION 22: FRIDAY, 1 MARCH 1912

Kept to see Dr. Shattuck.[115] Dr. Gambill[116] told me that Dr. Richard Cabot[117] asked Dr. Baldwin to see Rachel. She is to have Zander treatment, and Hydrotherapy.[118]

Slept well. Dreamed of cooking. It seemed as if she had to cook for a great many people, who kept coming in, and for whom her father made her cook.

Dreamed I said I couldn't do anything more; left her; said that the other doctors could now do what they pleased.

She felt blue all the afternoon.

I just worshipped mother.[119]

I am afraid I yielded to Jack.[120]

I could look at it to get my feet but I never could before.

Mother prevents her seeing what it is that she is concealing.

I often thought, after I knew what father was, if it had been mother I might not be her daughter.

Did once have the suspicion. Last summer.

I saw Rachel between 12:30 and 2.

Twice by putting my hands over her eyes I tried to get the secret, but both times the vision of her mother prevented. Once she seemed almost to push her mother away, and afterwards felt remorseful, but to no purpose. It seemed almost as if Jack were concealed behind her mother. At one time she did see Jack and her mother talking, seemingly about her; Jack was cross and angry. Always it is the vision of her mother that stands between her and the knowledge she is seeking.

To the worst things, and mix-ups, I could suggest about herself and her mother, she showed no emotional reaction.

She said her mother had no marriage certificate.

She had, of course, thought of adultery. At first, though, she thought her mother had a right to go with any man she chose.

The thought of not being her father's daughter, crossed her mind when she heard of a neighbor having an abortion.[121]

The thought of her life has been to conceal her knowledge of her father from her mother. She knew it would wreck her life.

SESSION 23: SATURDAY, 2 MARCH 1912

Didn't sleep well. Had the awful dream.[122]
Seemed to be going somewhere. As she walked grew weaker. Fell finally, and couldn't get up.
Thought last night of what I said. As to the lack of a marriage certificate, she remembered that her mother told the minister who married her in Worcester. Thought of Jack.
Wished he hadn't come in my life at all or he had lived and I could have had him.
Ever since I broke off with Jack I have thought of him.
No one ever knew it.
The morning was spent in getting free associations. It seemed always as if her mind was divided and one part of it was occupied with one thing; the other part would think now of one thing now of another and again of nothing at all. Jack is the center, however, around which all her thoughts circle.
Went to Zander: Massage prescribed.[123]

SESSION 24: MONDAY, 4 MARCH 1912

Dreamed she was back in the New England Hospital.[124] (She was there when she was about 17. They performed some sort of an operation on her left wrist. Also a gynecological one.) Seemed to be going through it all again. Has a strong dislike for Dr. Culbertson.[125]
Her father was in to see her yesterday. He fussed about the expense. He wanted her to go to the New England Hospital, but she refused.
Dreamed all about home.
Saturday night dreamed about mother.
I am all the time dreaming about Jack.
Mother used to say that Harry wouldn't do as he did if I hadn't encouraged him in some way; but I never did.
Put my hands over her eyes. Got nothing but more or less faint images of mother, and Jack, no, she only thought of Jack, she didn't see him this morning.

Do you dream of Jack every night? I don't know that I do, but sometimes I feel I do.

Told her she was dreaming most of the time, etc.[126]

She tried to stand.[127]

She can feel in her legs, but only some little time after touch. No Zander yet.

SESSION 25: TUESDAY, 5 MARCH 1912

Had the horrid dream last night.

Step-grandmother's boarder came in to see her.

They kept her in the nerve department till one yesterday. Dr. Baldwin again tried to open her hand. Dr. Gambill was there but didn't do anything.

Gave her a lot of exercises in Zander in afternoon.

Talked about sex, etc.

Cloud remains all the time.

Put my hands over eyes.

Struggled terribly, but finally saw mother, Jack, and two beds. Couldn't see what was in the other bed, eyes seemed strangely blinded.

Yesterday I thought nothing remained but dreams, to-day I think there is more. Miss Burleigh suggested that perhaps her mother caught them.

Has sensibility in legs but it takes some little time to perceive touch. She said she knows when I touched her but took time to realize it.

Told her to try to move when she felt the touch, she tried and I could feel, sometimes, a slight quiver.

Told me to-day that they told her mother at the New England Hospital she couldn't get married if they hadn't operated.

Last night when she would lie down she would have an awful feeling, she would stand it a while when it was like an external force and she would fling out of bed.

She still has nausea though it is better.

SESSION 26: WEDNESDAY, 6 MARCH 1912

Zander. Opened hand and washed it. Miss Heath, in the Office at the Front Door, is a member of the choir in Winchester.

Doesn't remember any dream, but the nurse said she hollered, "Don't look at me that way."

To-day she showed, for the first time, a real emotional melting. She cried, and the hardness of her chin broke, and quivered.

She said she had been unable to think of anything all yesterday but what she saw when I had my hands over her eyes. Said she slept very little last night. She said, "I can't do anything to-day."

SESSION 27: THURSDAY, 7 MARCH 1912

Zander. Dreamed but doesn't know what.

Thinking all the time of the same thing. It seems as if it can't be so even if I see it. It seems as if somebody wouldn't let me know.

Hands over eyes.

It is just as if I had my eyes closed and wouldn't look.[128]

Mother, Jack, room; mother tries to show her something.

She was lying down; couldn't tell whether on floor, or couch, or bed.[129]

It may be she found Jack and me in the same room together, and I wouldn't look at her.

Don't you think that's it? It may be, I don't know.[130] I will try till I do conquer. It seems as if I could know, but when I try I can't.

SESSION 28: FRIDAY, 8 MARCH 1912

Zander.

1) Dreamed she was a little girl learning to dance and someone knocked her down.

2) Dreamed she was in the ward; it seemed as if my wife were there; she brought up a man whom I wanted her to let hypnotize her; I wasn't there; my wife was talking.[131]

3) Dreamed she was in Beverly at her "aunt's." (Step-grandmother) It seemed as if I went to some place with that boarder; perhaps the theater.

Dr. Jennings asks about me, what I do, etc. He spoke of putting splints on.[132]

I put my hands over her eyes.[133]

It might be a paper telling we were married. (The thing her mother held in her left hand trying to make her look at.)

It might be a baby in both hands.

Now Jack is leaning over me.

Now there are other people coming in.

The secret lies in her hand?

It seems as if I could look I could know.

She feels she couldn't stand it. It doesn't seem as if she were ashamed.

It seems as if I could stand anything better than mother's disgrace. It doesn't seem mine.

Her mother told her she once went with a fellow whom others thought of as she did of Jack. But she does not remember that she told of any secret misstep. This was when she was warning her against Jack.

It seemed as if all the disgrace I had had, if anything more came I couldn't stand it.

It seemed as if mother were trying to make me look, but Jack wouldn't let me. Had her lie down. (By lowering the back of the wheel chair.)

Associations.

Jack—dream—his mother—ward—Dr. Jennings, etc.—home—card parties, etc.—feeling about it all—Jack—different places—letter I got this morning—I thought I'd never go with any other fellow—mother, etc.—father, etc.—how I thought of other fathers—as if I knew for a second what it was—

As if she held it in her left hand.[134]

If mother came round it must be Jack who is keeping me from it.

I wish I could have that feeling again; it seems as if I could drive it out of my feet. (She refers to the feeling she had when she became paralyzed.)

When Jack was leaning over her while she was lying on the floor, it seemed as if he had her hands, and as if he were trying to hold his hand over her mouth so she couldn't tell. He seemed to be trying to prevent her looking too.

Twice I tried to help her get the hidden thought, by holding my hands over her eyes, but both times she was unable to look. Her anguish was awful.

SESSION 29: SATURDAY, 9 MARCH 1912

Zander. Tired, put to bed at three. Dreamed, but remembers nothing.

Lies down.

Jack—Freda (Ella?)[135]—feels that when day-dreaming it is something like looking at Jack—how I tell you how much I cared for Jack, but wouldn't tell anybody else—my mind jumped back to Jack again and how this man from Beverly[136] looks so much like him—I never thought of it before—she went to Nantasket[137] once with Jack and two other couples; bathing all the afternoon, etc.; Paragon Park; home, etc.—if they had let him come to the house I wouldn't have gone out, they were to blame for that—saw him every night when he was home—wishing I'd never seen him, first, but since I have a wish I could have him—asked mother for proof; she never gave any but said she could, or would; girls merely referred to his reputation—

A troubled thought flashed by—saw the room, the bed, myself, but knew Jack and mother were there—could not place it—I know I have seen it so—it seems like a round room.

First she seemed to be dreaming, then she thought she was here to look and she knew she had seen it before. It was just as she was doing this that the cloud seemed to open for an instant and a "troubled thought" flashed by.

SESSION 30: MONDAY, 11 MARCH 1912

Dr. Jennings opened her hand Saturday, and again Sunday morning. He put in a wad which pained terribly and not being able to stand it she finally got out.

Her father visited her yesterday afternoon. He wants her to stay till she is cured.

Last night she dreamed she was in a factory. There were cookies and beside each cookie there was a pile of Jack-straws. Before she could have a cookie she had to take a Jack-straw off the pile. She did not succeed. (In amplifying later she said she seemed to be with her girl friend and two men, but this was indistinct.)

Dreamed about her father and what he said Dr. Jennings told him. (That she would be better off at home and that she could open her hand if she wanted to.)

Dreamed she was back in the telephone office. She seemed to be having hard work; she couldn't get the cords into the Jacks.

Had the bad dream. (All these were last night.)

Saturday night she hollered, "I never could like him."

I had her lie back in her chair.[138]

While reclining she gave me many associations mostly about Jack.

She described in detail about the time when she heard him say she was innocent. From that moment she began to think of getting rid of him.

She also described minutely the last day he was at her house, the pulling her down on the sofa, giving her a kiss, quarreling that night, telling him that things as they were suited her, i.e. she didn't want to have anything more to do with him.

She thinks that it can't be that she actually yielded because if she had she wouldn't have felt so badly at giving him up.[139] And the feeling of relief she experienced at his death, she thinks was due to the feeling that now a real temptation had providentially been removed.

But still the cloud persists.

SESSION 31: TUESDAY, 12 MARCH 1912

Zander. Jennings opened her hand last night and washed it.

Dreamed I was home walking around.

Dreamed she was with Jack again. She was in the Hospital. He came to see her. She told him what I thought it was. He said it was not so, that he would take me where it would be all right. She did not go. There was more to it but this morning she couldn't remember it. It was pleasant and when I woke up I was sorry it wasn't so.

Dreamed of brother. Dreamed of Mr. A. (Beverly boarder)[140] He came to see her yesterday but was not admitted because she had another visitor, a friend from her church.

She feels deeply against Dr. Jennings. Partly because he hurts her when he opens her hand, and partly because he sneers, she says, at me and my treatment.

Had her lie back in her wheel chair.

The troubled thought came last night about 6, and again this morning at about 7. Last night she was reading the Rosary,[141] and was just at that part where she sings before an audience. It flashed by. It startled her; it was like somebody gave her a hit.

Wished my hands would open out so I could show Dr. Jennings he didn't know everything.

Saw the man who assaulted her when she was 13. He has her on the floor.[142] Oh, I was just thinking of him and it seemed as if his face came right up to mine.[143] (He has troubled her a great deal. He follows her about. Whenever she goes to visit in Beverly he gets himself invited. She feels weak when she sees him.)[144]

Mother must have made me go over. (She used to make her go, and had not patience with her for feeling as she did.)

I know she sent me over for some thread once. He lives in Beverly now, and when mother used to go to visit Grandfather she always wanted to call on them and take me. I used to get out of it whenever I could. (He is a machinist, and used to work in the same room with Grandfather, U.S. Shoe, etc.)[145]

The last time he was at the house she had to go for milk and he went with her. She felt terribly, and when she got home she was so weak she could hardly stand.[146]

She has no memory for what happened after he threw her on the floor. Probably he raped her.[147]

SESSION 32: WEDNESDAY, 13 MARCH 1912

Zander. Had a night-mare. It seemed as if somebody had hold of her throat and she hollered "Let go."

Dreamed (I can't tell the other dream; I don't think it will have anything to do with that. I know it just as well as anything but I can't.) Finally she told it.[148]

Her turns[149] were on when she came, and started again Monday night.

Last night she dreamed that Dr. Jennings asked her why they came so often, and said he would have to examine her. She objected and refused. Finally he got a lot of doctors around, and a nurse, and said she would have to go away. It seemed as if they went on two rafts, she and the nurse on one, and the doctors on another; the nurse asked her if she consented but she still said no. They seemed to be on the ocean. At last the waves were so high the nurse was washed overboard. She took hold of a pole, but that broke and she fell into the water. She went down and seemed to be drowning. As she came up the doctors asked her if she had consented and again she said no. She seemed to be going up and down and the waves were buffeting her about. Finally she went down for the last time and stayed down. Then she seemed to be on a lonely country road, and was lame and weak. As she was walking along she met her brother and a dog.

He was surprised to see her. She asked him if they had missed her, and he said yes, but then they had thought she was dead. It seemed that she knew the way home but didn't want to go there. Her brother didn't know the way. But the dog knew and would keep going in the right direction. She would take him up and turn his head around, and set him down facing in the opposite direction but he would always set off in the right direction. She was glad she hadn't given in to the doctors. She seemed to have been away about a year and a half. She was sorry her brother took it so easily, when she woke.

She had another dream, in which she seemed to remember the one before. She was sitting in a chair on a bank, and a colored doctor[150] asked her why she hadn't told about when she was 13. She said she hadn't known about it till the other day. When he asked about it, it seemed as if I had told it to him and now he would tell her father. After he said that, I got up and said, "is there anything else you would like to ask, Dr. Johnson." She did this in the most sneering manner possible.

This was the last dream she remembers.

Lies down.

Johnson—the doctor—dream, etc.—Jack

She walked back and forth before this doctor because walking seemed to irritate him most.

Of course I know there is more, really, but I can't seem to get it. (Anent the assault at 13.)

Jack's face comes and fades away into somebody else's.

Last Thursday or Friday night she dreamed she was married to Jack. She went off and married him without letting her family know. Then he abused her. He fingered her, hit her, threw her down, on the floor, on the couch, had intercourse with her, perhaps half a dozen times. It seemed as real as it would have been in actuality. Somehow her mother seemed to know and said it served her right as she had warned her. She has been concealing this dream because it seemed to corroborate the suspicion that she had had actual relations with Jack.

It was very difficult getting both the long dream and this one out of her but at last she complied.

She was unable to recall anything more about the man who assaulted her when she was 13.

SESSION 33: THURSDAY, 14 MARCH 1912

Zander. Opened her hand last night and when it was done Dr. J[ennings] suggested splints but she snatched it away. Dr. Smith[151] was with Dr. J[ennings]. Dreamed she was in a room, mother was there, and the colored doctor again asked why she didn't tell about when she was 13. Again she thought I had told him, and she answered as before. She thought she walked back and forth in front of him to tantalize him, as before. The dream was practically identical with the similar one she had last night.

In one dream she was in a big house and didn't know how to get out. There were a number of people there who said that's easy enough follow us, but she got lost. It seemed hard to walk, as if she were staggering.

I kept dreaming I could walk.

The troubled thought came about 4. I was sitting there talking when the nurse said I must go to bed and just as she said it the thought came. It was just as if the cloud had come suddenly and disappeared.

Lies down.

Reproduces the scene of the assault as before.

Wishing you would start asking me.[152]

Put my hands over her eyes.

He has her by the throat, and has thrown her on the floor.

While she was reproducing this she had the troubled thought.

He would make me feel weak and faint and my head would ache and I would feel weak all over. (This was the way she felt whenever she saw the man who assaulted her, though she didn't know why till she remembered the assault, here.)

In the dream she seemed to be married 2 or 3 days and Jack was having intercourse with her all the time. It seemed as if that was all he wanted. (This was an addition to the dream she told me yesterday.)

While I had my eyes over her eyes she saw the neighbor and the room and herself on the floor, etc., but there was no interference by any vision of Jack or her mother.

SESSION 34: FRIDAY, 15 MARCH 1912

Zander. Dreamed about Mr. A. I know I was with him.

Dreamed about home.

In another dream it seemed as if I were in it.

Thought a great deal about the time at 13, but got nothing; it all seemed a blank.

Now, this man and the cloud seem identical.

Lies down. Sees man, room, bed, and herself on the floor.

I know he did have me by the throat, and when I tried to get up put me back; I know he did but I can't see it.[153]

She recognizes that what she saw yesterday was really so, but beyond that remembers nothing.

It seems as if mother were in his place now, as I saw her first, holding something in her hand. It seems to be in the same room. I see him and then mother; I think of Jack but it doesn't seem clear.

Wishing I was home.

This morning it seems as if mother were there.

Whenever I think of the room I think of her instead of him.

At this point I put my hands over her eyes.

Same scene with the addition that he tries to put her on the bed. She thinks he did but can't remember it yet.

She struggled terribly while reproducing this scene. Each thing that she sees she remembers was so, but she can get nothing in her memory that was not forced out of her while I had my hands over her eyes.

Her hand seemed very slightly relaxed.

SESSION 35: SATURDAY, 16 MARCH 1912

Can you think of it as of a game yet?[154] It's no game; of course I know it is true, I know that, but I hope that it isn't.

Dreamed she was home. Her hand was all right, and her feet, while not entirely well, were getting better.

In another dream she was hunting for something; I was there, and for some reason seemed cross. There was more but she couldn't get it.

Zander.

Yesterday she could remember the attack more herself; it wasn't so much like a dream.

You couldn't get anything more yourself?[155] Of course I can imagine it, but I can't remember anything more at all.

Lies down. Last night it seemed as if I knew for a moment where the room was, but then I dozed off and couldn't remember anything.

I now put my hands over her eyes.

She reproduces the scene of yesterday with the addition that he leaves her for a moment and tries to drag the bed to her; while doing this she gets up and runs but then he gets her again and with his hand on her throat throws her down again.

Scene changes and she sees her mother.

It seems as if it were there and I can't see it.

She never has been able to wear collars. When she had one on it seemed as if she would go crazy. She couldn't wear a chain unless it was pinned down at the back. She couldn't wear beads. It is only lately that she has been able to wear bracelets.

He held her hands as well as her throat.

Another detail came out to-day. When he had her on the floor, and had his face close to her, he kissed her, as if to tantalize her, she said.

SESSION 36: MONDAY, 18 MARCH 1912

Dreamed she was at home, but strange people were there; it seemed she was going to a train but missed it; hand was all right but went bad and she had to go back to the hospital.

There was a woman died last night and she dreamed she was in her place and they thought she was dead and she tried to let them know she wasn't.

Dreamed they were cutting her hand off but doesn't know what else there was in the dream.

Fell out of her chair Saturday and dreamed of it.

It seemed in the dream that she fell a great deal further.

Liked to swing, as a child, especially standing up.

Father came in Saturday and wants to see me.

Lies down.

See if you can remember anything that happened the day of the assault. Nothing.

Remembers she never did like him from the first.

Yesterday I thought and thought; it seemed as if I thought of nothing else all day, yet I couldn't get it, yet there seemed more.

Now tell me about it.

Went with me to get the milk about a month before the attacks this Fall.

Did he ever make any allusions? I remember once he said it would be a nice night for a walk I said yes if anybody cared to walk and I looked right at him.

In Beverly last Fall.

He is German and has German friends who live right opposite us.

Beginning last Summer has seen much more of him.

Was sick naturally from July 4 till October.

In Beverly told her aunt she wouldn't stay to supper if he were invited.[156] Before attacks began in Fall.

For a year after she left Adams[157] she never went to Beverly, didn't see him at all that she can remember. The following year she saw him, but infrequently. He has been at her house perhaps a half a dozen times this Fall.

Hands over her eyes.[158] I don't know how I can feel sorry when I know perfectly well there is something more and I can't look at it. (Saw Dr. Shattuck.) Got nothing more. Asked her how she felt at the lack of success.[159]

SESSION 37: TUESDAY, 19 MARCH 1912

Zander. Dreamed she was in a desert, all alone, sad and wanted somebody, but couldn't get anybody. It seemed as if she met people but they would turn their backs on her; she didn't know them they were strangers.

Had a troubled dream. People were in it but can't get anything.

Thought things over but didn't get anything more.

I would go up to them they would turn their backs on me; it seemed as if I were along and nobody wanted me.

Just as if I were alone and how you would feel if you were. (Feeling she had just before going to sleep.) It seemed as if father were one of the persons I went up to.

Hands over her eyes.[160] Adds he ties her. "If I can't get you on the bed I will do it on the floor." He gets her on the bed but she gets off. Lifts her dress to tie her knees. Lifts her dress again but something seems to stop him from going on. Goes out, gets rope, ties hands and legs. He leaves her tied a while.

She can get nothing more, every thing seems blank, as if she didn't know where she was.

SESSION 38: WEDNESDAY, 20 MARCH 1912

Remembers it all as she saw it yesterday. It wasn't imagination? "Why no, I re-member it happening."

Dreamed last night but remembers nothing. Zander.

Got her to the bed before he got the rope.

She did have a hope he didn't, but to-day she feels he probably did succeed.

Hands over her eyes. "I know it must be so."

Clothes up; draws down.[161] Beside her. Fingers between her legs.

"I can't help thinking there is some way out of it."

Hands very much looser. "Isn't it enough that I know it?"[162]

Chokes back crying. Seldom cries; didn't at mother's death.

He asked her to promise she would keep quiet.

SESSION 39: THURSDAY, 21 MARCH 1912

She remembers that what she saw yesterday was really so. Dreamed but re-members nothing.

Zander. I just thought till it seemed I didn't have any thinking powers left to think with.[163] I can't help thinking he didn't do it.

Didn't cry.

I don't remember anything it is all a mystery to me.

Hands over her eyes.

Same scene as yesterday. Everything seems a blank beyond what she saw yesterday.

SESSION 40: FRIDAY, 22 MARCH 1912

Zander.[164] Slept better. Dreamed but remembers nothing. Everything is as she saw it.

Associations.

rope—tied me—time—everything about that—men in the woods—man in the house—how I could have come home—him—wood—home—I know I hold things back—nurses—last night—home—brother—father—splints—church to—night—wish I could walk—letter I got from auntie—Bert and his wife—father, in Zander, how I wished he wouldn't come—Miss Burleigh—room again—letter from Henry's mother—Jack—other friends I have been with—Jack, etc.—the dream of Jack—just thinking if anything bad came in my mind how I could answer it—here—would I ever get out—home—father—different people—school—mother—what I could have gone to his house for—how it all came out, what it all meant—seems as if my mind goes to think of something and stops right short—rather it were anything than this—Mother said I was the closest mouthed.

Troubled thought: in Zander when father was there; and when sent to bed.

Associations

hand—my own hand—opening it last night—ward—doctors—somebody in—weak—will I ever be out doors again—Jack—time I've had with him—it seems as if all the time I am thinking of the room and those things come separate.

SESSION 41: SATURDAY, 23 MARCH 1912

Dreamed but remembers nothing. It wasn't troubled.

Associations.[165]

Room—him—tried to recognize it—home—now at home—mother—how she was sick and I was at the Nervine room—last night how I felt—when I

tried to go to sleep his hand would be on my throat—him—Henry—letter
from his mother and how I would answer it—times when he was at the
house—Jack—room and how it seemed Jack was there first—students, and
doctor, in the ward—dream I had about Jack—room and something else but
I couldn't get it—mother and how I feel she is right beside me—different
things I could have done to make her life happier, that I didn't think of then
but I do now—room, right on the floor, him and what he was going to do—
times I have seen him, how he acted, how I felt—room comes back to me
again—how it ended, how it could have happened and I not know about it—
his wife, and if he told her—if I can ever face him and not say something to
him—wishing my headache would go away—room saw it as I remember it,
how it happened—baby crying—somebody walking—thought of babies—I
thought of having them—how mother said she didn't want me when she was
going to have me—I thought if he did have anything to do with me, and I
had had a baby, how awful if would have been if I had had a baby—how my
aunt felt when she found no father (illegitimate) (this is aunt Eva in Worcester) Rachel was about 16 when she was told about aunt. aunt Nettie (Pawtucket)—Bert, illegitimate son of a friend (adopted)—auntie Eva, what she
was and yet how good her children turned out—room again, only what I saw
before—how I felt—if I could tell and not know I was telling, that I really
know all the time, oh! I can't express my feelings.

Lectured her.[166]

Oh! I wish you wouldn't ask me everything—nothing only my feelings—oh!
I can't—when you say such things my feelings are hard and stubborn—how
foolish I was to feel that way—it seems as if I could not think—if I could
have a good cry I might be able to think—girl and felt bad how I went in the
fields (to the Golf field, on a rock, woods, etc.)—rock, lay there—wouldn't
cry—wishing I could go there now—school—room, vivid, as if I were
there—him and how I dislike him—I felt if I could only see him I must do
something to revenge myself on him—assault, him, my feelings—my mind
just stays right there—I don't see anything but just what I actually know
now—I can't get my mind off it now—

Hands over her eyes. Got nothing more.

I know it must have been so—I realize he must have but just that I can't seem
to think of it as I do the first part of the scene; it seems as if I really knew
that—I was trying to realize it, trying to make myself see it—

While I had my hands over her eyes the thought came to her that she knew,
but, not the thought of what she knew.

It seemed for a second she did know, but when she tried to think about it she no longer could.

Thinking of how I felt, the last 3 days I felt funny, I don't feel like myself at all, I don't know why.

What a funny thing I did yesterday—letter, etc. (She was writing to a friend, when all of a sudden she found that for a few pages she had been writing her inmost thoughts and feelings, and not a letter at all. It made her so provoked that she tore the letter up and threw it in the fire.)[167]

SESSION 42: MONDAY, 25 MARCH 1912

Saturday night dreamed off and on, but couldn't get anything. Troubled dream. Slept well last night.

The girl who came yesterday has just become engaged. Rachel dreamed she told her at her home, and she had to tell her she was very much pleased, but she wasn't. It seemed as if Jack were there. In the dream when she told her it seemed as if she had lost her, as if she were dead. In reality she felt as she did in the dream, she said.

Had another dream in which she seemed to ask a simple question and woke hearing herself say she didn't see why it couldn't be answered without going through all those questions. I was in it.

Face flushed—she said it was burning.

Associations.

room—time—different things in the room and about him—everything just as it happened—yesterday and what we talked about—(tells me about her friend's engagement)—her—getting married—over girls who get married—Jack—different times I was with him—the last time he was with me—what a pleasant day we had—father, home, church—cantata—wishing I were there—here—Saturday morning—how it seemed for a moment I knew—I just thought of Dr. Putnam, I don't know what made me—room, here—I was trying to see how it came out and how it happened—legs—walking, going home—room and the way I felt now was the way I felt when I was lying on the floor—mother—telephone—it seems that as she lay on the floor she wondered if she would ever walk again—his life—Beverly—aunt and Mr. A. good traits he had but hoping he wouldn't bother me any more—(turned her so she couldn't see me)[168]—Jack, I was thinking of him—I was wishing he was alive—Henry and his mother—Henry's father sick—girl friend who is coming this afternoon—room—how disagreeable it was—it seems as if my mind goes off on something and I don't know what it is—I suppose it is the ending of whatever took place in the room—I was thinking when you put your hands over my eyes I knew for a minute and I was trying—home as it would have been then, etc.—school—15—how I felt—how father was followed—life—different times when he went off and I knew what he was going for—something came over me and bothered me but I don't know what it was—like a dream—I suppose it was realizing what he did—I was provoked at myself for not being able to get it[169]—woods, when 9—how I got home that time—it seemed as if the last part of that was gone too—dream of Jack too keeps coming to me, all the time I know I am thinking of something but I don't know what—I think of the room, but then there seems to be something else I keep thinking of—it seems so separate from the room that I was wondering if we got that if there were anything else we would have to get[170]—doctors out here—home—ward, etc.—letter I wrote—maybe if I had kept it all would have been cleared up—room again, I keep thinking of that—it seems as if I was thinking and then everything goes blank, just as if my mind stood still—thinking how Fay said father was coming in and was going to find out what was the matter, I wouldn't tell him anything, and he was going to find out.

Saw Mr. C.[171]

Thought about father, wondering if he would come in this morning—my mind dwells on those things, it keeps going over and over what we got; wishing I was home.

SESSION 43: TUESDAY, 26 MARCH 1912

Zander. Gertrude C. Dreamed it seemed as if she and another girl friend went skating, a fellow chased her, it seemed like fun and yet it was serious, finally he got her and they all went home, where she was met by her brother who told them her mother was sick, father said she wasn't. She went upstairs, and saw her mother in bed, she asked her why she didn't have a doctor, and she said she did, but when asked couldn't tell his name, then Rachel seemed to take her mother in her arms and walk around the room with her; there seemed to be a second bed and she saw her sister, looking as she would now, if she were alive. She asked her father why he didn't send for a doctor and he said he had, but it seemed to be a woman doctor and she thought it was only one of his "friends" so she sent for a doctor herself and when he came she woke up.

Another dream but remembers nothing except she woke saying "please tell me."

Dreamed of father; it seemed as if he was making fun of her and laughing at her.

Associations.

Skating—dream—different times I have been—yesterday and today my throat felt bad, as though there was something to tell, but what it is I don't know—father here yesterday—there seems to be something all the time but I can't get it; it did yesterday—Dr. Bucholz[172] in Zander yesterday (tried to open her hand)—book I was reading and the characters in it—Smiths, died, glad I wasn't there—dream and the man—I think of that but my mind is on something else all the time, I think of that too but it seems as if my mind were divided between these two things—thinking of that dream about mother—room—the last part of it that I know—it seems as if I think of Jack just as soon as I think of the room—his wife and how he has acted—woods—how hunting for that and the other was just about the same—I don't know what I was thinking about—Miss Burleigh—if she found out what she would say—I wish I could think that not everybody knows all now—first goes on one then the other, I can't seem to think of anything else—I think of it all the time, I keep searching for something—I wish that baby would stop crying—can't you get it some other way but this, I can't think.

Put my hands over her eyes.[173] Woods and room—"One of the men did it."—got the thought for a moment—

It doesn't seem to have any feeling only I know that is what I am after. It is just as if the cloud showed itself, I don't know.

Lies down. Associations. Richard—the man—room—woods—what they did, how I felt, etc. mother, if she ever really knew—woods—room—didn't she think then just as in the woods, wondering if she knew—it seems to me if anything had happened to a child of mine I'd know it, I was wondering if she didn't surmise—when I keep my eyes shut and lying it seems as if I were there—I think of the two rooms, I mean the two places—room—my feeling at the time—oh, when I get my eyes shut I am going through it again—times—mother—room and woods—I was just thinking of it—thinking when he was doing it in the woods—I keep going over it and over it and over it all the time—trying to relax, to let my mind go where it will—my mind is right on it all the time switching on to the two parts of the two scenes—if there was anything different I wouldn't mind so much but it just stays on the same thing[174]—every once and a while one of the men in the woods takes hold of my throat—I can't get anything different, once and a while I think of mother—it goes back right to the same thing—the two seem to be together to-day and it seems as if I couldn't have it so—I have accepted it but I get thinking of it just the same—just the same thing—dream of Jack—woods and room—I can't get my mind off of it at all—it was something about those two things but I don't know what it was—I know I feel I am keeping something back but I don't know what it is; it seems to be right in my throat only I can't get it out—just as if I wanted to tell something and couldn't.[175]

SESSION 44: WEDNESDAY, 27 MARCH 1912

Troubled thought came yesterday while in Zander.
Dreamed she was at home; mother scolded her and she cried and cried, then her mother told her that she didn't mean anything but did it for her own good.
Associations.
cry—like to cry—dream—how I felt in the room—last night—home—times again—here—uncle who was in to see me yesterday (Ned of New Hampshire)—"I'd never go home if brother went away."—I was thinking about the room and more about the way the thought came to me yesterday and how I couldn't get it—(reclines)—I was thinking last night I was trying to give up myself and how I couldn't—those two scenes—Jack—(pains in back)—it seems as if there were something on my mind all the time and I can't get away from it—it seems as if I were trying all the time; I find myself trying and straining at something—

> I was impatient here.

It seems as if I hadn't known myself at all and I was just finding out myself.
Home and the two times—oh, I was trying to make myself relax or do something to find it out—school life—work—thinking about myself—wishing I didn't feel as I did—blue—dream last night—wishing it was true—book I read yesterday—I thought of the men in the woods when they were doing that and it seemed as if they were right there again—Jack and wishing he were alive—those things—it seems as if I think of the men in the woods more than the room—I can't get anything only those unless I try to think—if I try to think I get different things—without trying to think it just stays on those things—goes back and forth from one to the other—room, saw him, lingers on this man—just looking at that man—it seems as if I was thinking of something else but when I go to think of it I can't get it—oh, I don't know what I was thinking about, I know I was thinking of those times, but what I was thinking about I don't know—ward, and how I hate to go back there—home how I wish I was there and quiet—those times—wishing I could get up and

walk—oh, I just feel as though I would go frantic not being able to get up—I was thinking if I could have a good cry I wouldn't feel so tight and I could think of things and let them come to me—I think those scenes, but it seems as if something else was there and troubling me but I can't get it— Did you ever pray?

SESSION 45: THURSDAY, 28 MARCH 1912

Zander. Dream she was in here, in the out-patient department, and had something to tell; but couldn't do it and went out and walked up and down outside; then went to Miss Burleigh but she looked so cold she wouldn't tell her; I came in and Dr. Waterman, we both accused her of different things, and she said, I won't tell anybody but I'll go home and tell mother; she did so. It doesn't seem that I dreamed what I told her, it was like skipping over that. Thought I was lying down, peaceful, thought if you were here I could tell you, it seemed that I realized I didn't know but I could think, and I thought how nice it would be if I could tell you then and not come up here in the morning. Dreamed I was crying, woke up feeling I must cry. Associations.
What is this thing?—I don't know—girl laughing—dreams last night— here—Miss Burleigh—it seemed as if she was cool—biting my finger nail— company and letter I had from father—Beverly—room—what we know— last night and how I felt—it seems as if everything just flies from my mind when I get up here—Zander and how I tried to walk—ward—
About 3 A.M. she woke suddenly very much startled, and found her right hand clenched. That frightened her too, and though she couldn't remember what it was that startled her, she strained and worked for over an hour until she finally got her hand opened. No one knows this.
I had her lie down and left her to speak or not as she chose. She was in this position about three quarters of an hour, and spoke twice. She said she could almost get it but it would slip away. The last thing she said was that it seemed all mixed up with a lot of other things.

SESSION 46: FRIDAY, 29 MARCH 1912

Zander. Dreamed but remembers only that it seemed to be about her right hand. Troubled. Felt yesterday she would have to uncover a lot of things to get what she wanted but she can't tell what they were.

Associations.[176]

Rope—rope they tied me with—room—home—how I am now—woods, men—birds—Miss Burleigh—home—house—friends—first came in here—hand—this room and looking at different things in it—last night in the ward—Beverly and letter—Jack—his folks—father and mother, how they opposed him—Mrs. S. (Henry's mother)—girl friend getting married—her and wondered how they would live—fellow she is going to marry—stopped—mother—wishing she was here—telephone—here—dream of Miss Burleigh and you and Dr. Waterman—choir and hoping I could be there Easter—book I was reading—clock striking—pain went through my head and things went black—last night—man walking—when I can't think of anything my mind goes back to this room and how you can have the patience, and then of myself—how foolish I am not able to know what I want—my feet—Dr. Waterman and Dr. Putnam—Nervine—Jack and the dream I had of him—those people talking—Dr. Jennings coming back Sunday—Dr. Gambill is going away—door—knob—Scrooge and Marley in Dickens—school—different things at school—home as it was then and mother—her, as I last saw her—father and brother—two times—in the room and in the woods—the time the thought came over me when you had your hands over my eyes—man who bothered me in the meadow and in Worcester—Aunt Nettie—meadow and Worcester—can't think of anything—baby crying—raining—wishing I could get out—ward—Dr. Baldwin in other room[177]—room and the woods—man as he is to-day and his life—what I would do if I met him—those two scenes again—(emotion)—wish I could stop biting my finger nails—whist party at home—head felt tight as if I couldn't think—home—brother's foot—wish I was home to take care of him—nothing—ward—Zander—birds—walking—here yesterday—Miss Burleigh—in the woods—different things about it—book—stops—home—oh, I don't know what I did think about—Jack—blank—people in the hall—it seems as if I had got to the end of what I know—those men—how the end was and what I told mother—uncle—"better for the folks if they boarded"—Dr. Baldwin—talking—I don't know; it seems as if I thought of something but I don't know—Zander—(questioned her about men and Jack)—something suddenly came into her mind, "I know it but I don't know what it was"—dreams—dreams I had when I was here before—about dreams stumbling one; jack straws; switch board—trying to walk yesterday—how it seemed I had forgotten how to walk—this room—brother would have to work out in this rain—oh, I don't know what I was thinking about—dream of Miss Burleigh—how good she had been to me—different people and how I would have to make some explanation to them—girl friends and how they keep wanting to know what the matter is—woods and the room, but it was just the same as before—the time the girls told me things when I was 15—school—studies and how hard they were for me and I couldn't seem to put my mind on them.

SESSION 47: SATURDAY, 30 MARCH 1912

Father was in to see her yesterday.[178]
Dreamed of being up here, but what she dreamed of she did not know. It seemed as if I were thinking just as I do here in the morning.
Dreamed mother was with her.
Telling of a time when she had a pain in her head and things went black she mentioned that it occurred once while in the Zander Room, and she nearly fell off the machine. She had been talking with the ward tender, about books she had read and liked. He caught her, and lifted her off.
Another time was Thanksgiving. She had knelt down to baste the turkey, it slipped and went on the floor and she fell. Cannot recall other circumstances.
Told her again about her sexual constitution, etc., which she took very well.
Have seen her forty-two times.[179]
Will see her for a half hour or so Monday.
Read letter; woman said, another place; landlady—my room no more, etc.

SESSION 48: MONDAY, 1 APRIL 1912

Has a temperature of 102. Can't come.[180]
Saw Eustis[181]: turns.
Talked a little with him about the significance of hysterical convulsions.

SESSION 49: WEDNESDAY, 3 APRIL 1912

Leslie C.; the other by sight.[182]
Right hand closed 15 minutes 8 P.M. Was trying to think of something.
Miss Wales, night nurse, told her she talked in her sleep, saying, "I can't think." I realized I was dreaming about here; the room and you.
Cried a little Saturday night. Miss Kelly, Head nurse, sympathized with her. She told her she was blue; that I had done all I could, and now it depended on herself, etc.

I know there is something there that is yet to come, but I didn't know what it is.

Was dreamy yesterday afternoon, but could get nothing.

SESSION 50: THURSDAY, 4 APRIL 1912

Zander. Dreamed she was in a desert and was all alone.

Dreamed, but remembers only that Miss Burleigh was in it and mother.

When she lies down now she feels as if somebody were on her but can't say who. She noticed this first Sunday afternoon after her visitors went. She tried 3 times to see if it were so and found it so.

I thought of my feeling before I knew it and how that explained it.

She does feel that it was the man in the room.

The reason she didn't tell this yesterday, forgot.

When she first lay down she had to get up at once she felt so badly. She thought about it, and then it seemed to be as though someone were on her, and at the same moment she thought of the man, and thought of what it probably meant, and then tried it again 3 times to see if she were right. At no time could she stay down any length of time, an irresistible impulse to get up came over her and without knowing what she was doing she would find herself up.[183]

SESSION 51: FRIDAY, 5 APRIL 1912

Zander. Dreamt of mother; were off together walking in the woods; was awfully happy.

Dreamed she was in bed without any pillows under her head; at last I came and put some under.

Lay down 4 or 5 times (4, 5, 7, and twice through the night) While thinking nothing would come, but the minute she would stop thinking it would come and before she knew what she was doing she would be up.

"It would come" means, the feeling of a man lying on her.[184]

3-4ths. hour.

SESSION 52: SATURDAY, 6 APRIL 1912

Zander. Dreamed of the fellow in Winchester who wants to go with her. "I was with him in some place."

Night nurse said I hollered out, "I can't do it." 2 A.M. Again, "I can't think."
Lay down once and got the same feeling. Jumped.
Troubled thought twice: right after leaving here; and in Zander.
It seemed to be the thought, the remembrance of the feeling of the man on her.[185]
Told her that hand and legs were substitutes for genitals. Showed picture of spinal cord; also schematic sections.

SESSION 53: MONDAY, 8 APRIL 1912

Got her hand part way open last night; after 1 P.M. Was lying on her back and for a moment knew the end and then her mind went to her hand, and it closed again.[186]
"I don't know it now at all."
"Afterwards it seemed as if I knew it and yet I did not know it; just as when you know a person's name and have it right on the end of your tongue and can't say it."
Father was in Saturday and she dreamed about him that night. "He said he tried to think I would get well but he didn't think I would." She dreamed she would show him he was wrong.
Dreamed last night of mother: "I was sleeping with her; I was begging her to help me."
Dreamed I was in someplace having a good time.
"Dr. Jennings said I could go to the clay-modeling class[187] if you were willing; I would like to."
Associations.
Showed her another scheme of spinal cord and brain; also female generative organs.

SESSION 54: TUESDAY, 9 APRIL 1912

Zander. Dreamed of mother. Dreamed of Jack; "It seemed as if he wanted me to do something but I couldn't do it." The nurse said I said, "I can't do it Jack." It seemed as if father and mother were in that dream. It seemed as if there were a baby in the dream; in a way it seemed as if it were mine and in a way it seemed as if it wasn't; it was all mixed up.
Dreamed about the words you gave me yesterday: "tree and woods"; it seemed

as if you gave those (the whole list) words over and had me give a different answer.[188]

Tried 3 times lying flat. It would start to come but then would go away.

Bucholz opened her hand yesterday, which hurt so she could think of nothing else.

SESSION 55: WEDNESDAY, 10 APRIL 1912

Zander. 2) Dreamed about Jack: We were living together and hadn't ought to and were hiding away from people; we were happy; brother had some connection with it; I woke up saying "Everett."

1) Dreamed of embroidering. (sleeping half a second)

3) Had the horrid dream but got nothing. (deeply sleeping.)

Tried twice when I went to bed and once this morning, lying down. The thought came but her mind then went to her limbs and she couldn't get it back. Showed her for comparison the association times.

Gave her James to read.[189]

SESSION 56: THURSDAY, 11 APRIL 1912

Zander. About 8 lay down and got the feeling of pressure and at the same moment her hands started to open and her mind went to them. She started up first but forced herself back; this was the first time she has done this. Tried again about 11; and at 4 A.M. but got nothing.

1) Dreamed of Jack: he was home and I was there and he kept asking me to do something; I was troubled; mother came in and said it served me right for going with him. I was crying in the dream.

2) Dreamed I was home and out boating on a picnic.

3) Dreamed of the telephone company but couldn't get anything.

SESSION 57: FRIDAY, 12 APRIL 1912

Zander. 1) Dreamed she was home and mother was trying to make her do things but couldn't and said she would have to send her to me but she didn't see how it was a mother couldn't make her do more than a doctor. She then got provoked with her mother and would not do anything and went off by herself. Father and brother were in the dream.[190]

2) Dreamed she was learning to be a nurse.

Lay down twice to try to get it; It seemed as if I could just about get it but couldn't hold it. I was thinking of it once, I was kind of dazed, it seemed as if I had it and when I came to myself I was disappointed because I thought I had it. I just had the feeling I knew. Had been studying half an hour. A girl next bed asked her a question and wanted to know what I had been doing the last ten minutes. (About 4 P.M.)

SESSION 58: SATURDAY, 13 APRIL 1912

Zander. Couldn't keep her mind on anything.

It seemed all the time that I knew just as well as anything but yet I couldn't get it.

Dreamed but remembers only that when she woke she felt a hand on her throat.

Questioned her in Socratic fashion as to the significance of the conflict in her mind, and as to the meaning of her dreams, with especial reference to the meaning of dreaming of me.

She agreed to go to the clinic for Dr. Putnam.[191]

Always wanted to be a nurse; wanted to be 18 so I could be but when I was they said I couldn't.[192]

Who are some of the people you have dreamed of? Henry, Mr. A., father, my aunts, Miss Burleigh, you.[193]

SESSION 59: MONDAY, 15 APRIL 1912

Dreamed last night: It seemed as if I was in the woods, and then it seemed I wasn't, but I kept walking and walking till I got lost. Woke up trying to find my way. Had a dream in the dream and thought it was a factory; this time it was a candy factory instead of a cracker factory; she thought of the dream of jack straws.

About 4 A.M., half asleep, hand half way opened. Had just thought before, I wish I could walk and show them.

Saturday night dreamed of going to the clinic and of them asking me all sorts of questions as to why I was this way, and when I couldn't stand it any longer I got up and walked.

Dreamed of father, thought he said I would have to go to the Nervine.

He was in Saturday afternoon and they argued. He finds fault; I ought to get well sooner; he said he was coming in to see me.

Dreamed about the choir but couldn't get anything.

The story the girls told when she was 15 started when a bad girl was going by; "man goes in a woman"; no, he sticks his "trunk" in; then she can have a baby in a year or two.

Lies down.

I used the words, "trunk," "fuck," "cunt," etc.[194]

Sick to my stomach; woods; room.[195]

"Yes, I know it."[196]

With this her hand opened. I held it and asked further questions. It had a very vile odor.

She remembered his doing it, then leaving her, and shutting the door. He said something but cannot remember what.

This was as far as she remembered.[197]

SESSION 60: TUESDAY, 16 APRIL 1912

Hand all right. Modeling class.[198]

Dreamed that I had my feet instead of my hand.[199] I was walking around the room; the doctors were curious, they were asking questions which I wouldn't answer.

Dreamed she was crying and was terribly frightened.

Dreamed of home, father and brother.

Dreamed a number of times and sat up in bed but what she had been dreaming she doesn't know.

Gets the assault more plainly but seems to be just exhausted on the floor.[200]

(Noticed a slight orgasm yesterday.)[201]

Lies down.

Turn your mind to the end, when he goes out and shuts the door and see if you can't remember what you did.

Seems like Summer.

I remember he asked me.

Always went up the back way.

In St. Vitus Dance I used to keep hollering, "I'll kill him." But they and I thought I was out of my head.

In a dream last night the nurse said I hollered out "Well I've told it anyway."

I think it was about that time (when the girls told) that they thought I was going to have the St. Vitus Dance again. Couldn't walk very well.[202]

When she had convulsions before, the doctors tortured her. (The house doctors and visiting doctors stuck pins in her and stuck their nails in under hers which she didn't know at the time but afterwards would hurt terribly. This was one reason why she was so afraid to have a convulsion here again.)

I am not going to tell anybody but I am going to let him know I know.

She can describe the room fully now and recognizes it as the one she saw in her dreams.

The last thing she remembers now is lying exhausted on the floor, glad he had gone.

She hated to tell it yesterday because she felt that if she told it she would have to know it. And after she told it, it seemed as if she felt she ought not to have told.

SESSION 61: WEDNESDAY, 17 APRIL 1912

Hand all right now but clenched up this morning about 2. I suppose I was dreaming about the assault but when I woke up I put my mind right on it and got my hand open. I just thought I couldn't help it anyway and I was bound to get my hand open.

I felt worse last night than when I first found it out. Cried a little.

Dreamed of mother; thought she was home with her. It seemed in a way as if she was accusing me of something and I was answering I can't help it. When I woke up I thought it was about the telling.[203]

I thought he would do something if he got the chance but I didn't know he had done anything.

She has no memory of his doing it any time after the event.

Had her lie on the floor.[204] Got nothing.

Ever since she had St. Vitus Dance she has had trouble with her legs. Then she couldn't walk at all.

I am so mad I don't know what to do. I would like to have him tortured. All her thoughts end in revenge.[205]

SESSION 62: THURSDAY, 18 APRIL 1912

Last night didn't go very well[206]; hand closed and couldn't sleep very well. I seemed to be afraid to go to sleep. When I closed my eyes I thought I was on the floor here and when I went to sleep I dreamed I was on the floor here. It seemed as if the man was there and you were there and you kept saying you haven't told me this and you haven't told me that, until you do you can't get up. He was standing and every time you asked a question I would look at him and I couldn't do it.

Zander. Slept from 2 till 3. Was thinking of mother all the time after that. In the dream it seemed as if she knew what the ending was but when she would look at him he would indicate "no". I wasn't on the floor at first but you put me there and then when you would ask me I would kind of know but would look at him. It seemed as if I wouldn't let her up till she had told. Woke up still lying on the floor. I got provoked and said something which woke her.[207]

SESSION 63: SATURDAY, 20 APRIL 1912

Dreamed she was home, sick a bed, mother was there; I was a child, I kept saying, mother I can't tell, and she kept questioning me and wanted to know what was the matter. It would seem as if I would start to tell but couldn't. I would make out there wasn't anything.

Had a box of chocolates and dreamed she was concealing it from the nurse. Woke up saying, "that isn't the right thing."

Dreamed I was in some place crying, alone, somebody had been cross and then said they didn't mean it. (Thursday I had analyzed her dream of me into its elemental significance.)

Thursday night she woke up knowing she had been dreaming about me and the thought came to her that she mustn't and she didn't dream any more. She did dream after that but doesn't know what.

Hand hasn't shut up once.[208] It doesn't feel natural yet but is getting better every day.

Remembers now that the last words of the man were a threat. "If you tell I'll do it again."

Father was in Thursday: glad.

Felt her genitals for the first time.[209]

SESSION 64: MONDAY, 22 APRIL 1912

Clinic. Hand feels like tightening up but can get it right out again.

Dreamed of going home to see her mother from the Nervine. There is a lady in the ward dying and she cries just as mother did. She seemed to be at home hearing her mother just as she did really.

Dreamed other things but remembers nothing.

Saturday night dreamed of brother. Father said Saturday that he wasn't going to let him come every Monday.

To-day I feel kind of smothered. (Has a very bright color.)

What came to your mind then? "I thought of when he was on me, that's all."

Closes her eyes and her mind immediately goes to the two times.

It seems as if I can't breathe with the heat; it seems as if I were burning up. It began last night (10) was thinking about the woman dying and having to come up here to the clinic. Was hot all night. Lies down.

Cried a little this morning about 1 or 2. That woman brought back mother. He put his hand over her mouth too.

This feeling of smothering always came before convulsions.

Feels like getting up and stamping and screaming.[210]

Richard T.

I just feel that I don't want to see it and I'm not going to. This ugly feeling came yesterday afternoon. A new nurse (Miss MacDonald) said yesterday noon that she could walk if she wanted to. Yesterday cloud came again at dinner time.

I keep thinking that I shan't look and I can't get my mind to think that I will look.

SESSION 65: TUESDAY, 23 APRIL 1912

Has the feeling when lying down but can stand it better.

Feels just that same smothering feeling.

Brother came in and she dreamed of him last night, and that father was scolding him.

Dreamed about Jack but can't remember what. Woke up with her hand on her throat.

Dreamed of clay modeling class; it seemed as if someone were breaking everything as fast as she made it.

Had other dreams but can't remember them.

Went to clay modeling. Sewed, but had to keep taking it out because she didn't know what she was doing.

It doesn't feel exactly like a cloud.

Had her write any words that came to her.[211] Very trembling. Refused to go on when she thought Jack might have done something too. (page 3.)[212]

She thinks Jack MAY have done wrong to her. Asked to be excused from coming to nerve room tomorrow.[213] Willing.[214]

SESSION 66: WEDNESDAY, 24 APRIL 1912

Says she feels pretty good.
1) Dreamed I was all alone in the woods at home. I was happy. Was reading.
2) Dreamed she was going along the road, saw a house which had had a fire, a girl came out and began telling tainted stories, she told her she ought not to, she took her home and gave her some clothes, it seemed as if she was playing the part of teacher. I remember giving her some words, I was analyzing them for her and telling her what they meant.
4) Dreamed that I didn't want to come up here but you made me and you were using words I didn't like and you became provoked and said if you don't tell I will get someone who will make you and Dr. Waterman came in and I was so frightened I got up and walked.
3) Dreamed, and called out, Jack; didn't wake up and then called out, don't hold my throat so tight.
Zander. Feels dazed and hot as if something were coming.
Put down her pencil before "My hand feels etc."[215]
"Feel cross and ugly, etc." page 4.

SESSION 67: THURSDAY, 25 APRIL 1912

Zander. Dreamed and I knew it till this morning but then I couldn't remember it. It seemed I was up here. You were here.
The woman in the ward died and I dreamed she was dead. She was standing on one side of the bed and mother on the other. They were talking but I do not remember.
Had other dreams but doesn't remember them.
Had the troubled thought. At night her hand feels tight but can get it open all right.

SESSION 68: FRIDAY, 26 APRIL 1912

Modeling class yesterday.
Dreamed she killed herself; took poison, went to the medicine closet and got it. Woke up just as she was dying. In the dream just felt unhappy. It seems as if

she was home. It seemed in the dream that she never could find out what was the matter and she would now have to kill herself. It seemed as if she had just got home; was glad; sat down and was thinking and thought it would be all over with and got up and went to the closet.

Never was allowed to cry at home. Father used to say things that made her cry and then would punish her. Mother weakly submitted, and did the same. This began in Winchester, when she was about 6. She got control of crying just after 9.

Told her she should cry. Saw Dr. Shattuck, Dr. Jennings, and Dr. Eustice. She is to be put to bed and screened. Nurses told to let her cry.[216]

SESSION 69: SATURDAY, 27 APRIL 1912

Zander. Remembered last night about 10 of being home after the assault knowing he did something and wouldn't tell.[217] Mother asked her what was the trouble. Remembers being home in bed sick and knew why but wouldn't tell mother. Remembers knowing he was the cause of it, but how she got home she doesn't know.

She would ask me what I did over there; she asked me what made me so long; I tried to keep getting up but she wouldn't let me; I don't remember just how I answered but I know I evaded her questions; I don't know that I told her afterwards, I know that I didn't tell her then.

Cried after she got back to the ward; and felt better.[218]

Remembers now that she knew it was something he ought not to do and was puzzling as to what it was he did.

Thus it came over her what he had done when the girls told her, etc. feels she had got it pretty well out of her mind when the girls brought it back then it was she put it out for she doesn't remember thinking about it afterwards.[219]

Dreamed she was in the woods, then was on the water, and lost her way; at last she asked a man, a sea captain, and woke up feeling glad she was on the right way.

In another dream it seemed she was in a jail, distributing a lot of books and papers to the men. "I came to Mr. T.[220] and I was glad he was there, then I thought that wasn't right and got him out." (She debated the pros and cons as to whether she should notice him or not a long while, and then made some arrangements with the keepers.[221]) "I seemed to be having a conflict in my wishes."

Dreamed of home; girl friends; eating good things of home cooking, etc.

It seemed in what she remembers that she tried to get up but her mother wouldn't let her; she said she was sick and wasn't able to.

When she tries to think how she got home she remembers waking up and finding herself in bed with her mother standing by.

Did remember he lifted up her dress. (She knew he had done something wrong but what it was she was unable to get.)

I now turned her attention to her childhood.

When she was about 6 she was forced to go to walk with her father one Sunday afternoon. He had her little brother in a go-cart. He put it on a raft and teased her by saying he was going to let it drift away. This made her cry. Then he sent her home through the woods alone, and told her if she hadn't stopped when she got home he would punish her. She kept getting lost and couldn't stop crying, but finally got home. He made her go to bed right after supper, without letting her play any, for a week.

Her father used to talk against her mother and that made her cry. Then he would punish her, sometimes not letting her go to a party a week or two ahead.

He would hide her cats for a few days and pretend he had killed them and when she would cry would punish.

Once when she was 4 and her sister was 8 they were invited in to dinner at a friend's after Sunday School. They went and for this they were whipped. She was put across his knee and strapped with his razor strop.[222]

She did not cry but was terribly angry and gave him such a look that her mother told her that he said he would never whip her again. He never did whip her, but was always punishing her in other ways for crying.

LETTER: FATHER TO EMERSON

28 April [1912]
Dr. Emerson
Dear Sir.

I was in to the Hospital to see Rachel Saturday and I found her down in the yard and it seems Dr. Smith had passed through the yard only a short time before I arrived and he came over to Rachel and asked her how long more she was going to stay in the Hospital and Rachel did not reply and then he said if you had any *spunk* you would get up and walk that was said before the others who were with her and Rachel is very *sensitive* and when I came she cried as if her heart would break and begged me to take her home.

Now it was lucky I was not there at the time for he would remember me for a long time to come and I can't see what difference it is to him any way how long she stays at the hospital for the Sup[erintendent] and I have had an understanding in regard to it and now Dr. I thought it best to tell you of this for I think they are undoing just what you are trying to build up she is very sensitive and her fealings [sic] are easily hurt and when they are it breaks her all up so she can't eat.

I remember well the advice you gave me in regard to Rachel when I called to see you and it seems to me that if every thing should [be] made pleasant for her at *home* it certainly should be at the *Hospital too.* I have a great deal of confidence in you and the talk we had cheared [sic] me up in regard to her getting better I see [her] every week and I try to chear her up and keep happy and also her friends that come to see her and it seems to [sic] bad that these *slurs* should be [illegible word] at her, she will not stay 5 min. after she can walk for she is so anxious to get home. I called the Sup[erintendent's] office and told the gentleman in the office about it. It was not the Sup[erintendent] I am accustomed to meet there and he said he would see to it. But I thought I would drop you a line and let you know what I think is up against what you are trying so hard to get her well.

I remain cincearly [sic] yours,
Henry C.

LETTER: FATHER TO EDITH BURLEIGH

28 April [1912]
Winchester
Miss Burleigh

Dear friend
I have just written a note to Dr. Emerson in regard to Rachel and I did not know [how] to get it to him only through you for I did not know his full name and I was anxious for him to know what I have learned in regard to Rachel's treatment in the hospital and will you please see that Dr. Emerson receives the note you may read it if you wish.

Thanking you for your kindness
Respectfully yours,
Henry C.

SESSION 70: MONDAY, 29 APRIL 1912

Moved her leg yesterday about 1 P.M. She was trying to think how she got home and something came over her and she moved her right leg, about 6 inches.

Dreamed she was in some place hunting for Miss Burleigh.

Dreamed she was home and brother was there sick and she was taking care of him.

Woke up crying but what she was dreaming of she does not know.

Saturday night dreamed of Dr. Smith. He had told her she could walk if she wanted to, and it had made her very angry and when her father came she cried and told him and vomited. She dreamed she was in Dr. S[mith]'s place and he in hers and she was telling him what he had told her.

Dreamed of the letter Miss Burleigh got instead of her brother; seemed to be sort of sorry he hadn't got it after all.

Had her draw a diagram of the house and try to remember end.[223] [Figure 2] I feel now just as I did in bed puzzling how I got home.

Saw Dr. Smith and told him I was glad he had done just as he had.

Had her close her eyes.

Just thought of another dream; I thought there was another girl in my place; I was looking at things in a different light and giving her advice as to how to get out of it.[224]

SESSION 71: TUESDAY, 30 APRIL 1912

Clay class yesterday.

Dreamed she was walking up a mountain, stumbling and getting on the wrong path, and when she got to the top she found the reservoir turned into a well, which she told the folks, but they laughed and wouldn't believe it, but they went and saw the same thing. (Jack.)

Dreamed something about the class.

Dreamed she had an operation on her throat, up here. It seemed as if I had had it and my throat felt better.

Has her mother's ring on the fourth finger of left hand.

For reference to the relation between "thrills" and "thoughts" see note book.[225]

SESSION 72: WEDNESDAY, 1 MAY 1912

Moved her leg about 4:30 (Was trying and had relaxed.)

Zander.

Dreamed and woke up crying, and saying, "I couldn't forgive him."

Lies back and closes her eyes. (See notes.)[226]

Moved her legs a little twice. (Mother is in the way. Perhaps her mother for-

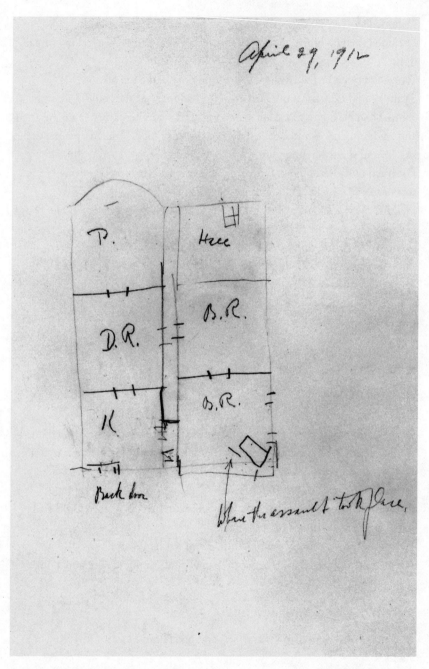

Figure 2. Diagram of the interior of the neighbor's house, "where the assault [at age 13] took place," that Emerson had Rachel draw, 29 April 1912 (session 70). Reproduced, with permission, from the Boston Medical Library in the Francis A. Countway Library of Medicine.

bidding her to go with Jack is the reason why she can't get the end now, because she doesn't want to give up thinking of him, and thus loses the thrills.)

"Times mother slept with me."

Noticed yesterday that she did not have her brother's ring on.

"I feel mother has something to do with my not telling."

"I feel if I could put up my hand and brush it away I could see it."

SESSION 73: THURSDAY, 2 MAY 1912

Zander. "Felt I was near it but yet I couldn't get it."

Dreamed I was walking around the ward. I cried a little before I went to sleep. Prayed.

Explained how I thought mother prevented by forbidding Jack; she doesn't want to give up Jack; transfers mother's forbidding to her own desires.

Lies back. Free associations.

See notes for shudders.

It seems as if mother acted suspicious.

Vision: father—Jack—mother.

Thought of going in the woods and whether I ought to.[227]

He came back in the room and helped me up, he threatened me as he helped me up, and helped me down stairs. He said he wasn't through with me yet. (Can move her legs.) Took her home to the gate and said if she told he would do it again, but if not he wouldn't trouble her. She staggered up the path and crawled up the steps. Sat in chair in kitchen a while and then went to bed.

Thinks she didn't answer her mother's questions.

Thinks she didn't know even then what it was that he had done, but whatever it was, knew it was wrong.

SESSION 74: FRIDAY, 3 MAY 1912

Can lift right leg but not left and can't stand yet.

Clay class yesterday.

Dreamed but couldn't remember. Towards morning though she dreamed she had a baby she was taking care of. It didn't seem to be her own. She was playing with it and feeding it. It was about a year and a half old. "I remember putting it to bed."

One of the patients said I was calling for mother last night but I don't remember it.

I went to her for trifling things but things that really bothered me I never could go to her with because with she never seemed to understand me.

Had her lie down. For shudders see notes.

Cloud last night. Felt accused because of telling.

Cried off and on all day and cried herself to sleep last night.

"It seems as if it were summer time."

"Wishing I had a sister."

"Mother sent me over with some pieces of silk."[228]

"He was in the dining-room. I don't remember how he got me into the bed-room. His wife was not there."

"I gave him the pieces of silk she sent there. Mrs. T.[229] was making a quilt."

"Blank again and then I see mother, father, Jack, just as I did yesterday."

Shudder—Door opened by Paul.[230] Arm, left, shaking. Thought she was in the room[231] and the man had returned.

"It seemed as if the thought just as I had hold of it slipped."

"Somehow it seems as if I didn't get up the next day."

"I have the feeling I told her. It seems as if I got up and went down stairs, I re-member being on the couch. It seems as if I remember telling her. It seems as if I saw Mrs. T. I was on the couch. It worked me all up to see her. She was questioning mother about it and she said it was all nervousness.

I know. I told mother he had lifted up my dress but I didn't know what he had done. She said people thought things so much they finally got to think so in reality.[232]

"I wouldn't have anything to do with Mrs. T."

"Mother said I was so nerved up I didn't know what I was doing." (Arm twitches less.)

"It seems as if I got better after a while."

She can move her left leg now, but cannot stand yet.

SESSION 75: SATURDAY, 4 MAY 1912

Can stand a little but is wobbly. Zander.

Remembers how she came down stairs: father brought her. She didn't get up the next day but the day after.

Dreamed she was in here and went home and went off by herself, on the mountain, was happy, reading, thought of being here, woke while still dream-ing of the mountain.

Night nurse said she called out, "I can't forgive him."

A patient said she said, "I want to be alone."

Arm twitching stopped soon after she went back to the ward yesterday.

Cried a little last night, and woke up and cried.

It seems as if every time I spoke of it she (mother) pooh-poohed it, and finally I thought I really dreamed it. I remember seeing him and I thought of it, but I thought of what mother had said and I tried to put it out of my mind but just how long it took I don't know.

Soon after it happened she saw him, and thought of it, and it made her feel sick, but thought what her mother said must be so, it was only a bad dream, and after a while put it out of her mind.

Began to come to the M.G.H. latter part of July '08. In ward G[233] five weeks. Her mother questioned her and it was hard to tell but when she had and wasn't believed, she shut right up.

The first time she saw him was about a week after. She was sitting on the piazza with her mother and he and his wife came over for a few moments and sat with them. As they were coming up the path her mother gave her a look as much as to say, "you stay." She did so but was so faint she felt if she should stand up she would faint away. She didn't speak and never looked at him when she could help it. She was trembling all over, and felt sick. After that she saw him as usual and in two or three times it went. It kept getting fainter and fainter until it had gone completely.[234]

SESSION 76: MONDAY, 6 MAY 1912

Is very much better.

Saturday night I dreamed that the wheel chair was broken and they wanted to fix it but I wouldn't let them. I was home and the chair was in the yard. Father.

Had another dream in which she seemed to be with her father.

Last night dreamed of being home with people, you were one of them, I stood it as long as I could and went off alone.

Girl friends, brother, and father were there.

Dreamed I was walking with brother.

Woke up about 4 feeling smothered; was dreaming but can't remember what. Had the feeling ever since.[235]

Lies down.

Woods—Did that make a shiver go over you when you thought of Jack? "Not much of one, I seem to be able to control myself better."

(It was about 7 or 8 in the Fall.)

"I can't see how mother made me go to him so much when I told her." (Almost cries.)

When Dr. Jennings saw her move her feet he said, "I'll be darned."

It seems now that I knew for sure what he had done when the girls told me, and that was why I felt so sick.

I think of mother again and how she acted, I can't get it out of my mind.[236]

"They'd say right out I never could get well by having it go through my mind. They'd talk together, and look at me and laugh."

Shudder—"I know now what it is and it doesn't have the effect on me it did." (Thought of him.)

St. Vitus Dance—Couldn't walk to school.

Onset: Got up from supper-table and started running and stumbling. Mother had to call in the neighbors, she couldn't hold me I struggled so. I knew what I was doing and I knew I was acting foolish but I couldn't help it. This started about a month after school began. It seems now that there was only about a year between the woods and the attack.[237]

"I asked her to get a baby. She said the stork brought them."

Thus it must have taken 3 months to put the "room" out of her mind.[238]

Can remember when my knees ached terribly.

SESSION 77: TUESDAY, 7 MAY 1912

Remembered this morning how she got home from the woods.[239] Got up and walked home. Mother asked her why she was so late and she said she had taken a walk. Went to school the next day as usual.

I remember coming from school, I think for flowers, so I imagine it was in the Spring.

Lies down.

Dreamed of mother, brother, and I sat down to supper. Brother dropped a pitcher of milk; mother started to wipe it up; I told her to let brother do it; then I got up and did it myself, and scolded her; I said she humored him too much.

Dreamed Dr. Eustice and you were talking together, and with me; he said well we are about through with you, and you said yes just as soon as she stops thinking.

It seems as if that summer mother began to scold me for being dreamy and wanting to be by myself.

Nervousness didn't start till I began school. We started French, algebra, and I couldn't seem to get on at all. I know teacher said I had changed, that I was quite different from last year. Soon after she started to school she had trouble with walking and had to ride.

I know that all that summer I stayed in the house and wouldn't do anything. My knees ached, etc.

If anything bothered me or troubled me I always put it right out of my mind and I remember soon after it happened I would think of it and put it right out of my mind.[240] It seems as if in a month she had forgotten it.

Mother told her in later years that she thought her menses had started when she was 15.

Mother took her to the doctor's 3 or 4 times before she told her she was taking her to get her menses flowing.

She wasn't especially dreamy or fond of being by herself before 10.

Brother came last night. Cried after he went.

SESSION 78: WEDNESDAY, 8 MAY 1912

Looks as if she had been crying.

Went to the toilet alone this morning. Zander.

Dreamed she was in the ward and was sent for from the superintendent's office. I was there. I said I had two things to tell her and the last was terrible. I seemed to have difficulty and she thought it must be something about her brother and tried to ask me if it were and woke up trying.

It would seem as if I was going along and everybody I'd meet would bring up things in my past and I would try to get away but I couldn't.

I dreamed something but I can't tell what, I woke up saying "I shan't tell anything more."

Cried this morning. Lies down.

He was in the superintendent's office. "Just you and I."[241]

SESSION 79: THURSDAY, 9 MAY 1912

Can walk very well. Feels better.

When I first went to sleep I dreamed I was playing with your children; after that I dreamed but I would not know what.

Zander. Cried this morning.

T. came about a year before assault.

Was 10 when assaulted in woods.

Saw Dr. Shattuck and Jennings.
She walked back.[242]

SESSION 80: FRIDAY, 10 MAY 1912

Clay class yesterday. Wishes she didn't dream so much.
Dreamed of being a nurse: it seemed as if I was in training.
Dreamed of me, mother, and brother. Woke saying, "I can not."
Dreamed I was walking and somebody kept bringing up different things why
I shouldn't walk, but I kept on.
The reasons were like pictures. It seemed like a woman in the dream standing
in front of her showing these pictures and then saying "now you can't walk."
Thought of mother. Woke crying.
Knew she had been dreaming and woke thinking about the word, "ask."[243]
When she is reading her mother comes before her like a flash with a reproach-
ful look.[244]
(Notes) In the room he put her skirt over her face.
page 24 While carrying her mother went out into the hall and saw it full of
smoke, and saw the red lamp.
When she was born she had a red mark on her face just over her right eye.
This lasted till she was 12 or 13. There is a slight scale there now.
Her mother told her about this about a year before she died.

EMERSON'S NOTES

Rachel C.—Monday (?) June 10, 1912
Vomits.
Fall occasionally. Sunday night when returning from church with father. Fa-
ther ugly about her going to Waltham Training School for nurses—
To go to Winchester and see father tomorrow. Rachel does not know.

LETTER: RACHEL TO EMERSON

30 July 1912
Winchester, Massachusetts

Dear Dr. Emerson:
I received your letter thanking me for the vase and was pleased that you liked it.

I thought would like to know that I am really going to school in the fall. I can hardly realize it as true.

We intend to break up here by the first of September then I am going to Mrs. Frost. They have given me a lovely room so I will feel at liberty to come there whenever I have time.

Last Thursday I was twenty three and father gave me a fountain pen and Mrs. Frost gave me five dollars which will help me out a lot.

I have all my outside sewing done and a great deal of my own.

The clay modeling class are going to have a picnic down at Nantasket beach next Wednesday. I am going to try to go.

Please remember me to Mrs. Emerson and little Mary.[245]

Sincerely yours,
Rachel C.

Part II "Dreamed she was a pure girl"

Chapter 5 Commentary:
19 November 1912–1 May
1913, Sessions 81–188

Emerson found this part of the treatment, encompassing 108 sessions stretching from November 1912 to the beginning of May 1913, "complex and persistently difficult," far more so than "the smooth account of the abstract theory" of psychoanalysis had led him to expect.[1] The success of the first part of the treatment, in which a history of two traumas— the men in the woods, the raping neighbor—was established, confirmed his view that the theory of repression with which he was working was true. Recovery of the patient's repressed memories, along with uncovering the mother's role in first suppressing them, had resulted in her recovery, and Emerson was confident enough that he was finished with her that he took the opportunity to write up a summary of the case, taking what he called a "bird's-eye view" of her life and the causes of her hysteria.[2] Rachel did well over the summer. She and Emerson exchanged letters, and she began nursing school in the fall.[3] When she returned to him in November complaining of nausea and vomiting, Emerson immediately suspected there were other pathogenic nuclei yet to be discovered. His suspicion proved correct. Three more traumatic "scenes," from Rachel's past and ongoing in the present, came to light, involving the boyfriend Jack, the brother, and the father. The process of bringing these to consciousness, however, led not to the recovery Emerson expected but, rather, to the patient's condition worsening dramatically. In the six months spanned by these sessions, Rachel was hospitalized three times.

Emerson was an early and ardent analytic chronicler of the family's many pathologies. The papers he published while treating this case, from 1912 through 1916, told of fathers who beat their sons and uncles who masturbated their nieces; of families in which not just one but several brothers solicited sisters for sex; of, like Freud's papers, frigid wives roused to passion only in extramarital liaisons with libertines. Emerson acknowledged that the family was a social institution, but maintained that "the fundamental family relation" was sexual.[4] He held that serious psychic consequences flowed from parental sexual irregularities, severe hysterias in the children most seriously among them. But, even if in many cases it was the pathological familial environment, not deficiencies inherent in individuals, that resulted in illness, it was the individual that psychoanalysis was suited to treat. Further, in writing about even the most disturbed of families, Emerson located the nub of the difficulties not in the facts of family relations having gone awry but in the interpretations family members arrived at as to why they had done so. His focus was consistently on the psychic conflicts generated by the disturbed family relations.

In these sessions, Rachel provided Emerson with a precise and harrowing account of her family's secret workings. If, in the previous segment of the treatment, trauma—the men in the woods, the raping neighbor—was something that occurred outside the family, in this segment, with its revelations of fraternal and paternal abuse and solicitation, trauma was located at the family's heart. Rachel's account, which implicated all the men in her life, was elicited against great resistance and at great psychic and symptomatic cost, every revelation accompanied by the appearance of new and debilitating symptoms: vomiting, aphonia, paraplegia, blindness, convulsions, amnesia, auditory hallucinations, and, finally, self-mutilation. "It is obvious that psychoanalysis is necessary for discovering the more intimate forms of family relationship," Emerson wrote, because in an analysis "all kinds of data come to light that remain otherwise entirely hidden."[5] Indeed, it took Emerson more than a year of intensive (though interrupted) treatment to elicit from Rachel the critical information regarding the brother and father. As he learned in these sessions, Rachel and her brother had been having sexual relations since childhood, with him accustomed to crawling into bed with her in the morning, the two of them tussling and wrestling, and, in the process, becoming sexually excited, all with the mother's

knowledge and tacit consent. The father, Emerson learned, had been masturbating her since she was seven years old, again with the mother's knowledge and
consent, and, just before she had entered treatment with Emerson, had offered
to pay her for having sex with him. Just as troubling to Rachel was her double
admission, near the end of this phase of the treatment, that she had begun to
masturbate after the father had started to abuse her and that she had been, as
the treatment continued, masturbating regularly.

Rachel's family, which from the outside might have appeared as ordinary as
any other, was thus pathologically endogamous, knitted together by incestuous
sex and secret complicities.[6] That the father, considering remarriage, was talking of marrying his deceased wife's sister's illegitimate daughter—or, in other
words, Rachel's cousin (session 83)—is a measure of how constricted and in-
wardly turned the familial ethos was. Although the whole family in principle
subscribed to it, only Rachel actually honored it; it was she who bore the brunt
of the familial injunction to stay home. Both the father and mother had ventured beyond the family for sex, but when Rachel had tried to do likewise, with
Jack, dire parental warnings were voiced and prohibitions put into effect. Both
the father, who was soliciting his daughter for sex, and the mother, who had
confessed to both premarital and extramarital liaisons, barred Jack from the
house and forbade her to see him. In this case, the usual conventions governing
forms of familial alliance were reversed. Rachel could fantasize herself in the
position of wife to Jack (session 108), but day-to-day she acted the part of wife
to the brother and the father, who entertained their own fantasy of her as the
perfect wife, as both domestic drudge—"come home and keep house," her
brother wrote her solicitously while she was hospitalized (session 163)—and
sexual object, the brother adding in this instance that he "missed the pillow-
fights" that were associated with their incestuous sex.[7]

If Rachel suffered the most under the pressure of the family system, she was
also the most faithful to it. She was faithful in not betraying the mother's secrets, and she was sexually "faithful," sending Jack on his way as she continued
to have sex with the brother and father. "I will stay right home always," she
avowed in her sleep one night, in the midst of a period during which she was
coming to terms with the knowledge that she had indeed slept with her
brother. The nurse who recorded her nocturnal soliloquies noted that she then
"talked a good deal about going home, and staying there" (Nurse's Notes, following session 118). Rachel found her way out of this morass only through the
medium of her illness. In April, she was able to remember that it was her father's
attempted solicitation of her the previous summer that had precipitated her

convulsions. Following several scenes in which she had asserted a familial claim on him, begging him not to go with other women, he had come into her bedroom, made "expressive movements," and "*offered her some money* if she would let him do what he wanted to," as if meeting her objections to his exogamy by asserting his endogamous rights over her (session 166). She was frightened and angry, and could only call on the brother—with whom she was at this point also having incestuous relations—for protection, asking him to get her a key for her room. This memory, however, was accompanied by the devastating realization that she and the brother had had sexual intercourse many more times than she'd previously been ready to remember.

How could she desire when desire was so tainted? Rachel's implicit question became more urgent as the momentum of the case bore down relentlessly on her own secret and inadmissible desires. It was wrong to want Jack, to want sex and babies, when the father and the mother "did so wrong, she and brother had too much of such desires and it was wrong to have it" (session 177). She had often thought, she told Emerson, "of how easy it would be for her to be bad," and the mother—whose words Rachel nearly always took to heart—had only underscored this, telling Rachel "that if she ever fell, she would go in the whole way" (session 112). Illicit sex, incest, premarital pregnancy—in the end, acknowledging that she masturbated mobilized the force of Rachel's punishing superego far more so than did any of the other of her transgressions. In masturbating, which she did frequently and fiercely, there was no other on whom to displace all the guilt-ridden desire she would be forced to claim as her own. As her masturbation became more explicitly the focus of the analysis, she raved, she beat her head, she tore out her hair, all, to Emerson's analytic eye, concrete instances of self-abuse and symbolical instances of self-punishment that served as alternative means to sexual satisfaction.[8] She woke one morning trying to bite her hand off so she couldn't masturbate anymore (session 175); she pinned together the sleeves of her nightgown in a futile attempt to stanch the practice (session 182). By the end of this segment of the treatment, we are left with the image of Rachel alone and wounded, her arm bandaged to conceal the damage she has done to herself, dreaming of cutting herself up and of destroying herself as she desperately tried to evade the insistent press of her desire.

FATHER AND SON

Within a week of writing Emerson, on 14 November 1912 (Letter, before session 81), that she was not feeling "extra well" and that hoped she could see him in order to straighten things out, Rachel was fully back into the analysis. Telling him her dreams and talking a good deal about the mother, whom she found was constantly on her mind, she also told him that something else was troubling her, that she had forgotten something or put it out of her mind. "I keep thinking all the time; and what I'm thinking, I don't know; but I know I'm thinking," she said (session 83). Observing, over several sessions, that Rachel's resistances were becoming stronger, Emerson suspected there was more pathogenic material concerning Jack yet to be found.[9]

For two months, over the course of thirty-one sessions, Emerson encouraged and exhorted Rachel as she looked at the question of what precisely Jack had done to her and, at the same time, explored the role of her own desire in their transactions. That she and Jack had had intercourse was quickly, though with difficulty, established. On the day it had first happened, Jack had come to her house around eleven in the morning. After making sure her mother was out, he tried, apparently unsuccessfully, to kiss her. He then fed her the large quantity of bonbons and stuffed dates he had brought along and, when she began to feel queasy, refused her water and instead helped her to a couch by the china cabinet in the dining room and held a bottle to her nose, telling her it would make her feel better. She lost consciousness. When she came to, she realized her dress was pulled up and that he was having intercourse with her. She felt powerless to move, and lost consciousness again. When she woke again, she was alone and dazed, and could remember only that Jack had said to her, while he had her on the lounge, "you didn't like the candy, did you, but I had to gain my point" (session 95).

Rachel's agony, as she retrieved the memories of Jack forcing himself on her, was immense. She began to vomit so constantly she was admitted to the hospital, on 5 December 1912, leaving after two days only because she wanted to go back to nursing school (sessions 94–96). However, although Rachel narrated the scene with Jack as an assault, with Jack possibly drugging her to insure her compliance, her ambivalence was manifest. The day it happened, she told Emerson, she decided to give him up for good while realizing, at the same time, she couldn't do so (session 90). As it became clear she didn't do so, and that, further, she had had sex with him again, this time in a room upstairs in her friend Ella's house, she lost the use of her legs and, paraplegic, was again admitted to the hospital (26 December 1912), staying for seven weeks, until mid-February (sessions 104–140). "*Either:* she *wished* it; *or* he *did* it" (session 100)—Rachel's formulation, in which her desire absolved him of any responsibility, and which at the same time precluded the possibility of mutual desire, captured succinctly the interpretive knot in which she was caught. The sex this time, she told Emerson, was far worse than when she'd been attacked and raped as a child, because this time she had wanted it, she had gone up the stairs with Jack (session 103). Thoughts of desiring Jack—of how hard it was to send him off when it was over (session 99), of being as a wife to him (session 108), of wishing he would do it again (session 109)—punctuated her long struggle to piece together her memories, and tinged the manifest story line of his force with the shadow of her own ambivalent but strong desire. Emerson had analyzed a dream of hers in which she had been shot three times by a pistol (interpreting the pistol as a penis) as expressive of her wish for sex, telling her "she *wanted* sexual intercourse" (session 87). It would be weeks before she could even begin to claim that wanting as her own.

Still struggling to resolve not only what happened between her and Jack—to retrieve a memory of the "actual deed" that transpired in Ella's house (session 106)—but also the question of whether she had wanted it to happen, Rachel reported a long dream of sexual assault and humiliation that led to the revelation, two days later, of her incestuous relations with the brother. In the dream, Rachel was naked, carried by someone into "a room full of naked men." The men were talking and acting obscenely, and, with the mother's permission, fingering her and having intercourse with her, laughing as they watched one another have sex. The mother invited the men into the room and chatted with them, doing nothing to protect her daughter. The dream went on for weeks, Rachel told Emerson; "it was as real as reality" (session 112).

The dream, if not "real," did capture something of the reality of the incestuous family structure that Rachel began to reveal to Emerson in its wake. Not only did the mother not object to the brother getting into bed with Rachel, the mother told her, it later came out, when the two were talking about the rapist-neighbor, that girls and their brothers did "such things" (session 134). Further, with her silence, the mother tacitly condoned what Rachel had not yet told Emerson, the father's sexual abuse of her, which consisted in his fingering her and having intercourse with her. In the dream and in the family, the mother thus acted as procurer, while enjoying easy relations with the men who were having sex with her daughter. Within the dream, everything—as in the family—was visible, others could look on, and it went on endlessly, for years. Rachel was the only one who appeared to suffer, while everyone else enjoyed themselves. In reality, only after a friend of Rachel's discovered the brother in bed with her did she begin to discourage, though not absolutely prohibit, her brother from coming into her room.

With this dream of procurement, the focus of the analytic work shifted from Jack to the brother. "Now came a tough time for both analyst and patient," Emerson wrote.[10] Rachel's revelations about her brother deepened her despair and triggered a fresh wave of symptoms. Her resistances, in Emerson's estimation, became even stronger. She began to dissociate, sleepwalking extensively, and a fever, which hospital physicians would eventually decide was hysterical, set in.[11] Rachel struggled with the question of whether she and her brother had actually had intercourse for the good part of a month.

SITES OF STRUGGLE

As Rachel's conflicts continued to deepen, bearing down ever more insistently on the family's forbidden secrets and, most significant, on the issue of her own desire, the sites of her struggle proliferated. Her intense "mental perturbations"[12] began to find expression not only in the consulting room but also in the ward, where she shouted out in her sleep; in a series of vivid and disturbing dreams; and in her own notes, which she began to keep for the first time.

Rachel's nocturnal ravings began the night before she told Emerson of her relations with the brother Everett (session 114). "Why did you do it?" she cried out in her sleep, calling out the brother's name as well. Following this, the night nurses recorded her words as accurately as they could. "I shan't tell," "no, no, no, no," "I know it's so, and I won't say so" (Nurse's Notes, following sessions 115, 116)—Rachel's loud cries, which disturbed the sleep of other patients on the ward, testified to the depth of her conflict as well as to her resistance to allowing it conscious expression. For a week following Emerson's suggestion that perhaps she and the brother had done it in their sleep (session 115), Rachel carried on the analysis largely in her sleep. By day, in sessions with Emerson, she said little, and Emerson complained, as he had earlier in the case, of getting nothing from her, of finding nothing new, and of making little headway in the treatment. By night, her conflicted feelings came tumbling out as she raved and talked in her sleep. She both angrily pushed the brother away and, as if acknowledging her complicity in the incestuous familial system, talked of returning home and staying there, of not being able to give him up (Nurse's Notes, following sessions 118 and 119). She admitted to knowing he did it, but was reluctant to admit it, both to herself and to Emerson. "I won't, I can't, and you can't make me," (session 116) she yelled out one night, an outburst Emerson saw as directed at him, even though she also called out the brother's name, and which he found "perfectly intelligible from the point of view of her repressions and my urging her, against her resistances, to tell all."[13] Once again, she had fused him with one who was abusing her, and once again he was aware of her having done so.

Shortly after dreaming of the appearance of "immense quantities of writing paper, which she felt she must write on" (session 120), Rachel began recording her dreams, which were at this point particularly vivid and plentiful. Her writing, which excluded Emerson from the dialogue they had established,[14] may have been in part a reproach to Emerson, punishment for his continued scolding (session 121) and for making her feel "a coward and a fool" (session 114). She may also have been striving for more autonomy in the treatment, both her writing and her dream of writing (session 126) possibly signaling a desire to write up her own case. Indeed, she continued to record her dreams for a ten-day period between hospitalizations when she did not see Emerson (following session 140). The first dream she recorded, of her writing being subjected to the unceasing criticism of a man who "would always find something that was wrong with it" and who made her do it over and over, might have been of Emerson; the dream ended with her being provoked and burning the paper, after which she was free and happy (session 123).

Yet another strong theme in Rachel's dreams had to do with snakes. Early in this segment of the treatment, Emerson hypothesized that the snakes she dreamed were coming out of her pocket were a symbolic penis, the pocket a vagina (session 85). Throughout, Rachel consistently associated snakes with the brother. She dreamed of him bringing her a basket full of snakes, which then escaped from the basket and spread out over the bed (session 123). She dreamed of vomiting snakes, and then associated to intercourse with the brother (session 163). "Mind goes *from snake to brother*," Emerson noted in the midst of the next session (session 164). Following a session in which she said next to nothing, claiming to have forgotten everything, she recorded a dream centered on a small bag she was constantly afraid she would lose. Meeting her brother on the street, she suddenly realized she was missing her bag. She went back to the house to find it. Unsuccessful, she emerged from the house to see the brother "sitting on the steps with it. He said I asked him to hold it for me. I was provoked," she added, "because it seemed as if he was trying to take it from me" (session 129). Emerson left no record of how he interpreted this dream, but it is suggestive that, during the next session, Rachel was able to retrieve a vision of her brother lying on top of her in bed, trying, perhaps, to take her bag from her (session 130).

Emerson thought that with the revelations about the brother that he had reached bedrock. Rachel was discharged from the hospital on the assumption, he wrote, that she would gradually become reconciled to what she had told him and that eventually "she would not feel so badly over what she had learned about her past."[15] Within a week, however, she was back to see him, still symptomatic—vomiting, transiently blind, hallucinating the mother calling, and losing her voice. Then, after telling Mrs. Frost, with whom she was boarding while attending nursing school, the causes of her trouble (leaving the incestuous relations with the brother out of her account), she suffered a grand hysterical attack, a violent convulsion in which she pulled her hair out and which abated only after she was practically anesthetized, given ether and morphine by a physician summoned to the scene. Though discouraged, Emerson persisted, buoyed, he wrote, "by Freud's statement of the time necessary, in some cases, to effect a complete cure." Assuming, once again, that more hidden complexes needed to be released, he embarked on "the next and last stage of the analysis."[16] Rachel was admitted to the hospital, this time the newly opened Boston Psychopathic Hospital, where she stayed for two months.

ANALYTIC MIDWIFERY

In the hospital, two further complexes quickly came to light. A dream in which someone kept opening Rachel's hand and picking bugs from it, followed by the telling of another in which "she was fooling with herself," a snake in bed with her, led—against great resistance—to the issue of her masturbation (session 145). Struggling through paraplegia and yet another severe convulsion to remember whether or not it was true she had "'played' with herself" as the dream had suggested, she finally was able to admit she had, and that "the snake seemed symbolical" in this (session 152). This established, she then turned back to the question of whether she and the brother had copulated more than once (session 164), when, with a violent start, she sat up in the middle of a session and, "after making considerable resistance," announced, "It was Everett, Father, and everything."[17] The father had put his fingers in her when she was about seven years old, she told Emerson (session 165), and from that point on she and her brother had had frequent incestuous relations. Rachel then said that, having in effect told all, she had decided to stop being stubborn, "for now she has nothing further to be stubborn about" (session 166).

That Rachel could characterize her resistance as stubbornness is evidence of the extent to which she had adopted Emerson's morally laden language of willfulness, compliancy, and goodness and badness as her own. Emerson entered this segment of the treatment proclaiming his intention to lay siege to her resistance, which, he later wrote, "turned out to be the greatest resistance of all so far met."[18] As he had earlier, he urged her "to tell all," and complained repeatedly when it seemed that little or no progress was being made in getting at her unconscious complexes. "*I did not break her resistance,*" he emphatically noted as she told him she could not break the promise she'd made to her mother not to tell (session 168). At one point, in the midst of trying to remember what had happened between herself and the brother, he noted with a touch of sanctimony that she "seems more amenable to reason" (session 134). At another point, he noted he'd used a dream of hers—in which, situated at home, she was trying to keep both the father and Emerson out, and from which she awoke remembering "the time her father tried to get her to do wrong"—to "prove her the Übertragung." "Think I succeeded," he added, his triumphant interpretation, in which he no doubt explained to her that he and the assaulting father were merged, both an acknowledgment and an enactment of the analyst's penetrating power (session 186).

A number of Rachel's dreams were expressive of her transferences to Emerson and the analytic situation. In several dreams she was able to withhold from Emerson the revelations he so persistently sought in the analysis. In one, she dreamed she was on trial, but when it was her turn to talk she "wouldn't say any thing. They were deciding what they would do with me" (session 137). In another, she dreamed she'd been burying things in a deep hole, and, just as she was about to bury the last thing, Emerson came along and asked what she was doing. She couldn't tell (session 132). She dreamed of Emerson as impatient and demanding, of him "trying to make her tell something which she wouldn't tell" (session 176), and of him allowing her five minutes in which to tell him what she'd been dreaming of (session 154). In other dreams, truth, and her capacity for honoring it in the analytic encounter, was at issue. In one dream, the punishment for not telling Emerson the truth was to be sent to analysis with him (session 114). Rachel admitted to Emerson she was tempted to lie, and that she would do so if it would make what had happened to her "not so" (session 158). "If she felt she was able to get out of all this by lying she would have done so," Emerson explained (Staff Meeting, following session 175). Forgetting was an alternative to lying; in yet another dream she was "going from place to place trying to forget" but couldn't (session 168). Her dream of once again being a child, but armed this time with a book in which she recorded "every thing that happened so I wouldn't forget them it seemed as if I knew I had forgotten and wasn't going to again" (session 139), may have expressed her wish to be a better patient, a patient who neither forgot nor lied. But it may also have expressed her wish she'd been able to circumvent the need for analysis altogether.

Emerson wrote that looking for Rachel's memories was "like assisting in childbirth" (session 87), giving voice to the maternal strain that had figured as counterpoint to the masculinist language of siege and attack so dominant in the first part of the treatment. By now, however, the maternalism was even more fraught than earlier. Two years later, writing of love and the philosopher's desire, Emerson reminded his readers—and likely himself—that Socrates "called himself a midwife,"[19] preemptively warding off the charge he had played the woman's part in his treatment of Rachel. As Rachel's desire for a good mother and her conflicts about whether she could have one became more explicit, she may have harbored hopes Emerson could either be one or provide her one. Dreaming she had been given a magic wand and told she could do anything with it, she started to make a mother but realized she needed a model: "So it seemed as if I took Mrs. Emerson but all the time mother was here with me then it seemed as if I made you take me out of there" (session 137), suggesting she felt Emerson both offered her the possibility of a good mother and interfered with her getting one. Rachel's dreams were replete with themes and images of the mother. In one, which may have embodied her struggle to achieve a coherent picture of the mother, she tried unsuccessfully to assemble a skeleton, which she knew was her mother: "Her one object was to get this together and she couldn't," Emerson wrote (session 82). The mother was constantly on her mind; at the same time, Rachel was "constantly *putting her out of her mind*" (session 82). Just as Rachel identified with the mother as object of the father's sexual and psychic cruelty, it being "as if what her father had done were done to her" (session 171), it appears she merged Emerson and the father, experiencing his insistence that she yield her secrets as a reenactment of the father's betrayals and solicitations. At many points in this part of the treatment, it is clear that Rachel was furious at Emerson, just as she had been at the father, and that she wanted "out," out of the hospital (she petitioned to be discharged from the Psychopathic Hospital, filing a "three day paper") and, at times, out of treatment (Staff Meeting, following session 175). Yet, when she imagined that Emerson might himself want out, she first allowed that he might "be tired of the case," adding "I know I am," but then stated unequivocally that she would "not have another doctor" (Letter, following session 141). The next day she had an attack that resulted in her being rehospitalized, once again under Emerson's care. Her illness resecured his devotion.

Emerson's midwifery metaphor points to a submerged and conflicted maternal theme. It is also suggestive, symbolically, of the possibility that at this point in the treatment an unarticulated and unanalyzed erotic joint-pregnancy fantasy shared by Rachel and Emerson began to crystallize. This pregnancy would produce multiple deformed births in the form of the snakes and bugs of which Rachel repeatedly dreamed, equivalent to the terrible deeds and wishes that would also come out. The question of pregnancy—had Rachel actually been pregnant?—assumed increasing centrality in Rachel's dreams and in the analysis in this segment, and Emerson, as midwife to Rachel's repressed memories, may at times have felt himself to be assisting as much as he was actively drilling and laying siege.

RACHEL'S FAMILY ROMANCE

As the treatment progressed, and as Rachel was able to acknowledge the various traumas she had been through, she felt progressively more isolated and alone. For example, having revealed the secret of her incestuous relations with the brother, she felt as if he were dead, even as if she had killed him. "Everett I told as little as I could," she wrote. "I won't tell any more" (session 132). With her mother already dead, and now, with the loss of her brother, she told Emerson, she felt completely alone (session 121). She felt the brother had betrayed her; through the medium of a dream in which they'd both agreed to take poison but only she did, she admitted "he was the only one she had loved." She reproached him for going back on her (session 173). She could feel toward him as she felt toward the rapist-neighbor (session 145), and she could bristle when she saw him. But she was not immune to his entreaties that she should return home to care for him.

As Rachel characterized one after another of the men in her life—Jack, the brother, the father—as sexual predators, she cast them off, experiencing a great sense of loss as she did so. The casting off of Jack and the brother was likely in part defensive, a means of disavowing the dimensions of her own conflicted desires for them, which were only elicited in the face of great resistance. Whether defensive or not, the consequence was her sense of abandonment and loss. Her dream, while she was hospitalized, of everyone in the ward having died, except for herself, and of looking unsuccessfully for a nurse to help her carry the bodies out, after which she started to carry them out herself, may be interpreted as one of several expressions of this sense of loss (session 139). Later, remembering what the mother had revealed of her own sexual misdeeds two months before dying, Rachel experienced anew the sense of loss she had felt upon her death:

"Patient feels now she has lost everybody, *including mother*," Emerson noted, adding, "and it seems more than she can bear, especially as it is all sexual" (session 167). Rachel's mother had sworn her daughter to secrecy, a vow Rachel struggled to honor, but both the content of her revelation—the mother characterizing herself as both desiring subject, in love with a man known to be bad, and as victim of the father's sexual brutality—and the fact it was transmitted as forbidden knowledge, which carried special weight in Rachel's family, likely prompted Rachel to once again defensively cast herself as having been abandoned.

Rachel's loneliness resulted from her having disrupted familial injunctions, implicit and explicit, not to reveal the family's terrible secrets. Extruded from the family not by the incest, brutality, and hidden secrets in themselves, for these were what knitted the family together, but, rather, by breaking the family rule, which held it was only wrong to tell, not to perform, these acts, Rachel tried in various ways to ward off the loneliness that was the central distressing affect she experienced. Her masturbation, for example, was not only a source of excitement, shame, and guilt, triggering ever more heightened demands for self-punishment, from tying her nightgown sleeves together to viciously biting her arm. It was also a source of solace for her loneliness. In addition, her dream of taking poison (session 121), of dying and of being happily in heaven with the dead mother, may be seen as a wish for reunion and restoration, just as her gathering the materials with which to kill herself, and mulling over whether or not to proceed, may be seen as a conflicted enactment of the same wish and, at the same time, a form of self-punishment. "Poison" may be seen as a powerful metaphor for the nature of the family's connections, capturing the quality of relationship where connection and caring are so intertwined with toxins that they cannot be partitioned out. By this line of interpretation, taking poison would restore, in a symbolic sense, Rachel's sense of connection to her family. Her masochistic biting, which appears at the end of this segment, similarly dramatizes the familial mode of connection. If incest can be seen as representing a consumption of one's resources, rather than a renewal and augmentation, by going outside the family, procreating, and extending the clan, then biting oneself is not only a vicious attack, reflecting the viciousness in family relationship, but also a symbolic means of consuming rather than expanding oneself.

In the midst of losing her own family, Rachel once again envisioned a new family for herself in which Emerson and Mrs. Frost as well as hospital staff and patients figured. The Psychopathic Hospital—with its many prominent psychiatrists, its staff of solicitous nurses, and its constantly changing patient population—offered her a suggestively rich cast of characters around which she reenacted many conflicts and issues of the old family. The psychiatrists, in general, acted the father's part. She knew they were critical of her and of the treatment Emerson was administering. She was a liar,[20] all she needed was to show a little spunk,[21] she was really insane,[22] her problem was not too much but too little sex (Notes, following session 141): the physicians' diagnoses in these instances were indistinguishable from the father's. Similarly, the father's contention that the treatment consisted in "hypnotism" (session 180) was congruent with the psychiatrists' suspicions of everything associated with psychoanalysis. Her dream of the psychiatrist Herman Adler waking her from her sleep so that she could watch him amputate a leg, following which he pulled snakes and bugs from the stump, which she found sickening, suggests that she cast him and his colleagues in the same sadistic mold as she did the father (session 159). In her dream life, she had her revenge, just as in actuality she had lashed out at the father in a series of retributive acts. Armed with a hypodermic, she dreamed of "making all the doctors do as she wanted them to. . . . injecting them with a fluid" (session 177). Although she could envision replacing her father with Emerson (sessions 126, 164), her dream of being at his home, where she was betrayed by his daughter, suggests that she was not entirely sure he would be able to provide her with a good enough family (session 135).

If the father in Rachel's family romance was a skeptical sadist, the mother—in the person of Mrs. Frost, the nurses, and the other women patients—was infinitely kind and intuitively understanding. She was able to tell Mrs. Frost, who acted as a surrogate mother, of almost everything that had happened to her (session 142). Where the real mother had been oblivious to Rachel's suffering, Mrs. Frost was attentive and concerned, summoning physicians to care for Rachel and contacting Emerson regarding her care. While hospitalized, Rachel was ministered to by a series of sympathetic nurses who also played the part of the good mother. One, for example, assured her that "if any girl had fallen she could start anew and everything would be all right" (session 165), countering the real mother's indifference to Rachel's conflicts over sexual morality with the possibility of redemption. In their reports to Emerson, the hospital nurses portrayed Rachel as a good patient, as, on one occasion, "bright and cheerful in the ward and in every way improved" (session 165) and on another as crying, but quietly, "so as not to disturb other patients" (session 170). In so doing they were allying themselves with Rachel against the ever-critical doctors, offering her protection from the father's disdain in a way the real mother could not.

Rachel cast the Psychopathic Hospital that was her home for two months in a familial mold, imaging it as a realm of illicit couplings that were at once secret and known to all. Sexual knowledge and fantasy circulated constantly among patients in the close atmosphere of the hospital ward; indeed, Emerson later observed that the hospitalized hysteric was prone to enter into "undesirable intimacies."[23] In the Psychopathic Hospital, Rachel unraveled the mystery surrounding the tickling of hands and stepping on feet that the boarder had engaged in around her mother, learning from a fellow patient that they signified a desire for coitus (session 176). Patients, she learned, dreamed of having sex with the doctors (session 167), and they traded in stories in which nurses, following doctors' orders, had sex with male patients (session 184). Fantasy and reality, conscious and unconscious thoughts flowed together in this sexually stimulating atmosphere, such that when Rachel caught a glimpse of the dream-doctor who was the object of her confidant's desire, she thought of her brother—and, likely, her own desire for him—and felt sick to her stomach. Likewise, the fantastic psychiatrist's prescribing of sex may have resonated for Rachel with Dr. Smith's judgment that she was suffering from a lack of sexual intercourse (Emerson's Notes, following session 141). So real to Rachel were her forbidden desires for a baby, which found expression in her repeated dreams of pregnancy, that she slipped when talking to a wardmate, saying that she too had been sick while pregnant. Rachel was puzzled as to why she'd said this. "Told this proved the content of her unconscious," Emerson noted (session 177). Refusing, in one session, to continue with the analysis, Rachel explained that in the hospital she felt as if "everyone was looking at her and knew" (session 174), her conflict expressing the tension between the secret world of analysis and the transparency—unacknowledged, but similar to that which prevailed in her family—that ruled on the ward. In admonishing Emerson "that if every thing should [be] made pleasant for her at *home* it certainly should be at the *Hospital too*," the father had unwittingly captured something of the ways in which the two spaces might have been imagined as similar (Letter, following session 69).

Toward the end of this segment of the treatment, once Rachel had imagined she had revealed all there was to reveal, a powerful struggle around sex, desire, and pregnancy ensued. She dreamed of being faced with a choice between two roads, one irregular and the other straight and narrow. She chose the second, but "bye and bye it got very narrow and she *jumped* it and met her mother and together they went off somewhere" (session 156). This dream of being bad was soon followed by one that she struggled to remember in which she was a "pure girl" (session 170). Repeated dreams of being pregnant followed, interspersed with several dreams of ascending to heaven to join the mother and at least one of being with Jack. It came out that Jack had taunted her, prior to the second time he'd forced himself on her, that she was already pregnant. What was she going to do about that, he asked (session 176). Her response was to wish and hope she were pregnant (session 177). Thoughts of Jack and babies, and of wanting him sexually, crowded her mind, but she thought it wrong, she told Emerson, "to *want* such things because father and mother did so wrong, she and brother had too much of such desires and it was wrong to have it." Later in the same session, she told him, "It does seem like a wish, and a dream, what Jack said, pregnancy, and a baby, all mixed up, and I can't connect it up." The acknowledgment and articulation of this conflicted wish was a mixed blessing for Rachel. She became aware that part of her present conflict over Jack, who by her account treated her rather sadistically, was due to her forbidden wish for a baby. At the same time, this clarifying realization was balanced by the self-reproaches it occasioned.[24]

PSYCHOANALYSIS ON TRIAL

On 15 April 1913, Emerson presented Rachel to the Psychopathic Hospital staff in an unusually long and contentious staff meeting.[25] Fourteen psychiatrists, two social workers, and several others were in attendance, all of them skeptics on the question of the efficacy of psychoanalysis, which, along with Emerson, was on trial in this forum. E. E. Southard, director of the hospital, had already warned Emerson that he was far too aggressive in staff meetings, and that the medical and social service staff of the hospital were "hardly used to the expressions of frankness which prevail in certain psychoanalysts."[26] A month later, Southard warned Emerson he should "abstain from all claims of medical insight into any case whatever." Southard's manifest claim that he was willing to give "Freudian analysis, dream analysis, and kindred methods and theories as wide a scope as possible in the Psychopathic Hospital" was undercut by the persistent hostility he directed at Emerson and his practice.[27]

Yet, although Emerson, his methods, and his expertise were criticized and roundly derided, he was allowed to continue with what all agreed was a highly experimental, even disgusting, treatment. The patient's biting and convulsions were of concern to the hospital staff, who perhaps realized that the "intercourse" that Dr. Smith said she needed and the "discipline" that Dr. Stearns prescribed (session 178) were of little use in treating the hysteric's array of symptoms. The psychiatrists were curious about psychoanalysis, and allowed Emerson to explain the course of the treatment in precise, almost day-to-day, detail, far more so than in any other case conference held in the hospital in its early years. Rachel, when questioned, defended Emerson and his treatment of her, assenting to the proposition that he had helped her and made things clear to her in a way that no one else ever had. Southard suggested at the end of the questioning that "it is somewhat comforting to feel that you are not naughty but that you are a case." He continued, asking, "Isn't it somewhat comforting to feel that it is a disease you are getting over rather than an immoral difficulty?" Rachel could only look down and bite her lip, perhaps feeling herself caught between the two possibilities Southard suggested.

There is no record of Emerson and the patient discussing the conference and the tough questioning to which she was subjected (in the midst of the proceedings, Dr. Herman Adler had acidly observed, "I suppose it takes psychoanalysis to find out whether she has eaten anything"). However, a dream reported two days later contained allusions to the argument among the physicians over which ward she should be on (the numbers 3 and 5) and suggested she experienced considerable anxiety about the conference and its implications, including multiple deaths and an element of appearing naked and adrift on a raft (session 178).

Despite Rachel's continuing wish to die and her only limited improvement, she was discharged on 2 May 1913. As Emerson told his colleagues at the staff meeting, "Of course I haven't the slightest idea as to how this thing is going to turn out in the long run. . . . I am in hopes that coming to consciousness she will be able to stand the strain, and perhaps if she gets a chance to work or gets something to do that her going home will open her future."

Chapter 6 Text: Sessions 81–188: 19 November 1912– 1 May 1913

LETTER: RACHEL TO EMERSON

Winchester, Massachusetts
14 November 1912

Dear Dr. Emerson,

You will be surprised to hear from me.

I am back here to Winchester for a few days as I haven't been feeling extra well or rather I have been having a time with my eating. I came here yesterday morning for a few days' rest. The doctor at the school[1] said it was nerves and tired out but I don't feel tired just the same.

I was talking with Miss Burleigh tonight over the telephone and she was bound I would come in to see you and that you could straighten things out so to please her I promised to write to you and you would let me know when you could see me although it seems to me so wrong to bother you. This telephone number is Winch. 2— and I hope it won't hinder you too much.

Sincerely Yours,
Rachel C.

SESSION 81: TUESDAY, 19 NOVEMBER 1912

Regurgitating.[2]
Transferred from baby hospital[3]—Girls talking made her sick. etc.
Chemistry.
Face return as last year.
To come in here—To see me.

SESSION 82: WEDNESDAY, 20 NOVEMBER 1912

Dreamed she had a skeleton apart and was trying to put it together. It seemed as if it were somebody she knew. Part of the time it seemed to be mother. It seemed as if she had to put it together in a hurry. Her one object was to get this together and she couldn't.
Feels as if she couldn't sit still a minute; like walking all the time, but if sits down to sew, can't do it.
Has a good many dreams, here another. It seems as if her mother was in her mind all the time. Everything that suggests a mother makes her think of her mother, "and yet I'm thinking of other things too."
It seems as if she thought of when she first began to think, and her whole life flashes through her mind at once.
Of course when I think of how mother might have helped my trouble, etc.
No matter what dream she has she always thinks of her mother when she wakes up.
Her mother is constantly coming back to her but she is constantly *putting her out of her mind.*
(Combating mother and desire for children)

SESSION 83: THURSDAY, 21 NOVEMBER 1912

Dreamed she was buried alive, was trying to get out.
Dreamed she was in a woods on a road and got down and put her ear to the ground, as though she expected to hear something. As though she expected a carriage. (This is what she first thought of on waking.)
Lying on back—dreamed 3 times—before could wake enough to turn over—funny feeling. "I seem to be thinking of something but I cannot tell what it is."
Often feels she has the thought but can't hold it and then has the suffocating feeling.

Feels as though she would like to go and hide herself—as though she were ashamed of herself.[4]

Father has entirely changed. It seems as though he changed some way to get around her.

He is lovable, etc. "Whenever I'm with him now he arouses all my ill feelings and I have no reason for it now."

All this (choking etc.) started November 4; had just got a letter from her father. He spoke of going with her Aunt (going to Worcester). He's talking of marrying Aunt Nettie's daughter (illegitimate born when Aunt Nettie was 15) She is about 47—a little younger than mother.[5]

"It seems like something I'm trying to think of like a name I've forgotten."

"It seems like something forgotten, or something I've put out of my mind and I'm bound not to think of."

"I say I try to think of it, and I don't try to and I do try to, I simply can't put my mind where I want to put it."

"I keep thinking all the time; and what I'm thinking, I don't know; but I know I'm thinking."[6]

SESSION 84: FRIDAY, 22 NOVEMBER 1912

"It seems as if I know yet I can't see it."

"It is as if the idea were in my stomach."

"My mind keeps going back to that Monday when I sat down."

"It seems right there ready to speak or tell and yet it doesn't come."

"Jack"—"Brother"—"Friend"—"Father"

SESSION 85: SATURDAY, 23 NOVEMBER 1912

Dreamed she was hunting for her apron. Out of her uniform (she was back at school) pocket, a big one in front, came snakes, food, and other things she cannot remember. She tried to empty pocket, but they kept coming. Awoke trying. Pocket symbolizes vagina and snakes penis?[7]

Monday morning, the day of attack, she saw some babies in alcohol.

SESSION 86: MONDAY, 25 NOVEMBER 1912

Dreamed she saw a lot of pansies and roses standing in big stalks. In among the stalks things seemed to be crawling about. As she thinks of it now, it seems as if they were snakes. The pansies seemed to be baby faces, and the roses were the faces of almost everyone she had ever known.

SESSION 87: TUESDAY, 26 NOVEMBER 1912

10–1 = 3 hours

Dreamed she heard a noise down stairs. She went down to investigate and found her friend Fay sitting in a chair. As she looked at her she heard 3 shots fired at her, she was terrified and told her friend to look out. But she seemed not to be afraid.

Dream and patient—bisexuality—pistol and penis etc.

Analyzed it for her, by Socratic method. Seemed to realize for the first time that she *wanted* sexual intercourse. A long session ended in the suspicion that Jack had had intercourse with her.

Every time she thought of sexual intercourse her hands would clutch up. There seems no doubt as to some sort of memory tending to return and so troubling her. Looking for it seems like assisting in childbirth. Resistances are enormous.

SESSION 88: WEDNESDAY, 27 NOVEMBER 1912

11–3:30.

Dreamed the house was on fire. The fire was somewhere in back hard to find. The two old ladies were gotten out, but one went back to get the cat. She was struggling to save the old woman and awoke.

Dreamed she was trying to make a word from the alphabet. Couldn't remember what the word was. (At first we thought it was "Jack"—later, in trying to face "it" she remembered it was "Babe")

Dreamed about Christian Science, etc. (In the afternoon, a woman had been trying to get her to have Christian Science treatment).

Followed her thought till it seemed certain Jack had had intercourse with her.

There was *amnesia* for from about 2 to 4:30 the afternoon he was last with her. *This was just a week or so before Thanksgiving. Terrible resistance* to looking when she was on the lounge, etc., where put by Jack. She is certain Jack is in it. After about 3 her mind went more or less blank and nothing more could be done. Resistance: "I won't look—there is no God, or he wouldn't let it happen—I don't know it and I won't know it." etc.[8]

SESSION 89: FRIDAY, 29 NOVEMBER 1912

11:30 A.M.

Lying down with eyes closed. Mind keeps going to lounge—"lying down ( ) getting up."[9]

"Was just thinking of "*it*" and something came over me that made me sick to my stomach." ("it" = lying on lounge) Keeps saying "no"

2 P.M.

Jack did.

But it comes as an unrelated fact. There is no connection, in memory, between this fact and anything else. The "dark space" is (or was) in *front* of the image of herself standing i.e. she saw herself lying on the lounge, then there was this "dark space," then she saw herself standing. This amnesia was of the fact that Jack cohabited with her.

SESSION 90: SATURDAY, 30 NOVEMBER 1912

10:30–2:30

Can't connect "it." No better.

Thinks Jack died the following July 4th. Dream = with brother, looking out of window—horse went up on sidewalk—Reached over hedge and ate hydrangea bush—Tipped carriage and turned and looked at it. "Well it's broke and he broke it."

When she thinks of the "lounge," (L) she thinks of the "darkness," (D) "the *fact* that Jack did it," (J) and "standing up" (S), i.e. four separate facts L D J S but when she looks at the "darkness" she can't see L, J and S.[10]

"If I could just see through that black space I'd know everything."

1:40 P.M. Jack got her on the couch a second time and it was then he had intercourse with her.[11]

He must have left her, for when she came to, she was alone, had an awful headache, and felt very dizzy. She didn't know even then what had happened. Her girlfriends came in to supper. *At supper she was nauseated at the sight of food and couldn't eat any.* They had potatoes and Jack wanted her to mash them but she wouldn't.

Jack wanted her to cheat at cards but she wouldn't and he got mad. She had done it before, for fun, but for some reason or other couldn't that night. They were eating candy all day.

Thinks they may have been eating it just before coitus. Girls said she looked sick and asked what the matter was.

She cannot remember what happened between the first and second times when Jack pulled her down on the sofa. Nor can she remember how he did it. She remembers she never dared to go with Jack again but she couldn't give him up. Without knowing why, she decided that night to give him up for good and all.[12]

SESSION 91: MONDAY, 2 DECEMBER 1912

Attacks continue.

Remembers: Jack's coming about 11—asking if mother was there—trying to kiss her—brother came—money to him—eating dinner, helping, pulling down on couch, etc., getting away first time———(blank except she "knows" what he did)———"come to consciousness and found myself on the lounge and -feeling awfully dazed—got off the couch not knowing where I was and feeling that way when I first came to." "It seems a faint memory that I got up and sat in a chair. The next real thing I remember was letting the folks in." "It seems as if I were sick at my stomach when I got up, but it isn't real pain." The couch was in the dining room right by the china closet [Figure 3]. "I had to pass by it to get to the china closet."

Had lunch that noon.

It seems as if she didn't try to remember what had happened on the couch. Remembers exactly when she came to and how she felt, but nothing *back of* that. Remembers his making several unsuccessful attempts to get her again after first time. After she got everything put away in china cabinet she went and sat down in same chair by window she sat in afterwards, and he got up and sat in other chair. Here her memory *stops sharp,* and she remembers nothing *after* that. She is lying with eyes closed trying to think. Put her hand to her head. What is it? "I thought of that Monday night at the school and something flashed across my mind but I don't know what it was." Couldn't sleep last night.

Fainted last night and Saturday night—about 2 A.M.

SESSION 92: TUESDAY, 3 DECEMBER 1912

Sleepless so long took 2 morphine pills and slept till 7:45!!! Scolded her. Lying down with eyes closed. Mind in room in Waltham.[13] "Oh, I know.

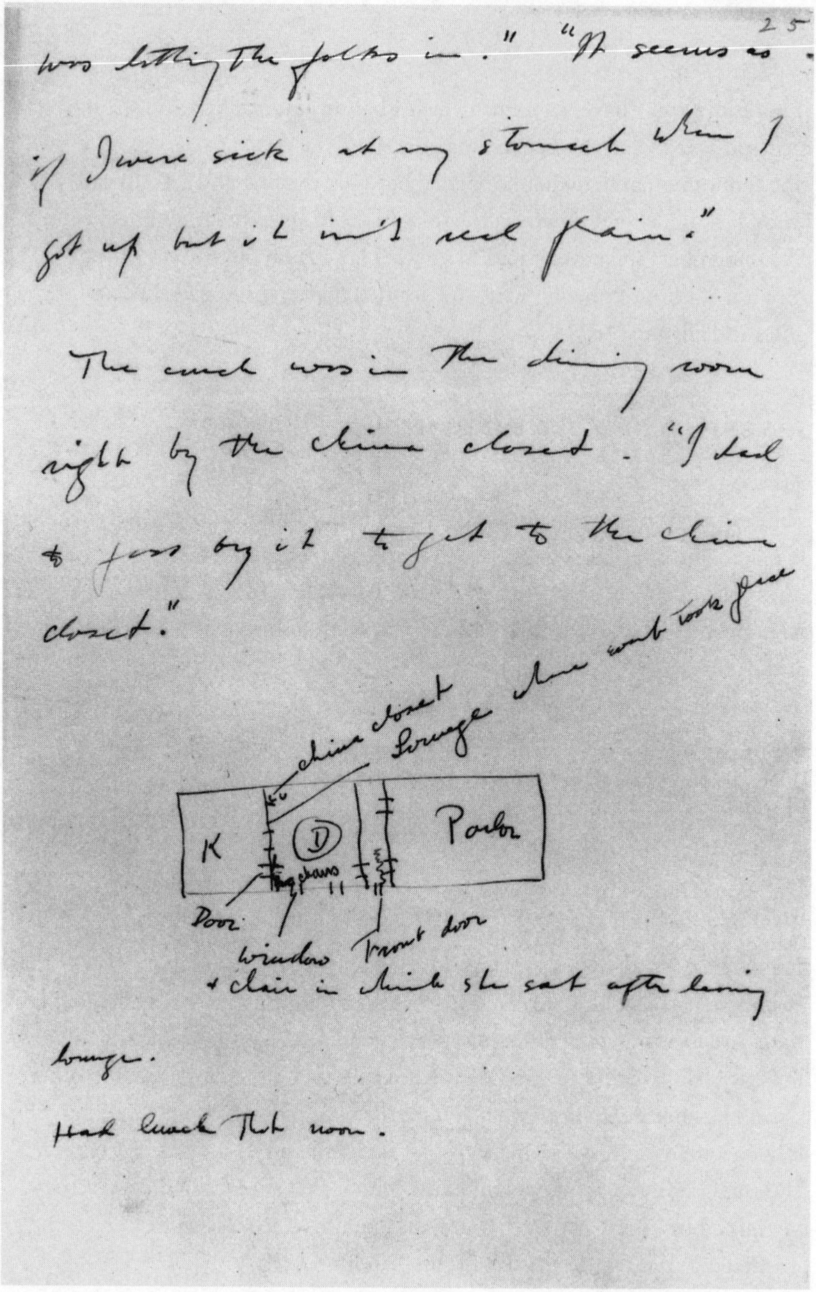

was letting the folks in." "It seems as
if I were sick at my stomach when I
got up but it isn't real plain."

The couch was in the dining room
right by the china closet. "I had
to pass by it to get to the china
closet."

china closet
Lounge where event took place

K   Ⓓ   Parlor

Door
window   front door
+ chair in which she sat after leaving
lounge.

Had lunch that noon.

Figure 3. Diagram of the interior of Rachel's house, "where the event [with Jack] took place," drawn by Emerson, 2 December 1912 (session 91). Captions, from upper left, read "china closet"; "Lounge where event took place"; "Front door"; "Window and chair in which she sat after leaving lounge"; "Door." Reproduced, with permission, from the Boston Medical Library in the Francis A. Countway Library of Medicine.

There were sash curtains that went way down to the floor. Down behind them was a box of candy of Miss Walcott's. I reached down and took a piece and that made me sick." "I hardly knew what I was doing." (Her conscious mind was occupied with dislike for chemistry.) It was a rocking chair in Waltham room; also in Winchester room.

Had to go out to see Mr. H., Miss Stevens' fiancé 3/4 hour.[14] When I came back she was sitting up. She had remembered *being* on the couch the second time. She kept trying to rise, but was dizzy and lay down again. Jack was standing over her and sitting by her, *asking* for something, she knew what, but didn't remember words. He was not using physical force, but she couldn't seem to escape. (Throat much quieter. Lies quieter.)

Had to go out to see Dr. Smith about Virginia F.[15]—1/2 hour. When I came back—still lying down. Had remembered how she got to the couch.

She was eating candy. Felt queer, not faint or dizzy exactly. Jack helped her to the couch, laughing at her for getting sick over eating candy. She wanted him to get her some water, but he wouldn't. Here her memory ends.

Jack brought the candy. (Drugged?)[16]

SESSION 93: WEDNESDAY, 4 DECEMBER 1912

When she reached home yesterday she remembered how she got to the lounge. She had been eating bon-bons and stuffed dates (tasted queer but kept on, seemed to want more [1/2 lb. box loosely filled]). Jack refused, said they were for her, and ate chocolates (2 pound box). Helped her to lounge—Refused to get her water—Wanted her to eat more. Held a bottle to her nose, which he said could help her. She felt worse, tried to push it away but felt powerless. *Then,* and *not till then,* the thought came to her, she wished she had obeyed her parents, she knew what he wanted. It seemed as if something dark came in her eyes. Did not sleep.

Cannot hold anything down yet. Is coming back Saturday.

SESSION 94: THURSDAY, 5 DECEMBER 1912

Slept an hour last night.

Vomited all afternoon.

During night, off and on, kept hearing someone call "Rae." Went out into hall several times to see. There is something in her mind that when she thinks of it is associated with a choking smothering feeling in throat. That is its *only* association. "I'm not trying to think yet my mind will stay right on some-thing."

She is lying with eyes closed reproducing superficial thoughts.

"I'm thinking of different things yet I know I'm thinking of that."

The thing she's thinking of seems to be the actual deed. When she thinks of Jack holding the bottle before her nose, "I then start to think what came next." She feels sick at her stomach. The thought flashed by her a number of times but she couldn't get it.

Dr. Lee will take her in the West Medical Service—Admitted at front door.[17]

SESSION 95: FRIDAY, 6 DECEMBER 1912

Remembered last night about 2 A.M.

Lost consciousness after Jack held the bottle to her nose; then came to enough to know he had her dress up, and then was having intercourse with her—she seemed powerless to move or escape. Then she lost consciousness again; when she regained her consciousness, she was alone, etc.

She also remembered that Jack said, when he had her in the lounge, "You didn't like the candy, did you, but I had to gain my point."

When she remembered, last night, the thing she was after, she felt as though she had lost all power in her arms and legs. She was perfectly conscious, but powerless. Soon, however, she pulled herself together. But even now (11 A.M.) she feels that if she should let go she would lose control as she did before.

She ate her breakfast this morning and kept it. She *was* nauseated, and it came up in her mouth, but she swallowed it again and held it down. It was quite different from the involuntary action of the stomach previously.

She thinks now she had forgotten again what we learned last winter, just after she applied as nurse.

SESSION 96: SATURDAY, 7 DECEMBER 1912

Forgot everything yesterday from 2 to 5. After she had her supper she went to the toilet, where she vomited. For a moment she didn't know why she was vomiting. She thought if she vomited they wouldn't let her go home so she set to, to think, and soon it all came back. Then she was frightened lest she forget again and thus couldn't go back to school. There was nobody in the toilet at the time and she didn't tell anybody, for fear they'd keep her. She was more than anxious to ask them to let her go today. She was afraid the Misses Frost wouldn't let her go back to school Monday if she didn't get back home today. She kept thinking of it off and on all night, though she did sleep well, and she thought of it again this morning. She ate her breakfast all right (cereal, toast, and coffee) and wasn't even nauseated. Her trembling also has much subsided. Dr. Rogers[18] gave me some *Ammo-nitrate*—Rachel thinks it the same stuff used by Jack. (Airey)[19] She is not absolutely positive however.

She realizes now, as never before, the necessity of being able to remember these events. She says she *knows* she will never forget them again. She said "I will not." This time it is no more "I will try."

Having had a taste of school, she is *very* anxious to keep on. Discharged this afternoon.[20]

LETTER: RACHEL TO EMERSON

Waltham, Massachusetts
10 December 1912

Dear Dr. Emerson,

I hardly know what to write to you.

They put me on very easy work but for all that it is all I can do to do it. I try to eat just as hard as I can but I have to force myself all the time and then I can't more than half the time keep it down not that I have forgotten anything but it simply makes me sick.

I wish now I had followed Miss Buttinger's[21] advice to stay away until the first of January when our real lectures begin then I would have got more of a hold of myself.

I have just written to Miss Burleigh and told her I was going to ask you some time when you have time if you would tell her every thing because I can't help but feel that she will feel different towards me. Maybe I am wrong but as I feel that way myself I can't think others' feelings would be any different. Besides I would feel much better if she knew and I have not the courage to tell her. Will you please do this?

If it wasn't for what others have done for me I should just drop this for unless in January when our real lectures begin my mind isn't different than it is now I will never be able to put my mind to them and succeed.

I know I shouldn't write such a discouraging letter to you but I couldn't do otherwise and be truthful about it.

Sincerely yours,
Rachel C.

SESSION 97: MONDAY, DECEMBER 16, 1912

Kept supper pretty well.

Breakfast vomited without nausea. Stringing popcorn last night and saying which kind of candy she would make—*stuffed dates and chocolate drops.* Walnut creams—*bon-bons.* Did not think of Jack. Had a dream just as she went to bed: "Just as if somebody had their hand over my mouth, but whether it was Jack's I don't know." Slept no more.

Every time she laid down after that she had a suffocating feeling, and had to get up. Head feels tight.

Dreamed more this week of a lot of hacks, like a funeral procession.

Another time it was like collecting a lot of flowers. It seemed as if I wanted to go some place and I had to cut my way through the flowers, but I couldn't make any progress.

Thought of other dream of flowers and how I interpreted it.

"It seems as if my mind never thinks of anything except what I want it to think of."

Feels numb, especially when she gets up in morning.

Lost her voice Thursday. (Called me up that night.) Couldn't speak about 10 A.M. till late in the afternoon when it came back gradually. Couldn't speak at all, even whisper. (Dreams about hacks and flowers same night. Friday night.)[22]

"I never thought of it before till you mentioned it." (Did Jack do anything more?) Ate breakfast, dinner, and supper all right a week ago Saturday. Ate Sunday breakfast, all right but Sunday dinner took with father and brother. And threw it off. It felt more like being sick at her stomach.

Went to bed at 7:30, slept till about 10 Sunday morning.

SESSION 98: TUESDAY, DECEMBER 17, 1912

Everything goes unless she consciously holds it.[23] When she relaxes it goes right out of her mind. Then it comes back as a terrible shock. Everything goes black: She feels faint, dizzy; all power leaves her, and she has to fight for strength. Then she thinks of what causes it, and Jack is remembered followed by the others (Jack seems the worst). Sometimes the memory comes back like a blow and she feels faint, etc. Fainted at school last week twice. Once had been vomiting badly. The other time had eaten ice-cream, was fighting off nausea, went up 2 flights, fainted at top.

Loss of voice was Wednesday, not Thursday.

Female blood: Urine test shows signs of starvation products.

When she tries to think of "more" thinks of Jack. Was with him at friend's house alone about 1 hour. She left them to see if they wouldn't wake up.

SESSION 99: WEDNESDAY, DECEMBER 18, 1912

Acetone and diacetic acid in urine showing starvation products. Lost 20 pounds since November 4.[24]

Kept her supper down all night by the most tremendous effort.

This kept her awake all night. Vomited at 7.

"I will not look at anything more."[25] Ate 4 times before she could keep supper down.

"I'd rather not eat than go through what I did last night."

"It seems as if there were something I was trying awfully hard to look at and all I see is what he did." (i.e. Jack's assault.) This much she knows: whatever it is it is connected with Jack. Jack and the friend's house keep coming. (Is lying with eyes closed.)

Keeps thinking how hard it was to send him off.

"My mind seems fixed on something. When you say a word my mind goes to that, so I can think of anything. I want to but all the time it is 'fixed' on something else and won't go anywhere." Last night sat by the house, thinking, but when she came to, would be unable to say what she had been thinking of: "Dreaming like." Feels now as if one part of her mind were dreaming about something but doesn't know what it is.

— blank— "you" etc.

Blank "Father" etc.

Blank "Father" and Mother dying

Blank *and* school

Jack and mind held—mother etc. T.—Blank—his wife—blank talking about eating. . . . Miss Frost—a kind of blank—as if I were going to say something and it went out of my mind—blank—Jack—last night—blank—Oh I don't know the blanks as often—blank and trying to think what it was—stops trying to think—starts—"Just as if I half-way thought of something." Home and Misses Frost—blank—Father—Brother—Christmas—blank—"I didn't want to look at anything more." "I was going to make myself [illegible word], so I wouldn't have to."—brother—blank—walk I took yesterday—

Ella R. (girl at whose house she saw Jack)—long blank—Jack and friend's house—Henry's house and first convulsion—Thought of "something": has no connection with anything.

What now? "Oh, I don't know. It seemed as if I had something but I couldn't get it."

With some of the "blanks," however, there goes a strong feeling that Jack and intercourse are some way intimately related to it.

Patient doesn't want to return tomorrow but will.

6:30 P.M. Telephone from Miss Frost: Patient lost voice.

SESSION 100: THURSDAY, 19 DECEMBER 1912

Lost her voice at 2 P.M. just after she vomited.[26]

Vomits, not nauseated, just the same, when she eats.

When, in her friend's house, Jack asked her what he had done that she was so cold, she said, nothing, only her friend didn't want her to go with him.

(Hence Jack would think she didn't mind.)

(Lying down with eyes closed.)

Either: She *wished* it; *or* he *did* it.

She is almost absolutely voiceless; I can just barely hear her.

She feels she might be able to "think" that Jack did it again, but she wouldn't be able to "speak" it. ("I might etc.")

Intellectually you do think it, don't you? "I don't know what else it could be, but I don't want to speak it."

Ella R. is studying to be a nurse. She is the girl at whose house she and Jack met.

Left 15 minutes. When I come back will talk. (11:55–12:10)

"Voice seemed to clear up." Blank at first then mind went to Jack and girl—"I know it looks that way" and then she started. What was it? What did you see? I asked.[27] Thought just gone again—saw just the cloud.

What do you see now? Whispers, "Just the same thing." Jack and the room? "Yes." What do you see now? "I think of the room now and it goes into a black space" i.e. her mind. Her mind stays in the "black space."

SESSION 101: FRIDAY, 20 DECEMBER 1912

Has her voice, but is wobbly on her legs. Ate her lunch, vomited, and got her voice about 2:30. Was lying down, thinking, in a sort of dream-like state, Miss Frost came in, startled her and she felt as though she had lost the use of all her body. Didn't dare to lie down again last night but it happened. Ate her supper, all right, also breakfast.

Persuaded her after a while to lie down on the couch.

Did not ask her to shut her eyes. After considerable effort the feeling and thought came to her of "upstairs in Ella's house."

"Open your mind."

"Take it upstairs."

"Look!" Then her mind closed. Above effort kept up 1 hour.

"I can think of upstairs but I can't picture it."

After the hour's effort she found it harder to "put her mind upstairs," and it "shut up" quicker. (Fatigue.) Explained that this was her first effort at voluntary attention and voluntary thinking.

SESSION 102: SATURDAY, 21 DECEMBER 1912

Went home and ate a little. Vomited then tired and slept 2 hours. Dreamed of doctors here, especially Dr. Waterman. Thought she wished there was some way in which I wouldn't have to tell them.

Tried to think of it last night, but couldn't.[28]

Today knows it was a "memory" yesterday, today it is only a "thought."

Looking now (is lying with eyes open) sees a "blank" but mind does not "close."

"I think of the 'blank'; then my mind goes to the room; then I think of what he did." But your mind doesn't close? "No."

"My mind seems awfully tight, yet I know I'm thinking of something underneath."

"How real the upstairs seemed yesterday." "I know that something happened there, but today it doesn't seem real at all."

Thinking of Ella's house and suddenly everything went blank.

"Just a feeling when I tried to look at it" (upstairs)— Did your mind close? "No."

"Feeling"—"blank"—"closing"—are different ways mind acts when thinking of "upstairs."

"I try to think of upstairs and a feeling goes all over me—something like those dizzy spells, numb." Also a trembling all over goes with this.

"You know perfectly well what is coming, don't you?" "Yes." You can bear it can't you? "I've got to that's all."

"I hesitate for a moment and then something has gone."

"I just thought I would look and just as soon as I did it closed."

"It doesn't seem as if I could make myself look at it."

"I saw upstairs like I did yesterday but then it closed."

"I think of down at her house and then I think of what he did." (Breaking up of continuity into elements, etc.) "I think of Ella's house; of what he did (in her own house) and going home."

"Something 'held' my mind, but I don't know what it was."

SESSION 103: MONDAY, 23 DECEMBER 1912

Saturday thought, just as she went to sleep, she wished she could forget it all. Dream: She was home, looking out of the window. A funeral procession came along. She thought of the old saying that a person lived as many years as there were hacks. There were three. She wished she didn't have to live so long. Then they stopped at her house and the man in the hearse got out and they took her and put her in. Then they buried her. She woke trying to call out. She went to sleep again, however, and slept till 10.

All day yesterday she was in a sort of dream. She had forgotten everything again. She even forgot an engagement she had with some girl friends to go to a concert in the afternoon. Her friend called her up afterwards.

Last night, about 7, Miss Frost asked her what time she was coming in on this morning. For a moment she was very much surprised because she had forgotten that she was to come in. Then she knew she had to come in, but didn't know why. After a while it came back to her that she had forgotten about Mr. T. and the woods, etc., but the whole thing didn't come, except momentarily, till this morning, when she remembered what Jack had done to her, and held it. Then she was provoked at forgetting.

"I was upstairs and just about to see something when my mind snapped shut."

"I thought of how I was trying to look at it and something kept pulling my mind away."

"I thought of upstairs again and it seemed as if I could see him plainer."

Saw father Saturday. He said in another year she would be crazy.

Thinks she didn't eat anything all day yesterday. Knows she spent most of the day in her room, reading.

Five bedrooms in Ella's house: father, mother, Ella, and a cousin. Separate rooms, one guest room.

Guess—When we went upstairs we usually went into Ella's—she had it fitted up as a sitting room (bed, couch, etc.) We often have been up there. We spent more time there than in any other room, usually.

It would have been perfectly natural to go up.

"I don't feel as I did Saturday but there is something that won't look."

After great effort:

"I can seem to see him sitting in that room, but I don't know whether it is just because I think of him and connect it up."

"I thought of up there; then I thought of downstairs and of him as awfully mad, and then she came in and I thought of something more but I couldn't put it together."

"I think of upstairs after that but I can't tell why we went up there or anything."

"I thought of downstairs again and his being awfully provoked and I can think of his saying something but I don't know."

"I think of upstairs and my mind snaps and I think of downstairs again."

"My mind seems to stay right there upstairs trying to connect it up."

Hadn't I better write to Ella?

"No. If you do I won't come in."

"I just thought it must be so, but I couldn't have it so."

"It seems so much worse than when I was a child and T. did it."

"I didn't *see* it."

"If I could forget it from afterwards I might be able to see it."

"I just think of him and of upstairs, and my mind just closes on it."

Well you know he did it now!

"I know he must have or I wouldn't feel this way."

"It is all I can do not to put it down in my limbs. When I go to look at it it is all I can do not to push it down in my body."

Almost lost the use of her legs but finally went home. To return Thursday.

Telephone message—Threatens to take morphine. Half in mind half in legs.

SESSION 104: THURSDAY, 26 DECEMBER 1912

Dreamed she was at a party. Girl friend—Glass case like an umbrella stand only as high as girl—Brother put her in case—Trick to get out herself—Entertainment. Woke helping her.

Thinks Ella out.

Legs went: admitted by Dr. Lee.[29]

LETTER: RACHEL TO EMERSON

Massachusetts General Hospital
Tuesday Morning [31 December 1912]

Dear Dr. Emerson:

Dr. Clymer[30] told me yesterday that you probably wouldn't be in to the hospital for a number of days so as I will I think be home before you come back.

This morning I can manage walking a great deal better. I have thought of most everything I think. If I can only keep them in my mind and connect every thing up but I don't care if I can only walk I would rather have it go anywhere except to my limbs.

I am going to write down what I know then when I forget it maybe that will help me to remember it. I have been sleeping very good and eating well. The only trouble is when my limbs get better I have trouble with my stomach but I have got so much and I will get the rest or walk any way.

I hope you will be well soon.

Dr. Smith said this morning he thought Dr. Lee would discharge me just as soon as I could walk well enough to go home so when he comes this morning I am going to ask him, as if I can get home I can do just as well as here.

When I left the school this last time Miss Buttinger said or asked me to have you call up Miss De Veber when I was able to come back and tell her so. I should have told you this before but I forgot it.

Perhaps I can go out tomorrow and if so or whenever I do I will telephone you.

If I could I would write every thing out to you but some how I can't get things straightened out.

I received a lovely letter from Miss Burleigh this morning.

Hoping you will soon be well and back to the hospital again. I am

Sincerely Yours
Rachel C.

SESSION 105: THURSDAY, 2 JANUARY 1913

(I haven't seen her for a week on account of ulcerated tooth)
Legs about the same.[31]
Remembers that Jack wanted her to let him have intercourse with her again (in Ella's room) and threatened her if she refused, i.e. said he would tell her father and brother and friends. She said he had forced her before but he wouldn't again. He said he would deny it and nobody would believe her.

She remembers she thought she would have to let him do it just before—I'll fill his threat and tell.

She remembers lying in the lounge with her head on her arm. She remembers his standing over her and then sitting by her and taking her by the arm and trying to get her to lie back and let him.

Remembers Ella was out of house. Does not remember the deed. When she tries to think "what came next" her mind "snaps shut." It is all she can do to hold what she now knows, before her mind. If she lets go for a moment it all tends to slip out. Then she feels worse in her legs.

SESSION 106: FRIDAY, 3 JANUARY 1913

Remembers when Ella came back.[32] Remembers getting up from couch awfully angry.

Cannot remember actual deed. Mind snaps shut as usual. Remembers how frightened she was and how she felt when Jack threatened her.

SESSION 107: TUESDAY, 7 JANUARY 1913

As she sat she gave a start and then said everything went blank for a moment, as though she were blind for an instant.

I have her lie down. She is trembling. Her eyes are closed. Every once in a while she gives a start and says it seems as if something flashed in her mind but she doesn't know what it is. She cannot remember Jack did anything more.

"My mind stood still and I felt tight all over as if something were holding me."

"It seems as if there was something I wanted to get and I can't."

"I thought of different things that had happened then my mind went blank and I thought of other things."

"My mind just seems to be going over Ella's house, then home, and back and forth all the time."

A sudden start ("it just shakes me") "I was thinking of coming downstairs. It seems as if it were in my body. I didn't think of it at all." (She is trembling all over.)

Lying very quietly has *a violent start.* "It seems as if I know—Yet I can't say it—I don't know what it is." Trembles, etc. Shakes violently for a long time.

Starts: "It seems as if my mind closes the minute I think of it—whatever it is."

"I thought of woods, I don't know why."

"What woods?"
"Near my house."
"Did you think of Jack?"
"No."

SESSION 108: WEDNESDAY, 8 JANUARY 1913

Dreamed she was trying to hide, sometimes herself, sometimes a 3-year-old boy whom she was taking care of. His stockings kept coming off and she had to put them on. Got a policeman to help her across the street.
Sometimes streets were wet and dirty.
Has thought she stood in relation of wife to Jack.
Vomited breakfast. Did not vomit yesterday.
Legs better.

SESSION 109: THURSDAY, 9 JANUARY 1913

Psychic blindness.
Seemed blind in a dream. Woke up, blind for a few seconds.
Blind this morning about 2 minutes. This about a week and a half or so.[33]
Dreamed she was upstairs and workmen tore away stairs. She couldn't get down. Someone put her in a rocking chair and threw her out the window, when she landed she woke. She didn't tell of this because she thought it would pass off perhaps.
"I think of different things that might have happened."
"That he did it again;
"That I wished he would;
"That he told mother and father.
"I think of that time how I hated him and in a way I didn't."
"I just thought of someone pulling a pillow out from under my head and making me lie flat. I seem to remember it as a dream last night."
It seems as if I just dwell down at Ella's house. I think of other things but it goes right back there."
Blind 11:03–11:11 "It just came back as though it cleared"
"What was it you were thinking about?"
"I don't know."
"I don't *feel* afraid."

Blind 11:30—"It seemed as if I tried to see something and it's just gone."
11:33[34]

SESSION 110: FRIDAY, 10 JANUARY 1913

Vomited a little after breakfast. Slept not. Legs about same. No blindness after interview.
Blind 11:42. "It's as if something were right over my eyes."
"I think it maybe." "What?" "That Jack did do something up in Ella's house."
Lies quietly, no trembling.
Headaches. There is no other feeling.
Sees some 12:15.[35]
January 11—Saw her for a moment in ward. Practically blind all afternoon—sight went as soon as she returned to ward. Went completely when she went to bed.

SESSION 111: MONDAY, 13 JANUARY 1913

Went to the ward to see her a few times. No change. Has not been blind.
Vomited a little. Legs not well.
Dreamed she was upstairs and couldn't get down. Lots of mice and rats about.
Told Dr. Smith about her psychic blindness.

SESSION 112: TUESDAY, 14 JANUARY 1913

Took a long while to get a bad dream out of her.
Dreamed she was naked. Somebody carried her into a room full of naked men. Her mother was there, in charge. The men talked and acted obscenely. They had intercourse with her. While one was having it the others would look on and laugh. The men came and went. Her mother let them in and talked with them. She would not help her to get away. She seemed to be there a long time: weeks or more. The men fingered her also. It was as real as reality. When she first woke she knew who the men were, but later forgot. Still repressing something.
Letter from father maligning brother—Brother came to see her.
Girl in ward tells of living in a house of ill-fame.

Her mother always said, when such a subject came up, that if she ever fell, she would go in the whole way.

She has thought how easy it would be for her to be bad.

SESSION 113: WEDNESDAY, 15 JANUARY 1913

Dreamed she was at the Frosts. They were sewing and had supper. But the food seemed mysteriously to disappear just as they were about to eat it. Then she went for a long walk and came upon an empty house. She went in. While there I came. She wouldn't let me in. I tried to look in (?) or get in (?) the windows. I seemed to make a mark on each window.

No change.

Blind yesterday noon about 15 minutes. Again in the ward.

Übertragung perhaps responsible for psychic blindness.[36]

SESSION 114: THURSDAY, 16 JANUARY 1913

Woke up crying twice, but couldn't tell what about. The nurse said she called out several times, "Why did you do it?" and also called her brother's name. Following this lead I learned that her brother had been accustomed to coming to her bed and getting in with her up till his mother's death.[37] Her mother made no objections. He would wake her by throwing pillows at her and then they would wrestle. Sometimes he would throw her and sometimes she him. Then he would get in bed with her and they would sleep together. They would get very excited. One morning a girl friend came before they woke up. Her brother said let me get out of this. When the friend came in she asked her who was in her room. She said *she* never would let her brother come in her room. She denied that they were undressed, said they both wore pajamas.[38] This story was preceded by the account of a dream. She was with a woman whom she did not know. It seems as if I came and asked something. She answered falsely. Then the man said "I will have to take you to Dr. Emerson tomorrow." At that they both were surprised, because they thought the man talking was Dr. Emerson. She felt she wouldn't go to be told she was a coward and a fool.

SESSION 115: FRIDAY, 17 JANUARY 1913

Eyes blind 11:37. I had just said, "Perhaps you did it in your sleep, perhaps he did it in his sleep."

Still blind at 12.

The nurse said she called out, and talked and mumbled in her sleep. She said, "I shan't tell"; she called out her brother's name and also spoke of her mother. Said she had rather kill herself than know, though she didn't suppose she could. Rather be sick.

Dreamed she was in an open pasture. There was no fence but she seemed to be held in by some invisible fence. It seemed impossible for her to get out. Dreamed she was climbing a mountain with someone whom at first she thought was her father. Later she didn't know who it was. When they got to the top, there seemed to be a high wall preventing any further progress, turning she found it was impossible to go back. She seemed to be caught.

She thinks the significance of the dreams is that at last she is caught.

SESSION 116: SATURDAY, 18 JANUARY 1913

Regained her vision about 3 P.M.[39] Vomited a little this morning. Legs about the same.

Dreamed she was at Miss Frost's. Her brother and Mr. A.[40] were in the summer house. She had a book she wished Mr. A. to read, so she went out. Her brother said he wouldn't but he did and was reading aloud to them. A postman came up the hill with a letter. He wouldn't come way up so her brother went after it. He wouldn't go all the way and the postman wouldn't come any nearer. Her brother then went nearer and seemed to try to get it but was in danger of falling over the hill. She woke calling out "Look out!"

After another dream she woke feeling she would rather be burned at once than be tortured slowly. The nurse said she called out, "I won't, I can't, and you can't make me."[41] She also called out her brother's name.

As was the case with Jack, so when she looked to see if her brother had done anything wrong to her, her mind closed, or snapped shut.

At other times something seemed to flash across her eyes but what it was she couldn't see.

NURSE'S NOTES

Rachel C. Talk in her sleep.
"No, no, no, no" (turned over)
"Say something"—mumbled
"Oh! dear I wouldn't stay there, not—"

"Oh yes, I am going to."

"Everett, won't you say something, can't you tell me about it? No, no, no, I shan't."

"You get her to tell me. I can't help it, Mama—"

"Can't you get it before it goes? You could if you tried."

———

All of a sudden sat bolt upright in bed, awakening other patients, crying out loudly. (10:30 P.M.)

———

"No, now, don't you see it? I have it! I got it! Leave me alone! Don't touch me! I won't! I won't!" (I attempted to awaken her, as she disturbed other patients. Took about 5 minutes, for when I spoke she answered in her dream. I finally got her to turn over and wake up. (Did not talk at all from 11:30–1:00).

"No, I won't. I won't. Leave me alone."

"Oh dear. What are those things?"

"Oh dear, dear, dear." (Did not talk at all from 2–3:30.)

"No, no, no, no."

"Oh, let me tell it please—Oh my head, oh my head."

"Everett stop! Please do."

"Why it would take me all night to figure that out—"

"I know it's so, and I won't say so."

"Mama you know it too. No, I won't, and I shan't do different."

"Oh dear, dear, dear."

"Well then in the morning, but I can't now, it makes me sick."

NURSE'S NOTES

Rachel C.

Saturday evening was the quietest she has had for some time. Did not talk out loud at all during the night. Slept well. Mumbled a little at times.

Sunday night report enclosed. A typical restless night. The conversation noted could be heard distinctly across the ward. She talked a great deal more, but mumbled her words. Could have jotted down more, had I not been busy with other patients—

Elizabeth I. Hansen

Night Nurse—Ward 16

SESSION 117: MONDAY, 20 JANUARY 1913

Vomited some, but with normal nausea. (Catamenial.).[42] No dreams that she can remember. Says she never will remember it, if it is her brother.
"What do you think about it?"
"I can't think: It is too big."

SESSION 118: TUESDAY, 21 JANUARY 1913

Forgot all about brother, etc. by the time she was back at dinner.
Vomited badly.
Another patient had convulsions: Rachel had violent convulsive shaking all afternoon.
Didn't eat any supper and only remembers about brother and what it was all about when she went to bed at night.
Almost got it, today, but not quite. Heard yesterday that the wife of the S. S. Supt.[43] was dead. Dreamed that the S. S. Supt. was dead and she and Everett were at the funeral. She saw his wife laughing, under her veil, and at first felt critical of them though she shouldn't because that was the way she had done herself. At another time dreamed of shoes. At yet another of a glass house.

NURSE'S NOTES

Rachel C.
Monday night. January 21[44]—Very quiet night. Mumbled some in her sleep off and on, but did not talk out loud at all. Slept soundly about 10 hours.
Tuesday night. January 22. Fell asleep about 9 o'clock. Talked a little off and on until 11.
"No, no, no, I will never go there again. I will stay right home always."
"Oh! Mama, please don't make me."
"I don't want to go there. I won't. I won't."
Did not talk out loud at all from 11–2. Then talked a good deal about going home, and staying there. (Was busy and unable to write down the exact words.)
About 2:45 sat up straight in bed, eyes wide open, body rigid. I went to her and asked her what she wanted. She had her eyes open, but was asleep, and did not answer me.

Tried to arouse her. Thought at first it was a nightmare—but she began to shake and tremble, and appeared to be in a sort of convulsion. Fought and tossed about in bed, did not grit her teeth, said she was going to get right up and go home. Clenched her hands, and arms became rigid, but whole body shaking as with a severe chill. Unable to arouse her at end of 10 minutes and reported to night superintendent, who saw about her 15 minutes later. Knew her name and was conscious then. "Spasm" lasted about 20 minutes but continued to shake for about an hour. Hot water bags, temp 105°. Given at axillae and abdomen. Said she did not feel cold at all. Fell asleep about 3 and has slept as quietly as a baby since then.

Elizabeth I. Hansen
Night Nurse—Ward 16

SESSION 119: WEDNESDAY, 22 JANUARY 1913

"Everything is as clear as can be."
"Look through that thin surface of deceit and see the truth. What do you see?"
"I suppose he did, but I can't see."
Thought of when she could wake and find him gone, and then when she would go first.
"It seems as if the tightness of my head was going away."
"It seemed as if I were tight all over and as if this tightness of my body went to my head, and it was on tight, and then passed off."
"It doesn't seem as if I were afraid to look now, but I don't see anything."
Got a letter from brother yesterday telling about his throat. (ulcer)
"I think of upstairs and my mind just closes."
"When I think of it my head goes tight and then it strikes my stomach."
"It seems as if it is that." (stomach convulsive)
"I can't get it and it just seems as if my head would burst."
"I'm thinking that must be it but I can't place it."
"Trying to place it and make myself know it well."
"Something happened, but I don't know when."
"I know he did but I don't know anything else about it."

NURSE'S NOTES

Did not talk at all until after 2 o'clock.
"No, I haven't."

"Oh, no, I won't. Oh, no."

"Now, stop that, don't do it again."

"Mama I won't, I won't."

"Everett, Everett."

"Oh dear, my head, my head." Mm—

"Don't, please. Now I'll go to Mama, oh, my head, my head" O——h!

"Ain't it horrid, I hate—"

"Oh I don't know, I can't read it, it's all mixed up."

"Well, I'm going home, I don't care, I just told a lie. I can't answer. I wish you would leave me alone, my head aches—"

"You know I hate you and why don't you go, you have always plagued me and I hate you. You have never been like a father. I have his brother, and I can't give him up."

"I can't, I can't."

"Oh, dear. Yes, I'll get up in a minute."

"Yes, I'll get up. I'll get up." (Sat up in bed and reached for her clothes. Hit her arm on the chair which awoke her, and she laid down again.) I said nothing but stood by bed and watched her.

A few minutes later.

"Is he gone? Is he gone?" I told her he was. Then "Now I am going to get up." She awoke and began to shiver some, complained of headache, soon fell asleep and slept well for the rest of the night.

Elizabeth I. Hansen
Night Nurse, Ward 16
22–23 January 1913

SESSION 120: THURSDAY, 23 JANUARY 1913

Dreamed that all sorts of things were coming out of the air shafts in the chimney, furniture, everything for keeping house, people, and finally immense quantities of writing paper, which she felt she must write on.

When she left me yesterday her head felt clear. She kept the awful thoughts in her mind. She ate her dinner all right and did not vomit. But about 4 her head got all tight again and memory seemed to go. She tried to eat her supper but vomited it all up, as well as her breakfast.

Lying down with eyes closed.

"I don't know it to place it. It seems as if I knew it and yet I don't."

Head aches badly and it hurts to keep her eyes closed.

"I just try to see what I did yesterday, for a second."

"I don't know what is the matter. I put my mind to it but I can't seem to think of it."

"When" "Oh, I don't know, when I think of that I just see him, that's all."

"Was it in the morning or at night?"

"I don't know anything about it."

"Oh I can't do it. I can't make my mind go there." "It seems as if I couldn't look at it because I don't want to."[45]

SESSION 121: FRIDAY, 24 JANUARY 1913

Saw her brother yesterday and hinted around, but by his replies felt reassured again. Scolded her for trying to hide behind brother.

Lies down with eyes closed.

Dreamed she was home. Took poison—died and was with mother.

Happy.

"I know well enough it happened." (aet. 16)

Image of mother and brother interfered.

Feels that with loss of brother she is alone as mother is dead.

Ate her dinner and did not vomit. Could not eat supper or breakfast. Awake most of the night. Has been running a temperature.[46]

SESSION 122: SATURDAY, 25 JANUARY 1913

Temperature 102. Pulse 120. Kept in bed. Vomited a little after dinner, badly after supper, more after breakfast.

Dreamed a great deal: Everett being in all, and mother.

Forgot it during sleep but knew there was something to remember this morning, and got most of it back. Remembers no further details.

SESSION 123: MONDAY, 27 JANUARY 1913

Temperature 101, pulse down. In ward. Has forgotten nothing. Brother incident perhaps—a little plainer.

Nothing new.

Legs not quite so reliable.

Did not vomit breakfast.

PATIENT'S DREAMS

It seemed as if I was in a very little room sitting down to a desk adding up figures. There were five men standing around me—just as soon as I would finish I
would pass the paper to them and it seems every time as if four of them would
say it was all right but when it would come to the fifth he would always find
something that was wrong about it and I would have to keep doing it over until
I got so provoked I burned it up and the minute I did it seemed as if they all
vanished and I was free and happy but yet I started crying and woke up so.
I thought brother was a little boy again and I was teaching him something and
mother was standing over me and forbidding me to talk to him but it seemed
as though he and I just laughed and kept on. Father came in then and carried
me off.
It seemed as if the ward was full of pairs of shoes walking around, they all had
some thing in them but I don't know what, some times they would be on the
beds other times on the floor. Some times it would seem as if I was under
earth there under boards.
It seemed as if I was trying to find my way in the dark through what seemed to
be a hospital. It seemed as if I couldn't find any one but a girl in a private room
and she was crying. I tried to get her to let me take her to the ward. She started
to come when it seemed as if the floor gave way and we both fell and it seemed
as if we never would stop.
Someone was making me cut glass.
I thought Everett came here with a large basket full of things and he began
showing them to me just as he began there was a whole lot of snakes started to
come out of the basket and they went all over the bed it seemed we tried to kill
them but we only got four or five and the rest got away.

SESSION 124: TUESDAY, 28 JANUARY 1913

Temperature 100 yesterday. Pulse 80. Vomited badly last night but not this
morning.

SESSION 125: WEDNESDAY, 29 JANUARY 1913

Temperature 100/pulse 120 (came to OP)[47]
Why is it you don't like music? She gave a sudden start and said, "Oh! I hate
music."

"When I hear it it makes me think of what I've been through."

Jack played a good deal.

Brother sings.

Mother had a great habit, playing began before got up. (She played sacred music most)

She can't stand church music. First noticed it last summer, was walking with a girlfriend and heard a hurdy-gurdy. It made her feel faint and this girl noticed it.

"I just think of brother all the time, it just stays in my head and I can't get rid of it, but I can't put it clear."

It seemed last night when she was just going off to sleep, that she knew it, but when she woke up enough to know it she didn't know it.

What are you thinking of now?

"I thought of that, then I thought of Jack at Ella's house, and I thought I heard music, then I thought of Everett."

What is it on your tongue to tell?

"I know there is a lot more."

"I feel like telling all, but I don't know what."

SESSION 126: THURSDAY, 30 JANUARY 1913

Temperature 101. Pulse 90+

Has not vomited and walks a little better.

Dreamed she was writing and woke up to find herself sitting up in bed, writing, but with wrong end of the pencil.

Dreamed her brother was dead and she had taken him to the woods and buried him.

Dreamed she had a different father and was with father, mother, and brother. After terrible effort got "it" a little clearer.

Her head felt as if it would burst.

SESSION 127: FRIDAY, 31 JANUARY 1913

Has not vomited. Slept well. Legs better. Temperature 101. Pulse 90.

Dreamed the stumbling dream: Seemed to be afraid, and running, up a mountain.

Feels as though her brother were dead.

Feels all alone.

Monday or Tuesday wrote down about Jack and brother. Otherwise can't remember what she is in the hospital for. Every morning takes about an hour to recollect.

SESSION 128: SATURDAY, 1 FEBRUARY 1913

Temperature 101. Pulse 120. Has not vomited.

Dreamed of her brother. Seemed to see pictures of him for every year of his life. Was trying to arrange them properly. Woke.

Dreamed she was at a concert.

Lies down and closes eyes.

Sees her room at one time but *cannot* see her bed at one time: i.e. Trauma. Sees room, brother, and herself at all other times and sees bed. Mind went from room at home to Ella's.

SESSION 129: MONDAY, 3 FEBRUARY 1913

In bed. Last night temperature 103–102, pulse 100(?).

Forgot it all yesterday 2–4:30 or so.

PATIENT'S DREAMS

It seemed as if I was up among the stars. There were a lot of people on one and it seemed as if they were all trying to leave that star and jump on others. Some would succeed and others would fall.

I started out to go to high school with a girl that used to live next house to ours. I had a small bag with me and I was afraid I would lose it all the time. I went to call for her and it seemed she wouldn't believe it was time to go but still kept on with her home lessons which she was doing. At last we started but I knew we would be late so I wouldn't hurry. Just as we were leaving her house it seemed we met brother just then I missed my bag and I went back in the house to find it but couldn't and as I came out again I found brother sitting on the steps with it. He said I asked him to hold it for me. I was provoked because it seemed as if he was trying to take it from me.

SESSION 130: TUESDAY, 4 FEBRUARY 1913

Temperature 100. Last night 103—102—101—Pulse 120—Vomited last evening.
Dreamed but can't remember. Ate good breakfast, no vomiting.
Slept till about 8. took till 9:30 to know. 1. Wondered why 2. To think of something 3. Gradually brother comes to mind. 4. Finally knows, in a way, as much as has already been gained.[48]
Lies down. "I can see this room but I can't picture the bed."
"I saw it all."
Saw herself lying on her back in bed with her brother on her.
Cries.
Says she hears music; sometimes so clearly she asks others if they hear it. It is a ringing, or humming, in her ears.[49]
When the bad idea struck her she winced as one at a dentist's does when his nerve is touched.

SESSION 131: WEDNESDAY, 5 FEBRUARY 1913

In bed. Temperature and pulse.
Dr. Smith instead of Dr. Lee ruled out nearly everything but isn't sure.
Has forgotten nothing. Vomited last night and this morning.
Dreamed she was burying something.[50] I was there and made her dig it up.
Dreamed it wasn't so.[51] Dreamed she was walking with brother at different ages.
Hears music faintly.

SESSION 132: THURSDAY, 6 FEBRUARY 1913

Temperature dropped 103–101, pulse 100. Vomited badly last night and this morning.
Dream—
Talked in sleep.
Still hears music occasionally.
The dream she had night before last was: she had been burying a lot of things in a deep hole. Just as she was about to bury the last I came along and asked her what she was doing. She couldn't tell and I found it. Woke up.

PATIENT'S DREAMS

It seemed as if I was with mother in a very old house. All at once it seemed that the house became glass—just as it did mother threw something over my head. I woke up trying to get it off my head.

Ella's room, his talking

PATIENT'S NOTE

Everett I told just as little as I could. I won't tell any more. My head will burst if I don't. I am going home. Make it clear: Stop playing.

(Thought she heard music.)[52]

Pieced together by what nurses and patients told her.

SESSION 133: FRIDAY, 7 FEBRUARY 1913

Temperature 103. Pulse 100. Still vomits.

Doesn't dare to let the memory of the last go, as when she does her legs feel worse. Has got nothing new. When she tries everything goes blank.

PATIENT'S DREAMS

I was trying to write a letter to my mother but it seemed every thing that I wrote was wrong so I had to keep doing it over. I woke up trying to write and crying.

It seemed as if I thought I was at a fire and my face was burning just as if it seemed I couldn't stand it any longer some one threw water on my face.

It seemed as if I was back to the Baby Hospital and had a number of children to wash and dress when I went to get the water it seemed to me to be full of dirt and bugs. I told the head nurse and she went to look but said it was all right and told me to use it. I wouldn't and tried to explain it to her. She said it would do the children good.[53]

SESSION 134: SATURDAY, 8 FEBRUARY 1913

Temperature 103.2. Pulse 100.

Has vomited a little.

Seems more amenable to reason.

Says her mother must have thought of sex matters because she used to speak of girls and their brothers doing such things (when she spoke of T.).

Still hears music occasionally. Gets it clearer but no more details.

SESSION 135: MONDAY, 10 FEBRUARY 1913

Woke yesterday morning feeling much relieved. Temperature 99+ about noon. Something seemed to come to her mind and when they took temperature it was 102–3. (See dreams.)[54]

This morning when she woke her head felt clear and did not ache. She felt there was more to see but she was no longer afraid to look, though she didn't like to. Temperature 97 or so. (see chart) (also see dream)

No trouble with eyes.

Feels weak. (Dr. Smith says due to fever)

Some surgeon shown about by Dr. S said he could imagine a fever due to the brain work of a president of the United States. Told Dr. S[mith] she didn't expect him to understand it but that was no reason for his being sarcastic. Since then he has been more civil.

PATIENT'S DREAMS

It seemed as if I was at your home and that you had a number of grown children. I went there with your daughter. After supper she was going some place with me. I went outside to wait until she got ready. I waited a long time and pretty soon her brother came out and I asked him where she was and he said she had gone over to a girl friend's. I was provoked and started for home. It seemed as if I only had my kimona and shoes on. I was pretty near home when I saw a lot of fire teams coming up the street. I then took my shoes off and went up beside a building. They stopped in front of me trying to find out where the fire was. They found it was in the building near me then everyone rushed in just then an old man came up to me with a little dog in his arms and asked me to exchange dogs with him as he thought the shoes I held was a dog. I woke up trying to get out of the heat of the fire.

It seemed as if I was sick in bed and Everett was trying to amuse me by dressing up in different clothes. It seemed he would come in the room dancing and mother would play for him. I would cry and then laugh. It seemed as if I didn't want him there but hated to tell him so.

Saturday, 8 February

I had a number of children and it seemed to me I was doing a lot of sewing and dressing them all up just as I had finished some man came and undressed them and put them in the bathtub saying they were too dirty.

I thought you ordered me off some place where I would be all alone. It seemed as if I knew why I was going and I thought I would not be afraid to know the rest of every thing.

Sunday night, 9 February

SESSION 136: TUESDAY, 11 FEBRUARY 1913

Temperature 99+. Up in night 102°.

Peaceful in morning but rebellious as day wears on.

Did not vomit yesterday or this morning. No nausea.

PATIENT'S DREAMS

It seemed as if I was in two persons first I would go with one and then the other but yet all the time I knew what each one was doing.

It seemed as if I was being pulled up a hill by a rope I was near the top when I became afraid and was going back just as I thought of it the bottom of the hill gave way and I either had to go on or drop.

Some thing about music, a church, father and mother.

SESSION 137: WEDNESDAY, 12 FEBRUARY 1913

In bed. Temperature 100.

Vomited last night but not this morning. Was reading but made no attempt to find out what set her off. Feels more peaceful in morning but as day wears on tightens up.

Is much disturbed by patients dying about.

"I want to go home."

Tears came to her eyes.

PATIENT'S DREAMS

It seemed as if some one gave me a magic wand and said I could make any thing or make any body do as I wished. The first thing I started to do was to make a mother but I had to have a model so it seemed as if I took Mrs. Emerson but all the time mother was there with me then it seemed as if I made you take me out of here.

Something about my dying and being buried.

At home with a number of young people. We were all eating.

It seemed as if I was at a trial. A number of different people were put on the stand when it came my turn I wouldn't say any thing. They were deciding what they would do with me when I woke up.

SESSION 138: THURSDAY, 13 FEBRUARY 1913

In bed. Temperature 100.4.

Did not vomit yesterday or this morning. Had 2 or 3 spells where she felt like crying and laughing together. Held in. Woke up last night doing it.

Head feels clear and she feels fearful in morning. She feels there are several more things to remember about brother.

PATIENT'S DREAMS

It seemed as if some one was trying to make me put a white apron on and I wanted a black.

Thought I was back to the school.

It seemed as if a number of my friends were all up to Jack's house there was a weding [sic]. I stood watching it and yet at another time it seemed as if it was Jack and I getting married we started to go off when mother saw us. I was awfully afraid and ran off letting Jack face her alone.

Woke up crying and laughing I don't know what over.

SESSION 139: FRIDAY, 14 FEBRUARY 1913

Temperature 97°.

Last night about 6 P.M. head suddenly cleared up and she dropped off to sleep. Has not vomited.

Feels fearful and resigned.

PATIENT'S DREAMS

It seemed as if every one in the ward was dead except myself. I was trying to find a nurse to help me carry the bodies out but couldn't and started to do it myself.

It seemed as if I was a small child again. I had a book and each day I would put down every thing that happened so I wouldn't forget then it seemed as if I knew I had forgotten and wasn't going to again.

Some thing about a fire at home, Everett and Henry S.

SESSION 140: SATURDAY, 15 FEBRUARY 1913

Temperature 97—

Has not vomited.

Head feels clear.

Took the Saturday morning class over to see her.[55]

Discharged Sunday, 16 February 1913.

PATIENT'S DREAMS

15 February

Thought I was playing and putting my thoughts into music instead of having to speak them. Then some way in the same room it seemed as if I found mother I remembered she had died and I couldn't seem to realize that she was alive. I was very happy but woke up crying.

It seemed as if I was whitewashing a fence but as fast as I would get some done some boys would mark it all up.

It seemed as if my sister was living and I was telling her everything. Everett some way was in the dream as a small boy.

16 February 1913

I was unpacking a number of trunks full of very old silk dresses. I was having great fun ripping them up and making them over.

Sunday night

Out on a ranch riding horseback and saying it didn't seem true I was there as I had always wished to live there. I remembered what had happened but thought as all the people were strangers to me I needn't be afraid they would know about me.

I was a small child again sitting on mother's lap and she was trying to make me say what my name was. I wouldn't tell her so she seemed to think I had forgotten but when she told me and asked me if it wasn't so I cried and said no but I can't tell. In the same dream I was going to be punished for some thing and I woke up trying to think of some excuse. Monday night.

Doing a washing but couldn't seem to get the clothes clean so went and got Everett to help me. Tuesday night.

Thought of mother playing on the organ as she used to. It seemed as if I was sick. Tuesday.

It seemed as if I was in bed and mother called me I tried to get up and go to her but then the bed began to sink as it seemed through the floor. I called to her but she wouldn't come I woke up hearing her laughing. Tuesday night.

There was a social gathering at Fay's house. I came in the room linking arms with Fay and laughing to find mother there when she saw me an awful look came over her face. Instead of going up and kissing her I went to shake hands she refused me but excepted[56] Fay's. Wednesday night.

Some thing about writing names it seemed as if some would turn black and some white as I would write them. Wednesday night.

It seemed as if I had morphine hidden away. I would go and get some once in a while and then I would take it myself. In some way some one found it. It seemed as if a pistol shot woke me up.

Thursday night.

It seemed as if I were in a church all alone reading. I fell asleep, some one woke me up and told me to look who was being married I did but I wouldn't believe it. I went up to the minister I don't know what I said but he refused to marry them then. Friday night.

Sewing up torn clothes. Friday.

Thought I was in the old home again all alone. Then it seemed as if Henry was there. I was cooking and he was helping. His mother came and then it seemed as if every thing went wrong but I don't know what happened.

I was on a vessel. I came up the hatchway it seemed from a lecture with my books just as I got to the top of the stairs I met mother talking with one of the doctors that gives us lectures. I didn't like it. She saw me but wouldn't notice me. Some how later I was at a table on deck and as I thought at first mother came up to me sick. I wasn't going to help her but the more I looked at her I knew it wasn't she but Aunt Gertrude in Beverly. Friday night.

Woke up crying a number of times and knew I was troubled over something but couldn't remember what I was dreaming about. Thought I was a child again and playing with snakes as I used to. I woke up but when I went to sleep again I thought the same snakes were all over my bed. Saturday night.
Thought this house was on fire and there were a lot of babies and dogs here. I was trying to get them out. It seemed as if I cared more about the dogs than the babies. I got afire some way. When I woke up I was downstairs getting a drink. Saturday night.
I was taking a walk with mother and I was telling her some thing. She kept interrupting me so it made it hard for me to tell her when I had finished she wouldn't believe me told me to forget it. It made me provoked. I went off and left her said something about I might have expected it. Saturday night.

SESSION 141: MONDAY, 24 FEBRUARY 1913

Still vomits.[57]
Eyes blind 5—10 minutes yesterday afternoon.
Auditory hallucinations. Music—hears mother call. (Answers and gets up and goes to her, before she realizes it is not so.)
Temperature 103 yesterday, 99 this morning.[58]
Evening: Telephone message from Mrs. Frost. Patient lost voice; "head feels like bursting," had gone to bed.

LETTER: RACHEL TO EMERSON

Winchester, Massachusetts
Tuesday morning
25 February 1913

Dr. Emerson:
Mrs. Frost told me this morning that she called you up last night. I am so sorry but I cannot help her doing it for I know it must bother you as you must be tired of the

case and I know I am. I have told her not to call you again and I hope she won't.
They mean well but are so worried. I try to keep as much as I can from them.
She says you want me to have another doctor. I don't know how you can say that
when you know physically I am all right.
I am feeling better this morning or at least my head is.
I hope you will forgive Mrs. Frost for what she said for I know well enough she
talked pretty hard.
As soon as I get my voice I am going to try to tell them in some way what has hap-
pened. I don't know how I shall but if I don't they will never understand what you
have done or why I will not have another doctor.

Sincerely,
Rachel C.

EMERSON'S NOTES: TUESDAY, 25 FEBRUARY 1913

M.G.H.
"I'll tell you another thing. It may be too gross and all wrong but I believe she
is suffering as much from lack of sexual intercourse as she is from thinking
over what has happened to her."[59]
Dr. Smith (House Physician)

EMERSON'S NOTES: WEDNESDAY, 26 FEBRUARY 1913

7:30 P.M. Mrs. Frost telephoned that Rachel had told her the cause of her trouble. She only wished she had done so long before. She still vomits and has bad
headaches.
8:50 P.M. Second telephone. Rachel has had a fit. Is all the time calling for her
mother.[60]

SESSION 142: THURSDAY, 27 FEBRUARY 1913

Dr. Dennett, [61] of Winchester, called me this morning to tell of his visit to
Rachel last night. Grand hysteria attack.[62] Pulled hair out of her head—Hand
clutching it. Neck drawn back—impossible to hold her in bed. Gave her
ether and hypodermic of morphine.
Saw her this afternoon at Psychopathic Hospital.[63] Face red from crying.
Generally twitchy—feels as she did when she had St. Vitus Dance. She has

forgotten nothing. She has told Mrs. Frost all except about her brother. She wrote it, and asked them not to speak of it to her and they did not.

Gave her something to eat at Psychopathic but she vomited it.

Had a little trouble with her eyes yesterday.

SESSION 143: MONDAY, 3 MARCH 1913

Both legs paralyzed during Friday night. Left hand closed up too, last night, but she opened it. Feels like closing today but she controls it.

Dreamed last 3 nights but cannot remember.

Has not vomited since Saturday. No trouble with eyes or throat.

Has forgotten nothing.

Hears music and hears her mother calling, occasionally, "Rae."

SESSION 144: TUESDAY, 4 MARCH 1913

No change, until, during interview, her brother was announced. It caused her considerable perturbation. When she started to see him her left hand was clenched and she could not open it.

SESSION 145: WEDNESDAY, 5 MARCH 1913

Paraplegic and left hand still contracted. No vomiting.

Had patient lie down and close eyes. Feels towards brother as towards T.

Dreamed last night that someone kept opening her hand and picking bugs out of it.

During analysis the memory of a dream she had either Thursday or Friday here, came back. After enormous resistance, told it ("Dreams come true"). Dreamed she was fooling with herself. Had a snake in bed with her. *Opened hand.*[64]

SESSION 146: THURSDAY, 6 MARCH 1913

Hand all right. No nausea. Hears music. Mother calling. Tells of playing with snakes as a child. Kept it up till 15. Mother used to punish her till she felt it did no good. Girl friends called her snake-charmer, etc. Used to go to woods, with book which she seldom read much, look for snakes, play with them, sit and dream. Remembers a boy who used to go with her.

Used especially to like to see mother snake open her mouth and swallow her young, when disturbed. Tamed snakes.

Boys killed one mother snake with many of her young, once, and patient saved six. Can't remember whether she put snakes to her face or not, but thinks she did. They used to bite her, and it hurt a little, but not much, and she didn't mind.

Remembers the dream when she had a snake in bed while she was fooling with herself but can't remember whether she used the snake for that purpose or not. Girls used to think it was nasty and loathsome for her to play with snakes.

SESSION 147: FRIDAY, 7 MARCH 1913

Dreamed all night about snakes. Thought they were in bed with her—on her, etc. Black adder chased her (10) and brother (6) 4 miles home—Killed by Arthur 2~3 days later—tore up steps to get at him. Used to wish she were a snake. Crawled under rocks in sort of caves on mountain (After she left school and had nothing to do—about 16.)

Suddenly thought of dream the other night and it seemed true (snake in bed with her). After telling this she could move her feet a *little*.

SESSION 148: MONDAY, 10 MARCH 1913

Paraplegic still.

Feels as if she had it right in her mouth to say but can't speak it.

Still hears music; and her mother calling.

Whenever she hears music always immediately thinks of that morning with her brother.

SESSION 149: TUESDAY, 11 MARCH 1913

Father here this afternoon.

Father used to hold her—pinch her, tickle her, fool with her breasts, etc. Talk badly, etc.

Vomited this noon.

Thought she moved her legs this morning when she first woke up.

SESSION 150: WEDNESDAY, 12 MARCH 1913

Vomited yesterday and this noon.

Condition unchanged.

Nothing new elicited.

SESSION 151: THURSDAY, 13 MARCH 1913

Moves her legs a little.
Vomiting increased.
Told her yesterday she had better look out, etc.
Still hears music and mother.

SESSION 152: FRIDAY, 14 MARCH 1913

On Ward III.[65]
Convulsion last night about 6—6 nurses and 2 doctors to hold her. Beat her
head upon the floor, tore her hair out by the roots, frothed at the mouth.
Fought off doctors and nurses. Had been dreaming.[66] All of a sudden everything was clear. She knew all that she was trying to recall. It made her feel
faint, she couldn't seem to bear it, "something snapped" in her "brain" and she
knew no more. The only thing she could remember of what she saw, was, that
it was true that she had "played" with herself, as the dream suggested. The
snake seemed symbolical.
Head is relieved, but still hears music and mother.
Can stand and walk, but wobbly. Has not eaten.

SESSION 153: SATURDAY, 15 MARCH 1913

Back on 5.[67] Slept well. Walks a little. Ate supper and break. Vomited dinner.
Saw an image of a man whom she went often to see and who always affected
her badly; told her mother, but didn't know why seeing this man made her
sick before dinner.
Still hears music and mother but it isn't so bad.[68]

SESSION 154: MONDAY, 17 MARCH 1913

Can walk.
Vomits badly.
Gets nothing new and connects nothing. Remembers what she did get.
Dreamed last night she was with the Frosts. I was there too and told her to tell
me what she was dreaming about. I gave her 5 minutes, but she couldn't re-
member.

SESSION 155: WEDNESDAY, 19 MARCH 1912

Ward III.

Shook last night and nurses were afraid lest she have another convulsion.

She felt as though she had something in her throat to tell; tried to tell Miss Davis,[69] but couldn't.

Remembered, with a shudder, that she did used to have snakes in her room. *Held 'em in her lap;* made 'em coil around chairs; into letters and figures (8); and her arms, etc.

Thought: snake, hypnotism, and of hypnotizing a girl. She and two other girls used to hypnotize a poor girl and make her do foolish things. (Last year at school). Patient got so she could do it herself, after a while. The girl got very much afraid of her.

Hears mother calling less. Music about the same.

SESSION 156: THURSDAY, 20 MARCH 1913

Ward III (in open ward).

Dreamed of a choice of two roads: one irregular, another straight and narrow. She chose to go on the straight one but bye and bye it got very narrow and she *jumped* it and met her mother and together they went off somewhere.

When she got very nervous (after St. Vitus Dance) mother used to play to her to quiet her.

Thought of music and then thought of man who used to trouble her. Had to tell her mother and then she would play then to calm her. Remembers first seeing this man *after* "woods."

Thought again of playing with snakes in her lap.

Been vomiting badly.

Hears mother calling more today and music less.

SESSION 157: FRIDAY, 21 MARCH 1913

Ward V. Walking all right.

Lying down with eyes closed. Piano going in assembly room. Patient suddenly starts up and says—"I know where I saw that man. He was the other man in the woods. I know about the music too. Mother was playing that morning." (i.e. when brother fooled with her.) She then sat up and lowered her head in her hands. I said, "What are you thinking of now?" She gave a sudden start

and said, "I thought I was at home, in my room, I had a snake in my hand."
In the next instant, she gave another start and when I asked her what the matter was she said her stomach had just "turned over," just after she thought of the snake. Last time played with snakes a year ago last summer. Vomiting began same summer.

SESSION 158: SATURDAY, 22 MARCH 1913

Head feels better. Doesn't hear music now, but thinks of it, and then of brother. Hears mother calling occasionally. Vomited badly in the night when she woke from the dream of dying.

Dreamed she was going somewhere with her brother. Suddenly she had a baby in her arms. Thus burdened she couldn't get along so well and her brother kept getting ahead of her. Then he would come back to help and though he said the baby was as much his as hers, she wouldn't let him have it. People kept speaking to her as she went along, but she doesn't know what they said. Her uncle then appeared on the scene and gave her a box of candy. He asked her to guess how much it cost and she woke trying to guess.

She woke, later, saying "I haven't lied." Then she remembered a dream in which it seemed she had lied, and she knew it, and knew why.

I had the patient lie down and close her eyes.

She has thought a good many times that if she could get out of it by lying she would lie. She said if she could only make it not so by saying it wasn't so she would.[70]

As for her brother (dream) she thought it might mean that because she had been with her brother she had a baby.

She was afraid to look lest it turn out to be what she thought it was (i.e. masturbation). But she did finally get it. She saw herself, she said, all the times she had masturbated.

SESSION 159: MONDAY, 24 MARCH 1913

Still vomits.

No longer hears music.

Heard mother call her once today.

Dreamed Saturday night she was burying a snake, but it kept coming up. She tried to kill it but couldn't. Seemed to remember the saying that a snake couldn't be killed till sun-down. This was in morning and it seemed she couldn't stand it to have it alive all day. Woke up, sick and trembling, as snake stuck its head up.

Dreamed last night that she was asleep and Dr. Adler[71] came and woke her up. Told her to get up and see him amputate a man's leg. She did so and he cut off the leg just above the knee. Out of the stump he pulled out a lot of snakes, bugs, and insects. It was sickening.

Seeking explanation, patient acknowledges she thought the dream of having a snake in bed with her must be that she had masturbated herself with the *tail* of a snake. Cannot remember it, however. Masturbated mostly with hands but once with a syringe. Did it from 7–8 to 17–18 about.

Patient seems in good condition in every way except for vomiting. Remembers that she was first sick last summer when someone wanted her to go in and see the snakes at Revere Beach. Vomited at night. Saw her brother Saturday. While troubled it was not so bad as before. Patient thought of possible meaning of snake—masturbatory dream either the next day or day after the dream. She has been thinking about it ever since but could not clear it up.

SESSION 160: TUESDAY, 25 MARCH 1913

Still vomits.

Hears mother calling occasionally.

Does not hear music.

Dreamed she was wading in muddy water trying to get through it to clear water beyond.

Dreamed she was taking pins and needles out of her body. They seemed to be in the flesh.

Dreamed she was eating and had to keep taking things out of the food.

Had patient lie down.

After a while she said she remembered having a snake in her room and doing something with it but what she doesn't remember.

Finally she remembered that the dream of playing with herself with a snake was true. She remembered she was about *15*.

Thinking about it all made her feel sick at her stomach but did not vomit.

SESSION 161: WEDNESDAY, 26 MARCH 1913

Cried and wrung her hands yesterday afternoon. Heard music, and her mother calling, dreadfully, *but not since.* When she woke up this morning remembered "the dream" but thought it only a dream. Vomited badly all day.

SESSION 162: THURSDAY, 27 MARCH 1913

Vomits.

No hallucinations.

Dreamed she was building a house with colored cards.

Had patient lie down.

Thought of everything and more—snake turned into brother then thought of Jack, T., men in woods etc. Finally remembered again that it was true about the snake—but next instant it seemed like a dream—so it vibrated quite a time—finally she felt it really was so. Whenever she thought of it as real she was sick at her stomach; when it seemed like a dream it was a relief. "Everything" seemed to come before her.

When she thought of it happening at 15 she also thought of 19 (aet.)

Dreamed she was back at school trying to do something but couldn't.

SESSION 163: FRIDAY, 28 MARCH 1913

Vomited—heard mother this morning. Had a *horrible dream.*

Difficult to get. Finally got her to lie down.

Dream: of *everything* she had been through. With brother 7 or 8 times.

Thought she was vomiting snakes. Mind went from vomiting snakes to intercourse with brother.

Had a pillow-fight with patient just before going to bed.

Had a letter from brother: hopeful she would soon be well and could come home and keep house. "Missed the pillow-fights."

"I feel just like two persons. One thinks it was so (i.e. snake episode) the other thinks it a dream."

Feels she is stubborn and won't look at anything more than she has to.

Thought of snakes and then of brother

SESSION 164: SATURDAY, 29 MARCH 1913

Vomited, but not so badly.[72]

Has heard mother and music a little.

Dreamed she was back at school.

Dreamed she was with brother

Dreamed she was a little girl again and I was her father

Lies down.

Mind goes *from snake to brother*. Finally *remembers* she used snake. (Was in bed aet. 15.) *Thought* of other times with brother and was afraid to remember lest it turn out they had copulated more than once.

SESSION 165: MONDAY, 31 MARCH 1913

Nurse said that while she still vomited it was steady growing less for the last few days. She is bright and cheerful in the ward and in every way improved. Patient said she hadn't slept much. Felt better, especially this morning, till about *ten* when something flashed across her mind and made her vomit violently, and this morning vomited as badly as ever.

Had her lie down—After a while *started*. "It was that thought." *Started violently* and *sat up*.

"It was Everett, Father, and everything."

Father put his fingers in her when she was about 7 after that Everett "right along."[73]

Last night the nurse told her if any girl had fallen she could start anew and everything would be all right. "That was why I felt so much better this morning," said the patient.

When the patient had told me about her father she said "I can't help resenting it, you would." Has had no hallucinations today—but last night heard her mother once and heard music. (not during the day)

Did not dream last night only slept an hour, she said. Saturday night dreamed she was back at school trying to do something, or catch up, but couldn't.

SESSION 166: TUESDAY, 1 APRIL 1913

Vomited a little at supper but not much; not at all today and ate breakfast and dinner.

Slept well. Dreamed she was hunting for a knife to cut off her hands with. Woke up biting her hands.

No hallucinations.

Lies down: further details brings out the fact that her father followed her to her room, a year ago last summer, and making expressive movements, *of-*

fered her some money if she would let him do what he wanted to. She was terribly frightened and drove him out, and put a chair in front of her door. When her brother returned she told him father hadn't been acting right and asked him to get her a key, which he did. *That night she had the first return of the convulsions before she began to come to see me.* This scene was preceded by several in which she had begged her father not to go on with women, as he had been doing, and as he had done before her mother died. He always joked, however, and told her he earned his money and would do as he pleased, till she upbraided him about his actions before her mother died when he got mad. She is very angry towards her father and cannot forgive him. She is absolutely certain everything is true that she has remembered. Only she remembered she had played with herself and had had relations with her brother much more than she had at first remembered. It seemed her brother as about 9 and she 13 when they began. She doesn't think they did anything wrong after her mother's death. But it was pretty frequent before.[74]

She still feels somewhat nauseated when talking about all these things, but not badly. She said her head felt much clearer, light even, as if it were far away, or she was. She has no headache.

She says she has decided to stop being stubborn, since yesterday, for now she has nothing further to be stubborn about.

SESSION 167: WEDNESDAY, 2 APRIL 1913

Sleepless.

Vomited at noon: This morning a patient told her a sexual dream she had had about one of the doctors here. It made no particular impression at the time and was forgotten. At noon, this doctor came into the dining room. He reminded her of the dream. That made her think of her brother and of "everything" and turned her stomach. She felt she must hold in before the doctors. She had finally to leave the table.

Last night she remembered what her mother had confessed to her about herself and about her father about 2 months before she went to the Adams Nervine. It made her feel terribly. It had something to do about her mother's early sexual misdeeds and she made her promise not to tell. She said she would return to haunt her if she even told. Her mother was a spiritualist and went to mediums, etc.[75] Patient feels almost as if she believed as her mother did. She really is afraid lest her mother return. (Origin of a delusion?) Her father hurt her mother in some sexual misdeed.

Patient feels now she has lost everybody, *including mother*, and it seems more than she can bear, especially as it is all sexual. Heard her mother calling her in the night, but has not today, and has not heard music.

Her mother told her she couldn't keep these things to herself any longer. (She never *listened* to anything from her daughter however.)

SESSION 168: THURSDAY, 3 APRIL 1913

Heard mother last night some, but not today and no music. Slept 2 hours with hypnotic after that sleepless.[76] Dreamed one of the patients was running; she was running after her; I was chasing her, or both, with a long pole with a ruler on the end of it. I said if I didn't catch her I would be punished in some way. But I didn't catch her.

Patient spent the rest of the night trying to make up her mind whether she would tell what her mother told her, or not. She feels she could not tell without the next instant regretting it and afraid lest her mother really return to haunt her. *I did not break her resistance.*

When her mother told her it stunned her. She went off for a long walk and didn't come back till bedtime. Ate no supper. Just as she left the room her mother said "You won't tell?" and she answered, "I never broke a promise yet." Nothing was even said about all this afterwards.

Mother told this about 2 months before death: Just a little while before patient went to Adams Nervine.

   Query! Was this after Dr. Putnam and Miss Burleigh tried to tell Mrs. C. about sex? (January 4 1910).[77]

After mother told her she was cross. Mother said she was changed.

Mother's confessions recalled things to patient but after a while they were crowded out of mind again.

Has feared inheritance. With brother.

PATIENT'S DREAM

4 April 1913

I was going from place to place trying to forget but I couldn't as it seemed as if everyone knew some way. I got discouraged so took my life. Then it was as if I traveled a long ways and went through a lot of trouble I don't know what. At last it seemed I got to the end and asked some one where I was they said it was heaven then I went in search for mother I found her. I asked her if I had done right she said yes. Just then it seemed as if someone separated us and put fire between us and said if I could go by that I could be with her. I wouldn't after that have anything to do with her but turned and went with this person. Thought I was burning holes in my flesh and putting something in them. Playing with snakes as I used to. Mother was scolding me but it didn't seem as if I cared for I answered her back and she got provoked.

5 A.M. Dreamed my promise was taken away from me so that I was free to talk as I wished. I was really happy. I woke up then and decided to talk everything out, then I went to sleep and when I woke up again I couldn't speak.

SESSION 169: FRIDAY, 4 APRIL 1913

Aphonic: since this morning.[78]
(See dreams)
Was thinking yesterday afternoon whether she could forgive her mother or not. Wrote out what her mother had told her and was thinking whether she would give it to me or not.

SESSION 170: MONDAY, 7 APRIL 1913

Voice returned Saturday morning. Dreamed Friday night she and her mother were swimming together in dirty water. (Fresh water in distance) Her mother kept trying to drag her down. Dreamed she was a pure girl. (Had difficulty in remembering it.)

Saturday night dreamed she was buying cloth—same as before—was with mother again, walking. Dreamed she was doing something to her father as punishment.

Dreamed of falling stars. Seemed to be right in amongst them.

Didn't sleep any last night.

Did not hear mother call or music Saturday or Sunday but has today.

Vomited, but not badly, Saturday, and even less Sunday, but today, vomited badly at noon.

Bit her right forefinger yesterday afternoon, after Fay left.

Visual hallucinations of mother yesterday. Thought she saw her standing right in front of her. (6 times about)

Had one today, while lying on the couch, answering my questions.

Last night imagined she was in Heaven with mother, and brother.

Tried to get out of it, but the minute she gave up trying, merged back. No hallucinations of music; where none are mentioned none were had.

Finally has given me the note about mother in sealed envelope.

But would not *tell*.

Bit off part of a needle this morning and accidentally swallowed it. (blunt end)

Says she wants to go insane; she wants to die.

Nurse says she is crying a good deal, but quietly, so as not to disturb other patients.

PATIENT'S NOTES

8 April 1913[79]

She[80] told how she used to go off with this friend of hers. She loved him but knew his reputation was very bad. She knew when she gave in to him but could not seem to help it. Then later after she was married with a roomer we had in Springfield.

Father would make her have sexual connection a great deal more than she wanted or at le[a]st from him. He would handle her very rough, make her stand up with out any thing on. He would not wait any time at all after a child was born before he would demand satisfaction. She said the way he did it and the leng[t]h of time was terrible.

SESSION 171: TUESDAY, 8 APRIL 1913

Vomited supper; ate no breakfast; kept dinner down.

Dreamed she and brother were in front of a furnace. This ran into a dream where she went into a room, followed by her brother. Hanging from the ceiling was a large bunch of grapes. Soon a lot of people came in and said there was one grape missing. She had it in her house and when they demanded it she would try to open her hand to give it up, but every time she tried it gave her an awful pain in her head and she woke up trying.

Associations brought out thoughts of heaven, when there were fruit trees, etc. and mother.

Overcoming tremendous resistances. She told of her father abusing her mother: standing her naked and having coitus so; doing it a lot of times through the night; having coitus right after the baby was born (terribly painful); putting his fingers up when having coitus; pulling it in and out a great many times—

As to herself: had relations with a man before she married. "In a way she loved him and in a way she didn't."

When patient was about 10 mother had relations with a boarder, who lived with them about a year.[81] When mother told her that patient could stand no more and left. Never, after that, had much to do with mother.

Patient told her mother she didn't like the boarder; mother looked scared and asked why; then told.

Did not read note given by patient yesterday but made her tell me.[82]

A few hallucinations of mother this morning but one this afternoon: saw her just before she came to me. No hallucinations of music.

Mother committed adultery; cf. automatic writing last year at M.G.H.[83]

Took patient about a month to forget all this. Told her she was identifying herself with her mother and it was as if what her father had done were done to her.

SESSION 172: WEDNESDAY, 9 APRIL 1913

Has vomited, but not badly. Has seen mother only once, this morning. Bit herself in right arm 4–5 times last night.[84]

Revengeful and cruel: tore her father's shirts all up—about 15. Often wanted to kill him; Thought how easy it would be to do so with knife, pistol, and poison. Dog and skunk put them on father's clothes and spoiled them. Cut holes in his jackets so he would lose his money. Started to set the house on fire several times. Once had cotton soaked in oil and took it to his room and lighted it. Just before she went to Nervine and before mother confessed[85] she knocked the lamp over. They thought it accidental. When she was 8 told a lie on girl-friend so she got whipped every night for a week. When it was found out her mother whipped her. Father slept very soundly and she tied him to the lounge to make him mad. Put soap in the brown sugar so father got it in his mouth. Put salt in sugar.

Feels like biting, has felt it since Monday. Bit finger Sunday afternoon.

Feels like throwing herself on the floor and yelling and screaming and tearing her clothes.

Has changed much in the last 2 years, she says, never used to let anything go that anyone had done to displease her. Would try to pay 'em back.

Tore up a shirt waist she was trying to make last summer.

April 8, 1913

She told how she used to go off with this friend of hers. She loved him but knew his reputation was very bad. She knew when she gave in to him but could not seem to help it. Then later after she was married with a roomer we had in Springfield.

Father would make her have sexual connection a great deal more than she wanted or at least from him. He would handle her very rough, make her

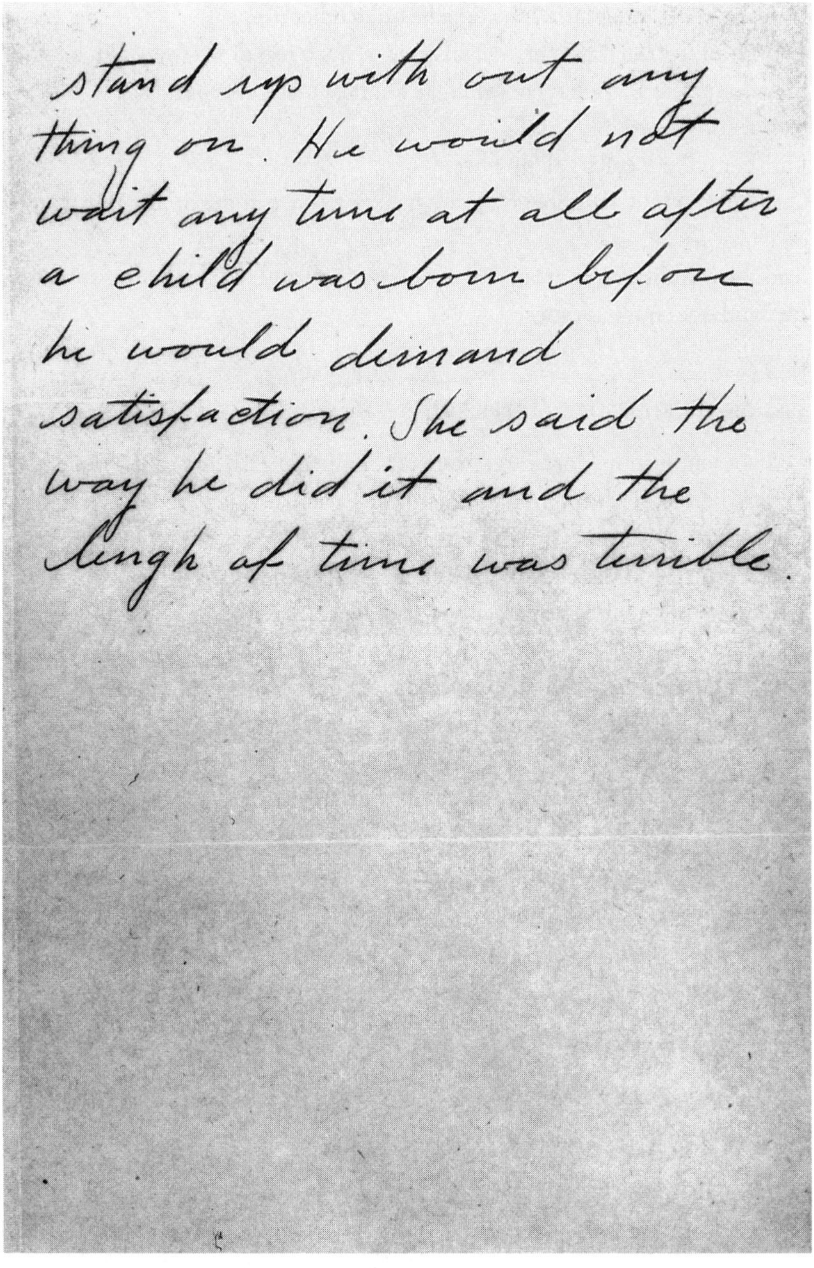

stand up with out any
thing on. He would not
wait any time at all after
a child was born before
he would demand
satisfaction. She said the
way he did it and the
lingh of time was turible.

Figure 4. (*continued*)

Threw a book at her father the time he offered her money.

Kept thinking she was in heaven all night—not a real dream, she said, because she wasn't asleep. Then there would be a sort of blank space and she would sort of come to biting herself.

Tore her father's collars all up once.

She has been told a number of times that she frothed at the mouth during convulsions.

Said she couldn't make me understand how cruel and revengeful she used to feel, and does now, at times.

SESSION 173: THURSDAY, 10 APRIL 1913

Did not vomit supper or breakfast. Did not bite herself, though she woke up finding herself on the point of doing so three times.

1) Dreamed she and her brother agreed to take poison together. She took hers but he didn't, and she reproached him because she said he was the only one she had loved and now he had gone back on her. She woke up thinking she was dying.

2) In the next dream she thought she was going to heaven, climbing a long flight of stairs. Finally she got there and was being shown around by a guide. Nobody she knew. Then he said she must see Hell and they started downstairs, after a while she couldn't go any further, and began to fall. She woke falling.

3) Dreamed she was masturbating herself.

After she had told these dreams and said they were all she remembered I asked her if she knew one of the symptoms of pregnancy. She said yes, vomiting. Then it developed that she had dreamed something about *pregnancy,* and a *baby,* last night, and again when asleep in the roof garden this morning.[86] I had her lie down but she couldn't get it connected—once she said she didn't like to think about it because she thought of her brother. She had it twice last night, once between 1 and 2 and again after 3.

After this dream she thought she was in heaven for about an hour.

Felt sick when nurse woke her this morning and vomited dinner. No hallucinations except saw her mother last night just before she went to bed. Has neither seen nor heard her mother today nor heard music.

Told me yesterday she put a snake in father's bed.

Said today she sewed his clothes up several times.

SESSION 174: FRIDAY, 11 APRIL 1913

No hallucinations. No imagination of being in heaven. Vomited this noon badly and as she did so thought for the first time since she was with me of what we were after yesterday. (i.e. meaning of pregnancy dream)

Bit herself twice, but not so very badly. (Shoulder)

Dreamed she had a baby in bed with her, dressing it up. The baby looked like a little old woman patient here. Said she had been very ugly to the doctors. She felt ugly here (cried and felt badly) and after a while refused to go on with the analysis. Company coming, she went back to the ward.

Got the feeling yesterday that everyone was looking at her and knew. After she left me she thought over everything, what she would do etc., and it looked black.

SESSION 175: MONDAY, 14 APRIL 1913

Ward III. Taken this morning.

Woke up about 5 A.M. biting herself. For an instant knew she was *trying to bite her hand off so she couldn't masturbate anymore.* She knew, too, in this instant that she had just been masturbating in her sleep, and had been, more or less frequently right along. The next instant the thought went out of her mind. But she had to get up and go to the W.C. and just when she got there, it all was plain again. She knew she had been masturbating; she knew that was what came before her eyes when she had the convulsion; she knew that was why she was nauseated (she was disgusted with herself). She knew about the pregnancy dream; and all together this was too much for her—*She fainted.* She was easily brought around, however, by the nurse giving her some water. When the doctors made their morning visit she told them she knew why she bit herself, but refused to tell it. They put her in ward III.

Has had no more hallucinations.

Vomiting decreased.

Dreamed she was with Jack last night.

STAFF MEETING

15 April 1913[87]

Dr. Southard, Dr. Adler, Dr. Stearns, Dr. Myerson, Dr. Maisch, Dr. Thom, Dr. Krout, Dr. Emerson, Dr. Norton, Dr. Walton, Dr. Daley, Rev. Dr. Groves,

Dr. Hanson, Dr. Kent, Dr. Solomon, Mr. Carpenter, Mrs. deVauriac, Miss Atkinson.

Rachel C., No. ———, Voluntary, presented by Dr. Myerson.

DR. MYERSON: The diagnosis has been hysteria.

DR. EMERSON: I feel that an explanation is due for showing the advantage of my work being dwelt upon, and it is necessary because I cannot do it in conjunction with anybody else who is observing it, observing it auditorily, at any rate. I would be perfectly willing to do the work in a glass cage—

DR. SOUTHARD: Provided that people didn't throw stones.

DR. EMERSON: Yes: but the patient only gets to give me this confidence because she gets to have, after a good deal of effort on my part, a perfect confidence that I would stand by her no matter what happened. Then there is another point that I wish to speak of before I enter in to this work, and that is, scientifically and psychotherapeutically it is necessary for the patient to overcome her own resistance, that is to say so far as any therapeutists may claim for this work, it only takes place when the patient does understand the situation. Any part of discovery on the part of psychoanalysts is useless so far as helping the patient is concerned. Scientifically, also, it is bad to work up a whole lot of theories in your own mind and then try to inject them in the patient. One is open to reproach if he does put these things into the mind of the patient, therefore, so far as I am able to control my work, I have never suggested anything to the patient, but advised one rule that whenever I could to help the patient overcome her resistance. I urge and urge the patient to overcome that, whatever it may be. This patient has been worked with by a good many different institutions. The social service department at the M.G.H., has been interested in her, and there a little work was done but nothing like the real psychoanalysis was attempted, though some attempts were made at hypnotism which were unsuccessful and afterwards she was sent to the Adams Nervine as you have already heard. She was referred to me because she was having convulsions, such as she had here a short time ago, and these convulsions coming on again after a remission of some two years frightened her so much that she came to the social service department and they referred her to me. I began to work on her January 24, 1912, and, knowing that she was very sensitive to any investigation in the direction of sexual lines, I was, for a long while, very careful about how I brought such subjects to her mind and I skirted around the surface, so to speak, for a long while. She had resisted all efforts of every[one] who had tried to help her before as to whether there had been any process in her life that could be troublesome in that way, or in any other way, for that matter, connected with sex. January 24, as I said before, I began to work on her and I saw her two or three times a week pretty constantly until February 19, when I became discouraged at the slowness of the process and I became impatient at her refusing to tell me what was obviously going on in her mind and troubling her very deeply. She would close her eyes at my suggestion, but would immediately open them again. On February 19, I became impatient and followed Dr. Freud's idea of putting his hand on the forehead of the patient and pressing and telling them that an idea would come to their mind. I modified that and stood behind her in that way and put both hands over her eyes, holding her head in my hands, and I said— "Now keep your eyes shut," of course she had to with my hands over her eyes, "Now tell me what you see?" and then I got the first fact there is in that direction, the resistance that she manifested was very marked, her mental agony certainly was tremendous, but after a while she acknowledged that she saw certain things in her childhood that were obviously connected with childhood experiences. She saw several things mixed up. The first one was a neighbor who lived near her when she was about the age of sixteen [sic]; another was an experience that she had had in the woods when she was younger. I insisted in my impatience in holding my hands before her eyes, and I insisted that she tell me the things that came to her mind. Finally she did tell me that when she was about ten years old, she was pursued by a couple of men in the woods near her house and assaulted, one of them playing with her, another attempting more. This had disappeared, she claimed, during her consciousness. The fact that she had told anything of that sort seemed to her so terrible that she then refused to have anything more to do with me, or this work, and it was with very great difficulty that I was able to persuade her to come back. I did, however, and on February 23, while holding my hands over her eyes, and insisting that she tell me what she saw, she suddenly became paraplegic, both legs, and her left hand, contracted in the following fashion with the thumb held. She was admitted to the M.G.H., and from February 23, until April 15, I saw her practically every day. I felt that I really ought not perhaps to have put my hands over her eyes; I felt that I ought not to have touched her in trying to get her to conclude what she saw. I thought I had produced more resistance into her consciousness, and from that time on I have never touched a patient. On April 15, she recalled this specific event of the assault of the neighbor when she was 13, and with the clear consciousness of the focalized event, she put her hand to her head and opened her left hand and it remained open from that time on; she had no more trouble with the contracture. She had absolute amnesia, however, for anything that followed and was somewhat paraplegic, and had remained paraplegic. I urged and urged that she remember what had happened and, after a great deal of urging, on April 2, she finally remembered a few details and moved her legs slightly. From that time on, her legs came more and more under her control and she was discharged from the hospital on May 11. I want to say that in any work I had urged a certain level and if the patient insists on going home it seems advisable to let her do so; trusting that if I had reached the bottom of things that she will then be all right; fearing if I have not she will then have further symptoms. The social service department arranged to give her an opportunity for study, going to school and given a chance for doing better work, but in June I had a note from her and saw her again when she complained of vomiting; June 10, also complained of falling down occasionally. November 19, last, the year she returned to the hospital, she complained of this vomiting. My suspicions, of course, were directed toward a lover whom she had been very much interested in and who had died a month or two before she had her first convulsion and before she went to the Adams Nervine. At the last day, however, I had not come to any conclusion in work in that direction. This time, however, when she returned I again urged her to remember more clearly any relations she may have had with this lover and in the process of this on December 5, she began to have auditory hallucinations. She heard people calling her by her name. She heard those things for some time and the situation became so strained that I got her admitted to the M.G.H. again where she stayed a couple of days and was discharged December 7, during which time she had remembered of the lover succeeding once in having improper relations with her. On December 10, she wrote me that she was still vomiting and that she was in no way completely recovered. December 26, having seen her between the 10th and 26th frequently, she was again admitted to the hospital because she had again become paraplegic, losing the use of the legs. From that time on the situation became very difficult. On January 7, she complained of being as if blind. On January 9, she had an actual occurrence called an attack of hysterical amaurosis, and then she acknowledged that for the last week and a half or two weeks, she had been having blindness every now and then but had concealed it, thinking it would pass away. Still seeing her every day and urging her that she would tell anything further in her consciousness that might be troubling her, I got no further practically, but on January 16, the nurse reported that during the night she had called out her brother's name and said—"Stop" and "Why do you do so." Without any further resistance from her, however, on asking her what that might signify, she immediately told me that her brother, four years younger than she, and that it had always been the habit for them to play together in the morning and sometimes the night. That the brother would awaken her by throwing pillows at her and they would then have a wrestling match, they would fall together on the bed and that afterwards sometimes they would sleep in each other's arms. She did not think there was any harm in it, but she heard her mother remark one day that she would be glad when those children grew up. One day a girl friend came and found her brother there and said she wouldn't let her brother come into her room and that brought her to the consciousness of the significance of this fooling and from that time on the practice was broken up. From January 16, on, she began having high temperatures, I have a chart here of the temperatures she ran at the M.G.H., and my suspicions were in the direction of relations with her brother, and during the time that she was having these high temperatures, my urging and my efforts were towards making her remember any possible connections in her mind as to the experience that she had with her brother. They made some of the tests there, not being a medical man I don't know all of the tests that they made, they made a Widal test, a blood test, they tested her for T.B. and various other tests, all this time these temperatures were taken by officials at the hospital, or the nurses, and all I had to do with her was to see her as I do here. On January 22, the patient said, "I know he did it but I don't know when." January 4, she said it was about when she was 18, and nothing further was I able to get at the M.G.H. On February 4, she began to have auditory hallucinations of music, started as a sort of ringing in her ears, or humming. February 10, she was discharged.

DR. SOUTHARD: On February 4, she had a temperature of 104.

DR. EMERSON: The temperature had dropped in two or three days to 97. After they had made all the tests that they felt necessary and finally regarded it as highly probable hysterical temperature, and as she was insisting on going home and making life miserable for the attendants in asking to go home, they agreed to risk it and take a chance on letting her go home. She had no temperature after going home and when she was admitted here she had no temperature. February 24, 8 days after she was discharged from the M.G.H., I had a telephone message from the people where she was staying, who told me that she had lost her voice and I saw her that same day and she told me that she had been blind the day before and had auditory hallucinations of music and heard her mother calling her. She used to answer these voices and disturbed the people where she was staying. On February 25, I had 2 telephone messages from the people where she was staying, the second of which informed me that she had a convulsion. They called in a Dr. Denny of Dorchester[88] who gave her a great deal of ether and a hypodermic of morphine and, as far as I could make out, he and the nurses spent most of the time trying to hold her down to the bed. She was persuaded to come here voluntarily by bringing her to the telephone and hearing me tell her that she must come here as it was the best place for her. On the 27th I saw her here that afternoon and nothing further had been learned but that night she was paralyzed during the night. Her hand was clenched but she would open it again. She was still having auditory hallucinations, both of hearing music and of hearing her mother calling her. On March 4, while visitors were on the ward I was seeing her in one of the little rooms, a nurse came in and said that her brother was waiting for her. She seemed to be in a certain tenseness rather than activity. I got up immediately to allow her to go to her brother and I noticed that her left hand was again clenched. I asked her to open it and she was unable to. She went out and saw her brother and the next day she told me she had dreamed the night before that she had been masturbating. She then opened her hand and she has not had any more trouble with the contracture so far as I know. She has told other things almost incredible in regard to snakes, but I will not go into that for they may or may not be realities. On March 4, I saw her next on Ward 3, where she had been placed because she had had a convulsion the night before. Then she was able to work, she was able to stand up. She told me that everything, and of course a great deal more than I have told, had come to her mind the night before and simply overwhelmed her and the next instant she did not know what had happened. As a matter of fact, she had had a convulsion. I was unable to get any further through her resistance until March 21. At that time she recalled and said, "I know about this; I know why I heard music." She said her mother was playing and she remembered her brother and she had played with each other. From that time the hallucinations of music practically disappeared. They disappeared immediately so far as a close connection with this occurrence was concerned and she had only a slight return of it. It is interesting to know that on March 22, she admitted that she had lied and she knew why she had lied and in questioning her she said that if she felt she was able to get out of all this by lying she would have done so, but now feeling that it was necessary to be controlled she had overcome that inclination. On March 24, while with me, and during my effort to overcome her resistance, she had another sort of a vision in which she saw her brother, her father and everything all at once. Having penetrated that instance it was learned that her father had merely handled her perhaps improperly at the age of 7, and from that time on she had played with herself more or less and her brother and she had been playing in this way all the time, practically. In the meantime I might say that she had been vomiting every morning. This was stopped April 1, and she admitted that she had been hunting for a knife to cut her hand off and woke up with that impression. On April 2, she remembered, or at least told that she remembered, that 2 months before her mother died, her mother had called her into her room and had confessed to her a whole lot of her past life, her relations with her husband and with other people, etc., which she felt that she could not bear to hold in any longer. With that confession of the mother she has practically lost all hallucinations of hearing her mother calling her. On April 4, she had aphonia which remained the next day. On April 7, she bit her forefinger when a visitor was with her. On April 8, she told the whole story, as she remembered it, that her mother had told her, and on April 9, she bit herself some four or five times in the arm, I had a photograph of them. On April 14, she told me that at 5 o'clock yesterday, in the morning, she awakened biting herself. She explained this by saying that she awakened finding herself masturbating herself and the next instant the dream came to her that if she bit her hand off then she could not masturbate any longer. The thought left her as soon as it entered her mind and she was obliged to get up and go to the toilet, and while there the thought also came to her that that was what came before her eyes the night that she had the convulsion,

March 14th, and she remembered too that the connection between the dream was the cause for her self-disgust. However, she was still right up to April 14, off and on masturbating herself entirely unconscious so far as her verbal consciousness was concerned. She was then again, and rightly, put on Ward 3 because of the biting, and that so disturbed her that she immediately handed in her three days' notice, although I urged her to stay longer, and she is going tomorrow or the next day, whenever the three days are up, so I thought it would be well to present her at the staff meeting today. Of course I haven't the slightest idea as to how this thing is going to turn out in the long run, but I am in hopes, considering the character of the girl, now that she knows that for a long time she not only hasn't had an inclination, but in a dreamlike state she has satisfied that craving, she ought now to be able to control it. I am in hopes that coming to consciousness she will be able to stand the strain, and perhaps if she gets a chance to work or gets something to do that her going home will open her future.

QUESTIONED BY DR. SOUTHARD:
Q. So you are going, Miss C.?[89] (Nods head in the affirmative.)
Q. Do you think it is the best thing to do?
A. I don't feel in a condition to work.
Q. You do or don't?
A. I don't.
Q. You have decided to go?
A. Well, I have put in my notice.
Q. It is your serious intention to go?
A. (Looks at Dr. Emerson.)
Q. Do you think you should stay here under different conditions? Is there something we could do that would be better?
A. No.

DR. ADLER:
Q. What is it you told me this morning?
A. I said that I put it in on the impulse of the moment but I knew that I wouldn't bite myself again.

DR. SOUTHARD:
Q. You knew that you wouldn't?
A. Yes.
Q. Are you quite sure?
A. Yes.
Q. You think it is just as well to go?
A. I think I might just as well. (Looks down.)

Q. Then as I understand it, you are intending to go?

A. Yes.

Q. But it was an impulsive act, your saying it?

A. Yes.

Q. I thought there might have been more or less persuasion by Dr. Emerson.

A. I wanted to be home before this but he told me it would be better here than home. When I came here I didn't want to stay—I didn't want to sign the paper.[90]

DR. SOUTHARD TO DR. EMERSON: What do you now think?

DR. EMERSON: I am undecided. I think perhaps it would be better for her to stay.

DR. SOUTHARD:

Q. What are the advantages of going?

A. There are no advantages. I haven't any home; if I had I wouldn't hesitate a moment. If I go out I will have to go to friends.

DR. ADLER:

Q. I wish you would tell us just what you said this morning. I want to know just what you thought of. You said this morning that you handed in your notice in haste and that you would like to go back on Ward 5, but if you couldn't go back on Ward 5, you wouldn't take your notice back.

A. I don't remember saying that.

DR. SOUTHARD:

Q. Take your notice back anyway?

A. I don't want to.

Q. What do you want?

A. I want to go back on Ward 5 if I stay.

Q. If you can't go back you want to go?

A. As far as my wishes go, yes.

Q. Is there anyone else to consider?

A. I don't know—I know I won't bite myself again.

Q. You said that you weren't well enough to work?

A. I said I wasn't in condition to work.

Q. Why not?

A. Because I can't control myself.

Q. Then you don't know that you are not going to bite yourself again. (No reply—Looks down.)

Q. Do you think you are better?

A. I am much better.

Q. Well enough to work, perhaps? Or is there some doubt?

A. (Hesitates.) I have put in my notice now and I am ready to go.

Q. I am afraid Dr. Emerson's indecision has something to do with it.

DR. EMERSON: I can make a decision.

DR. SOUTHARD:

Q. Wouldn't you do exactly as Dr. Emerson says?

A. (Hesitates.) Yes. It is plainly up to Dr. Emerson.

DR. EMERSON: I think she had better stay a while longer.

DR. ADLER: On Ward 3?

DR. EMERSON: That's up to Dr. Adler.

DR. SOUTHARD:

Q. You don't like Dr. Adler, do you?

A. W-h-y———— y-e-s.

Q. I mean really?

A. I know he thinks he's doing right, but I know I shant bite myself again and I shant have another convulsion.

DR. ADLER: I feel that I can't be sure of it as long as you say you haven't got control of yourself.

DR. SOUTHARD:

Q. Supposing you go back and do bite yourself?

A. If I go back on Ward 5 and have a convulsion you will put me on Ward 3.

DR. ADLER: The only reason for Miss C. being on Ward 3 is that we can observe her a little better. We have only one night nurse on Ward 5 and 3 on Ward 3.

A. I was much nearer the night nurse on Ward 5 than I am on Ward 3.

DR. EMERSON: It is so complicated that I don't really get the point.

DR. SOUTHARD: Ward 3 versus Ward 5.

DR. EMERSON: If it doesn't interfere with the hospital routine, I think she would be better on Ward 5.

DR. ADLER: Why?

DR. EMERSON: I am inclined to agree with her. I don't think she will bite herself again and I don't think she will have another convulsion. The reason that I am a little more confident this time is that when she came to her consciousness instead of having a convulsion she fainted.

DR. ADLER: But all these things, convulsions, biting and all that, happened on Ward 5. You really have been only a short time on Ward 3.
A. Yes, I know, but up on Ward 5 I can sew and on Ward 3 I can't do anything and the patients irritate me and everything.
Q. How about that vomiting?
A. I haven't eaten anything lately, so I don't know. It was much better.
Q. I suppose it takes psychoanalysis to find out whether she has eaten anything.
A. I haven't eaten anything since Sunday night.
Q. Don't you think it is possible for you to have eaten something and not remembered it?
A. Yes, but I don't think I could forget it. (Picks at sweater greater part of time.)

DR. SOUTHARD: Is there any extreme objection to her going back to Ward 5?

DR. ADLER: None at all on my part, if she will get along all right.

DR. SOUTHARD:
Q. You don't bite other people, you never had that impulse?
A. I never bit anything until I bit my hand and I only did that twice.

DR. SOUTHARD: Amnesia for the other four or five times.

DR. EMERSON: Four or five times for that one occasion. Three times; she bit her finger once, another occasion four or five times on the arm, and another time on the shoulder.

DR. STEARNS:[91] I think it is very surprising that Miss C. seems to do these things when she is on a quiet ward.
A. I should have done the very same thing if I had been on Ward 3.

DR. SOUTHARD: I wonder if this is so.
A. I told Dr. Emerson to move me back.

DR. ADLER: The nurse might have got there quicker on Ward 3.

DR. SOUTHARD: Your point is, Dr. Stearns, that a number of patients on Ward 5 react in an impulsive way.

DR. STEARNS: Whether or not it is intentional or whether or not it is real, I think the apparent discipline has a good effect.

DR. SOUTHARD: Your opinion is that Miss C. needs a little more discipline than she thinks she needs.

DR. STEARNS: I think it was rather wise for her to come to Ward 3. I don't see why she differs from any other patient in the hospital. We have had a number of patients transferred from 5 to 3.

DR. MYERSON: I think in this particular case perhaps it would be a good step to transfer her to Ward 5.

DR. MAISCH: Miss C. has undoubtedly improved a great deal on Ward 5, but I am still quite a bit worried about her.
Q. What causes you the bother? The things you eat?
(No reply.)

DR. MAISCH: On Ward 5 we haven't quite as many nurses as on Ward 3 and if she is going to keep up this vomiting I think for her own good she ought to be where someone could get to her at once. If she gets sick to her stomach the nurse might be able to do something at once. I would like that vomiting to stop.
A. Dr. Maisch, my vomiting has been much better.
Q. You told me yesterday that you vomited after each meal.
A. You asked me yesterday and I told you that I had not, but I told you that I had refused my breakfast and supper.

DR. MAISCH: Miss C. is quite sure she is not going to vomit and quite sure she is not going to bite herself again. If I were quite sure that Miss C. is certain about the control that she would manifest over the vomiting, I would be convinced to send her back to Ward 5. She improved very much there and appeared quite happy. You must have chewed your arm quite a bit, it was black and blue from the wrist up to the elbow.
A. I woke up and found myself biting it. I don't know how much I did.

DR. SOUTHARD: Dr. Emerson has really in your own mind helped you a great deal.
A. Yes. Certainly.
Q. No one else has done anything?

A. No.

Q. He has made all things clear to you?

A. Yes.

Q. You think this will be a permanent cure.

A. I don't mind so much if the vomiting stops right off, because I can control my feelings about some things.

Q. The vomiting has been a relief to you?

A. Yes.

Q. You would still be relieved by vomiting?

A. I don't know, I just simply can't keep it down.

DR. SOUTHARD: Dr. Emerson, are you still undecided as to whether she should stay or go?

DR. EMERSON: I think it is better for her to stay.

DR. SOUTHARD:

Q. What do you think about it?

A. I will do just as Dr. Emerson says.

DR. EMERSON: She has no home to go to and the two old ladies that she would be staying with would be quite disturbed about it and it might lead to another convulsion. The only other place she could go to is to the house of a friend of hers who works.

DR. SOUTHARD: What is the longest interval in which she was apparently cured, but has later relapsed?

DR. EMERSON: I think from the time of her mother's death in March 1910, until February 1912.[92]

DR. SOUTHARD:

Q. You were quite well?

A. Yes.

Q. Not a sign?

A. From the time that I came back from my mother's funeral. I had a convulsion that day.

Q. Do you suppose you could get rid of those head movements?

A. It is much better.

Q. Has Dr. Emerson explained those to you?

A. (Looks down.) No.

DR. SOUTHARD: Dr. Emerson, how long do you want her to stay?

DR. EMERSON: It is uncertain.

Q. If you should be free from these things for a fortnight or three weeks, do you think your strength would be again so that you could go, and then you would call it a cure?

A. It's a cure now as soon as I can keep my food down.

Q. It is somewhat comforting to feel that you are not naughty but that you are a case. Isn't it somewhat comforting to feel that it is a disease you are getting over rather than an immoral difficulty?

A. (Looks down—bites lips.)

Patient dismissed.

Discussion

DR. STEARNS: Does everybody agree?

DR. MAISCH: I don't know whether I should or not. I am inclined to hesitate.

DR. ADLER: I think it is hysteria. I am not quite sure whether she ought to stay or go. I think it is a little mistake to have her hear so much of the discussion. I think it will exaggerate somewhat further in her mind the importance of having been moved from Ward 5 to Ward 3 and, while this is a way of discipline, we try to avoid having it appear so. She thinks it is a very important thing and the doctors could not agree.

DR. SOUTHARD: If she hasn't any more judgement than that it doesn't matter.

DR. ADLER: I don't know whether she should go back to Ward 5 or go home. I am quite willing to have her go back if Dr. Emerson wants her to. I don't believe she is very much improved.

DR. WALTON: I suppose it is hysteria, but the whole explanation of treatment is too much for me to discuss. I think that if that woman is only to be cured by dragging out the disgusting details; for my part, if a patient tries to tell me that I say, "Let up on that, I don't want to hear about it."

DR. EMERSON: I am very glad that point is brought up because it seems to me to be a very important one; it seems to me that on the condition that the symptoms are so severe—she was having at one time five convulsions a day and she reported that she broke her hand twice in convulsions.

DR. ADLER: She broke her hand?

DR. EMERSON: She broke her hand.

DR. ADLER: Did she?

DR. EMERSON: The social services worker said she bruised her hand greatly, but in any case she has been put down and out both by the convulsions and paraplegia.

DR. SOUTHARD: She seems to have had everything. Paraplegia, vomiting, aphonia, blindness, auditory and visual hallucinations; if she is relieved of all these symptoms by this, it was then worth it, otherwise not.

DR. WALTON: I can only say that if she can be cured by it why of course that justifies it; if not, I will feel a great deal towards that subject as Huxley says about vivisection; "It is necessary, therefore, someone must do it, but I can't do it."

DR. MYERSON: I think it is a case of hysteria. I think the cause of symptoms is interesting if it is true. I mean if it is really the cause of the symptoms. I believe that hysterics are liars myself. I wouldn't take her story about her father or mother or anybody else. I have seen hysterics get well with or without treatment and I have seen them improve with or without treatment. I don't see enough improvement in her case to warrant that she is cured.

DR. SOUTHARD: How many hysterics have been seen by the members of this meeting who have been absolutely cured?

DR. WALTON: I don't remember any.

DR. SOUTHARD: I think 9 years is given in epilepsy by Turner for some reason, I don't know what. Does anyone know what the literature says? We must look it up.

SESSION 176: TUESDAY, 15 APRIL 1913

At staff-meeting.[93] To stay.
After she went back to the ward heard her mother calling a good deal
for 10 minutes. Ate dinner but vomited a little. Did not bite herself last
night.
Lying down. Dreamed of the dream of pregnancy. As she was lying there she
started: "I don't know why I should think of that man we had for a boarder,
his face just loomed up in front of me."

One of the patients told her Sunday night the meaning of tickling hands and stepping on feet (i.e. desire for coitus) and it brought back the fact that that was the way this boarder did, not only to her but also to her mother. She complained about it to her mother and she laughed.

She remembered that when she was in Ella's room that last time with Jack and he was tempting her, he asked her what she was going to do now she was pregnant. She was terribly frightened, but denied it.

"It kind of seems as if the dream had something to do with what Jack told me."

"I think of one, then I think of the other, and it kind of seems as if they draw together, and I can't get how they would go together."

"I know what he said made me dream that."

"I know it is that because my stomach is all upset now thinking about it."

Woke herself up last night saying "I won't" knew she had been dreaming that I was trying to make her tell something which she wouldn't tell.

Remembered she had had pregnancy dream a good many times.

SESSION 177: WEDNESDAY, 16 APRIL 1913

Vomited some but not much.

No bites—No hallucinations.

Dream: Started from here and went home. Then started out alone and came to this mountain. I didn't know why it was so dark. I was searching for something. At last I got to the top. I seemed to be above everything in this earth. Then it seemed as if a ladder came down from heaven—and it was light up there. There were people up there—Mother, father, Jack, Everett. Just started to go up when I decided to come back. It seemed to take more courage to stay. Dreamed she was making all the doctors do as she wanted them to. Had a hypodermic needle and was injecting them with a fluid. Dreamed of snakes one time but doesn't know what it was. Something about fire in another dream but couldn't get 'em plain.

Had patient lie down.

After a while she suddenly remembered another dream: Dreamed of having a baby like the one in Ward V. She thought she didn't care now whether she had a mother or not as she had a baby to love. Many times her dreams are of giving birth to a baby, but last night she just had it.

Started: much resistance, "nothing to do with dreams or anything else." Finally: Thought of Jack, and babies, and wanted him sexually. Thought it wrong to *want* such things because father and mother did so wrong, she and brother had too much of such desires and it was wrong to have it.

What did you think of then? "I don't know why I should have said it but Mrs. D.[94] (Sunday) after we went to bed was talking about her children and babies, and she said she never was sick when she was pregnant—I said 'I was' but she couldn't understand and so I said I was thinking of something else—but I don't know what made me say it." (Told this proved the content of her unconscious.)

After Jack told her she was pregnant, that time, she often dreamed she was and would wake terrified and trembling, sick all over. She used to ask her mother, in roundabout ways, to find out if she could, how one could tell, but her mother always avoided the subject. The first time she associated vomiting with pregnancy was the summer before she first saw me, probably before July 4th when a young married friend of hers was visiting her and was sick and told her it was because she was pregnant.

Good color—seemed better—still on Ward III.

"It does seem like a wish, and a dream, what Jack said, pregnancy, and a baby, all mixed up, and I can't connect it up. It seems foolish if I've been dreaming that and a thought could make me sick."

She didn't vomit this noon till at least 10 minutes after dinner. She was sitting down at the time. A doctor whose wife was a patient came and asked to see her arm. He undid it and was asking her if she knew why she did it, etc., finally he asked if she didn't hear him, and then she seemed to sort of come to, and was sick, held in a while, but finally had to go to the toilet and vomit.

SESSION 178: THURSDAY, 17 APRIL 1913

Ward V.

No biting. No hallucinations. Vomited dinner. *But* after dinner was lying dozing in a chair "dreaming" when (about 2:30) it came over her that what she was dreaming was: *being pregnant.* Then she remembered that after Jack told her she was pregnant, she thought of what had already happened and thought she might as well have a baby anyway, and so began wishing and hoping she were pregnant. She knew, too, that the content of her daydreams was "pregnancy." She did not know vomiting was a sign of pregnancy till her friend told her, and when she told her that seemed to bring her own desires to her mind and made her sick.

Is not certain she will not vomit, because she thinks it was associated, too, with moral self-disgust.

Dreamed she and her brother were on the elevator together. She pressed the button 5—The elevator went right on up through the roof. She pressed the button again and it went back to the basement. They did this 3 times when her brother got off. Then she found herself in a raft, naked. Somebody told her her brother was dying with heart disease. But she had no clothes on, till finally someone brought her shoes in a boat. She got to shore and went to this house. When she got in, the telephone rang and she told them to lie and say she wasn't there. Then she ran upstairs to 5 and found her mother with a baby in her lap. Her brother and another baby, for he was a baby in the dream, were on a bed together (second telling the other baby was on top), they seemed closely knit together and she had hard work to get them apart. Her brother was having a convulsion and blood was foaming out of his mouth. She took him (and threw the other baby on the floor—second telling) and started for the doctor. She met Dr. Stearns in the stairs and said she was afraid he was dying. Dr. Stearns said he thought he was dead and that was why he came. Then he began asking about her relatives.

Dr. Stearns much distressed her last night by "insinuating" she needed discipline. He said something about her biting herself being insane, etc. After he left she had a screaming and crying spell and refused to go to bed, at about 9 threw herself down and went to sleep. Dr. Stearns came and told her she could go back on 5 in the morning if she were quiet. Except for the noise everything on III is better than on V—food and nurses.

SESSION 179: FRIDAY, 18 APRIL 1913

No bites.

Dreamed of being in heaven 4 times. Second dream was of being with brother *Thought* she was in heaven, several times this morning.

Heard mother several times this morning. Mother was reproaching her for having told, etc.

Ate supper and breakfast and no vomiting—Dreaming at dinner; called out of it by another patient and knew she was dreaming of being pregnant (and everything else) and was sick, and knew why.

Had eggnog this morning and did not vomit.

Does not feel so badly at father.

Is very much better.

Dreamy spells come on involuntarily.

SESSION 180: MONDAY, 21 APRIL 1913

Very well Friday afternoon and all day Saturday.

Saturday night letter from father criticizing her, "Hypnotism," etc. Said if she didn't get well soon she would kill him as she had her mother. She wished he would die, and put it out of her mind.

Dreamed she was doing things to her father as used to.

Sunday "saw" mother a good deal.

Miss Davis.[95] "Jealous" etc.

Vomited supper. Vomited today.

Can't seem to stop dreaming today.

SESSION 181: TUESDAY, 22 APRIL 1915

Vomiting badly.

Dreaming and seeing mother.

Dreamed of going away with Mrs. D.[96] They seemed handcuffed together till they got outside when she saw her mother in the sky and started to rise towards her. As she rose she had to keep dropping things to get higher. The things she seemed to be dropping were the things she had been through and done. Finally she came to a cloud and had to drop something, but woke trying, for she couldn't seem to let go.

Later she dreamed she was in the woods. There was a great bowl, hewn out of granite. She had a great fire in it and was burning all the snakes, when suddenly one jumped out and into her mouth. She woke trying to get it out, and it was about half out. She was awfully sick and had to go to the closet and vomit.

Later she "imagined" she was with her mother. She thought she was in bed with her and they were talking together.

Just before the snake-in-the-mouth dream she was sucking her thumb!

Told not to lie in her face!

SESSION 182: WEDNESDAY, 23 APRIL 1913

Vomited, but not so badly.

Has seen her mother some, but not so much.

Dreaming better.

Dreamed she went to a Spiritualist meeting to talk with her mother through mediums. Her mother told her to leave the hospital. She came back to get her things and did leave but just as she stepped outside the door she fell into a deep hole, and woke, falling.

After this dream she woke, finding herself just about to *masturbate*. (Or else just had?) Felt like biting herself. The next dream was of torturing somebody. After 3rd dream woke up shaking, but didn't know why.

Twice after this woke finding herself just about to *masturbate*. Did not suck her thumb.

Is going to pin the sleeves of her night dress to control her hands. Patient acknowledges having masturbated a great deal lately. Some nights, she said, it would seem as if she would hardly get to sleep before she would begin, and every time she woke up, she would be starting again. Some nights were worse than others.

SESSION 183: THURSDAY, 24 APRIL 1913

Got her hands out—Woke up once taking her night dress off. Woke up 2 crying and laughing and shaking and shivering (thinks she masturbated). Ate neither supper nor breakfast. Nauseated by failure. Sick all morning. The last thing she remembers thinking of just before vomiting dinner was of her failure last night. "I'm discouraged, and deep down in my heart I don't want to try." (Last thing she said just as she left.)

Has seen her mother but not so much. Thought she was in heaven last night.

SESSION 184: FRIDAY, 25 APRIL 1913

Vomiting some. Saw mother, but less.

Dreamed of a bag of marbles. Playing with them and put them in bag. Someone told her to take them out and they rolled all around the floor, and rolled together like quick-silver. They kept bursting and things kept coming out of them.

Dreamed of being at home. Dreamed of cutting herself up. Cut off her hand, leg, etc. "It seemed as if I was two people, and I was lying on the table, yet I was standing then cutting myself up." Cut herself all up. Woke chopping her body up.

Has no consciousness of masturbating but thinks she may have.

Heard story, through Mrs. D. (a patient), that night nurse had had relations with a man at a doctor's orders.

PATIENT'S DREAMS

Friday Night

Bugs all over me and people laughing and crying around me.

Trying to run.

Killing snakes and taking the skins and making a dress. I just got it finished when all the snakes seemed to come to life.

Mother came at the same time.

Something about getting a letter written in blood.

Sunday Night

It seems as if I came out of myself and tried in a number of ways to get rid of my old self.

I was on a table and I was trying to raise myself but couldn't get up. I was crying.

SESSION 185: MONDAY, 28 APRIL 1913

Vomiting about the same.

Dreaming about mother and heaven and pregnancy, and what she had done, and had done to her.

The following night she dreamed of destroying herself.[97]

Sunday night dream. 1) Tried to cut it[98] up but could make no impression.[99] 2) Tried to set fire to it with a torch. 3) Tried to drown it but could float. So got a boat and brought it to shore and 4) tried to bury it, but couldn't dig deep enough, earth kept filling in, she woke.

Woke masturbating 4 times Saturday night. Orgasm woke her. *No dreams* she could remember.

Saw mother most Sunday. Didn't eat much.

Father masturbated her at 7.

She began soon.

Mother told her and brother 10 and 6 not to masturbate.

Woods at 11.

Brother at 12 till 16. *First* memory was *last* time.

T. 13.

Jack 19~20 etc.

Relieved at his death but didn't know why.

SESSION 186: TUESDAY, 29 APRIL 1913

Vomited less this noon—Was blue and cried a good deal this morning.
Dreamed all night about the door. Seemed to be trying to fix it so I couldn't
shut it. First she arranged it so when I tried it came off the hinges; then she
arranged the knob to come off; and other way she couldn't remember. Once
the door seemed to be at home and she was trying to keep her father and me
out. (This came out in second telling) When she woke she remembered the
time her father tried to get her to do wrong.
Used this to prove her the Übertragung. Think I succeeded.
Saw her mother a good deal this morning. Once with me.
Did not catch herself masturbating and thought she had not.
Dr. Adler told me to do as I thought best.

SESSION 187: WEDNESDAY, 30 APRIL 1913

Better. Thinks she did not masturbate. Dreamed she was being hanged.
Rope = T.
Thought of man she and brother found who committed suicide so. How she
wished she had, etc.
Dreamed she was trying to find something to dream about that didn't mean
anything, but couldn't.
This noon kept everything in her mind, while eating, bound she wouldn't
vomit.

PATIENT'S DREAMS

1 May 1913
Mother coming to me and telling me you would tell things I had told but that
she forgave me and to come with her and never mind.
Taking the tablets, dying.
In the woods with Jack. He turning to Everett. Some one saying now you will
be able to lay on your back.
It seemed as if I was back to school and looked at the babies in the bottles
which I didn't want to then it seemed as if I went from there to a room a long
ways off and from there to woods then back to home in bed as if I was sick. It
seemed as if every thing was dark all the time.
Something about painting a bed white.

Cutting meat and a lot of cats and dogs around me in some way they couldn't eat it so they started to eat me. I was happy and yet it seemed as if I was in pain.

SESSION 188: THURSDAY, 1 MAY 1913

Did not vomit much last night; did badly at breakfast, not at all this noon. Saw her mother twice this morning.

6:30 last night nurse let her in room where medicines were, to get a cathartic.[100] After getting her pill the nurse took up a bottle and said, "How would you like to take this?" It was corrosive sublimate, and marked poison.[101] In the moment the nurse's back was turned, she took two tablets. Saturday night and this morning were spent in struggling against the temptation to take them. A lot of times she started to do it when something held her back. Finally, at 10 A.M. she threw them down the water closet and from that time began to feel better.

Woke sucking her hand once. Used to do that till running sores.

Does not think she masturbated.

Started when I spoke of the tablets and asked her what that meant. She did not intend to tell, she said. Wrote these notes down last night.

The dogs were biting her legs; the cats jumped on her shoulders and were scratching and biting her face and neck.

The bed was black.

Written her brother to come after her tomorrow night—dreads meeting him.

(Brother came and got her at noon May 2)

Discharged.[102]

Part III "My mind is just making my body sick"

Chapter 7 Commentary:

16 May 1913–6 March 1917,

Sessions 189–292

This last segment of the analysis spans four years. Two weeks after her discharge—once again, in Emerson's estimation, apparently cured—from the Psychopathic Hospital, Rachel was back in treatment. She saw him regularly from 16 May 1913 through early August, when he went on vacation; she resumed treatment in October 1913, and saw him with some frequency until mid-May 1914. From then until January 1917, the analysis lapsed—one session and several letters notwithstanding—to be taken up again, in a final flurry of twenty-two sessions that began with her admission to the Massachusetts General Hospital.[1] Three letters spaced over two years round out the case. When last heard from, in August 1921, Rachel was a tubercular patient in a state sanitarium in Dunseith, North Dakota, planning, upon her recovery, to marry her thirty-five-year-old fiancé.

This portion of the case is the least well documented of its three parts; we have only Emerson's daily case notes from which to reconstruct its progress. For reasons that are obscure, Emerson concluded his published account of the case with Rachel's discharge from the Boston Psychopathic Hospital (coinciding with the end of Part II in this book), although she was back in treatment with him a mere two weeks later. That is, even as he was writing up and publishing the case as if it were finished, he and she were carrying on the analysis in much the same manner as they had previously, with sessions scheduled three to four times a week. Throughout this segment of the case, Rachel was adding new symptoms to her repertoire, most serious among them self-mutilation—using a knife to cut her breasts and wrists—and Emerson may have felt that the treatment was spinning out of his clinical and theoretical control. His note at the end of session 199 suggests he was confused, with new and distressing material emerging and already-broached issues still unresolved: "Complex: confession of mother; questions she asked; Jack, Henry, Mother's seducer, Father, Brother, babies; pregnancies, how to tell; fear—."[2] Emerson's decision to bring the published case to premature closure, and to append an extended theoretical discussion to his session-by-session narrative account, may have seemed to him the only—or, alternately, the most prudent—choice, given that he may have felt his grip on it imperiled. Whether, a year or two further into the case, he could have written about it using the language and concepts of psychoanalysis available to him at the time is open to question. There is some evidence he was thinking that Rachel's difficulties were characterological, that, to put it anachronistically, she suffered not only from hysteria but more fundamentally from an intractable character disorder.[3] It may be that he prepared the article's theoretical excursus, in which his frustrations with Rachel and with the limitations of psychoanalytic technique in treating her were everywhere evident, at the last point at which it was possible, intellectually and emotionally, for him to have done so.

FAILURES OF PSYCHOANALYSIS

In 1915 Emerson published his first remarks on psychoanalytic failure. "At first it was thought," he wrote, "that hysteria was due to childhood sexual traumas, repressed." But the early analytic formula—"release the repressions, allow sublimation to take place, and the patient was cured"—had not, he wrote, proved universally efficacious. Patients "were not cured and sometimes not even helped much," he continued, invoking no patient in particular but with the case of Rachel likely in mind.[4] In her case he had assumed from the start that the release of her repressions would bring complete recovery,[5] while in fact what he was witnessing in 1914 and 1915 were partial, and repeated, recoveries with the concomitant appearance of new and ever more troubling symptoms. It is not unreasonable to assume he was, at the least, discouraged and that, at the worst, he felt himself defeated by the refractory nature of Rachel's illness. Not curing a neurosis, he wrote, invoking Freud's authority, might in some cases represent "the best practical solution of an unbearable situation,"[6] which Rachel's increasingly appeared to be. "When the present conflict is completely won complete recovery will supervene,"[7] Emerson optimistically wrote at the conclusion of the published article on her case, but, as must have been clear while he was writing, the present conflicts—in particular, those concerning both the brother and masturbation—showed few signs of imminent resolution.

That Emerson did not as fully document this portion of the case may have been due not only to discouragement with its progress in particular but also to a more general—and, by 1915 or so, increasingly apparent—disenchantment with several critical aspects of Freudian psychoanalysis. The extent to which he was ever philosophically and technically fully in accord with Freud is open to question; recall, for example, his discomfort with free association—later to be known as the "fundamental rule" of psychoanalysis—for what he saw as its aimless quality and, more important, the surrender of analytic authority on which he felt it was premised.[8] By 1915, his dissent from Freudian orthodoxy centered on two issues: psychoanalytic ethics and the transference. Even as his disagreements sharpened, however, he continued to consider himself every bit the psychoanalyst. He read widely in the literature, helped to organize psychoanalytic meetings, abstracted German language papers for American journals, and published his own psychoanalytic papers. His 1916–17 paper titled "Some Psychoanalytic Studies of Character," for example, presented several colorful and sexually detailed vignettes of men suffering from what Freud called aberrations of sexual desire. It was written in a distinctly Freudian vein, the case material refracted through Emerson's reading of Freud's *Three Essays on the Theory of Sexuality*, published in 1905, and, it is likely, his essay on narcissism, which appeared in 1914.[9] Narcissism, perversions, incest fantasies, and a fixation on sexual fore-pleasures figured in the men's pathologies, all of whom were Freudian types—one, outwardly normal, could overcome his sexual inhibitions only in the presence of pretty girls, but the image of his mother and of his wife, whom he loathed, "prevented actual intercourse"; another, a successful professional, nursed by his mother until age eight and introduced to fellatio at age ten, was an avid collector of obscene books and pictures who was fixed, Emerson argued, at the autoerotic stage of sexual development.[10] In this article, and in another, also a clinical paper, published in 1918–19, on the successful treatment of a woman who suffered from the delusion that everyone thought she was immoral (she habitually looked "where she 'ought not to'"—at men's abdominal regions), Emerson wrote from within psychoanalysis.[11]

Characterizing psychoanalysis as a marginal and beleaguered therapy, Emerson showed no hesitation in rising to its defense. He readily defended the necessity and autonomy of psychotherapeutic practices, and made clear he wanted to preserve them for medicine against the claims of "quacks and quasi-religious organizations."[12] Still, he was voicing his disagreements in an ever more direct register. In 1914, Emerson could slightly misconstrue Freud, without acknowledging he was doing so, in writing that the latter considered "usefulness and serviceableness to society . . . the end and purpose of a psychoanalysis"[13]; Freud was not one to think in terms like this of social utility. Further, Emerson could assert, again without signaling his disagreement with Freud, that psychoanalysis was, at bottom, "really elementary moral instruction and training."[14] In subsequent papers he was more combative. Abstracting Freud's 1915 "Instincts and Their Vicissitudes," Emerson "ventured a word of criticism" at the end, suggesting that the paper "lacks in not giving sufficient emphasis to the fundamental social character of all psychic processes."[15] Freud "seems to think ethics has no place in psychoanalytic procedure," Emerson wrote in 1916[16]; or, countering the view that psychoanalysts had no business with ethics, he asserted their fundamental importance. Standards of good and bad were, he held, mobilized in psychoanalysis, even if only unconsciously. By 1919, he was proposing that the unconscious was a vast domain—his understanding of it was topographical—that properly consisted in two parts, one the more familiar repository of impulses, instincts, and cravings, the other "a part capable of training and education." There must be a portion of the mind "capable of learning lessons, of being trained," he maintained, suggesting that it be termed the "subconscious,"[17] a term Freud had used early on but had subsequently subjected to criticism.

Emerson's stance on ethics and educability was in some respects complex, deeply grounded in philosophy. For all his talk of morals, he was no adherent of conventional morality. Indeed, he maintained it was the hysteric's overestimation of such morality, the fact that her impossibly strict ideals—in his experience the hysteric always having "the highest of ideals"—conflicted with her all-too-human desires, that lay at the root of the disease. He was enough the analyst to write that the desires in themselves were not open to change; the analytic task was to "clarify the conflict by making it conscious." A wide chasm between ideals and acts characterized hysterics; they were blind to their "own limitations and absolutely unaware as to just where the conflict really lies." The function of analysis to convince the patient, he wrote, "that virtue consists in virtuous acts, and not in barren purity of thought."[18]

This capacious conception of psychoanalytic ethics and technique was compatible with Emerson's more patently pedagogical orientation, on display in this and other cases. He consistently countered the sexual ignorance of his hysterical patients with facts and instruction. "Told her the facts"; "talked with her and told her about sex, etc."; "told her of possible sex connection"; "explained the sex act somewhat"—scattered through his case notes is evidence of his project of sexual enlightenment.[19] He had no difficulty, in the analytic encounter, wielding the authority of the enlightened schoolmaster; this was but the other side of the haranguing analyst, the miner of buried gems who would not be put off his quest. By contrast, there are hints that he viewed the authority of the analyst proper—the authority embodied in the transference—as slightly illegitimate, akin to what the hypnotist or suggestive therapist conjured up in "abnormally intensified" fashion to dominate his patient as he went about insuring her "personal dependence" on him.[20] In conceiving of the transference in almost uniformly positive terms, Emerson was unwittingly envisioning it as but a variation on hypnotic practice, in which, as John Forrester has pointed out, the sleeping patient was by design subjected to—and cured by—the doctor's magisterial authority.[21] Emerson was thus attributing to the *analyst* the necessarily charismatic power that the suggestive *hypnotist* exercised over his patients—even though Freud had emphasized, fully ten years earlier, that there was "the greatest possible antithesis between suggestive and analytic technique" and that he himself had given up both suggestion and hypnosis early in his practice.[22] In hypnotism the relations of authority between doctor and patient that, in analytic practice, would be "both reinforced and displaced" were nakedly on display, to Emerson's evident discomfort.[23]

Emerson's handling of Freud's 1915 paper, "Observations on Transference-Love," suggests he interpreted the newly named phenomenon of transference-love as, in effect, the distilled essence of transference. As such, he shrank from it as he did from hypnotism, the latter, as Freud noted, replicating the love relationship. Abstracting Freud's paper into English, Emerson not only left "love" out of the title but also opened his summary with a definition of transference as "the situation where a female patient falls violently in love with the physician," with both moves rendering what Freud termed the "sharply circumscribed" problem of transference-love coincident with the problem of the transference in general.[24] Further, although Emerson invoked the violence of the female patient's love, Freud referred to the "violence" of transference-love only once in his paper, near the conclusion discussing the woman of "elemental passionate-ness" who could tolerate no psychical substitutes for the analyst's actual love. From such women, he wrote, "one has to withdraw, unsuccessful." That is, al-though Freud argued it was with "highly explosive forces" and "dangerous mental impulses" that the psychoanalyst dealt, the only violent women in his paper were those he considered untreatable[25]—with Emerson's maneuvers here suggesting he thought of Rachel likewise. At the same time, in another pa-per Emerson was championing "disinterested love," a concomitant of a Jame-sian pluralism or ethical idealism, as a psychoanalytic ideal and an implicit al-ternative to the violence of transference-love. The only desires mentioned in this paper are those of the philosopher.[26]

In this segment of the analysis, it was not that Rachel was proffering her love to Emerson in any of the registers Freud noted in his paper. It was rather that he either ignored or did not recognize her criticisms of him and doubts about him and the treatment—the negative transference. But it mattered little to Freud whether the transferential bond was affectionate or hostile: both, in Freud's words, were indicative of the emotional tie that constituted the transference.[27] The negative transference, so indistinct a phenomenon to Emerson's mind, was what in particular ensured the distinction between psychoanalysis and hypno-sis, for while the positive transference might appear a variation on hypnosis, as Freud pointed out, only the negative transference could take account of the pa-tient's resistance. Suggestive therapy, he wrote, did not allow the analyst "to rec-ognize the *resistance* with which the patient clings to his disease and thus even fights against his own recovery."[28]

Several of Rachel's dreams in this segment of the analysis were expressive of her conflicting wishes toward Emerson. In one, she dreamed he gave her "an or-dinary string with a lot of knots in it which I told her she was to untie. As she did so the string grew heavier and heavier until it became a rope." She then had Emerson tied up in the rope (session 191). In another she dreamed she had Emerson's baby, but that he was trying to take it away from her (session 201). In still others she was angry at him, but, characteristically, placated him. Similarly, her extended struggle to remember what sort of surgery she had undergone at age nineteen may have been one way she was able to express her anger and con-fusion about the analysis. The surgery—most likely pregnancy related, possi-bly an abortion—was, like the analysis, an operation that was to have cured one condition but which had serious postoperative complications. In a letter written to the social worker Edith Burleigh in the midst of the struggle, Rachel announced her intention to leave treatment with Emerson and to spend quiet time in the country with an aunt who "will ask no questions," because, as she said, "I cannot get any relief. . . . my mind is just making my body sick." It seemed to Rachel as if both parties had lost faith in the efficacy of the treatment. She felt Emerson was discouraged. And she felt angry at him, both for not knowing quite how despairing she was and for accusing her of contributing to her illness by not trying (Letter, following session 260). We have no record of how Emerson responded to Rachel's criticisms of him and the treatment. It is doubtful that he recognized them as transferential, for he held that even the positive transference was not completely established in her case. Had it been, had her libido been freed from the brother and father, he would have ensured it did not become attached to himself. "It is necessary, of course, that the *libido* is not allowed to become again fixed, this time on the analyst, but is transferred to more general, perhaps non-sexual, objects, such as is the aim of the highest, broadest, and best education," he wrote, with these words retreating to the safety of the schoolmaster's position as he short-circuited any possibility that the transference neurosis would be allowed to develop.[29] This is not in itself so remarkable; only in 1914 had Freud named the transference neurosis, explaining that it was an artifact of analysis, an illness in which all the formerly disparate transferences were organized around the figure of the analyst.[30] What is remarkable, however, is how tenaciously Emerson clung to his view of the transference as hypnotic effect. In 1930, delivering an address at the annual meeting of the American Psychoanalytic Association, "Some Remarks on Transference," he traced a wholly positive lineage for the transference, organized around statements culled from Freud's early papers—and a reference to Freud's later *Group Psychology and the Analysis of the Ego* (1921), in which the identity of it and hypnosis were asserted—while at the same time suppressing any reference to Freud's repeated attempts to distinguish between the two phenomena.[31]

INCESTUOUS DESIRES

Thus, there are signs that Emerson was withdrawing from the analysis by 1914 and 1915, publishing his final words on it even as it continued to unfold. Although he persisted with Rachel, he appears to have been at a loss about how to handle her worsening condition. He began to enthusiastically underline as he recorded her words, a concrete expression of his excitement when he sensed she was improving. He appears to have been somewhat alarmed by the onset of severe dissociative symptoms,[32] and noted, perhaps as a reassurance to himself, that "Dr. Stearns thinks whole picture hysteria" (session 247)[33]—the diagnosis he was beginning to doubt. On at least one occasion, the criticism of a colleague—Dr. Taylor,[34] who looked in twice during a session with Rachel and voiced doubts about his urging her on—prompted him to let Rachel go "without telling all" (session 219).

"Telling all" in this segment of the analysis brought Rachel and Emerson ever more squarely onto the terrain of incestuous desires, of babies both real and fantastic, of family alliance gone awry and Oedipal prohibitions violated. If Emerson implicitly cast Rachel as the Freudian woman of elemental passionateness, he may also have cast her family as "children of nature"[35] who, in their consistent violations of the usual boundaries between fantasy and reality, and in their refusal of any Oedipal order, appeared insufficiently socialized, even civilized. How was he, as fledgling analyst, to make sense of a family so structured around incest as this one, a family in which the daughter could dutifully play the wife's role and, in finally foreswearing that, harbor dreams of leaving home to set up housekeeping with her brother? Mrs. Frost, an ordinary outside observer, thought in light of everything Rachel told her about the family, it wouldn't have been very wrong for Rachel to kill herself (session 218). Emerson was more measured, encouraged that Rachel had finally renounced her father by this point in the analysis. The brother was still loved, he noted, a circumstance that would have to change before she would recover.[36] Yet, as the analysis progressed, the dimensions of that love appeared to increase, not diminish, and it is possible his doubts about whether she would ever get better did as well.

Emerson may have been correct in his assessment that Rachel had already renounced her father, but her anger at the father only intensified as she remembered more about the onset and nature of his abuse. The abuse started in a tender domestic scene. As a child Rachel would crawl into the parental bed on Sunday mornings, staying near her mother. The father would rise to stoke the fire; the mother would get up; and the father would then return to bed, lying on top of her (session 204). It became his practice to lie on her regularly; at age 13 or 14, she recalled, he started having intercourse with her. In this segment of the treatment, Rachel remembered that the mother caught them several times, and that she reproached not the father but Rachel, telling her she would be disgraced by it and that no one would believe her in any case. Further, the mother did nothing to put an end to the incest, instead commanding Rachel not to tell anyone of it (session 213). As Rachel pieced together a picture of the incestuous sex—remembering first the father's lifting her nightdress, then the feeling of his "trunk" against her, then his actual penetration (sessions 208 ff.)—Rachel oscillated between rage at her parents and self-blame at herself for initiating the sex. She began to cut herself in the midst of pulling together the particulars of the incestuous scene, the first time using a kitchen knife to make a two-inch gash on her left breast (session 200). She also began to take morphine, perhaps as a sedative to ward off the agitating visions, thoughts, and memories (session 204). The drug, however, may at the same time have predisposed her to a mild delirium in which those same visions and memories could have become more intense and frightening.

The father's sexual involvement with the woman Rachel referred to as "aunt" was increasing through the period covered by these sessions, with Rachel telling Emerson that the two had registered at a resort hotel as "man and wife" (session 212). At the same time the father could taunt Rachel for walking out with a man in the evening, asking her "if she had got another fellow and was going to get into trouble again"—his implicit message that her virtue was better protected at home (session 189). The father was continuing to solicit Rachel through these sessions; rebuffed by her one night, he insinuated that she and Emerson were sexual partners, the scene of psychoanalysis a sexual one (session 197). The father's accusation that if she wouldn't have him she must have been having Emerson accurately captured something of the transferential currents that so unsettled Emerson. On the one hand, Rachel dreamed repeatedly of having someone's baby—whether Emerson's (session 201), the father's (sessions 204, 214), or the brother's (session 206). On the other, in a number of dreams she called on Emerson to stanch the father's—and her own—desire. Emerson caught the father, who was chasing her, in one (session 207), while in another Emerson restrained her, holding her so she could not go to the father—precisely the accusation the father had leveled (session 213). Rachel dreamed of asking Emerson to help her (session 232), then of him agreeing to help only if she would tell all, an unreasonable demand she could not meet (session 233). Several days later the father wrote her saying he wasn't getting married after all, and asking her to return home and keep house for him (session 236). With whom would she cast her lot? Her dream the night following the father's lewd insinuation suggests the question was a conflicted one for her. Two men wearing badges—"one with hell the other peace" written on them—came to her, each trying to entice her to join him. Hell offered her money and said pleasant things, while Peace looked sad and merely motioned to her to join him. She first joined Hell, the father, starting to go down a ladder into a hole in the ground with him, but saw something and screamed. She ran to join Peace, who like Emerson picked her up, when she was awoken by a pistol shot (Patient's

Dreams, following session 196). Emerson kept her from the father, but in her dreamlife, and in her father's imagination, reality intruded in the shape of the pistol-penis.[37]

Rachel's conflicted desires for her brother were of an intensity Emerson judged almost delusional, with her eventually all but convinced she was pregnant by him. She both wanted to have sex with him and knew she shouldn't, was both angry at him and filled with yearnings for him. One night, for example, he came into bed with her, hugged and kissed her and caressed her breasts, making "expressive motions" before getting a hold of her legs. "She nearly gave in to his wishes," Emerson wrote, adding she wished she could have (session 192). Many times she thought of running off with him; "I thought I'd like to keep house again and just have him," she admitted (session 201). A dream in which she attempted to rescue him from the temptations offered by his drinking and gambling friends by taking him home and putting him in bed in her room suggests that her imaginative world was as constricted by incest as was the father's (session 200); both of them could cast the family as an especially virtuous space safe from the depredations of the outside world. Rachel turned over the possibility of leaving Boston for Chicago, and dreamed of being out west with Jack, but she couldn't leave (Patient's Dreams, following session 196), dreaming the next night of the father and brother in her bed. Tales of girls who had babies by their brothers reached her (sessions 198, 201), stimulating her thoughts of wanting to do the same.

Rachel began to enact a fallen woman scenario in this segment of the analysis, staging a drama of defiance that was at the same time a fulfillment of her mother's prophecy that, having erred with the father and brother, she would come to no good. Her defiance took the form of going for rides in automobiles—"autoing"—with men or groups of men, some of them married, who fondled her and at least one of whom supplied her with opium (session 224).[38] Rachel went for her first ride in the midst of intense conflict over her desires for her brother. Just before she joined a married Mr. D. in his car for a two-hour-long ride, Mrs. Frost had told her a cautionary tale of a servant girl who had gotten into trouble with her brother, which stimulated Rachel's thoughts of doing the same. The auto ride with a forbidden man was both an enactment of her conflicts, a substitute for the flight with the brother she desired but on which she could not in reality embark, and a temporary escape from them. Rachel was at this point filled with thoughts of killing the father and brother, then herself, the brother because "it wasn't right to go off with him." And she was filled with thoughts of being bad, of trying prostitution, and of cutting herself and "being terrible." That night, after vomiting her supper, she went to sleep only to wake at 2 A.M. and cut herself with a kitchen knife. She also dreamed of the auto ride, of running down people but not hurting them, and of the auto flipping over and her making love to the man—she "was kissing and talking love to him" (session 201).

Rachel identified the feeling of cutting and masturbation as the same (session 204), and, with respect to the former, told Emerson that as a child, when angry, she "just had the desire to cut" (session 201). She would get scissors and cut—paper, the brother's hair and her own, and, while suffering from St. Vitus Dance, herself. Five months later, at a time when she said she was "in a dream most of the time," she told Emerson that she dreamed of cutting herself. "It seems as if it would be a great feeling to slash and cut herself, as if letting the blood flow would relieve her brain," he wrote (session 231). She attempted to control the pure desire from which both the masturbation and the cutting stemmed by behavioral means, tying her nightgown sleeves behind her back to stop the masturbation and locking herself in her room, away from the kitchen knives, to stop the cutting. Cutting, Emerson wrote in the roughly contemporaneous article on the case of hysterical self-mutilation he had treated, "was a sort of symbolical substitute for masturbation."[39] Although he did not record what he said to Rachel about the cutting, he did, early in this segment of the treatment, point out to her "the double significance of her symptoms," telling her they represented both satisfaction and punishment. Rachel replied that she had thought the same thing a week earlier (session 190). Emerson was enough the student of Freud to recognize the pleasure in the pain, quoting the latter's *Three Essays on the Theory of Sexuality* to support his contention. "It has also been claimed that every pain contains in itself the possibility of a pleasurable sensation," Emerson quoted Freud as having written, a position Rachel's equating of masturbation and self-cutting underscored. Later in the same paper Emerson quoted Freud on "the psychic participation in the perversions": "The omnipotence of love nowhere perhaps shows itself stronger than in this one of its aberrations," referring to the "most repulsive" of the perversions.[40]

For much of 1913 and 1914, Rachel worked intermittently as a telephone operator at the Massachusetts Homeopathic Hospital[41] while living with quite a high level of symptomatic distress. She suffered from increasingly frequent and severe episodes of fugue and amnesia, which Emerson loosely called "somnambulism." She suffered as well from dissociative symptoms, such that Emerson wrote "splits" several times in his notes, and an emphatic "Double personality" once. Memories of having had a gynecological operation at age 19, after Jack died, crowded her mind. There was much evidence, to her mind, that it had been an abortion. Jack had accused her of being pregnant as he forced himself on her the second time, and her periods had ceased for a long time after she had had intercourse with him. The mother had thought her pregnant, and had given her tansy, a bitter herb that was known as an emmenagogue.[42] Rachel attempted to go to the New England Hospital to find Dr. Emma Culbertson, one of the surgeons who had operated on her, but she went into a fugue, and was later unable to recall where she had gone instead. She had been told at the time that the operation had been to remove a structure, and, in the context of the analysis, was able to remember a good deal of the ambiance surrounding the operation. The doctors questioned her searchingly, her mother looked on her reproachfully and "kept wondering why," and both parents talked late at night in secretive, hushed tones about her. She had convalesced at home for over a month, the thought she'd had an abortion intruding. But the question of what precisely she had undergone was settled neither at the time of the operation nor in 1914.[43]

Rachel's only contact with Emerson from May 1914 through mid-January 1917 consisted in one session and two letters. In February 1915, she came to the Massachusetts General Hospital to find Emerson, and told him that she was doing well and had been relieved of the worst of her symptoms. In a letter to him written in October the same year, she told of feeling well and of her excitement at undergoing training to be a nurse. Shortly thereafter, however, her condition worsened, and she dropped out of training, to work in a small private sanitarium run by the kindly Dr. Patch.[44] At the time she made no effort to contact Emerson, and did not see him until she was picked up by the police in January 1917, wandering around Brookline in a fugue state, and taken to the Psychopathic Hospital. The final ten weeks of the treatment, from mid-January through early March 1917, were largely focused on her anger and punishing self-recriminations over an affair she'd had with a married man named Harry T. Aspects of the affair repeated earlier patterns and conflicts. For example, Rachel claimed she didn't know he was married while at the same time admitting that the two had used a "secret stamp" to identify their letters to one another in order to hide them from his wife (Nurse's Notes, following session 277). That is, just as with the brother, she both knew and didn't know he was by law—real or psychic—unavailable to her. Further, this Harry, like Jack, forced her to have sex on a lounge with him, a recent scene that Rachel could nonetheless barely remember (session 282). Eventually she was able to remember Harry T. telling her, after he locked the door, that they wouldn't be interrupted and that she would have to do as he wanted (session 290). She struggled, but he, like Jack, told her that her protestations were useless, that no one would hear them and "she would only get tired out" (session 291). Still, she loved him, and she went into a fugue state after renouncing him. Throughout these weeks, she was extremely distraught, and was apparently taking a variety of drugs, some of them administered by doctors, some by one or another of her lovers.

The confusion that runs through Rachel's narrative treatment of her relationship with Harry T. is suggestive of a displaced narrative concerning her feelings toward Emerson. In a dissociated state one evening, she rambled first about her lover: "You see I liked Harry—I knew I hadn't ought to talk so much to a married man and be with him so often." Then, a minute or so later, she turned explicitly to Emerson: "Why did I go to Dr. Emerson. He won't understand. He can't you know he can't" (Nurse's Notes, following session 279). The account she addressed to Harry T., telling him how much she loved him, of all that he had and how little she had, of how he forced her to do his bidding—she later remembered how he "tipped her over in [a] chair" (session 290)—and of how she was complicit might be seen as expressing transferential feelings about her and Emerson. "One moment I hate oh how I hate you, the next well you know. . . . I don't see how you can go into your office every day and not go crazy knowing the tortures you put me through there": these words of rage and disappointment might well have been addressed to Emerson (Letter, following session 283).

Emerson's notes ended abruptly on 6 March 1917, with a mini-recovery of a memory about Harry T.'s seduction that appears to have yielded clarity. But Rachel was unable to function fully, and told Emerson she was going to the Adams Nervine Asylum, where she had been hospitalized before she had begun treatment with Emerson. There is only scant evidence documenting what might have happened to Rachel after the treatment's end. Her letter of 28 August 1917 suggests that she and he had been in contact by mail. She was working as a nurse, but was down and depressed, doubtful she could ever again be open and tell—let alone even know—what was on her mind. "I have got so in the habit of putting matters out of my mind if it is anything disagreeable that I do it before I know what I am doing. Usually over night."

Rachel's rather remarkable letter of 6 January 1919 to Emerson represents a veiled repudiation of him and psychoanalysis. Working hard as a nurse in a cancer ward, Rachel wrote to Emerson that she was virtually cured—not by the

years of psychoanalysis she had undergone with him but by visits to an os-
teopath for a bad back. "He not only cured my back," she wrote, "but it seemed
as if all the nerves were loosened and all the tenseness that I held myself in just
vanished. I can't tell you how different I feel of course I have my blue days but I
get over them the same as anyone else and best of all things stay clear in my
mind and I have no more half-thoughts." We are back here to the days of railway spine, running the movie of the history of trauma backward, to the mid-
nineteenth century, rendering psychoanalysis altogether superfluous.[45]

The case closes with a warm and affectionate note to Mrs. Emerson in which
Rachel related news of her upcoming marriage, delayed while she was ill with
tuberculosis. Her fiancé was "thirty five, tall dark hair and eyes." Five years previously, in 1916, Rachel had written to Emerson that she couldn't "think it fair
what ever I really want to do either my health or some thing has to stop me"
(Letter, following session 270). Whether or not her bitter prediction was realized in this final instance remains unknown.

Chapter 8 Text: Sessions 189–292: 16 May 1913–6 March 1917

LETTER: RACHEL TO EMERSON

5 May 1916
Winchester, Massachusetts
Sunday evening

Dear Dr. Emerson:
Everett came Friday much sooner than I expected but as he had to get back to work I could not wait very long so I told Dr. Adler I would write if I did not see you.
I went up to see Mrs. Frost yesterday. They will not hear to my staying away, so I shall go there in a day or two for a short time anyway.
I am feeling just about the same but I wish more than ever that I had done what I hesitated about doing the other night then every thing would be past.
I received a letter Friday from Miss Burleigh. It must be beautiful to feel about things as she does if only I could.
Father has been here most of the afternoon. They have all gone to church together this evening so I am alone which seems good.

Sincerely yours,
Rachel C.

SESSION 189: FRIDAY, 16 MAY 1913

M.G.H.

Vomiting. Visual and auditory hallucinations of mother. Mother comes to her and tells her what to do when she is puzzled dress-making. Last Saturday mother came to her in dream, told her it was a dream, that brother was sick and for her to go to him. Went next morning and found he was sick with "quincy sore throat."[1] Almost has a delusion that mother *really* comes to her and advises her. Has fainted 3 times at dressmakers and once at home. (last night) Last night she felt as she did when she had the convulsion; went to toilet and got a glass of water; went back to room and walked until finally she *had to give up* and laid down in bed. (11 P.M.). Didn't come to till after 12.

A week ago last Wednesday walked home with Clive L. Met her father. Introduced him. He left. Father asked if she had got another fellow and was going to get in trouble again. Laughed and insinuated. Following this she walked home by herself in a sort of daze—Felt sick at supper and afterwards vomited badly. Since then has vomited a good deal.

Sunday morning lost the use of her legs some time, but after trying and trying, got them back. In the afternoon walked from 3 till after 7. Monday night started to think of brother. (whether she started him sexually) Put it right out of her mind.

Dreamed last night she was falling. Has had a good many dreams like nightmares. Has masturbated a few times, but not much, she says. Has not bitten herself.

Dreamed she masturbated herself with a snake.

PATIENT'S DREAMS

Friday night 16 May 1913[2]

I was running up and down stairs Everett was with me at last I ran out-doors there was a hole in the earth I went down it. There was a funny house there I was looking in all the rooms I came to a closet I tried to open the door. There were cats mewing some place I got the door open just as I woke up.

Thought the hired man had me hanging by my hair I was begging him not to let me drop.

Saturday night May 17

Thought the dress I was making I sewed up all wrong was trying to rip it every thing went wrong.

Sunday night May 18

Going boating tipping over being at the bottom of the sea, seeing all kinds of fish, collecting all kinds of animals.

Thought I went to church found mother singing in the choir, then it seemed as if she had a baby in her arms also a piece of paper which she was reading. I started to cry and had to leave.

Rolling down hill as we used to the last time I got to the bottom mother came and took me away with her telling me to come away from trouble. She then changed to a young girl very pretty I tried to see her back again as she really was I couldn't she was laughing at me.

SESSION 190: MONDAY, 19 MAY 1913

Seemed brighter; walked briskly.

Fainted twice yesterday. 5 A.M. and 5 P.M.

Still vomiting.

Masturbated once or twice.

Got up and got a knife last night.

Head ached badly in morning and brother, who was there, combed her hair. (about 11) Suddenly had a memory picture of him in bed with her when she was about 9. Then she thought of sexual connection and "everything else" and jumped up saying she was nervous. He wanted her to go boating with him and another man named Kitchen but she refused.

Told her of the double significance of her symptoms: 1) satisfaction, 2) punishment. She said she had thought of that herself about a week ago.

Saw her mother but evidently the hallucination is not so vivid as it was.

Mrs. Frost is talking of sending her to Chicago. Rachel has friends there. The first time she had aphonia was when Dr. Putnam was treating her. The first time paralysis was with me. 1st vomiting summer before coming to me.

SESSION 191: THURSDAY, 22 MAY 1913

[Word associations. See Figure 5.]

Monday night dreamed she was sitting in a bed of flowers. Her father came along with a hose and watered them and spoiled them. He laughed because he knew he was going to spoil them.

Last night dreamed brother came with a whole lot of button-holes and threw them on the bed. She started to make them, when the button-holes changed

Word	Asso.	T	Repro. + Remarks	May 22, 1913
head	mind	1⁴	my own	
green	grass	1³	✓	
water	fond	2²	✓	
to sing	choir	1³	✓	
dead	mother	1⁴	✓	
long	way	2	✓	
ship	water	5³	—	
to pay	I didn't hear it	5-3	money	
window	he or	2¹	hear 2 gloss	
friendly	oh, I think I knew I...	16³	I thought I gave anything	
to cook	meals	2¹	—	
to ask	deny	9²	✓	
cold	heat	3²	✓	
stem	flower	2⁴	✓	
to dance	oh, I don't know	15	✓	
village	home	2¹	✓	
lake	home	2¹	✓	
sick	well	3	—	
pride	my own	4	✓	
to eat	vomit	5	✓	
ink	writing	1⁴	✓	
angry	myself	3¹	—	
needle	sewing	1²	✓	
to swim	fun	3²	✓	
voyage	I don't know	16	—	

Figure 5. Jung's association test (Jung 1909), administered by Emerson 22 May 1913 (session 191). Subjects were instructed, upon hearing the word in the left-hand column, to "answer as quickly as possible with the first word that occurs to you" (Jung 1909, 441). The subject's

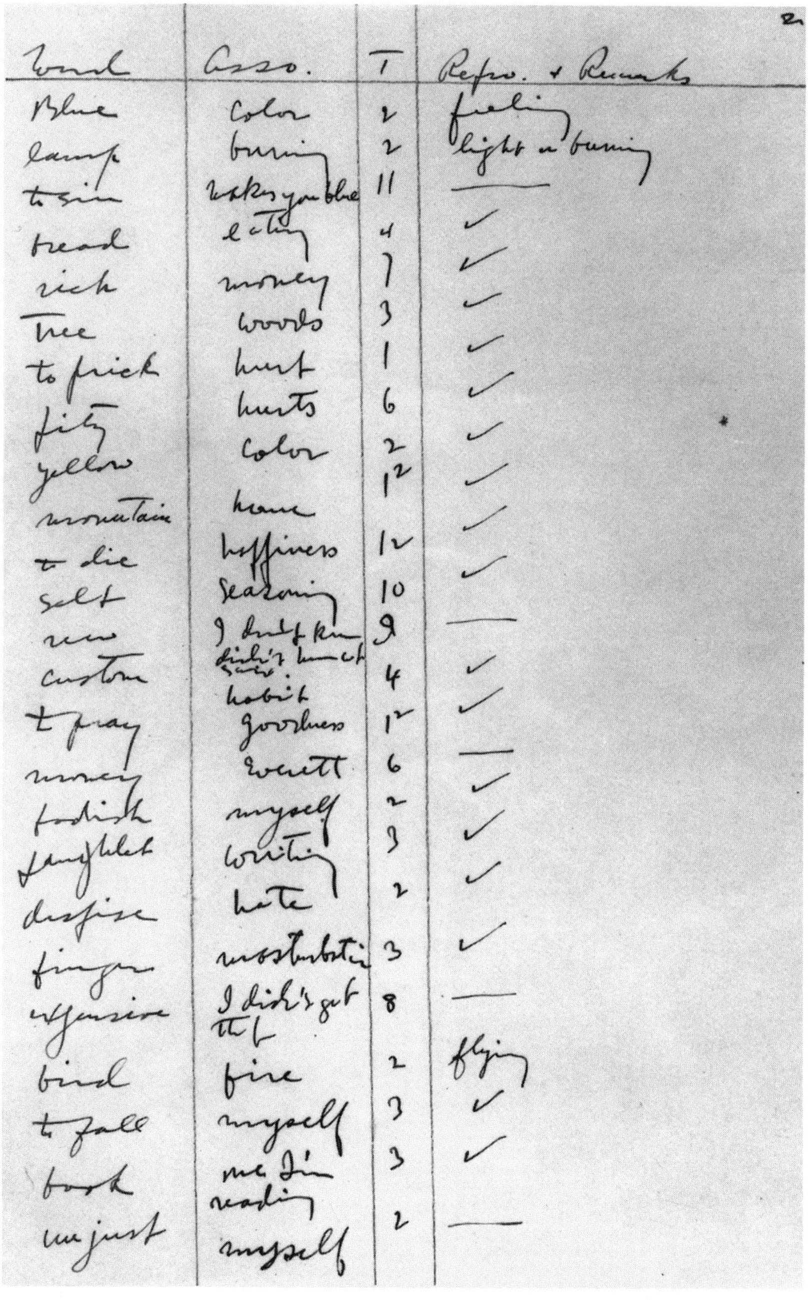

2

Word	Asso.	T	Repro. + Remarks
Blue	Color	2	feeling
lamp	burning	2	light or burning
to sin	makes you blue	11	—
bread	eating	4	✓
rich	money	7	✓
Tree	woods	3	✓
to prick	hurt	1	✓
pity	hurts	6	✓
yellow	Color	2	✓
mountain	name	1^2	✓
to die	happiness	12	✓
salt	seasoning	10	✓
new	I don't know	9	—
custom	didn't hear it / same / habit	4	✓
to pray	goodness	1^2	✓
money	Everett	6	—
foolish	myself	2	✓
pamphlet	writing	3	✓
despise	hate	2	✓
finger	masturbation	3	✓
expensive	I didn't get that	8	—
bird	fire	2	flying
to fall	myself	3	✓
book	me I'm reading	3	✓
unjust	myself	2	—

Figure 5. (*continued*) reaction time, measured in fifths of a second, was recorded in the column headed "T." Words, Jung explained, "are really a kind of shorthand version of actions, situatic .s, and things" (444). Note some of her responses: to "friendly," "I don't

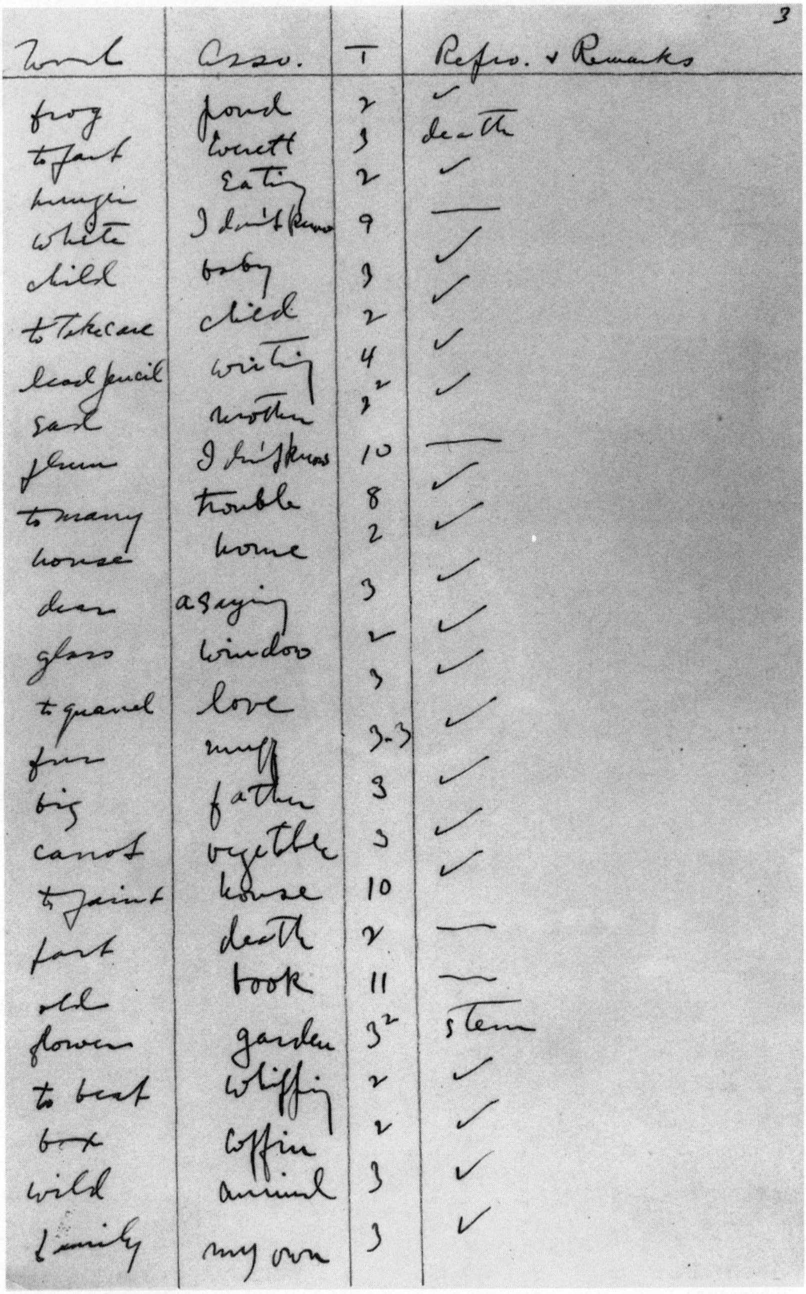

Figure 5. (*continued*) know, I can't think"; to "to eat," "vomit"; to "to die," "happiness"; to
"to think," "myself"; to "to marry" "trouble"; to "to quarrel," "love"; to "to fear," "thoughts";
to "ridicule," "father"; and to "to abuse," "myself." Reproduced, with permission, from the

Word	Asso.	T	Repro. + Remarks
to wash	clothes	1²	✓
cow	milk	1	✓
friend	Enemy	4	✓
luck	good	3	✓
lie	deceive	9	✓
department	School	6	✓
narrow	way	2	
brother	Evcutt	1²	my own
to fear	thoughts	2	——
mother	my own	2	✓
false		300	——
anxiety	worry	4	✓
to kiss	brother	5	✓
bride	marriage	2	✓
furs	girl	1	✓
door	hire	5	✓
to choose	right	5	✓
hay	farm	3	✓
contented	happy	2	✓
ridicule	father	5	✓
to sleep	dream	2	✓
month	this month	7	——
nice	I don't know	17	——
woman	another	3	✓
to abuse	myself	3	——

Figure 5. (*continued*) Boston Medical Library in the Francis A. Countway Library of Medicine.

into links of a chain that enclosed brother and her. Then lots of people came and the chains enclosed them. Then the people disappeared and the chain came back on her bed. Then the closet doors opened, and bureau drawers, etc., and in her clothes there were people. These people surrounded her bed. She woke up crying.

Dreamed I gave her an ordinary string with a lot of knots in it which I told her she was to untie. As she did so the string grew heavier and heavier until it became a rope. Then there was something she doesn't remember. The next thing that she remembers is that she had me tied up in the rope. I started to try to get out when she woke up.

Everett has a sore finger (in reality) so I cut it off (in the dream) and it seemed to grow large and I was making experiments with it. ("I was cutting it up more—I had bottles there.")

Thought brother was dying. Thought he was dead. Was all ready for the funeral when he came to life again. I gave him something again and he died, he kept coming to life, and finally father got onto what I was doing and I woke up.

Dreamed snakes and mice were all over me. I wasn't in bed. I was in the car at one time and snakes and mice were there too. It was all mixed up.

Masturbated 6–8 times Monday night. Fainted twice yesterday 12 noon and 10:30 P.M. Brother called last night—got $2.

Vomits but can eat raw eggs.

Still sees and hears mother.

Monday father called and was scolding about her sewing, etc. She told him about his going with bad women.

PATIENT'S DREAMS

Thursday night, 22 May 1913

Thought I had all the lace curtains down on the lawn in the back of the house. I was trying to walk in between them. Then they all turned black and out of the holes in the lace worms kept coming. I caught a lot and put them in a hole I dug. Everett came and tried to help me. We got discouraged then sat down on the curtains and was eating them saying it was the easiest way to get rid of them.

I went to a meat market and asked for tripe they didn't have but the man wanted me to take frankfurts. I got provoked.

I was in a strange room with a big bed and a small one. I was in the big one mother was there crying and a man. It seemed as if every thing every once in a while would become covered with blood. There was a dog there I wanted them to let me have it but they wouldn't.

Horses running wild in the woods then at home doing something to my room.

Friday night

Thought I was being weighed trying to subtract my present weight from what it used to be. I couldn't do it.

Oiling a floor but couldn't get the spots out. Then putting dirt on it and planting seeds.

It seemed as if I was crossing a field by jumping from stumps it seemed as if I was going but yet I stayed on the same stump all the time. Then it seemed as if I was trying to paint the picture as I stood there.

Dreaming I dropped and really finding myself on the floor.

Thought I went to Dr. Mack[3] she told me what I wanted to know.

I spoke to mother in reality. Mother somehow had awful cuts and I was binding them up.

SESSION 192: SATURDAY, 24 MAY 1913

Fainted once yesterday morning. Masturbated most of the night and bit her upper arm a little.

Did not see her mother so much yesterday but was angry with her for crying so much. Analysis of dream of mother showed she wanted to torture her—said so. This led to brother. He came for some money last night but she refused him. She was in bed, when he came. He sat on her bed. Laid down, etc. Said he wished he had never grown up. He hugged her and kissed her and she him. He made expressive motions "It was his actions." It seemed he caressed her breasts and got hold of her legs, etc. It brought everything back to her mind and she nearly gave in to his wishes. She wished for a moment she would do as she wanted, etc. Finally he left.

She was lying in sofa in hospital while telling this—Felt dizzy—Felt like fainting but didn't.

Brother's finger was bleeding(?) cut(?)—It was sore and he showed it to her last night.

Did not vomit last night but did badly this morning.

Present complex—conflict—is about brother.

PATIENT'S DREAMS

Saturday night 26 May 1913

Going through the house and in every room finding a ladder except in my own room. Then in some way I would go out and come into my room not by the door, as it seemed as if I was trying to find it.

Back to the Psychopathic but yet it seemed as if it was heaven. Mother was there with Everett as a baby. Every one was ringing a bell so I ran back home to get one then tried to go back and fell hitting my leg so I couldn't walk. The ground started to slip away from me. I woke up just as it seemed as if I saw hell.

Tying our two cats' tails together. Everett undid them scolding me then he tried to make me drink some thing after a while I did and then every thing turned beautiful. We were walking in the air over people.

Went over all that happened with Everett the other night.

Something about the hospital being afire and it seemed as if I had two bodies trying to get them there to burn. You took one away from me. I still tried to carry the other but being mad and tired I couldn't and started crying.

Sunday night

Had father buried all but his head then bringing every one I knew to see him wouldn't give him any thing to eat.

Making a lot of aprons.

Taking all the dishes I could find and breaking them also the windows, screaming as loud as I could then I ran out doors and came to this pond of blood just alive with dead cows I crossed by jumping from one body to another. Then it seemed as if some thing took me up and carried me back to my bed.

Going to mother's grave, finding it empty. I took off all my clothes getting in the box putting the dirt over me. Then snakes began to come and worms winding them around me to make a dress. Trying to get out of the box again.

SESSION 193: MONDAY, 26 MAY 1913

Sunday night. Dreamed she was hunting for her mother in her grave. The grave was empty and she couldn't find her. So she got in the box and was trying to get the dirt over her. Then a lot of snakes and worms came in and she tried to make a dress out of them. She tried to wind them around her, then she was skinning them.

Dreamed she was running and breaking dishes and windows, then started screaming and ran out doors and came to a pond of blood with a lot of dead cows in it. Ran around it, couldn't get across. At last got across it by jumping from one cow to another. Then somebody picked her up and carried her back to her bed.

Saturday night dreamed ladders started in the middle of the floor and went up through the roof of every room but hers. She was locked in her own room, hunting for a door to get out. Finally got out through the wall—It seemed as if she went out and came back again but wasn't satisfied because she couldn't find the door.

Brother came Sat 3:15 paid back $2. Wanted to know why she acted so diff[icult?],[4] etc.

Father came yesterday. "Auntie" stayed in room.

Fainted twice Saturday 4:30 (after brother) and 4.

Fainted once yesterday 10.

Masturbated a lot Saturday night. Vomited badly right along.

Dreamed last night of being pregnant. Thought she was different from everybody else and could have a child without intercourse. She thought something about the way Jesus was born. Different people in the dream: Jack, Everett, Mother, "I'll be her and she'll be I." When she woke up she thought of blood. Father wanted her to go with him and Everett to put flowers on mother's grave.

SESSION 194: TUESDAY, 27 MAY 1913

Dreamed she was picking flowers. I came and she was angry with me. Then she gave me some flowers to make up for her angry feelings. But I wouldn't take them and she woke up trying to get ways of making me accept.

Dreamed the kitchen was being painted. The walls were green and the floor in squares. She thought she was glad the walls were not red.

Dreamed of being pregnant.

Some girls came to see her last evening. Playing cards, she couldn't seem to say what she wanted to. At times said 'no' when she meant 'yes,' etc. At other times seemed unable to talk at all.

Last night was very nervous. About 12 had a big flow of menstrual blood. Lasted only a short time and then stopped. She felt so nervous she knew she would masturbate if she left her hands free so she tied her sleeves; but got out; then she put on mittens but got them off; then she tied her hands behind her back and after that slept a little.

She fainted this morning about 4. She was up walking around.

Dreamed she was having great trouble with her sewing machine. (She had broken a lot of needles in the afternoon and also a wheel.) She thought she was taking her machine apart and fixing it. Then in some way it changed into her body and she was cutting it up. She cut off her legs, arms, hind, etc. and was cutting up the trunk. Then she seemed to be taking needles out of her body and putting them in the machine. She woke—After this she had another dream, which she cannot remember. Then she seemed to go into a sort of dream, more like a day-dream, and when she came out of this she had *cut her right ankle* with a *pen-knife* she has for ripping with.

Did not bite herself.

Is thinking of going West (Chicago) but doesn't want to leave her brother and father.

Has vomited just the same. Has not seen mother so much. Dreamed of mother last night. She seemed reproachful and when she woke thought it was because she had told me.

SESSION 195: WEDNESDAY, 28 MAY 1913

Has not fainted and did not vomit till she reached hospital this morning. Has not masturbated or cut herself.

Dreamed last night she was lying on a board and I was sitting in a chair questioning her. I moved my chair about, circling her.

During a dream-like state she took everything out of her drawers, closets, trunks, etc., off the bed and bureau, and put them in the middle of the floor. She did not move the pictures off the walls but did off the bureau. *She tore her brother's picture to bits.* She has no idea as to why she did all this, but thought perhaps she was hunting for something. She had been searching her mind all the afternoon and evening for her repressed memories. She did not go to bed but sewed nearly all night. Slept a little in her chair towards morning. 'Twas then she dreamed.

She has been thinking of going away; yesterday she said she thought of going to some hotel and being a waitress during the summer.

SESSION 196: THURSDAY, 29 MAY 1913

Used to try to kill her brother when she had St. Vitus Dance. Played with snake to show off before "William."

Pulled her clothes all out again. Caught herself doing it again last night. After that felt mad and knew she'd masturbate if she did not tie her hands and did so.

Fainted about 8. Mrs. Frost there. When she came to called out her brother's name.

Dreamed she was being chased by boys in the woods.

Told how T. used to give her candy and take her to amusements.

Had a picture of her brother about 6 she 10. Thinks that was when they began intercourse.

PATIENT'S DREAMS

Thursday night 29 May 1913

Thought I went to Chicago and when I got there all the folks were sitting in high chairs. I said I thought you were all grown up they said no we went back to children again so then I wanted to just then mother came and said no as I would be too much bother. A fire then started all the others vanished but mother and I couldn't get out. Mother burned to death and every thing was burned from me.

It seemed as if two men came to me both with badges one with hell the other peace. They both wanted me to come with them the one with hell kept offering me things [in Emerson's hand: took things out of pocket—money (father)] and saying pleasant things while peace looked sad and motioned me to come. I did not know what to do. Then we went out doors and there were two holes in the ground each with a ladder one going down the other up. I decided to go with hell but just as I was going down I saw some thing which made me scream and I ran back to peace he picked me up then a pistol shot woke me up.

Up to the cemetery everything was brown and dead. Starting to plant seeds. I went with Mr. Kitchen to an entertainment we danced for a while then a man came on the stage and did some magic tricks. He would give you anything you asked for so I went up to him got what I wanted. Mr. Kitchen wanted to know what it was I ran home he after me.

Saturday night

Thought the sewing I had finished Mrs. Frost brought to me all ripped up saying I had not done it I denied it then you came and said as she did and told me it was another disillusion.

Was walking along the street came to a market in the window was a large cake of ice and on it was a baby I went in and demanded to have the child taken off.

Catching birds, then somehow my ring grew large and I was putting them through it.

Pregnant dream.

Sunday night

Thought I was with Jack out West.

Back to the school in a lot of trouble, then it seemed as if I was shut up in the closet with the skeleton.

I had two children in my arms trying to kill them drowning, cutting, biting, hiding.

In the woods as a child then as I am now. Back in our yard, up in my room.

Trying to write a letter then my hand got paralyzed.

I was going to bed found father and Everett in my bed.

Some thing about seeing a great load of grapes and wanting them.

SESSION 197: MONDAY, 2 JUNE 1913

Fainted Friday night and yesterday morning. Put everything in middle of floor this morning. Has vomited as usual.

Thursday noon kept her dinner down.

Thursday night told father she wouldn't see him again. Met him and he wanted her to come to his room. Locked her in but she got key away from him. One thing led to another. He insinuated things about her relation to me. (see second dream) Talked with him till she lost her voice.

Yesterday saw mother—battled 3 hours—Fay came—cross—cried—felt better—girls came and better. After girls left went to bed. Kept seeing father, mother, Miss Burleigh and me. Morphine.

Started to masturbate once and after that tied her hands behind her back.

SESSION 198: WEDNESDAY, 4 JUNE 1913

Not vomiting so badly.

Fainted yesterday 2 A.M. about 15 minutes. Was dreaming badly. Thought she was a girl again teaching a Chinese boy to read as she used to do. It seemed as if he and I went to China. He used to say we'll go and I seemed to be living [illegible] just what I used to do.

Seemed in heaven.

Thought that Mrs. Frost had died. Breaking up housekeeping and father came in and bought the house and I went to the woods and got in some water and was drowning.

Thought she was trying to see what would kill guinea-pigs. They became surrounded by snakes which killed them. Went out in the yard and played with one snake.

Didn't sleep at all last night. But took no morphine. Felt like it but did not masturbate.

Free associations. "It seems foolish, I didn't know why I thought of it, but I thought I had a lot of eggs and was smashing them—time when I got mad with mother and did smash a lot of eggs. She found me with the snakes and scolded me and wanted me to go for some sitting eggs—I went and got them with the intention of breaking them when I got back, she had to pay—and I smashed them 1 after 1 on kitchen floor. Think of snake in our yard now, how it stays around there and I can do anything with it I want to—it brings back the thought of what I did with a snake. I don't like it. I think of other cross things I did to her (mother). Used to put snakes in the hen-house. She wouldn't dare touch the snakes and would call me. I wouldn't touch them till I got ready.

I was thinking that sometimes when I didn't know what I was doing I could take something and end it all.

Was going over last night everything that happened the afternoon mother confessed.

Mother standing in front of her.

She may reproach me for Everett.

If I could stop seeing her I could think of something.

There seems something more connected with mother's confession. The mother-image keeps coming to her and looking reproachfully at her. It seems as if mother wanted to tell her something. As a matter of fact, patient left mother when she was confessing and refused to hear all she wanted to tell. She left when mother was still talking but cannot remember what she said. A number of times after that when mother tried to talk again about it, she "shut her up" or left.

When home, between being at M.G.H. and Psychopathic, patient heard of a girl (14) having a baby by her brother. It was common talk and the brother was said to have confessed.

SESSION 199: FRIDAY, 6 JUNE 1913

Mother's confession, last words, brother, Henry.
She was talking Thursday about Henry. Always quoting him. He used to pretend to come to see Rachel. "I used to tell her I wish she wasn't married then she could have him."
She sent Henry after her that night. (confession)[5]
I thought of what I did last night. I was kind of dazed and I wrote a letter to you I had the poison. (strichnine).[6]
Yesterday repeated last day in somnambulism. Mother confessed Henry and Jack wanted to know. Why I couldn't care for Henry as I did for Jack. She enjoyed [?] this fellow in Worcester, while she had relations with to [sic] Jack. She told her if she didn't look out he would get her.
Patient did blurt out something when she left. (The scene of all this is the confession)
Sees mother and hears her. She seems [illegible] like saying, "Ah! Rachel!"
I knew I asked mother the early part of that afternoon about babies and what she said made me sick. She asked me why I asked her about such queer questions. Dr. Putnam wanted someone in the Social Service to explain things to me and I wouldn't listen and I asked her what it meant and she said I ought not to talk about such things.
It was some idea. I knew one couldn't have a baby without connection and I asked her if one had to have a baby, and how long it took, etc.
Complex: confession of mother; questions she asked; Jack, Henry, Mother's seducer, Father, Brother, babies; pregnancies, how to tell, fear—[7]

SESSION 200: MONDAY, 9 JUNE 1913

Dreamed Friday night that she was sailing through the air (on something). Came to a city that at first looked beautiful, but as she looked it changed to bad, and kept changing back and forth to beautiful and bad. When it was bad, she saw her brother there. He was walking along the street. There were other fellows there tempting him to drink and gamble and such things as that. It seemed as if she followed him and was visible or invisible as she chose. She tried to take him away from temptation. Finally picked him up and carried him home and put him in her bed with her mother. It was my room.

Was at some social gathering. Contest. Had to say alphabet. Got to w. Woke up thinking she was in a well.

It seemed as if she killed herself in some way. Came back and told me her mother did want to tell something, etc. Miss Burleigh and I wanted her to stay, etc.

Yesterday morning seemed like a room with a great steeple in it. Out of the steeple came snakes. The air was filled snakes were all around her and she woke up screaming.

Something about Mrs. Frost being killed.

Cut herself—2″ her left breast—yesterday morning. Kitchen knife. This was before the dreams. It was after this that she went to sleep.

Masturbated yesterday morning after cutting.

Didn't know how long pregnancy was. Thought it was a number of years. Dr. Putnam, Miss Burleigh, and Miss H.[8] set her thinking. Asked mother how long it took. Mother wouldn't tell her.

Asked her how anyone would know. "She looked at me awfully strange."

Fainted for a short while just after she knew she had cut herself. Seemed as if she were thinking of blood.

Heard her mother playing yesterday afternoon and came downstairs. Could see her sitting at the piano and asked Mrs. Frost before she realized it wasn't so.

Blood—cats—menstruating—babies—bring them Everett—cut on his finger—fixing it (Saturday)—bit myself—Him—coming up in my room Saturday.

Threw an egg on the floor.

Note from Father.

Dreamed of a necktie—something about it hanging her. (she is making one for Everett).

Told Everett she was going to kill herself. He wouldn't leave her till she promised not.

SESSION 201: TUESDAY, 10 JUNE 1913

Cut herself (2 A.M.) Right side. Had locked door but got up and went down to kitchen and got kitchen knife.

1st dream. About auto ride. (Went in afternoon with married man) Repeated it in dream. Running down people. Ran right through a store, but didn't hurt anything. Finally auto turned over and she made love to man—was kissing him and talking love to him. Woke.

2nd. Thought she was all undressed and on top of a bush in front yard.

3rd Dreamed of killing her father.

After this got control of her feelings, as she thought, and then it was she cut herself.

Has had lots of times the thought of going off with Everett. Had it last night, about 10:30—11. "I thought I'd like to keep house again and just have him."

Has thought of prostitution—New York and other big cities.

Mrs. Frost told of a servant girl who got in trouble with her brother. They remembered how white she looked. They told how this girl went off with her brother it was their servant. This made Rachel think of going off with her brother 6:30 lasted about an hour. Was thinking about the 2 when she started in auto ride. Gradually forgot it in ride but when she got back 9:45 began thinking about it again. Went to sleep thinking about. "I just buried my face in my pillow and made myself stop thinking about it." Some days she thinks of it a lot and other days not at all.

Mr. D.—man who took her on auto ride.

"Think of killing myself. Think of killing father and brother before myself."

4 or 5 times a day perhaps—some days more than others. After I left dinner thought of killing brother because it wasn't right to go off with him. Often thinks of father and his actions. Did not masturbate.

Fainted twice last evening.

Vomited supper.

"It's just entered my mind but I'd put it right out, I couldn't think of it." i.e. about being bad.

Mother said if any girl has fell she would rather have her die, but if she did live she might go ahead and do as she had. Says she has this thought all the time. This comes, then the thought "Why shouldn't I?"

First only ever felt like cutting and being terrible. After she got to her room. When she was a child and got mad used to get the scissors and would cut paper. Just had the desire to cut. Cut brother's hair off and her own. Did cut herself in St. Vitus Dance.

PATIENT'S DREAMS

Tuesday

I was taking pins out of Everett and he doing the same to me. Then I thought it was a dream and asked him why I should keep dreaming that dream that it must mean something and that I shouldn't tell about it.

I started to come to the hospital I got on the elevated train it went off the track all the people fell with it but when it was falling I jumped out mother appeared and caught me and threw something over my head I could feel myself going up and down when she uncovered my face I was in a beautiful garden sitting among flowers she stood watching me when a man came up to me and asked me if I didn't know my father, mother got mad hit him and he disappeared then she picked me up and threw me as it seemed out of a house after that it was as if I lived and yet I didn't.

A man came into my room and was building a chimney on my bed on top of me I would kick it over as fast as he would build. He got mad started to choke me.

Everett was dying and I was trying to get a Doctor. People would keep coming into the room laughing I was crying and trying to get someone to help me. Then we were on a raft on top of a train going awfully fast something happened and we fell off.

Wednesday night

Thought I cut my stomach and took out a baby from it knew I hadn't ought to have it wanted to bury it but it cried so I couldn't I was undecided what to do.

I was in a room with nothing but blackboards in it I was writing and drawing pictures then a bed came in the room someone undid my hands and I went to sleep.

Something broke in my head. Then it seemed as if I had a tub full of eggs and some one was pouring blood over them to color them. Then some way I had your baby and you were trying to get it from me.

Praying them perfectly happy every thing being changed.

Thought father came to see me bringing Everett in too telling me something about disgracing.

SESSION 202: THURSDAY, 12 JUNE 1913

Cut herself last night lightly 3 times on right wrist. Fainted last night and this morning. Vomits her eggs now.

It came out finally why her mother looks at her so: Her father used to get in bed with her; lie on her; etc. She would try to get away and would call to her mother only then would he go. Mother would look reproachfully at her, as if she could help it if she wanted to, not accusing openly but really. Father was doing this when she first came in to M.G.H.: Apparently it has been his practice all her life.

This came to her in the car this morning. She has thought of it before, but never when with me. When she thought of it before, it never stayed with her but went out of her mind again immediately.

Remembered when brother was 3 or 4 and she 7 or 8 she played with his genitals.

SESSION 203: FRIDAY, 13 JUNE 1913

Has had no inclination to bite or cut herself.

Did feel like masturbating but tied her hands and did not.

Saw her mother a little last night while half-asleep, but no other time.

Fainted last night.

Seemed just about to think of more about her father when dropping off to sleep but would wake feeling badly.

SESSION 204: MONDAY, 16 JUNE 1913

Fainted Saturday evening at Gertrude C.'s—said to be a little like the old convulsions only not so severe. Her father had come to Gertrude and complained of Rachel's treatment of him, etc. She got madder and madder, wished he were dead, thought of the pain in her side and wished she had stabbed him etc., finally fainted.

No cutting—no biting—no masturbating.

Saturday night: Dreamed she was dead and in a coffin. As they were carrying it to the grave one of the men stopped and fell and let her drop. The coffin split open and she struck her head against something which brought her to life. Then everybody started having convulsions at seeing her.

Dreamed she was eating snakes.

Dreamed she was with her brother.

Sunday night: Dreamed she was lying down, trying to get away from her father. There was a baby in the dream, but what the connection was she does not know. Whenever she thinks of her father and tries to think of what he did she gets so angry she feels like tearing and cutting him, then herself—She cannot think of what he really did—to say it. Took morphine yesterday morning and last night.

Saw her mother yesterday but not today and not Saturday.

She has not masturbated but she identified the feeling of it, biting, and cutting, as the same.

She says she started it all by crawling into bed with her father and mother Sunday mornings when a child. Her father used to plague her so she would stay near her mother. But then he would get up and build the fire; then her mother would get up, and she would go to sleep again sometimes. Then her father would come back to bed and she would find him practically on top of her, etc.

SESSION 205: WEDNESDAY, 18 JUNE 1913

Fainted yesterday in Jordan Marsh's.[9] Has not cut, bit, or masturbated herself. Got a letter from father.

The thing she tried to get, and failed to get, this morning was, the *actual meaning of coitus by father.* Whenever she went to look everything went black or blank. Her mother also stood in front of the memory. Her mother used to tell her not to tell as nobody would believe her. Used frequently to talk about it, mother telling her she dreamed it, etc.

"I want to get well and do things but I can't face that."

SESSION 206: FRIDAY, 20 JUNE 1913

Dreamed Wednesday night she had sexual relations with her brother then she had a baby. At first it seemed as if the baby were born as usual then as if it were given her. She tried to destroy it, then she was running away from somebody and was trying to protect it. Then she woke and was terribly angry. After that she bit herself slightly on right upper arm. Fainted too. Did not sleep last night. Lies down.

Remembers mother accused her of wrong relations with father. Either one morning when she found them together or the house she made her confession. "It seems as if it were right on the edge of my mind all the time but if I go to say it I can't say it and if I go to think it I can't think it."

"I cannot say it. I remember it in my throat, so to say, but I can't speak it." (Intercourse with father) "When I go to look at it it seems as if I fill right up with angry feelings." "When you spoke of pain it made me think of a dream I had the other night." After great resistance I got out the following dream of Wednesday night, after dream of brother and before biting.

Dreamed she was cutting her genitals to get out a child. Then her father appeared and cut her genitals some more and got the child out and then they both seemed to be trying to cut the child up to destroy it. Then she tried to put it back in her body but was not able to. She felt that it was wrong.

SESSION 207: MONDAY, 23 JUNE 1913

Condition unchanged. No cuts and bites. Dreamed Saturday night her father was chasing her cat, whose tail was on fire. I was chasing her father. Her father caught the cat and cut his tail off. I caught her father and was choking him. She then got her cat which changed in some mysterious way into a baby.

SESSION 208: TUESDAY, 24 JUNE 1913

Condition unchanged. No bites, cuts, or masturbation. Fainted a short time 7:30. Did not sleep. Lies down with eyes closed.
Terrible resistance.
Remembered *pain* in genitals. Practically got memory of act, but finally went off into a sort of half dream. Half with mother half here.
Mrs. Frost telephoned she seemed disturbed, and memory troubled—To see she comes in tomorrow.
She knew yesterday, for a moment, what she was after, then it went again.
She almost got the whole thing today. She remembered her father in bed with her. Trying to get away from him. He got her night-dress up. Scuffling, and all but got *it*.
Brother has been discharged.

SESSION 209: WEDNESDAY, 25 JUNE 1913

Confused—no other symptoms.
Remembered finally father prevented her from calling mother. (Reason she sees mother so much is: she called, or started to call for her all the time, longed and prayed for her, but she didn't come then, now she comes in imagination and prevents the dread)
Remembered feeling his "trunk" against her genitals but can not remember the insertion.
Almost got it today. Her mother seems to be in it.
Her feeling against knowing it is tremendous. First she feels she would like to tear and rend her father in her anger, then it turns against herself. She is one mass of anger and will-not-to-have-it-so. She "wants" to face it, but cannot.

Told Mrs. Frost this morning it was about her father and she couldn't face it. She can feel it almost come and then go into her legs—she kept rubbing them they became so numb.

Neither bit, cut, nor masturbated. Was in a more amenable mood.

Walked and walked yesterday afternoon.

SESSION 210: THURSDAY, 26 JUNE 1913

Slept occasionally last night but had a series of seeming nightmares—She would think it was so (father incest) then not.

Woke herself saying "I know it." Then saying "it isn't so."

At Fay's house had a sort of faint. Wanted to tear her clothes and hurt herself but they held her hands. It was not so severe as usual.

SESSION 211: MONDAY, 30 JUNE 1913

Has not injured herself. Did not faint until 4 A.M. today. *Legs ache*—sharp pains, etc. since Friday.

Last night got to place where she gave up in mind and body. Today got the next move when father lifted night-dress last time. When she goes to look at what comes next, everything becomes blank.

She sometimes remembers standing up afterwards but mind skips essential thing.

LETTER: RACHEL TO EMERSON

6 July 1913
Sunday afternoon

Dear Dr. Emerson:

Mrs. Frost told me she called you up Thursday morning but I could not come in as my legs were so bad and I couldn't walk well.

I can walk much better to-day otherwise I am about the same.

I go out to the hospital to-night so as to start work tomorrow morning.

I have Wednesday morning off but will have to be back to work at one.

Friday I got everything for a second I think, and my head felt so relieved but then it went and I can't get it again.

Yours Truly
Rachel C.

SESSION 212: WEDNESDAY, 9 JULY 1913

Morphine Thursday night, Sunday night, Tuesday night. Cut her breast Friday night.

Friday 11 A.M. knew it for 15 minutes. Was at Fay's and father called. She was lying down and refused to see him.

Dreamed last night her father did have intercourse with her.

Is dreaming of cutting, torturing, father, etc.

The thought causes the fainting.

Has been dreaming of having babies—once by father. (Friday night)

Yesterday, at the board (telephone operator at Homeopathic Hospital), thought she saw a baby sitting in the middle of the floor and began to feel faint.

Legs have pained her terribly. Thursday fainted several times during the day because her legs pained her so.

Father was at Bass Point with "aunt" Sat and Sunday nights. (Registered as man and wife)

"It seems as if I knew it when I took the morphine."

Used to faint just before going to Nervine. Used to faint when she saw her father; when anyone talked of pregnancy, etc.

"All the pains in my legs seemed for a moment to come to my genitals and then they went right back."

SESSION 213: FRIDAY, 11 JULY 1913

Dreamed Wednesday night of a train wreck. Her mother seemed to come out of every car. Her father was there and she wanted to go to him but I was holding her and wouldn't let her go. Everything seemed to be on fire. Her clothes were.

Last night "it" seemed to come from her legs into her throat. It seemed as if she would choke, and couldn't breathe or swallow. It started about 5—got there at 8 and lasted till 4 A.M.

No self-injury—no fainting. Lying down with eyes closed (keeps opening)

Coming from my legs to my throat it stopped on the way in my genitals, i.e. pain or "it." (Last night)

It seems as if she gets it for a moment but can't hold it.

Finally got it.

Mother caught them. Accused her and blamed her for it all. Said now she knew why she went off always when her father did (when she was tracking him). Accused her of incest with brother Everett. Remembered father had had

intercourse with her a good deal but can't remember each time. Knew it all—
but when I tried to get her to tell it all repressed some of it.

Said her legs were all right now.

"I won't see it. I want to die. I wish I were dead."

SESSION 214: TUESDAY, 15 JULY 1913

Better until yesterday. Began dreaming again. Gertrude S.[10] came out to hospital to see her. Talked of mother etc.

Dreamed last night she had a baby and father took it away from her. Mother
seemed to be cutting herself up in a table. Mother told her, the afternoon she
confessed, that her father had said she followed him. Knows her father had intercourse with her many other times.

SESSION 215: THURSDAY, 17 JULY 1913

Decidedly better. Legs better; head better.

Tuesday night

Woke up sucking her left arm (made it sore, used to suck blood)—Was
dreaming of a baby. Thought there was a baby in bed with her.

Before that dreamed her father was chasing her and woke up just before he
caught her.

Dreamed she was with mother in heaven.

Fainted for a short time Tuesday night.

Remembers other times with father but all in a lump—cannot differentiate.

Feels so terribly angry that if she should let herself go she would scream con-
tinuously, and throw her legs and arms about in a convulsion.

Forces her father out of her mind but every once in a while something reminds her of him and all her terrible feelings surge back.

SESSION 216: SATURDAY, 19 JULY 1913

Better. No self-injury. No morphine. Fainted for short time last night. Legs
better. Head better.

Dreamed she was going to hospital. Saw baby on steps. Picked it up. Refused
admittance. Mother came took baby from her. Woke up at home and father
seemed beside her.

Thursday night—dreamed she was at switchboard. Things kept coming out of the jacks. The room was filled. A doctor came she told him she couldn't get out because the room was full.

SESSION 217: MONDAY, 21 JULY 1913

Cut her right leg a little Saturday night. Fainted just before. No other symptoms.
Knows there were other things with father but cannot remember them.
Thinks he began coitus with her when she was perhaps about 13.
Had a strong fight last night not to take morphine—Did not.
Dreamed she was in a chain crawling in and out of the links. The links were rope, snakes, and other animals.
Remembered her father and mother gave her a gold bracelet on 18th birthday. Henry was there. Refused it. Forced on her. Burnt it in stove. Father angry. Told him he knew why.
Remembers often destroying money he gave her from 10 on.
Thinks the discovered coitus was after Jack's death, *before,* 1st convulsions.
Knew Jack about 6 months. Just knew him at 18.

SESSION 218: WEDNESDAY, 23 JULY 1913

Has not fainted—no self-injury—getting on all right with work. Vomits. Legs better. Sitting by the death-bed of Mrs. Frost (86) this 3 A.M.. Told her all she knew. Was trying awfully hard to remember rest about father. Suddenly seemed to know it but couldn't speak it. Mrs. Frost said afterwards she couldn't make her speak for half an hour. After she came out of this state she knew she knew it but couldn't remember. While she knew it, head felt clear, and felt generally all right. When she told Mrs. Frost her trouble and how she wanted to kill herself Mrs. Frost said she didn't think it would be very wrong. So she went to her room and got some dichloride she took from the hospital, but she couldn't bring herself to take it.
Wrote her father if he didn't stop talking about her she would tell things on him, that she knew more than he thought.

SESSION 219: FRIDAY, 25 JULY 1913

Fainted 2 yesterday. No other symptoms except vomiting. Remembered rest about father. Wouldn't tell all. Mother did catch them a number of times. Not all relations at home. Promised not to tell.

Dr. Taylor heard some; looked in twice—doubtful about my urging her, etc. Therefore I let her go without telling all.

SESSION 220: TUESDAY, 29 JULY 1913

About same—no injuries—but faints and vomits.

Thinks father began when she was about 13 or 14—remembers 3 or 4 times mother found them.

Used to ask mother to lock her up, to let her go away, etc.

Can't become reconciled. Mother used to talk a great deal about it in days she found them. Made her promise not to tell. Told her she would be disgraced and looked down on.

Got a letter from her father which she hadn't opened.

Wrote out all she could remember of what she got Friday—Did not bring it in however.

Chauffeur at hospital won a doll asked her to dress it—dreamed—baby—father etc.

LETTER: RACHEL TO EMERSON

1 August 1913
Massachusetts Homeopathic Hospital

Dear Dr. Emerson:
I did not come in Thursday because I did not feel able to and I am not coming in tomorrow. My voice is quite a little better so that I worked for a while this morning but I feel so cross all over that I just can't come in tomorrow and talk about those things so please don't feel angry with me and I will try to come in Monday. I will anyway whether I feel like it or not.

If it isn't all right for me to come Monday would you please let me know at Mrs. Frost's Sunday.

Sincerely yours,
Rachel C.

SESSION 221: MONDAY, 4 AUGUST 1913

Cut her legs last Thursday night.

Says she feels different now than ever before: i.e., feels all the things as if electricity were flowing through her.

Has had several sort of fainting spells = stiffened but was conscious. Can't become reconciled.

SESSION 222: WEDNESDAY, 6 AUGUST 1913

Very much better. No self-injury. Slept well night before last. Last night sleepless. Thinks she fainted during the night. Was walking around—and came to[,] found herself on the floor.
Feels afraid most all the time. Alternates between *fear* and *anger*.
Man (Hospital Chauffeur) who has been showing her marked attentions came to Winchester after her and practically *proposed*. (Refused absolutely) She was thinking about it last night.

SESSION 223: FRIDAY, 8 AUGUST 1913

Better—no self-injury—no fainting, vomiting same.
Last night had a very bad dream and woke saying *"I am not"* (pregnant?[11])—felt nauseated and vomited. As she did so felt the presence of her *father*.
Since she was in Wednesday had not seen mother. After this, however, saw her mother occasionally. Knows (last 3 days felt this) there is something trying to come to her mind; represses it; vomits.

POSTCARD: RACHEL TO EMERSON[12]

3 August 1913

These are some pictures that were taken. The cross is where the office is. I hope you arrived safely.

Sincerely,
Rachel

LETTER: RACHEL TO EMERSON

18 August 1913
Winchester, Massachusetts

Dear Dr. Emerson:
I don't know what to write or at least I can't write it.

I feel a little happier tonight in a way as I saw Everett this afternoon and I did want to see him so much. He is down here for a few days.

I haven't seen or heard from father again.

My work is going along fairly well most of the time.

Three or four times before you went away I raised up quite a little blood but thought it was caused by strain of vomiting so much so I didn't say anything about it to you but in my talk Tuesday night over the telephone with Miss Burleigh I told her as Sunday it was quite bad. She had me promise if it happened again I would call up Dr. Putnam and tell him. I was all right as far as that went until Saturday and then I kept raising a little at a time off and on all day and until yesterday so last night I called Dr. Putnam up. He thinks most likely it is just what I thought but said if it didn't stop to call him up in a few days (or any way). To-day I haven't seen any thing at all and I feel better so perhaps it has stopped.

I have that same dream again quite often but I never can get it or clear anything up. It makes me so sick at the time (or I suppose it is that) that I can't think of it at the time. I have some fairly good nights. I don't see mother so much only hear her.

There is no use of my trying to write any more as I can't write how I feel or what I want to tell you. I wish I could just let myself go and cry then maybe I could think for myself.

Mrs. Frost is much better but isn't out of bed yet.

I hope you are enjoying your vacation.

Sincerely yours
Rachel C.[13]

SESSION 224: FRIDAY, 3 OCTOBER 1913

Still vomits.

Admits going with men autoing at night.

Admits they fondled her some. Once man gave her opium. Took it after she got home.

Taken morphine.

SESSION 225: WEDNESDAY, 8 OCTOBER 1913

About the same. Vomits some. No other symptoms.

Mr. "Furbush"[14] sent her some more opium but she destroyed it, she said.

She said she didn't masturbate very much.

Not menstruated since June 2. Often has bad pains.

SESSION 226: TUESDAY, 28 OCTOBER 1913

Left leg numb and heavy—has had to drag it. Saw father Sunday. Doctor sent for her—father has a touch of Bright's Disease[15]—to Worcester. Couldn't eat with him. Took brother with her. Father wants her to keep house for him. Last night dreamed of him and Brother. When half awake seemed to see father standing in door with a baby.

Can keep raw eggs in stomach. "Eggs—hens—what comes from them—babies, but that doesn't have anything to do with it."

When vomits, it starts in her head, queer feeling, as if tight, forehead and scalp, then goes to shoulders and head feels clear. When reaches stomach it turns over. Thinks it does have some relation with father but can't say what. No morphine or opium. While the men pester her, has not been out.

Sees her mother some days quite clearly. Catches herself talking with her.

SESSION 227: THURSDAY, 30 OCTOBER 1913

Felt perfectly well all day yesterday till night. Kept breakfast and dinner down. Vomited supper.

Dreamed I had something she wanted and tried to get. Woke with her hands closed, as if she had got what she wanted, but *burning* as if on fire. She put them in water for some minutes. Dreamed of father holding a baby, etc. as before.

Last night dreamed she was a child again in bed with brother.

SESSION 228: MONDAY, 3 NOVEMBER 1913

Dreamed last night she was injecting something into a man's arm. As she did so, mother came out of small hole. She was trying to insert the instrument (oil can) in and she felt like vomiting. Woke up and did vomit.

Brother lost job. Suspected of stealing. Father wrote this morning accusing her of mother's death and blaming her for brother's troubles and asking if she would atone. Brother trying to get money from patient.

Fainted yesterday for a few minutes—Felt at first as if she were getting numb and losing use of limbs—Fingers stiffened. When fainted, *relaxed*. Was all right soon.

Feels as if she ought to do as father wishes, but will not because of what he has done.

SESSION 229: WEDNESDAY, 5 NOVEMBER 1913

Dreamed night before last that she was filling a lot of shoes with something, what, she doesn't know. Then they disappeared. Everett was there—Somebody accused her of making away with the shoes. At first she denied it, then she acknowledged it, waking, hearing herself say, "I took them."
Last night could not sleep—Everett was on her mind.
I suspect she thinks she has committed an abortion. Either she has or she has not. Free association brought the idea of the dream of injection in arm, etc. Thoughts seem centered on Everett. She may have been pregnant by her brother, or she may think she was in a phantasy.
She *never* lies straight and flat on the couch. Her legs are *always* half flexed. She won't shut her eyes. She is staring as if she saw something terrible.
Night before last dreamed she was torturing herself.

SESSION 230: FRIDAY, 7 NOVEMBER 1913

Dreamed she was pleading with her father.
While typewriting yesterday wrote 4 or 5 lines "mother—mother," etc.
Often wakes up at night crying, "I can't do it—don't, I won't," etc.
Feels at times like screaming or strangling—just catches herself in time.
Still vomits—but no other such serious symptoms.
Has taken no morphine or opium.
Often wakes from dreams thinking she is crazy "I know I'll go insane, and you know it too."
Is working outside to pay her brother's ether bill,[16] his doctor's bills. Sent him money today. He has a job now.

SESSION 231: TUESDAY, 11 NOVEMBER 1913

Was unable to work Sunday because her mother appeared so vividly before her she could not see the board. She wanted to scream and stomp. Went home.
In a dream most of the time. Mother would come to her and tell her to do things. She was making some underclothes for Everett, for Christmas, and mother stood over her and told her to cut up one of them, which she did, into bits.
Does queer things: finds herself sitting on the floor and does not know why.
Finds she has let her hair down, etc.

Just before her mother comes feels faint, and trembles, then that passes and she seems to be with mother.

Feels as if she were two persons: 1) with mother; 2) normal.

Dreams of cutting herself. It seems as if it would be a great feeling to slash and cut herself, as if letting the blood flow would relieve her brain.

Has not menstruated since last June.

Dreamed of digging wells and filling them with water.

SESSION 232: THURSDAY, 13 NOVEMBER 1913

Letter from father, 10:30 P.M. Struck dumb.

Dreamed last night she had a baby. Then the man who offered her opium was in the room and took the baby. Then her father came and tried to get it away. Then they were out-doors, going up a hill, quarreling, one trying to get the baby from the other. At the top they were just about to fall over a precipice, father had baby and threw it to her. She awoke crying.

Dreamed she was kneeling by her mother with her head in her lap crying and begging for forgiveness.

Dreamed of me asking me to help her.

Keeps seeing her mother. Things lose their outline and turn into mother. Here, this afternoon, she said the chair turned into her mother "I have seen her a dozen times." Vanishes, today, when she stands up. Doing her work since Sunday.

SESSION 233: TUESDAY, 15 NOVEMBER 1913

Double personality[17]

Saturday left hospital 1:30 telling operator she was going home. When she came to found herself in Cambridge, Harvard Street, near Miss Burleigh's. Then she took car for Winchester and got there about 6:30.

Dream: mother told her to go to her grave and dig her up—did so and found her heart and opened it—found face of a man inside. (Looked mostly like Tom the chauffeur—last Summer's follower) 15 or 16 after father had teased her almost beyond endurance etc—Revolver.

Dreamed I was there and told her I would take the pressure off her head if she would tell me all. She felt she couldn't so I went off and left her.

She feels as if she had done wrong or were afraid to tell. "I feel like two persons and the one cannot control the other."

SESSION 234: THURSDAY, 20 NOVEMBER 1913

Tuesday night ate supper and did not vomit.

"It might mean I was pregnant and did something to stop it."

Questioning her she finally got waked up (got up and went by window) and remembered that after Jack told her she was pregnant she did not have her turns for a long while and mother gave her tansy and different things to start her again. Did not remember this before and felt sick now at remembering it.

Dreamed the other night she was pregnant but seemed to know she was dreaming and yet thought at the same time that it was true.

She is afraid lest it be time and will not let her mind think freely.

SESSION 235: FRIDAY, 28 NOVEMBER 1913

Monday afternoon started for here 1:30 came back 4:30 not knowing where she had been. Did not come here.

Is all the time on her guard. Keeps saying to herself , "It isn't so—I won't have it so," etc. (probably pregnancy) What of it if you were pregnant? "It wouldn't trouble me if I didn't remember it."

SESSION 236: TUESDAY, 2 DECEMBER 1913

Got up and walked to other side of room—"I was thinking of when father said I'd rue the day I ever saw Jack. Then I thought of how mother looked when she gave me the tansy and I thought I saw her looking at me like that just now."
Mother hallucinations.

Wanted to split at 11 but fought it off so hard—made a movement as if to vomit—was thinking of pregnancy.

Father wrote her this morning, saying he wasn't going to get married and wanting her to keep house for him.

Feels her mother tells her what to do and she has to do it. Tells her she can't sleep all night and she can't.

Walked in and out of Boston before she came to me. On the verge of splitting ever since 11—wouldn't lie down or close her eyes lest she lose control.

SESSION 237: THURSDAY, 4 DECEMBER 1913

Quieter.

After a while would lie down and close her eyes.

Mind went to time Jack told her she was pregnant. Mother's reproachful looks etc. The exact things not clear because of interference of mother's image. Father came to see her yesterday. Last night dreamed there was a locked door between her and her father. Her mother seemed to be standing between them.

POSTCARD: RACHEL TO EMERSON

28 November 1913

I made a mistake this afternoon when I said I would have next Monday off. I have Tuesday instead.

Sincerely, Rachel

SESSION 238: MONDAY, 8 DECEMBER 1913

"Split" Friday. Last remembers went to supper—woke up 10:30. Had written a letter to father and one to me. Was so provoked tore 'em up.
"Split" again last night.
This morning about 11, one of the nurses came in and for a while she thought she was her mother—she said, "Oh, why won't you let me tell?" She afterwards thought she had told her something and asked her to tell her back. The girl said she hadn't told her anything but Rachel said she lied, etc. She was furious for a while but finally came to.
The interview ended with: "I can't tell it. I thought I could, but I can't."

SESSION 239: WEDNESDAY, 10 DECEMBER 1913

Wrote a letter to me Monday night in dream-like state, telling "it." Struggled with mother about posting it. Struggled all the way to box and back (actually posted it, but can't remember whether she addressed it or not). When she got to her room seemed to wrestle with mother. At one minute knew it was a dream, next it seemed real. Finally choked her mother and killed her. Fell on bed and slept. Seemed relieved since.
Dreamed last night she was in a drug store buying something to make her menstruate.
Dreamed she cut her legs off and the bed was full of babies but she couldn't get away because she had no legs.

SESSION 240: FRIDAY, 12 DECEMBER 1913

Dreamed she was at a banquet. She couldn't eat anything because the food she saw all the others eating was filled with worms she awoke vomiting.

Bed—mother—Jack—home—looks—now—eat—worms—snakes—woods—Everett—here—dream—mother—picture—nothing—will—deny—speak—crying—speaking—mother—room—bed.

SESSION 241: TUESDAY, 16 DECEMBER 1913

Operations in hand and vagina at time she thought she was pregnant. Operation performed without her permission. Mother did not know she was going to dispensary and Hospital. At New England Hospital two weeks.[18] Had hemorrhages so Dr. Stevens[19] was frightened and went right to mother Dr. Culbertson performed operation.

Dr. Stevens and mother refused to tell patient for a long while why or what operation was. Threatened to go to hospital and find out brought mother to tell her finally. Mother probably believed her pregnant.

Probably patient and mother both believed an abortion had been performed. Saw mother Saturday morning and fainted.

SESSION 242: THURSDAY, 18 DECEMBER 1913

"I didn't———do it"?

Do what? etc. Perhaps she wants mother back to tell her she didn't do what she seems accusing her of.

Was better yesterday.

Somnambulism this A.M. 7:30—9 (told 'em she had awful headache—true) Walking, walking as if searching for something. Went to Coolidge's Corner. Came to every 10~15 minutes, etc. Doing now as she did when mother was giving her something to menstruate and looked reproachfully at her—i.e. going off and dreaming.

Feels if she could only have mother back long enough to tell her something wouldn't mind if she did die again.

Constantly finds herself saying "I didn't do it"—waking from sleep; under breath; etc.

SESSION 243: MONDAY, 22 DECEMBER 1913

Knows her mother is accusing her of something—(to be connected with "I didn't do it").

Once, all sitting around table, mother reading something about bad girls—patient made some remark, mother said, looking right at her, "People who live in glass houses shouldn't throw stones." Father said "Don't be cruel Nora"—At another time said now I know why you have been out with father. Mother locked her in her room one night to prevent her going with Jack. He put up a ladder and she was with him most of the night—nothing done—but bed was not slept in and then mother came in morning and saw it and said "something done" but couldn't understand it.

Has these terrible feelings when mother appears before her.

SESSION 244: FRIDAY, 26 DECEMBER 1913

Better Wednesday.

Dreamed last night she wanted the note she wrote me and came to my house to get it. Just as she got it in a bureau drawer her mother appeared and said something that frightened her terribly. There was something else to the dream but can't remember it. Then she went home, got a box out of her bed and threw it out the window. Woke up sick and vomited.

SESSION 245: TUESDAY, 30 DECEMBER 1913

Found herself writing to her mother last night. Part of it had been all torn up. She read, "I don't suppose you'll believe me."

Dreamed she was imploring her mother to forgive her. She remained obdurate. Finally she offered her Everett, who was a baby, and just as her mother seemed hesitating she woke up.

As she lay today with eyes closed she saw a vision of her mother standing by her in the kitchen. Later she saw herself in the woods. Next she thought of snakes.

SESSION 246: TUESDAY, 13 JANUARY 1914

A week ago dreamed she was going to have a baby. When she woke thought it was really so. Two days later, when with Frosts, often caught herself just about to tell them. The thought keeps coming now but she knows it isn't so.

Last night dreamed she was killing her mother by choking her.
Seeing mother very vividly last week.
Somnambulistic Sunday 2–10.

SESSION 247: THURSDAY, 15 JANUARY 1914

A process very like a delusion formation seems to be in progress of formation.
The patient is constantly afraid of something about to happen. In trying to
explain it to herself she has thought that perhaps what she was thinking about
was that she was going to have a baby. From this point of view the thing about
to happen would be the "baby." When she first thought of this as really so, the
other day, at the Frosts, she was disturbed at the idea because it was also unreal. Now she finds herself accepting the idea as real for longer or shorter periods and then coming to think she did wrong to allow herself to dwell with
such a thought. "In a way I know it isn't so," she says, "but yet I feel it is real."
Dreamed last night she was in heaven with her mother.
Feels she wants to see her mother to tell her something. What, she doesn't
know. Often catches herself saying, "I didn't do it." Dr. Stearns thinks whole
picture hysteria.

SESSION 248: MONDAY, 19 JANUARY 1914

Somnambulism.
When she left me Thursday went to see a sick friend at Huntington Memorial
Hospital—*Remembers leaving* but nothing till one A.M. in bed. The next day
heard from a friend in Winchester that she had been with her to the theater
(Boston—"The Whip") *Has no recollection of it at all.*
Dreamed Saturday night she knew where she had been Thursday and all
about it. Couldn't remember it however. Vomiting better today.

SESSION 249: WEDNESDAY, 21 JANUARY 1914

No somnambulism.
"Somebody knows," asks people if they know. "I don't know."
Dreamed Monday night Dr. Cady[20] and Dr. Southard accused her of something.
To clear herself she had to tell what was really so. Felt relieved. (Dr. Southard's
son scarlet fever at hospital. Saw him and Dr. Cady). Dreamed of father.
Bit herself early in morning, to wake herself so she wouldn't see mother

SESSION 250: FRIDAY, 23 JANUARY 1914

Dreamed about the abortion and sometimes thought it was not so—once thought it was.

Almost got it today, whatever it is. Mind went to operation, then home, after, on the lounge, and "what she told me." (Mother)

SESSION 251: TUESDAY, 27 JANUARY 1914

Dreamed she went to see Dr. Culbertson and she told her it was all right, it wasn't so.

Somnambulism yesterday: started for New England Hospital in afternoon to see Dr. Culbertson but doesn't know where she went; doesn't think she got there.

Every once in a while seems to catch herself talking with her mother but can't tell what she is saying.

SESSION 252: THURSDAY, 29 JANUARY 1914

Sees mother less.

Somnambulism Tuesday afternoon and evening.

Remembers now that, at first, for 2 or 3 days after the operation, took everything to be as Dr. Gray[21] and Culbertson said (i.e. removal of a "structure") but doctors came and questioned searchingly, her mother acted and looked suspicious, mysterious, and sorry, and reproachful. She kept wondering why. When she got home she had to lie on a lounge for about a month. She could not walk and her father used to carry her upstairs to bed at night. She would often doze or be half asleep in the evening and hear her father and mother talking about something in whispers, and they would stop as soon as she would seem to awaken. It seemed as if she knew, in a way, when half asleep, what they were talking about, but when she woke completely and would try to think what it was she couldn't. She had already got suspicions about the operation, at the hospital owing to the mysterious actions of the doctors, and wondered if the operation were merely the simple thing Dr. Gray had said. She asked her mother but she would never tell her, always turning her off, telling her to ask Dr. Culbertson if she wanted to know. The idea "abortion" did enter her mind, and she thinks it was due to something she had heard. (She was unable to walk for a month or more. Whenever she moved, intense agony) But she does not think this is what is troubling her now. She thinks she is going insane, because she feels like doing such queer things i.e. singing, laughing, or shouting, for no adequate external reason. She feels that something is going to happen, something terrible, her head feels as if it would burst, at times.

She dreamed last night she was at some place. The name was under some labels and she was trying to pull them off to find out where she was.

Dreamed her father told her she must take some medication, and offered her if only she could choose where it would go, to do its work, so she chose that it would go to her head. She woke before taking it.

Went to Dr. Stevens first at New England Hospital because of trouble with hands. Then she was very nervous, and had terrible pains, etc., so Dr. Stevens asked her to come to the private office. There she was treated for every trouble, by packing, etc. also by electricity. Here Dr. Stevens discovered the "structure." (Mother knew nothing of all of this. It was at time of menstrual stoppage) Wanted her to go to hospital for operation on hands and also on vagina. Patient went to have hands operated on and told mother morning she went expecting to stay only one night. This was the first mother knew her going to any doctor or hospital. Then Dr. Gray operated on vagina *without permission,* and she had such a hemorrhage, Doctor Stevens went right for mother

SESSION 253: MONDAY, 2 FEBRUARY 1914

No somnambulism—though almost this A.M.

Conflict now all in head. Feels if she doesn't get it she will go insane and if she uses part of energy, which now goes to keeping her sane, to assist in knowing, she would then go insane.

$$\text{Energy} \begin{cases} \text{1) energy of knowing} \\ \text{2) energy of keeping sane} \end{cases} \text{Conflict.}$$

Feels as if she could have convulsions, or paralyses, or any of her old symptoms if they did not repel her so now.

SESSION 254: WEDNESDAY, 4 FEBRUARY 1914

Thought for a moment, yesterday, that what made her think so constantly of her mother was that she actually tried to tell her something, once, and mother wouldn't listen, but turned a deaf ear.

Thought, last night, "It has come."

This morning was told by a girl how she had a baby and was caring for it. Thought, and almost said, catching herself only just in time, "I wish I had done that with mine."

After the operation Dr. Stevens asked her pardon and tried to get her to forgive her but she wouldn't speak to her.

Mother would believe but father would investigate.

Room-mate said she talked in sleep: "I won't go back" and she said, perhaps, "I won't go back to that time and think of those things."

SESSION 255: FRIDAY, 6 FEBRUARY 1914

Almost had "it"—did have it before she knew she had it—then tried to say it, but before she could say it, it went to her stomach and she felt like vomiting, and then her mind went to her head, then she had lost it.

Another time: mind in lounge, seemed to be listening to mother and father. Suddenly everything went blank.

Another time: thinking of it and suddenly everything went *black* = blind for second. Woke up last night hearing herself say, "I know it." The engineer, who went with her some last summer, seemed to be standing over her and made her tell him. When she woke far enough thought it a dream and everything was as before. For the few seconds she seemed to have it, her head felt clear and light.

Is dressing a doll for fair: dreamed the doll came to life. She didn't understand it since she knew it was only a doll.

Dreamed she was in a long dark passageway, with Tom.[22] Suddenly everything became brilliantly light.

Feels she is going to know it, but *before* she can know it, something must happen, *what* she doesn't know.

SESSION 256: TUESDAY, 10 FEBRUARY 1914

Saw father Sunday and asked him if she had had an illegal operation.[23] He said no, and then got mad and couldn't talk any more about it. He said, "You know all you're going to."

Picture in her mind: lying in bed in hospital a week after operation with feet up to stop hemorrhage. (Dreamed she was vomiting blood.) Felt like vomiting and had to go to toilet where did vomit.

SESSION 257: THURSDAY, 12 FEBRUARY 1914

Tuesday night dreamed a great deal about blood: vomiting it; seeing people cut up and bleeding; seeing blood; is it in head.

Mother told her *something*. She tried to deny it but was not believed. Can see her shaking her head. Talked in sleep last night: "Let me explain." "It wasn't so."—"Jack"—"Mother."

It is in her forehead today.

Last night dreamed she was trying to find beds for hundreds of babies.

Thought of something today but instead of telling, *bit her* tongue.

SESSION 258: MONDAY, 16 FEBRUARY 1914

Dreamed the letter she sent me which I didn't get, was returned by her mother. It was bloody and nobody else would take.

Running a temperature.

Saturday 101°. Sunday 103°. Monday 102°.

SESSION 259: TUESDAY, 24 FEBRUARY 1914

No change. Always saying "no" etc. to herself—shaking of head = "No" (?)

Aunt Eva came to Frosts Sunday. Said Rachel looked and acted just as she did when sick before (i.e. at operation). Worked her up so she went to her room and went into a somnambulism.

Dreams of having her legs, arms, hands cut off.

Dreams of being killed and killing others.

Dreams of drowning herself.

SESSION 260: THURSDAY, 26 FEBRUARY 1914

When about 10–12 found a dead snake—cut it open to see where the little snakes which came out of snake's mouth's came from.

Gets no further.

LETTER: RACHEL TO EDITH BURLEIGH

1 March 1914
Brighton, Massachusetts

Dear Miss Burleigh:—I was pleased to get your letter it did seem so long since I had heard from you. I am sorry to hear you are not feeling well and I hope you are

feeling better now. I wish I could come to see you but I am not going to as I know
you have enough trouble with out my coming and bothering you with mine. I have
been going to Dr. Emerson right along but I cannot get any relief. I have kept up
just about as long as I can and work, my mind is just making my body sick. Now I
am planning to go down to Rhode Island to an elderly aunts of mine that lives way
out in the country I can go there and wander wherever I please and she will ask no
questions and I can be alone with my thoughts, it may seem wrong to you for me to
give in to my desires but I have thought and thought until it seems as if I didn't
have any thinking powers left. I feel all the time that some thing awful is going to
happen I don't suppose I can really know but it does wear on me so. Dr. Emerson
says I will not lose my mind but I think if he really knew how my head feels and
how hard it is for me to keep my mind straight I don't think he would be quite so
positive, it may be he says it to ease my mind I don't know. He told me to come
tomorrow I told him I shouldn't and I shan't go if I could go and say I felt better
and could say what was bothering me you don't know how glad I would be as I
know he must be more than discouraged of course he says if I really wanted to
know I could and that makes it all the harder to have him think I am not trying.
You will say when you read this will I never receive a cheerful letter from that girl
and I won't blame you if you do.

I do hope you will get interested in your work again as you were afraid you wouldn't.
We are awfully busy as the hospital is more than full. There is a substitute coming
to relieve me.

I know it is too much to ask you to write again soon but I will love to hear from you
when ever you can spare the time.

With a great deal of love,
Rachel

SESSION 261: FRIDAY, 27 MARCH 1914

Does not see mother so much. All her thoughts seem to lead up to death-bed
scene with mother. Has forgotten all about it herself but told by father that
when she was taken to the bed by the nurse, her mother seemed to gain consciousness, at sight of her, and said something, or mumbled something. Neither father nor brother could understand, but Rachel threw herself on her
mother and had to be taken off.[24]
Woke up this morning singing, was in a happy dream. As soon as she was
awake, she remembered, and it was as if she had been hit on the head. She lost
consciousness and fell to the floor—Came to in a few minutes. "It is as if
someone had done wrong and were hiding."

At times loses sight for short while. It comes and goes—Sometimes can't hear. Still keeps saying "I didn't do it," "It isn't so" etc.

SESSION 262: WEDNESDAY, 1 APRIL 1914

Old attack Sunday night. Knew a moment before what she is repressing. *Friday.* Remembered that Mrs. R.[25] was thought to be pregnant and doctor found it wrong—Ella told her and she was relieved. This was after her own operation, she thinks. Mrs. R. got her to go to hospital and Dr. Stevens. Saturday. In Filenes saw a woman who reminded her of mother—fainted. Knew—Brought it all back.
Felt all day Sunday she was liable to have an attack. When she came to was so mad forgot everything else and for a while forgot about it. In attack bit arm; bruised, ground teeth and *broke one.*
Sunday slightly aphasic.[26] Stumbled on words.

SESSION 263: FRIDAY, 3 APRIL 1914

Woke this morning saying "I have got it."
Had patient lie down and close eyes.
Saw T. a week ago. Wasn't so afraid of him as used. Fainted last night at work.

SESSION 264: TUESDAY, 7 APRIL 1914

Lying down with eyes shut.
Suddenly sat up.
It was what mother said when dying. Seemed to reject what she had said many times before. "All the other times she accused me—came all at once."
What did she say? "I know it isn't so—I didn't do it."
Later: "It is what she thought."

SESSION 265: THURSDAY, 9 APRIL 1914

Fainted Tuesday when back at hospital. Bit herself last night.
Said she was out intending to drown herself but decided to try some more.
Hears her mother talking to her but can't get what she says.

SESSION 266: MONDAY, 13 APRIL 1914

Got a letter from father Saturday about 11:30. He accused her again of killing her mother. He said if it hadn't been for all those things that had happened she wouldn't have died—She knew then what it was that was troubling her. She sat thinking about it. When she came to it was after 3 P.M. She knew then, for a little while, what she had been thinking of but later lost it.

SESSION 267: TUESDAY, 21 APRIL 1914

Dreamed last night she was on the couch hearing her mother accuse her. She tried to defend herself, but instead of speaking seemed to vomit.
Remembers her mother used to hold this over her.
The last few days has come to the conclusion that whatever it was her mother accused her of, it must have seemed true, at the time, or she would have defended herself against it.
She remembers that she was lying in the lounge and heard what her mother said, it stunned her like a blow. She couldn't sense it. She couldn't keep it in her mind to think of it. It came back, at times, but she couldn't think of what it meant. *This happened about 6 months before her first convulsion.*
Last evening she remembered when lying on the couch at home after the operation, hearing her father say, "I don't believe Rachel would do such a thing." She knows her mother was accusing her of having had an abortion but could not remember the words.
Dreamed someone was beating her. Legs and thighs black and blue.

SESSION 268: THURSDAY, 23 APRIL 1914

Feels the reason her mother's accusation moved her so was because it reminded her of something else, forgotten, but true.
Dreamed she was washing a baby but couldn't get it clean.
Though her father, when she asks, says her mother told him nothing, he must have believed it because he has often told her she had better look out or she would get in trouble again.

SESSION 269: TUESDAY, 19 MAY 1914

No change. Wanted some medicine to make her menstruate.
Dreamed she was in an ambulance with a baby. The ambulance kept turning

over. When it did so she would throw the baby up in the air and catch it when it came down, unhurt, because the ambulance had turned over in the meantime.

SESSION 270: FRIDAY, 26 FEBRUARY 1915

Came To M.G.H. Went to Dr. Stevens about not menstruating. Wanted to know how much I had told her.

Symptoms remaining: bad pains in abdomen, breasts, arms, etc. "just as if something were tearing," visual and auditory hallucinatory images of mother; occasional fainting, vomiting very much diminished, practically gone; no menstruation in over a year. No paralysis, convulsions, amaurosis, aphasias, contractions. Very well all summer, till October or November.

LETTER: RACHEL TO EMERSON

8 October 1915
Friday evening

Dear Dr. Emerson:

I think you will be surprised to hear where I am and how well I am feeling.

I am taking up a maternity training out to the Talitha Cumi Hospital, 215 Forest Hills Street Jamaica Plain.[27] I am on my seventh week and got my cap last week so I am beginning to feel a little bit like a nurse, I love my work very much of course out here we have many sad cases and at first it made me feel badly but now I get along much better.

I did not want to let you know where I was until I felt pretty sure I could go through with the training and would be accepted but I know you will be pleased to know how well I feel and every thing.

I hear from Mrs. Monroe quite often I love to get letters from her.

Brother is doing nicely now in Winchester.

Father is still in Worcester and is very good to me.

I hope you had a pleasant vacation this summer.

We all take turns to be on call, last night was my turn and I wish you could see the baby a little girl weighing two lbs. and five oz. she is just perfect.

Please remember me to Mrs. Emerson.

Now I must close as it is time my light was out.

Sincerely yours,
Rachel C.

LETTER: RACHEL TO EMERSON

3 March 1916
Framingham, Massachusetts

Dear Dr. Emerson:
Possibly by this time you know I have left the Talitha Cumi Hospital.
I have been here in Framingham at Dr. Patch's[28] for the last three months.
It broke me all up when I had to give up my training and it has been just all I could
do to bear up and settle my mind to any thing, every thing seemed blank and as if I
was doing every thing in space but lately things seem brighter and it isn't quite such
an effort to do or say things pleasant.
If I can stop being bitter it will help out a lot but I can't think it fair what ever I
really want to do either my health or some thing has to stop me.
Dr. Patch is more than good. He knows I haven't been well and is just as kind as he
can be.
I meet some very pleasant people here so that helps. Every two weeks I have twenty-
four hours off so I can go away for over night.
You have been so kind to me I feel I ought and want to let you know how things are
going.
I hope this finds you well.

Sincerely,
Rachel C.

WEDNESDAY, 17 JANUARY 1917

Seen at Mrs. Scott's—Palmer Greenhouses, Newton Street, Brookline.

SESSION 271: THURSDAY, 18 JANUARY 1917

M.G.H.
Dreamed a man stood at the foot of her bed and tore a cat apart—She feels,
consciously, as if she would like to tear her head apart. Unconsciously—her
genitals—Feels like biting herself and tearing her hair out.
Harry T. is on her mind—can remember nothing else.
Was picked up in Brookline a few weeks ago by police—didn't know where
she was and taken to Psychopathic.[29] Has been discharged from Dr. Patch's
Sanitarium. Trouble began last October.

SESSION 272: MONDAY, 22 JANUARY 1917

Broke down last spring—2 weeks—Dr. Raynes[30] (Psychopathic) thinks father has been at her again.

Bit herself (left arm) last night. Feels "divided" front and back brain.

SESSION 273: WEDNESDAY, 24 JANUARY 1917

Received a letter Monday noon from Cyrus W. Wouldn't read it till night. When she did read it went off into dazed state and destroyed it. Said it made some sarcastic remark about Harry T. She now thinks she remembers the two men met in Winchester.

Did not come out of dazed state until yesterday noon. While in it told Miss Campbell[31] not to touch her as she was dirty. At one time said "I didn't do it. You know I didn't do it Campy."

As she lies on couch stops and looks off into space, but then can't get it.

When she was picked up in Brookline said she was looking at cars and all she could see on the sign was Hell in flaming letters. She asked a policeman to help her. Told him my name but couldn't tell him where I lived or where she wanted to go.

While in dazed state thinks food poisoned because everything tastes bitter.

SESSION 274: MONDAY, 29 JANUARY 1917

Remembers Cyrus W. "tempted" her a great deal. Hugged, kissed, put hands on breast, etc.

But Harry T. she "cares for"—remembers he "met" her at Sullivan Square helped her in car—exchanged names—came to Winchester etc.

Remembered everything last Wednesday night and jumped up to write it down but forgot it before she could write.

Dr. Clymer's trianol "so much better"—Got Clymer to prescribe veronal today.[32]

SESSION 275: TUESDAY, 30 JANUARY 1917

Slept pretty well on bromide. Dreamed she took her picture out of her pocketbook. A man tried to take it from her. At the same time it seemed as if the picture were herself in some way, and when he tried to take it, it felt as if a knife were being stuck in her.

Remembers being in Cyrus W.'s office last summer when he locked the door and said he was going to force her to marry him. He did force her onto a couch but no further—mostly talk, etc.

She was much disturbed, however, when he returned about a month later and said he would behave himself. Conflict: feeling for him being passion, should she marry him or not.

SESSION 276: WEDNESDAY, 31 JANUARY 1917

Wrote letter to Cyrus W. last night, in a state of absence, thinking she was writing to brother. Miss Campbell brought it in this A.M. She described her attack some time ago as a typical opisthotonos.[33] Slept pretty well.

SESSION 277: THURSDAY, 1 FEBRUARY 1917

Miss Campbell gave me attached notes.

Patient remembers, uncertainly, that he was married; about the "secret stamp-anchor"; about being alone in tents, etc.

LETTER: RACHEL TO CYRUS W.

30 January 1917
Tuesday evening

Cy:—I am writing this not knowing where I am going to send it but I am going to telephone tomorrow to you know *who* and see if I can't locate you for you have *got* to help me.

I have not been working for the past three weeks. What the matter is I can't explain to you but you can guess if you *try*, part of it. You know I begged you to leave me alone you knew what you were doing at the time and it would serve you right well if I brought you into this more instead of trying to shield you but I suppose it is because I do not care for you as I wish I did or as I do for the party you mentioned in your letter. What you said in your letter I can not remember as I wasn't feeling well that night and I have done some thing with it (yes I know you will say I have laid it around but I haven't as I have looked and looked I must have burned it.) I would rather do almost any thing than ask you for help as I know *all too well* I will hear from it later. I can not think so you will have to think for me. What do you know about Harry T.? Where does he live in fact every thing, you owe it to me, if you don't—well, I would remember some time then I rather think I would make you remember some things.

You couldn't keep away from Boston could you?

Please excuse pencil writing for various reasons. Do Cy answer this as I want you too (nothing more). You will be glad in the end and no one will be wiser in the end for you know.

NURSE'S NOTES

1 February 1917

Wednesday afternoon while lying on the bed with eyes wide open, but speaking more like one in a dream Miss C.'s conversation *ran like this*.

Could you care for a married man?? Did you ever?? Well you see it was up at the tents[34]—I didn't know he was married—not until long afterwards— he did not care for his wife and I didn't either. She was not nice to him, spoke of him as my husband, not calling him by name as my mother would have spoken of my father. His name is Harry. I met him first on a car. He introduced himself. Folks home did not approve of him. Said he was not all right or he would not have done that. I did like him though. You remember when soldiers were down in muster field—we used to sit on the stone wall and watch them and he enjoyed the music so—why did I not introduce him to you? Ah well Dr. Patch would not have approved of it—and then the girls were jolly, but you see I could not go out doors much so he had to come to tent of course I met him some times down at Framingham. He took me to see his little girl and I loved her. She liked me too, but his wife didn't.

I don't believe I shall be a tent nurse next summer—of course as tent nurse I can do more as I please, but I won't be tent nurse next summer—ah well there is a reason why—I must take that key back. If they get him of that they will be crazy.

We had a secret stamp which we used for our letters. It was an anchor. Of course if he didn't use that his wife would know.

It would be awful to be married to anyone you didn't love, wouldn't it. Did I love him?? Goodness I don't know. Well yes I guess I did, if he were here now he would rub my head and stop the aching. He gave me some stuff once for my head—

Then during night: "Ah that night, that night. Is it any wonder I dread it—" And later:

Say if any one left Framingham at 11 they would be in Boston at 12 wouldn't they—

SESSION 278: MONDAY, 5 FEBRUARY 1917

Had a slight attack Saturday night. Is thinking a great deal of the tent some night—in imagination sees father and then Harry T. on sofa.
Wrote to somebody but doesn't know whom.

SESSION 279: TUESDAY, 6 FEBRUARY 1917

No special change.
Father and Harry change places in the lounge in Tent—then everything goes black.

NURSE'S NOTES

We couldn't go up on Washington where people would see us, his wife might see—glad I got those two walks straightened out in my mind, Ah the walk on Washington St. and the walk in grove. I wish I had more of that medicine he gave me. Girls said I was distant, would not tell them things. If they only knew—I had my reasons. He was all right until that night honestly he was— He was just lonely and I was too. I didn't like Cy so I had to tell him I couldn't be with him, but you see I liked Harry—I knew I hadn't ought to talk so much to a married man and be with him so often. But that Sunday when he came and father came too, I was so afraid, ah that night. Ah that night, that night, why did he do it. He was peculiar all that night, down by river and all. Of course I knew he should not have written, but I couldn't help it. You know those moonlit nights in grove. Do you blame any body for wanting to be there, but I knew I should not have been. Why did I go to Dr. Emerson. He won't understand. He can't you know he can't. Why did I not fight it out myself— why didn't Jack live and I would have married him and never had all this trouble. Ah when he tipped my head back. I suppose that is what makes it ache so now—I was so tired, just as I am now—then he thought I wouldn't know because I had that old medicine, but I did know—Ah I suppose that is what is wrong with my head. I did care for him. No one will believe me—because I did do wrong they won't believe me—wish God would take me—wish I were a baby again with mother nothing to worry about. Just brother and I. Wish they would go to Harvard St. Medford—I'm going when get better.
She has repeated several times about the medicine. Said it was in thin glass bottle.

Then during night. Ah that night, Ah that office, that night in that office, Ah it hurt my arm so—Ah that night in tent. Ah that office, I didn't want to sleep in office—knew office was no place to go to sleep—and Ah my head—Latter repeated very often—and 4 times in tired excited state: I didn't want to go to sleep that way.

PATIENT'S DREAMS

Rope ladder
Snake—note in mouth
Swimming to islands and devil pushing me off.
Tearing calendars off, man on chair, myself in ferry.
Pancakes.

SESSION 280: WEDNESDAY, 7 FEBRUARY 1917

Remembers a little more about Harry T.

SESSION 281: THURSDAY, 8 FEBRUARY 1917

Remembers he wanted her to go away with him and at first she agreed to. Then refused. Telephoned—remembers everything but act on couch—cried.

NURSE'S NOTES

Saturday Afternoon
You know the back way. He thought that was fine. He didn't have to come up front driveway. Ah that night. Were you ever up in 8th story of a building looking down at night. It is pretty. I know I shouldn't have gone up. Well I didn't. He knows I care for him, but I suppose it is not right to wish any body dead—Ah then my head ached so—goodness that was after the 18th—I don't know—how he rubbed my head—Ah that muster field. I wish they would stop and then he would go home—(We could hear some music playing from the country club). Wouldn't it be fine if there should be a war and we should enlist as soldiers where war was on in [illeg.] He thought if he could go as a soldier and I as a nurse. He was all right then honestly he was—I wonder if I had gone off with him that time would it have been all right or not. Ah that night when he came to tent wasn't he mad at my phoning. Wish he didn't

have conscience, suppose he is doing what he ought to do now—even if he doesn't like to—She can thank me she has him yet. Suppose she didn't know about my head—I know why he didn't want anyone to see us in city. I know why he made that excuse to go up in office, I know. Lucky he didn't do more—Ah I wish I had some of that medicine. It was quiet, it is that medicine that makes me forget—Wish I could go to work—yes that time you thought just a little bit too much—you promised—I will not take any more of it—well, I suppose you will have your will in that—I will not take it—wish I had not shown you that back entrance. Ah I know Dr. Patch will see you—I can't help it if I do care for you—

Dr. Emerson if this is of any help to you I have more of it, but have no chance to write it as Miss C. is right here with me—If you care to ask me I can tell you the rest of it this A.M.

[signed by Nurse Campbell]

SESSION 282: MONDAY, 12 FEBRUARY 1917

"Forgot" Friday afternoon and legs went bad; remembered Saturday and re-gained full use of legs.

Bit back of right hand badly this A.M. at clinic.

Promised Harry at first she would run away with him. He gave her $50—then she telephoned him she wouldn't and he came up next night. Can remember fully now being forced on lounge but cannot remember actual intercourse except for a "second."

SESSION 283: TUESDAY, 13 FEBRUARY 1917

Remembers now that she came to Brookline village to see Harry T. off on his way to Michigan. It was after he left that she saw the cars marked "Hell"—Mind is filled with regret and conscience pains at having kept on with Harry after she learned he was married.

LETTER: RACHEL TO HARRY T.

14 February 1917

Dear Harry: I have no right to say dear but I am going to for the last time. I am much braver and stronger away from you than with you as you will know.

I was sick or I should have answered your letter in person. You say there isn't any God only the one we make ourselves but who ever it was they kept me from seeing you until it was too late.

Oh Harry if you care a little for me (as you would want little Ella cared for) forget and let me alone until I can master myself. Then I am going away. Try to make the best of it and once and for all *I will not* go away with you.

I am going to get well.

I am going to work and you must, you must when you have nights home be with Ella and your wife. Traveling as you do makes it easier.

Oh my head my head Harry how it aches. If I had only been strong when I first knew I had no right to be with you. Why did you deceive me all those months or even if you had just done right. That pain then to you wouldn't have been anything to what I am going through now. You have your health, your mind, your work, your money, and your home such as it is and if you did as you ought you could improve it, while I, every sound, in fact everything in fact reminds me of some thing, rolled up tight in my head.

One moment I hate oh how I hate you, the next well you know. You are to blame you knew I was lonesome you worked on my sympathies. I don't see how you can go into your office every day and not go crazy knowing the tortures you put me through there and well there is no use for me to go into any more details. Each one settles for their own doings.

You made me promise I have kept it so we will let it be. But I will do as I said I would even if I break my promise so if I do you yourself will be to blame.

I am leaving here. There will be no use to write.

Good-night and good-bye.
Rae.

SESSION 284: WEDNESDAY, 14 FEBRUARY 1917

After leaving clinic yesterday went to 5 + 10¢ store on errand about 11 A.M. Cannot remember what she did till she came to at 6 P.M. on Washington St.—Miss Campbell called me to ask where she was—

SESSION 285: THURSDAY, 15 FEBRUARY 1917

Wrote a letter last night—got her to read it—"Torture" makes her have a "pain" in genitals and all through. Can remember nearly all now—showed great resistance to reading tried to tear it up.

SESSION 286: MONDAY, 19 FEBRUARY 1917

No change.

SESSION 287: TUESDAY, 20 FEBRUARY 1917

Remembers a little more = i.e. going to see his wife.

Got a letter from him last night asking her again to go off with him. Threatening to get someone else if she wouldn't. Now says his name is R. Wrote and told.[35]

It was something he *said*, as he tipped her back in chair, that troubles rather than anything he *did*. It refers to Woodside.[36]

SESSION 288: WEDNESDAY, 21 FEBRUARY 1917

Remembers that night in tent was the next time she saw him after learning he was married. Remembers he undressed her! Remembers she lay down on the couch again and didn't care whether he was there or not—but *cannot* remember coitus.

Walks up and down like a caged beast. Left back way. Miss Campbell follows—comes back and says she can't manage her.

SESSION 289: MONDAY, 26 FEBRUARY 1917

Keeps saying "I ought not to have gone there." But does not know where "there" is, or why she ought not to have gone.

SESSION 290: TUESDAY, 27 FEBRUARY 1917

Remembered finally what he said when he tipped her over in chair i.e. (after locking door) "Now we won't be interrupted as we were in the tent and you must do what I want."

Walking up to tent: He told her he had not told her he was married because she wouldn't do what he wanted, but now she must be as a wife to him. She said she wouldn't.

Remembered going to a restaurant in Chinatown with him and leaving because of coitus with half-nude women, etc. He turned to other man and said "next time."

Can't remember what happened between taking medicine and fully undressing with Harry's help.

Says "promise" made when he was forcing head back on lounge, she sitting on floor prevents remembering (can't remember what happened between falling on floor and sitting with back to lounge.)

SESSION 291: WEDNESDAY, 28 FEBRUARY 1917

Remembers now struggling on floor, rolling over, his trying to get her dress up, etc. His saying it didn't matter how much she struggled, she would only get tired out, and nobody could hear, etc.

SESSION 292: TUESDAY, 6 MARCH 1917

Remembers now that she did promise Harry if he would let her go that time she would go with him to some house and let him do as he pleased. This clears up office scene. Remembers also that he did try to do something in tent before he helped her undress wholly and that although she wasn't sure at time yet she didn't care. (Houses and that man's face still came.) Is going to Adams Nervine.

LETTER: RACHEL TO EMERSON

28 August 1917
1462 C—— Ave.
Allston, Massachusetts

Dear Dr. Emerson:—

I received your letter, it was good of you to answer so quickly. Of course I feel I have a friend in you but some how when you hear from one it seems more real.

How I wish I could talk free and unburden myself of all my thoughts, "have a regular house-cleaning"[37] as I might say how much better I would feel. I have got so in the habit of putting matters out of my mind if it is anything disagreeable that I do it before I know what I am doing. Usually over night.

When we were up to New Hampshire we stayed at the Intervale House a number of days. It was one of the prettiest places we visited.

I left this case last Saturday morning as it seemed as if I could not stay and be pleasant any longer, but Sunday morning they phoned asking if I wouldn't come back for a while as she was very much up set and wouldn't keep the nurse that relieved me so I am here again.

They expect to move almost any day now so I am very busy but after we are more settled I am coming in to see you but I will let you know when.

Sincerely Yours,
Rachel C.

LETTER: RACHEL TO EMERSON

6 January 1919
Good Samaritan Hospital[38]
Brookline, Massachusetts

Dear Dr. Emerson:—
Thank you for your kind letter and invitation to come and see you as I have refused so many times but I did not want to see anyone when I felt so depressed and down hearted.

Last spring I fell and hurt my neck and back quite badly so that I was unable to even sit up for over two months. I was advised to try osteopathy which I did. He not only cured my back but it seemed as if all the nerves were loosened and all the tenseness that I held myself in just vanished. I can't tell you how different I feel of course I have my blue days but I get over them the same as anyone else and best of all things stay clear in my mind and I have no more half-thoughts.

I am at present on the cancer ward it is very hard but I enjoy my work and the nurses. Just now we have extra work as there are a number of the nurses out sick with influenza.

Yes I had a very pleasant Christmas considering that I had to be here all day as I did wish I could have spent it at my brother's home but I couldn't.

Father is still in Worcester but is not at all well.

A number of weeks ago I went over to the Psychopathic just to see you but was told you did not go there now.

Please remember me to Mrs. Emerson and I will come to see you both some evening when I have late hours.

New Years Greetings,
Yours Sincerely
Rachel C.

LETTER: RACHEL TO MRS. EMERSON

6 August 1921
State Sanitarium
Dunseith, North Dakota

Dear Mrs. Emerson and all:

I intended a number of months ago having Miss Campbell write you but she has been so busy and now I am able to write myself.

In April at Lake Park Minnesota. I was taken ill brought home after a while. The trouble all seemed in my spine. They took X-rays and found what they claim to be tubercular trouble in the lumbar vertebra's [sic]. Some days I am able to move with out much pain then others it is quite bad. At home it was almost impossible to take the cure so Doctors and all thought it best for me to come to a sanitarium so I have been here a month now. The pain is letting up but my evening temperature still stays they claim here there is slight trouble in the right lung but I won't believe that as I never cough or raise. Shortly when able I am going to St. Paul Minnesota to Juliett and Chittendon bone man and have a jacket made thus I will be able to be up and around some. My it will seem good.

It is here the most beautiful spot in all North Dakota situated at the foot of the Turtle mountains. I am on an open porch with twelve other patients we surely can see about twenty six miles way past the next town. It is in the northwestern end of the state and fifteen miles from the border.

At present there are ninety patients and eight nurses but those at the cottages take care of themselves.

The doctors and nurses are all very nice and more than kind.

I was so happy all winter as I was to be married this November but now I think it but not to consider it till I am fully well if I ever am I surely get discouraged. I am very fond of my friend he is thirty five, tall dark hair and eyes. His home is in Le Roy Minnesota so I suppose that will be our home some time.

I have wished so often I could hear from you. Miss Campbell often speaks of you. How I wish she could have seen the children.

I suppose you are at Intervale now and having the nicest times. Is the doctor with you?

Please excuse this awful writing but being in bed is not a very good position for writing.

Miss Campbell wished to be remembered when I wrote.

Give my love to the children.

With love,
Rachel C.

Chapter 9 Afterword

There can be no doubt that Rachel C. was a difficult patient and that treating her would have presented challenges to any analyst at any time. By the criteria of early-twentieth-century psychiatry and psychoanalysis, and in the estimation of everyone who came into professional contact with her, she was without question a hysteric. Even as her condition worsened and new symptoms—dissociations, amnesias, and hallucinations—appeared, the question of her diagnosis was not revisited, so strong was the consensus this was a case of hysteria.[1]

Psychiatrists disagreed among themselves at the time about the treatability of severe hysteria in general and, more particularly, about whether psychoanalysis was the right treatment for it. Within psychoanalysis, by contrast, the view that hysteria in all its many manifestations was perfectly suited for analytic treatment prevailed.[2] Emerson, while subscribing to this position, was not without reservations about some of Rachel's characteristics and her suitability for undergoing psychoanalysis. He judged her to be of a relatively simple-minded mentality, and he found her resistance to free-associating enormous. Some of his disappointment and dissatisfaction is evident in the case notes, expressed primarily around the issue of whether or not she would be able to associate and break through the resistances. She herself often felt she was neither strong enough nor courageous enough to do so and to fully cooperate with Emerson. Neither analyst nor patient could acknowledge, let alone analyze, negative feelings about the other; strikingly, in the published version of the case Emerson gave vent to his frustrated and even angry feelings toward Rachel. Ninety years on, contemporary analysts might be better equipped to understand the nature of her self-defeating behavior and, more generally, interactions between the two with sado-masochistic overtones. Transference-countertransference issues around patients who have been victims, including the issue of the therapist's frustration and possible reactive anger and sadism, are better theorized and understood now than in Emerson's day. Still, it is worth emphasizing that by both historical and contemporary standards, this patient, with her history of early and ongoing pathological family interactions, including incest, would have presented challenges to anyone.

It is unclear what Emerson gleaned from his readings and practice on the question of the role, prevalence, and treatment implications of intrafamilial seduction and abuse. In Freud's thought, there was no doubting the significance of actual seduction, though he was unsure whether he was over- or underestimating its prevalence.[3] Psychoanalysis as a discipline had not yet begun to translate Freud's elaboration of the role of fantasy and fantasized seduction into a praxis of continuous suspicion that "it didn't really happen." Emerson was working at a time when the model of repressed trauma leading to hysterical symptoms was still regnant, but when other models—involving fantasy, the Oedipus complex, repressed incestuous wishes—were moving center stage. Emerson appears to have been aware of this from the moment he embarked on his analytic career, declaring in 1911 that Freud had "changed his opinion as to the importance of early sexual trauma," now believing, he continued, "that it is not sexual excitements that lead to illness, but the attitude the patient takes toward such experiences."[4] And, although he shortly thereafter invoked "the incest impulse, or in more general terms, the 'the father complex,'" citing Freud's *Three Essays* in doing so,[5] he never once explicitly mentioned the Oedipus complex in any of his published or unpublished writings, a puzzling omission in light of the fact that his American contemporaries were using the term as early as 1913, if not before.[6]

Emerson was working, in this case, with a modified repressed trauma model, seeing the patient's conflicts buttressing the repressions. His readings in the analytic literature and his clinical experience treating hysterical young women nurtured his expectation, at the outset, that he would uncover some sort of sexually tinged trauma. It is not clear from the clinical record how prepared he was to handle the history of sexual assault and incest Rachel reported, nor is it clear that he understood the full import—for the patient's symptoms and for the treatment—of the ongoing active sexual solicitations, which, especially in the later stages of the treatment, were centrally implicated in her decline and the ultimate failure of the analysis. Emerson was eventually willing to credit Rachel's reports of her relations with her brother, characterizing the sex between them as "incestuous." And, late in the treatment, he overcame a good deal of his skepticism regarding what she told him regarding the father, referring in print to the latter's solicitations and "manustupration" of her.[7] Yet, while persuaded of the reality of the fraternal incest and paternal solicitations, he appears to have shied from fully engaging with either, and, more to the point, with Rachel's memories of intercourse with the father. Further, in light of the escalating intensity of Rachel's expressions of desire for her brother—the brother, he wrote at the end of Part II, "is still loved"[8]—Emerson may have been reluctant to consider the family constellation Oedipally, in the register of wishes, fantasies, and desires that he interpreted as *echt* Freudian. That is, it may have proven easier to conceive of Oedipal arrangements and desires in the realm of the symbolic—as in the instance of a young woman, filled with hate for her sadistic father, who engaged in an Oedipal repetition in contracting a "trial marriage" with a man for whom she harbored the same contempt[9]—than to watch an actual father and actual daughter act them out.

Emerson continued to practice psychoanalysis through the 1920s, seeing patients, teaching and delivering lectures, and serving in various capacities in psychotherapeutic and psychoanalytic organizations. He also addressed himself to a larger public, explaining the treatment of ordinary nervousness through "mental analysis," dream interpretation, and moral education in a popular book published in 1918.[10] From the start, Emerson's relations with his medical and psychiatric colleagues were somewhat embattled, as is evidenced in the skepticism toward psychoanalysis and his practice of it aired at the Boston Psychopathic Hospital staff meeting as well as in ongoing tensions with hospital personnel recorded in his case notes. His relationship to psychoanalytic orthodoxy was likewise strained, his disagreements with Freud voiced in print and, as important, his understandings of it increasingly limited and idiosyncratic.[11] Emerson's marginality only intensified in the 1920s as, on the one hand, psychiatric and neurological enthusiasm for a rigid organicism flourished[12] and,

on the other, professionalizing psychoanalysts—locally, nationally, and inter-
nationally—established formal structures governing training and practice,
which, in the United States, largely excluded nonmedical practitioners. Although the Boston Psychoanalytic Society, organized in 1928, would accept,
amid controversy, several nonmedical applicants and practitioners as members,[13] for the most part nonphysicians were excluded, from 1926 on admitted
to membership only upon pledging they would neither practice nor call themselves analysts. Emerson, so much at the center of psychoanalytic practice in
Boston before 1920, is not listed among the society's early members.[14] He died,
in 1939, in a disciplinary limbo, claimed by neither psychology, which had become increasingly experimental since the time he had earned his degree, nor
psychoanalysis, in the official record of which his once-thriving practice would
leave no trace.[15]

This case, which opens so promisingly and closes so equivocally, is open to a
number of readings and interpretations. Some might wish to celebrate Emerson as a heroic pioneer, well intentioned and persistent, who cared deeply
about his patient and established a solid therapeutic alliance with her. Others
might condemn him as rigid and inflexible, tied to his theory and set on uncovering, at any cost, what he was certain were the repressed traumas responsible for her hysterical symptoms; in the grip of a sado-masochistic relationship
with his patient, he could not help but push her to regress and dissociate, leaving her worse off in the end than she had been at the beginning. This is a case,
perhaps like many psychoanalytic cases, where one can easily say, "If only . . . "
If only Emerson knew then what is known now about the treatment of trauma;
if only he had had the emotional wherewithal to listen to Rachel's disguised but
persistent negative feelings about him and the treatment; if only he entered
more fully into her imaginative world—how much more he could have learned
about intense transferential currents constitutive of their relationship. In a mix
of praise, regrets, and condemnation for Emerson and his treatment of Rachel,
there is room for discussion and considerable disagreement on how best to understand the nature, course, and appropriateness of this analysis.

Chapter 10 Patient History and Case Chronology

This chronology has been compiled from information in the case as well as from a four-page-long chronology, prepared by Emerson sometime in early 1913, that follows. As the patient's history did not unfold sequentially in the course of treatment, this is meant as a reference for readers. Note that dates and ages may vary from information in the sessions, some of which was subjected to revision over time.

CHRONOLOGICAL DATA

1889   Patient born (25 July).

1893   (Age 4) Brother born.

1896   (Age 7) Probable beginning of father's sexual abuse and of patient's sexual play with brother.

1897   (Age 8–13) Fractures on seven different occasions.

1899   (Age 10) Sexually assaulted by men in the woods.

1900   (Age 11) (Fall) St. Vitus Dance, lasts approximately one year.

1902   (Age 13) Raped by neighbor, Richard T. Mother insists she has imagined it.

1904   (Age 14–15) Withdraws from school after learning from girls of the sexual act. (February) Meets Henry. (Spring) Discovers father's infidelity.

1906   (Age 17) Menarche.

1907   (Age 18) Relationship with Jack, who seduces her then dies (December). (March) Working regularly as a telephone operator (through March 1908).

1908   (Age 18–19) (March) First convulsions, following mother's accusations of sexual wrongdoing and pregnancy. (May) Gynecological surgery, possibly an abortion. Meets J. J. Putnam while hospitalized.

1909   (Age 19) (October) First contact with Massachusetts General Hospital. Treatment by hypnosis and psychoanalysis.

1910   (Age 20–21) (January) Admitted to Adams Nervine Asylum. (March) Mother's terminal illness, confession of her own sexual infidelity to Rachel; swears her to absolute secrecy and threatens to come back and haunt her if she tells anyone. Dies March 1. (May) Convulsions cease; patient discharged from Adams Nervine. Returns home to care for father and brother.

1911   (Age 22) [birthday is July 25] (Summer, c. 4 July) Convulsions return, with nausea, vomiting, and sleeplessness.

1912   (Age 22–23) (24 January) Begins treatment with Emerson.
       January 1912–May 1912 (Part I); patient at M.G.H., 23 February through 11 May.
       November 1912–May 1914 (Part II); patient at M.G.H., 5–7 December 1912, 26 December 1912 to 16 February 1913; patient at Boston Psychopathic Hospital, 27 February to 2 May 1913.
       February 1915–March 1917, sporadic sessions (Part III); patient at M.G.H., 18 January to 6 March 1917.

1913   (Age 24) Revelation of ongoing sexual solicitations by father and brother.

1915   (Age 26) Last phase of training as nurse; works as nurse in various hospitals.

1916   (Age 27) (December) Brought by police to Boston Psychopathic Hospital in dissociated state.

1917   (Age 28) (March) Last session with Emerson.

1919   (Age 29) (January). Letter to Emerson, informing him she is working and doing better after a brief course of osteopathic treatment.

1921   (Age 32) Last known contact; letter to Mrs. Emerson informing her of engagement, with marriage delayed on account of illness (tuberculosis).

EMERSON'S CHRONOLOGY OF THE TREATMENT[1]

Jan. 24, 1912	Began.
Feb. 19	*Put my hands over her eyes.*
Feb. 23, 1912	*Paralysed and Contracted.*
April 15.	*Hand opened*
May 2.	*Moved her legs a little*
May 11	Discharged from the M.G.H.
June 10	Note on vomiting and "falls occasionally."
Nov. 19	Returned—vomiting.
Dec. 5	*Began auditory hallucinations.*
	"Rae"
Admitted to M.G.H.	
Dec. 7	Discharged
Dec. 10	Letter
Dec. 26	Admitted M.G.H.
Feb. 16 1913	Discharged M.G.H.
Feb. 27	Admitted Psychopathic.
March 4	Bro[ther] called—*hand contracted.*
March 5	See notes—*opened hand.*
	Dreamed she was fooling w[ith] herself.
	(snakes.)
March 14	*Convulsion last night about 6 pm*
	Can stand and walk.
March 21	*Remembers mother played.*[2]
March 22	Dreamed she had lied—wake saying she hadn't, etc.
March 31	"It was *bro[ther], fa[ther]*[3], and everything."
April 1	Dreamed she was hunting for a knife to cut of[f] her hands with.
	Woke up biting her hands.
April 2	*Mother's confession*
April 4	Aphonia. Ret[urned] next day.
April 7	Bit her right forefinger yesterday
	Vis[ual] hal[lucinations] of mo[ther] about 6 times.
April 8	*Confession* as *to mother and fa[ther].*
April 9	Bit herself on r[igh]t arm 4 or 5 times, last night.
April 14	*Knew why she bit herself*

Ward III.

1913

Jan 7	"as if blind" for a moment
Jan 9	*Psychic blindness.*
Jan 16	*Called out bro*[ther]'s *name,* etc.
	Blindness.
Jan 22	"I know he did but I don't know when."
Jan 24	"I know well enough it happened (aet. 16).
	Has been running a temperature.
Feb 4	*Hears music-ringing or humming in ears.*
Feb 16	Discharged from M.G.H.
Feb 24	Blind 5–10 min[utes] yesterday. *Auditory*
	Hal[lucinations]
	Hears music and *mo[ther] calling.*
	Tel[ephone] message-P[atien]t had *lost voice.*
Feb 25	Letter.
Feb 26	*2 Tel[ephone] mess[ages]. P[atien]t had a fit.*
Feb 27	Dr. Dennett-telephone-ether and hypodermic.
	Morphine.
Feb 29	*Paralysed* and *hand closed,* but opened it herself.
	Auditory hallucinations: music and "Rae."

NOTE OF SOME PERSONS MENTIONED IN THE CASE

Mother

Father

Brother, Everett, four years younger than patient

Henry S., friend, met when she was fourteen; lived next door to family. Gave him up in October 1910. Electrician.

Jack (Dick in published account), lover, died in 1907. "Drummer"

Richard T., neighbor who raped her at age thirteen; lived in Beverly, near "aunt"—step-grandmother—c. 1912–onward. Friend of grandfather's. Machinist.

Mr. A., boarded with "aunt" in Beverly

Ella R., friend

Mrs. Frost, housemother

Harry T., married lover, 1916–1917

Cyrus W., rival to Harry T.

Notes

1. Emerson 1912–13, 386.
2. James Jackson Putnam (1846–1918), M.D. Harvard 1870; Instructor (1874), then Professor of Diseases of the Nervous System, Harvard Medical School (1893–1913); founder of the American Neurological Association (1874); head of Neurology at Massachusetts General Hospital (1874–1909); Freud's most ardent American disciple. See Hale 1971b.
3. On the notion of the "specimen case," see Ellenberger 1970.
4. Burnham (1967, 6) notes that not a single American review of *The Interpretation of Dreams* was published in the United States.
5. Meyer 1905a,b. Both cited in Burnham 1967, 6, 18–19.
6. Meyer 1906; cited in Burnham 1967, 19.
7. Hale 1971a, 138. Morton Prince (1854–1929), M.D. Harvard 1879; neurologist and psychotherapist, on the faculty at Harvard Medical School, Tufts College Medical School, and from 1926 to his death, in the new Department of Abnormal and Dynamic Psychology at Harvard (Hale 1971b, 319–20). Prince's journal was more open to psychoanalysis than most others at the time. The author of a well-known study of multiple personality, *The Dissociation of a Personality* (1905), Prince's relations with Freud and psychoanalysis were tense; see Hale 1971b and Marx 1978, as well as Jones's recollections (Jones 1959, 187–88) and his correspondence with Freud (Paskauskas 1995).

8. Putnam 1906.

9. Though he judged it "an adverse one": Jones 1945.

10. On the Boston school, see Hale 1971a, chap. 6; Hale 1971b, 11 ff.; Burnham 1967, chap. 2; Gifford 1978a; and Caplan 1998.

11. William James (1842–1910), M.D. Harvard 1869. At Harvard, he taught comparative anatomy and physiology (1872–1880) as well as philosophy and psychology, becoming professor of the latter two in 1887 and 1889, respectively. James was the author of the monumental *Principles of Psychology* (1890), considered by many to be the discipline's foundational text.

12. Gifford (1978a, 344) lists the following as having met at Prince's house from 1906 to 1908: Prince, Putnam, Jones (although it seems he did not visit Boston until early 1909), Münsterberg, Boris Sidis, Hall, James, Holt, George Waterman, E. W. Taylor, and E. E. Southard; Burnham adds Isador Coriat, August Hoch, Meyer, Emerson, and F. L. Wells, among others, to the list (1967, 25–26). Jones moved from London to Toronto in 1908; Prince invited him shortly thereafter to address the group, which he did on one occasion, reporting to Freud that he had expounded the latter's theories and answered questions for four hours, and commenting on the Americans' "colossal ignorance": Jones to Freud, 7 February 1909 (Paskauskas 1995). See also Jones's letter of 10 December 1908, on Jones's appraisal of the American scene, and compare his less caustic—and less interesting—autobiographical reflections (Jones 1959).

13. Hale 1971a, 5–16.

14. G. Stanley Hall to Sigmund Freud, 7 October 1909, cited in ibid., 17.

15. Ibid., 177–224, esp. quotation 177. The Clark Lectures were published in *Am. J. Psychol.* 21 (1910): 181–218; they appear in the *Standard Edition* as *Five lectures on psycho-analysis* (Freud 1910 [1909]).

16. Burnham 1967, 38; Hale 1971b, 38.

17. Details of Emerson's life are drawn from Taylor 1982.

18. A.M., Harvard, 1905.

19. Emerson 1907.

20. The Emerson Papers contain notes Emerson made on fourteen cases treated in Ann Arbor in 1910 and 1911. In four of these he used a version of Jung's word association exercise. See Duberman 1977 for an account of one of these cases.

21. Emerson was quite conversant with the psychoanalytic literature by 1911, as evidenced both in a paper he published and by his interventions following a discussion of a colleague's paper (Clinical Society of the University of Michigan, 1911). Noting the "large field under cultivation by psychoanalysis," Emerson said, "Obviously I could use all my time merely reading titles" (Emerson 1911, 210).

22. Emerson to Putnam, 4 February 1911, Putnam Papers.

23. Massachusetts General Hospital (M.G.H.), Blossom Street, Boston. Founded in 1811, open to "persons of any race or creed suffering from acute non-contagious diseases" and "unable to pay doctors' fee," the M.G.H. was one of the city's preeminent institutions. Maurice Gerstein, *Medical Directory of Greater Boston,* 4th ed., Boston, 1913–14. Taylor (1982, 44) notes that when Emerson was appointed a consultant to the Department

of Medical Social Service one year later, he was given an office, "a third-floor dressing cubicle in the corner with a curtain, a table, and two chairs."

25. Elmer Ernest Southard (1876–1920), M.D. Harvard 1901; Bullard Professor of Psychiatry, Harvard Medical School, and first superintendent of the Boston Psychopathic Hospital. Largely skeptical regarding psychoanalysis and what he perceived were its exaggerated claims, he was open minded enough to appoint Emerson to the hospital staff. See Lunbeck 1994.

26. Brill 1909, 1913.

27. On the enthusiasm, see, for example, Jones to Emerson, 15 March ? : "How do you like the new Zeitschrift, which I suppose you have received safely by now?" Emerson Papers.

28. Read (1920) mentions Emerson's published work on hystero-epilepsy and includes six of his papers in an impressively complete bibliography of early analytic publications. It is possible Emerson was not much read, as there are no citations of his work from 1920 through 1997 in psychoanalytic journals (including *Contemporary Psychoanalysis, International Journal of Psycho-Analysis, American Journal of Psycho-Analysis, Journal of the American Psychoanalytic Association, Psychoanalytic Quarterly,* and *Psychoanalytic Study of the Child.* Otto Fenichel (1945, 267) cites several of Emerson's papers.

29. McDougall to Emerson, 23 December ?, Emerson Papers. William McDougall (1871–1938), Oxford psychologist who moved to Harvard in 1920; a pivotal figure in attempting to take cognizance of Freudian and Jungian ideas within the context of academic psychology.

30. The group met on Friday afternoons, and was the forerunner of the Boston Psychoanalytic Society (Burnham 1967, 38). Formation of the group is discussed in Putnam to Emerson, 17 December 1913, Emerson Papers.

31. Freud 1912b, which appear in June; Putnam to Emerson, 19 June 1912, Emerson Papers. There is no evidence that this suggested mutual analysis ever materialized. Putnam wrote to Freud the previous year (30 September 1911) that he had "started on a Selbstanalyse," relating to him intimate details concerning his dreams, fantasies, and sexual relations with his wife. "I am glad to hear that our few attempts at analysis have not left you with a bad aftertaste. Self-analysis is a never ending process that must be continued indefinitely," Freud responded several letters later (Freud to Putnam, 5 November 1911), Hale 1971b. On Putnam's "self-analysis," carried on in print, see Jones to Freud, 13 September 1913; and Freud to Jones, 3 January 1914 (Paskauskas 1995).

32. McDougall to Emerson, 23 December ?. Emerson Papers.

33. Breuer and Freud 1893–95.

34. Strachey 1958, 86. It is not clear in any case with whom Emerson might have undergone a personal analysis. For an incisive reading of the papers, see Friedman 1991.

35. Emerson 1912–13, 406.

36. Coriat 1917. Isador Coriat (1875–1943), M.D. Tufts 1900; overlooking Emerson's presence as a fellow practitioner, he later wrote, "for years I worked alone" (Coriat 1945, 6). See Sicherman 1978.

37. However, Freud held that the case of Dora ended prematurely. Cases mentioned in Freud's papers from the 1890s, with which Emerson was also familiar, appear to have

been brief, as do those mentioned in correspondence with Fliess, which Emerson of course could not have read.

38. Freud 1904 [1903], 254.

39. Freud 1913, 129.

40. Freud 1914a, 1915.

41. See, for example, Freud to Putnam, 8 July 1915 (Hale 1971b).

42. Charles W. Birtwell to Emerson, 23 April 1912; Birtwell to Putnam, 23 April 1912. Emerson Papers.

43. Emerson 1913–14b; see also Duberman 1980, on the same case. Louise Kaplan (1991, 553) notes that Emerson's paper is the first of delicate self-cutting reported in the literature.

44. Freud 1910a.

45. Abraham 1922, 22.

46. Emerson 1918–19.

47. Freud 1912a, 107, n. 2.

48. Freud 1910 [1909], 33.

49. Emerson 1913–14e, 197.

50. Friedman 1991; Laplanche and Pontalis 1988, s.v. "transference."

51. Mahony 1986, 90–99. The notion that dreams and daydreams offered means of grasping transferential currents had appeared in the American technique literature by 1916 (Jeliffe 1916, 41).

52. Hale 1971a, 459–60 and endnote. The clinical record cited by Hale is no longer available.

53. Emerson 1913–14b. He closed the article as follows: "While fourteen months, without a relapse, is too short a time upon which to base any prophecy of the future, yet it does give a certain ground for hope" (54).

54. Stern 1921. By the late 1950s, a shift toward reconceptualizing the role of severe trauma in pathogenesis and toward a renewed attention as to how psychoanalysis and psychoanalytic psychotherapy could be used in such cases can be seen in the literature. See Simon and Bullock 1994.

55. We have contacted scholars and archivists worldwide and have found no such similar material, though of course it is possible some may exist and turn up by some fortuitous turn of events. Several cases, one quite extensive, from the early 1920s are to be found in the papers of George Wilbur (Archives of the Boston Psychoanalytic Society and Institute).

56. On social workers' and others' beliefs that there was indeed widespread domestic abuse of adult women and children, see Gordon 1988.

57. Emerson 1913–14e, 199.

58. Emerson 1915b, 426–27.

59. In an undated note to himself, filed among the handwritten notes for this case, Emerson wrote: "Seriousness of symptoms and seriousness of origin: i.e., *adequacy* of *cause*" (emphasis in original).

60. Emerson was in general alert to the different registers in which material surfaced in this treatment. For example, in the Detailed Account (session of 20 February 1912) he noted, after Rachel remembered having been raped, that "she declared the things she had told

me had really happened, only she had forgotten them." He continued: "I was more assured of my position" that she had indeed repressed, not fabricated, the events, because of this. Two weeks later (session 24), he noted he "told her she was dreaming most of the time." The next day, he wrote that "yesterday I thought nothing remained but dreams, to-day I think there is more" (session 25), perhaps signaling a shift in his take on the reality of her dreamlike memories. In subsequent sessions, he asked her, variously, with reference to the scene of the rape, "Was it really so? . . . Is it not all imagination?" (session 34, n. 153) and "It wasn't imagination?" (session 38). Several days later, he noted "that what she saw yesterday was really so" (session 39). Later in the case, the task of evaluating the veracity of her memories became more problematic.

61. The notes Freud made for three months of his year-long treatment of the Rat Man have been published in Freud 1909, where they can be compared to the published version of the case.

62. Ibid., 159. See also Freud 1912b, 113–114.

63. Freud (1912b, 113) allowed that "taking notes during the session with the patient might be justified by an intention of publishing a scientific study of the case." This was, to be sure, Emerson's intention; he wrote in the first paragraph of the DA that "a detailed report of each day's study and treatment will be given . . . ending with an abstract scientific account."

64. DA.

65. Emerson 1912–13, 1913–14d, 1913–14e.

66. Freud 1905 [1901], 16.

67. Rieff 1963, 9, 12.

68. Freud 1905 [1901], 16–17.

CHAPTER 2

1. On the writing of case histories, Kiceluk 1992, 1996; Michaels 2000; Rieff 1963; Wyman and Rittenberg 1992.

2. Breuer and Freud 1893–95, 160.

3. Breuer and Freud 1893–95, 161.

4. Kiceluk 1996.

5. Breuer and Freud 1893–95, 291.

6. Freud 1905 [1901], 12.

7. Freud 1905 [1901], 16.

8. Greenacre (1975, 712) writes that "taking notes, which I generally do quite rapidly and automatically, facilitates rather than distracts me from listening to the patient. . . . Some of my colleagues have told me they found note-taking not only distracting but of little use after the hour."

CHAPTER 3

1. Handwritten notes for sessions 13 through 76 have not survived; see Note on the Text.

2. Emerson 1912–13.

3. Freud 1913.

4. Emerson's handwritten notes, which he abstracted from the German, are titled "Further Suggestions as to the Technique of Psychoanalysis." Although the dates of his notes are unknown, it is likely he read this paper as he did others of Freud's as it was published. Two pages of these notes, which run to six pages, are devoted to what Freud wrote regarding money and fees. "Free treatment is not often successful," Emerson noted. "Many resistances grow out of it. With young women it is the Übertragung." Emerson may at this point have been weighing whether the fact he was treating Rachel without charging her fees was a hindrance to her recovery, as Freud's paper suggests: "The absence of the regulating effect offered by the payment of a fee to the doctor makes itself very painfully felt; the whole relationship is removed from the real world, and the patient is deprived of a strong motive for endeavouring to bring the treatment to an end" (Freud 1913, 132). Still, Emerson wrote, "one can carry the condemnation of money too far." He then crossed out this sentence, ending what he had to say about money with a free translation from Freud's German: "There are occasionally poor patients who can be benefitted." Emerson revisited the issue in print, writing that he was "inclined to take issue with Freud on this point" (Emerson 1913–14c, 291). Emerson noted that "the relation between patient and psychoanalyst is purely personal, and only if the patient is very rich is it of no importance to him as to how long his treatment is to continue. While, on the other hand, if the analyst gets a fee for every interview, it is to his interest to keep the thing going as long as possible" (ibid.). There is evidence in letters from patients to Emerson that fees were an issue, and that patients, as well as those paying for their treatment, could object that his were too high. One statement, dated ? February 1913, for eight "professional visits" and four "consultations" with the patient's husband, amounted to $50.00, which, the husband complained, was unfair: "It seems you should not charge for the 4 consultations. I have always been able to consult with my doctors on cases *without* charge and feel you should *treat* me as well as other physicians." Two months later, the husband, a manufacturer, wrote to Emerson that his bill was "not satisfactory to me being more than I understood between us. I can't afford to pay it and will be willing to pay what is right" (23 April 1913, E. W. B. to Emerson, Emerson Papers). What Emerson's usual fee was is unclear from this exchange.

5. Emerson changed Jack's name to "Dick" in the published account of the case. *The Random House Historical Dictionary of American Slang* (ed. J. E. Lighter [New York, 1994]) gives "a fellow, esp. if foolish or peculiar" as one first meaning for *dick,* and is appears that as late as the 1930s and 1940s it was used as such. It is not clear what, if anything, Emerson intended to convey with this choice of name. *Dick* means "thick" in German; his choice may have represented a consciously sly or unconscious reference to Rachel's possibly having been pregnant by Jack/Dick.

6. Session 22.

7. Emerson 1913–14e, 201.

8. Harry, whom she met at age eighteen; not the same as Henry S., her first boyfriend, whom she met at age fourteen (session 6).

9. Emerson 1913–14e, 202, citing Brill 1909, 100. The felicitous phrase is Brill's; the SE translation is slightly different (Breuer and Freud 1893–95, 282).

10. DA, session 20.

11. "It is highly probable that her suspicions as to his faithfulness, too, were untrue, being based on insufficient evidence. True or not, however, she believed her father bad in a sexual sense, and hated him accordingly" (Emerson 1912–13, 406). There is nothing in the case notes to suggest Emerson shared his suspicions of Rachel's story with her.

12. Emerson discussed this issue in Emerson 1913–14e, 185–86. According to Freud, he wrote, conflict "is the situation out of which rises hysteria. Is this the situation in the present case? That it is can hardly be open to doubt." Emerson's stance on the centrality of conflict was well enough known that Martin Peck (Peck to Emerson, 31 August ?, Emerson Papers) could write that he was reminded "that in your cases, you are apt to consider such 'traumas' . . . , only in the nature of exciting causes, and look for some more fundamental repressed conflict in addition."

13. Forrester 1990, 51; Freud quotation from Freud 1905 [1901], 35–36.

14. Forrester, 1990, 51, building on Lacan 1985, 65: " ' This is all perfectly correct and true, isn't it? What do you want to change in it?' " Emerson gave no indication he had read the case of Dora, but, given the extent of his reading, it seems likely he would have. Meyer (1906) called attention to Dora's tendency "to furnish superficial sham explanations," an observation similar to that Emerson would later make regarding Rachel.

15. In a paper on the issue of the differential diagnosis between epilepsy and hysteria, Emerson proposed "that the epileptiform seizure is of the nature of an orgasm. An orgasm is a sudden, explosive, discharge of nervous energy, raised to the breaking point of nervous tension. I should like to generalize the idea of orgasm. Ordinarily, of course, it is confined to the sexual sphere." He went on to write that one patient's "convulsive-like impulses" were closely associated in his mind with sexual ideas (Emerson 1915–16, 327–28). Read (1920) highlights this contention of Emerson's.

16. DA, 100.

17. DA, 102.

18. DA, 100ff.

19. Emerson 1913–14e, 185, quoting Brill 1909, 198.

20. Emerson 1913–14e, 198.

21. Ibid.; on Freud's position in the transference, see Forrester 1990, 53–54.

22. Southard to Emerson, 15 February 1913, Emerson Papers.

23. Southard to Emerson, 5 July 1913, Emerson Papers.

24. Emerson referred to the notebook in session 71: "For reference to the relation between 'thrills' and 'thoughts' see note book." In session 80, he referred to "p. 24" of these notes, suggesting he recorded a good deal of information in them. The pagination suggests that these notes are not the missing handwritten notes for these sessions; notes for sessions 1 through 12 amounted to seventy-one handwritten sheets. In addition, as noted earlier, during sessions Emerson wrote on sheets of paper, not in a notebook.

25. In the last paragraph of the DA, Emerson admitted that he'd probably "blundered in putting [his] hands over the patient's eyes at all . . . the analysis might have proceeded

more expeditiously and successfully if I had followed Freud more closely and not attempted to force matters."

26. Emerson 1913–14e, 195.

27. Ibid., 195, 198. In reporting his treatment of Miss A., the self-mutilating hysteric, Emerson (1913–14b) sounded a wholly different tone, noting her "natural intellectual ability"
(44) and writing that he'd explained "each step in the analysis to her." Miss A. was in
treatment for one month; Emerson wrote that "no special technique was required to
gain the facts" of the case; "simple questioning" sufficed (53).

28. Emerson 1913–14e, 203.

29. Emerson 1913–14e, 198, 196.

30. Note that these—"encourage," "exhort," "reproach," "threaten"—are the verbs Emerson himself repeatedly used to characterize his interactions with Rachel.

31. Emerson 1913–14e, 196, 195. The first mention of his insistence on her keeping her eyes
shut appears in session 5, in the midst of her free associations: "wishing you wouldn't
have me keep my eyes shut."

32. DA.

33. "This was a modification of the method first used by Freud, where he pressed the tem-
ples of his patients and told them that at the moment of pressure they would see something and think of something which they must tell and which would be important for
the analysis." In his published account, Emerson wrote that he did not use this technique regularly, and that he used it in this case only because it was so difficult. He renounced the practice in treating other patients (Emerson 1913–14e, 196–97).

34. Creelman 1902.

35. Ibid., 157–60. See also 161–86, where Hugh is hypnotized and seduced into marriage.
He thinks he's dreamed that he was wedded, and then discovers that Miss Grush has actually had a ceremony performed while he was hypnotized.

36. Thanks to Christopher Bullock for this formulation.

37. DA.

38. All details and quotations from DA.

39. Emerson 1913–14e, 196.

40. Ibid., 185.

41. Sándor Ferenczi would later report that he prohibited a patient's habitual leg-crossing
as she lay on his consulting room sofa, convinced that she was masturbating by pressing her thighs together. "I explained to her that . . . she was carrying out a larval form
of onanism that discharged unnoticed the unconscious impulses and allowed only useless fragments to reach the material of her ideas." This move eventually "permitted the
discovery of most important traumatic causes for her illness" (Ferenczi 1927, quotation
191).

42. Henry C. Baldwin, (1895–1915), M.D. Harvard 1884; Neurologist at M.G.H.

43. Emerson wrote that "at first I was much disturbed by interruptions, but as the work
went on I noticed the patient was herself not cognizant, so far as I could tell, of such interruptions as are frequent in the examining rooms of an out-patient department. I explained this by the patient's *almost absolute self-absorption*" (Emerson 1913–14c, quotation, 290; emphasis in original).

44. Emerson 1912–13, 406.
45. Cf. Freud, on the conflicts a woman can experience between desire and duty: "Nothing protects her virtue as securely as an illness" (Freud 1908, 195).
46. Alpheus Felch Jennings, M.D. Harvard 1910; House Officer, Massachusetts General Hospital.
47. Freud 1910b, 221–27. Summarizing his treatment of Miss A., Emerson wrote that "another course which would have been not only futile but actively harmful was also avoided. I mean the assumption that what the patient was suffering from was lack of specific sexual satisfaction and advising sexual relations or masturbation" (Emerson 1913–14b, 54).
48. DA, session 22.
49. The first mention of her lying down appears in session 28; in sessions 29 through 32, and in session 36, Emerson mentioned that he had her lie down, after which it was presumably standard practice. In session 42, he mentioned that he turned her so that she wouldn't be able to see him.
50. Emerson 1912–13, 403.
51. Ibid., 400.
52. DA.
53. Emerson 1912–13, 403
55. Emerson 1913–14e, 197–199.
55. The phrase "tender mother role" is Freud's: Freud to Ferenczi, 13 December 1931, in Falzeder and Brabant 2000, 23; cited by Forrester 1991, 61.
56. Emerson 1913–14e, 197.
57. Ibid., for the mining metaphor; and 197ff. on the transference.
58. Ibid., 197.
59. Compare Freud 1912a, which appeared in German in 1912, and which Emerson cited in the published case history, with Emerson 1913–14e, 203–4 esp.
60. Emerson 1913–14e, 203.
61. DA. Emerson never expressed sentiments this harsh in print. But, while he could allow that "it is no easy thing to renounce one's father" (1913-14e, 205), he attended, in print, very little to Rachel's often-expressed desires for her mother (see Mahoney 1986, 35–36, on Freud's slighting of the mother's role in the case of the Rat Man).
62. Emerson 1913–14e, 203.
63. Ibid.
64. Ibid.
65. Staff Meeting, Boston Psychopathic Hospital, 15 April 1913; in chapter 6.
66. Menninger 1961, 137.
67. DA.
68. Morton Prince to Emerson, 17 February 1913. Emerson both underscored the offending word and added another sentence, concluding the first part of the article using the precise words with Prince supplied him: "The recovery, however, was only apparent." In a quiet reproach to Prince and his meddling, Emerson added that "the worst symptoms, the *contracture* and the *convulsions* . . . have never returned." It is likely he wrote this shortly after receiving Prince's letter, which was accompanied by proofs of the article.

On 26 February 1913, Rachel had a grand hysterical attack, after which she was hospitalized. It is possible Emerson interpreted this as another reproach, leveled this time by Rachel.

CHAPTER 4

1. "From that time till last summer she had remained free from both convulsions and vomiting." After her mother's death, she "determined to get well," to care for her brother, "for whom she felt a mother's responsibility. . . . Whatever the determination had to do with it, she did start gaining, right off, and was discharged, in just two months, the convulsions having ceased" (Emerson 1912–13, 385–86).

2. Adams Nervine Asylum, Jamaica Plain, Boston; founded in 1873 and opened in 1880, "for the benefit of such indigent, debilitated, nervous people who are not insane," inhabitants of Massachusetts. The institution also received paying patients. It was relatively small, with forty-nine beds, thirty-eight of which were for women. Thirty-one percent of the 219 patients admitted in 1910, the year Rachel was admitted, received free care; the occupations of patients ranged from manufacturers and merchants (male) to dressmakers and telephone operators (female). Adams Nervine Asylum patient records no longer exist (Managers of the Adams Nervine Asylum 1910).

3. In his handwritten notes, Emerson recorded that he next asked her, "When was the very first time?"

4. I.e., the first convulsion. Emerson wrote that "the patient was referred to me because of convulsions, persistent nausea, and sleeplessness." She attributed her first convulsion "to the nervousness she felt at a 'bad test' "—most likely an employment test—and to "the 'terrible' chief operator who 'scolded' " (DA).

5. Emerson would later revise the date of the mother's death to 1910, and the time elapsed to two years.

6. St. Vitus's Dance (after St. Vitus, a martyred Christian child [245–313 A.D.], the patron saint of epileptics and dance) or Sydenham's chorea (after Thomas Sydenham, English physician [1624–1689]), an acute toxic disorder of the central nervous system secondary to rheumatic infection, usually seen in girls younger than the age of fifteen. Often mistaken for hysteria, its symptoms included involuntary movements and agitated emotional instability (Campbell 1981, s.vv. "chorea," "Sydenham's"). Emerson referred to the condition as "St. Vitus Dance"; we have as well, in the interest of consistency.

7. "Mother dead 3 years this coming March" (handwritten notes).

8. Emerson filled in more details later, noting when he wrote up this session that Rachel had been suspicious of her father for some time. "When she was about 16, she knew. 'I followed him one night.' She said two years ago she read a postal a woman sent to her father asking her to meet her at a certain square. . . . She followed her father to Boston; she saw him meet the woman and go off with her." Father brought this woman home, expecting Rachel would serve him supper, which she refused to do (DA).

9. "She could remember how she hated him when she was five. Her mother told her it was so, she said, when she was three" (Emerson 1912–13, 387).

10. "In hysterical somnambulism thinking of suicide and looking for poison" (DA).

11. A later correction, penciled in, in Emerson's hand.

12. Penciled in, in Emerson's hand.

13. "She said she thought he was a hypocrite" (Emerson 1912–13, 388).

14. Emerson wrote, "I asked her to shut her eyes and tell me what she thought of when I gave her a certain word: I started the Free Association with the word (1) Cloud" (DA).

15. "First suspicions of feelings against father when in Brightwood" (handwritten notes).

16. In response to Emerson's asking, "What do you know about badness between man and wife?" (Emerson 1912–13, 388).

17. "Spells first 2 at 19 or 20 in Telephone Company. St. Vitus Dance at 11—Father mocked her etc." (handwritten notes). "But talking about these matters does not relieve her" (DA).

18. Most likely a class at school, in a system of "manual training . . . designed for training in the use of tools and materials but emphasizing training in wood carving as a means to this end" (*Webster's Third New International Dictionary* [Springfield, Mass., 1986], s.v. "sloyd").

19. In handwritten notes, "other men."

20. In parentheses, inserted above the text, Emerson wrote, "Discussion about sex" (handwritten notes).

21. Infection of the mastoid bone, adjacent to the ear; in the preantibiotic era, a common sequela of middle ear infections.

22. Henry S., Rachel's first boyfriend.

23. "Told her if he were she he would look out for him" (handwritten notes).

24. "Was in Nervine January to May 1909" (handwritten notes).

25. "Birthday 1889. 22 July 25, 1911. Mother died March 1, 1909" (handwritten notes). George A. Waterman (1872–1960), M.D. Harvard 1899; neurologist and psychotherapist; Instructor in Neurology, Harvard Medical School. See Gifford 1978b.

26. "Fall of 1900, til about 1901" (handwritten notes).

27. "This girl was the origin of her suspicions" (handwritten notes).

28. Emerson, in DA, titled this segment "Free Associations," and wrote that they "hardly came as smoothly, or as 'free' as they read. I had to urge her continually to tell about what was in her mind. My method was to say 'Next,' 'What now,' 'Now,' etc. The content of the associations is entirely her own, but to get them at all required much psychic effort on my part."

29. Vomited or regurgitated, probably a mixture of partially digested food and bile.

30. "Knowing her feeling against her father, and assuming her nausea to be perhaps a sort of moral disgust at his sexual misdeeds, and hypocritical religiosity, I asked her if the nausea had not come from having to sit at the table with him" (Emerson 1912–13, 388–89).

31. "But while moral disgust might lead to nausea, it was certainly no adequate reason for the convulsions which followed. To find an adequate cause for that I must search much further" (ibid.).

32. "Felt cloud, blue, but not so heavy as now, about a year ago. About last 4 July. Vomiting started about this time too" (handwritten notes).

33. "Starting on another tack, I asked her about her first knowledge of sex" (DA).

34. "Knowledge of sex made her sick all over and felt like throwing up. Was nauseated, didn't vomit" (handwritten notes).

35. "The Übertragung has commenced" (DA).

36. The Austrian-born American psychoanalyst Abraham Arden Brill (1874–1948); M.D. Columbia 1903, translated Jung's lectures, "The Association Method," which were delivered at Clark University in 1909. They were published in *American Journal of Psychology* 21 (1910). The association list appears in Jung 1909. See Figure 5.

37. Number 99 of 100 words in Jung's list is "woman" (Jung 1909, 440).

38. Winston Churchill, *The Crisis* (1901), a fictionalized rendering of the Civil War; Augusta Jane Evans, *St. Elmo* (1867), and the best-selling *Beulah*, the tale of an orphan girl who finds both faith and love (1859). Chronicling "the anxious and conflicted coming-of-age of a young southern woman in the late 1850s" the book "is a classic *Bildungsroman*"whose popularity owed something to the growing vogue for the "psychological" or "subjective" novel (Fox-Genovese 1992, xii, xiv). Evans's novels were still popular at this time; her 1864 novel, *Macaria, or, Altars of Sacrifice*, was reprinted into the twentieth century (Faust 1992), and her 1902 novel, *A Speckled Bird*, sold 100,000 copies within a month of its appearance (Drew Gilpin Faust, personal communication). Elements of the plots in her books as well as in her life are very suggestive when considered alongside Rachel's story. Evans writes of women—fictional and real—who share profound ambivalences about marriage, work, and the proper place of religion and science in moral life; further, these women pass through periods of crisis (war, loss of love, disease) that generate the narratives (novel, biography, case record) they have left behind. Rachel's drama is distinguished from those of her literary counterparts primarily by the fact that her crisis is framed by the concepts and vocabulary of scientific medicine. Her literary precursors, by contrast, drew to a greater degree on Victorian themes of the "struggle for faith." Rachel was possibly aware that her literary heroine committed suicide in 1909.

39. "[Discussion of spells]. I worry over every little thing" (handwritten notes, brackets in original).

40. "I asked if she could remember anything she was especially worried about at this time. She said she was worried about her relations with Dick. (He was the one who died.)" (Emerson 1912–13, 389). Note that Emerson referred to Jack as "Dick" in the published account.

41. In response to Emerson's questioning her about Jack's character (DA).

42. " 'Did he ever take any liberties with you?' I asked, 'or insult you?' 'No,' she answered" (Emerson 1912–13, 390).

43. I.e., traveling salesman.

44. "I asked her if she thought it was right to go with such a man, against her parents' wishes" (DA).

45. " 'And his death was a great shock to you?' 'No, I was rather glad; I felt relieved.' 'Why?' 'Well, I had already thrown him over before he died' " (DA).

46. " 'So when he went that night, I told him he needn't come again' " (DA).

47. I.e., the hospital (DA).

48. Creelman 1902.

49. The third of four dreams remembered from the previous night.

50. I.e., Adams Nervine Asylum.

51. "Just after she came back from Pawtucket [unintelligible] . . . and thought she was going insane" (handwritten notes).

52. "Smoke—fire—different fires I've seen—how I felt. Repulsive feeling toward father came on about when she had St. Vitus dance. She left school" (handwritten notes).

53. I.e., suffering from St. Vitus Dance.

54. "Associations" (handwritten notes).

55. I.e., dancing.

56. "My mind." This was in response to Emerson's asking for free associations (Emerson 1912–13, 391). Note that this is the first time Emerson made a note of a silence.

57. " 'You can tell if you will,' I asserted," Emerson wrote (ibid.).

58. Rachel may here have been reporting the so-called globus hystericus—"the sensation of a ball or globe that arises in the stomach area and progress upward, being finally felt in the throat where it produces the feeling of strangulation" Campbell 1981, s.v. "globus hystericus."

59. This is the first time Emerson alludes to a joint discussion and interpretation of a dream.

60. "I asked her about her mother" (Emerson 1912–13, 391).

61. "(The patient was sitting with eyes closed.)" (ibid.).

62. " 'What do you see now?' I asked" (ibid.).

63. " 'What thoughts?' " (ibid.).

64. " 'It looks as if something were being concealed,' I said" (ibid., 392).

65. " 'What for?' I asked" (ibid.).

66. I.e., the mother.

67. With a pencil, Emerson drew a line between "insulted" and "assault."

68. "She wears her mother's ring on the fourth finger of her left hand" (DA).

69. "I asked her to close her eyes, and tell me what she saw" (Emerson 1913–14).

70. "She tried to turn the course of events by saying . . . " (DA).

71. "It was only with the greatest difficulty that the above information was gained. It was next to impossible to get her to keep her eyes shut, or to get her to tell what was in her mind. Becoming impatient at her refusal to keep her eyes shut, I stood behind her and put my hands over her eyes, and demanded that she tell me what she saw" (DA). In the published account, Emerson wrote, "Despairing of ever being able to persuade her to look voluntarily, I put my hands over her eyes, and told her to look and tell me what she saw" (Emerson 1912–13, 392).

72. "The details of what all this meant I was unable to determine. At first she refused ever to come back, threatening suicide, etc.; but finally she became somewhat reconciled" (DA). In the published account, Emerson wrote, "She felt terribly at the apparent corroboration of our suspicions" (Emerson 1912–13, 392).

73. "She had twisted and turned and writhed terribly, while I held my hands over her eyes, but I insisted that she look and tell me what she saw. This required great 'psychic effort' " (DA).

74. The published account then reads, "but made her responsibility . . ." (Emerson 1912–13, 392).

75. "I had promised not to question her further if she were unwilling" (DA).

76. The published account of the assault stops here, leaving out the details of the rape. That account in general plays down or omits direct and graphic language about rape and assault. It continues with "then her mind turned to the room again. In the room she saw the neighbor again" (Emerson 1912–13, 393).

77. The published account again breaks off at this point; none of the rest of the paragraph appears in it. "The man" refers to the neighbor.

78. "In her chair, as she told me this" (DA).

79. "I told her I thought we had now got to the bottom of her trouble and told her so. I told her that now she had relieved herself by telling these terrible things which had been on her mind, that she would probably have no more attacks. I was the more assured of my position because she declared the things she had told me had really happened, only she had forgotten them. How she could have done so, she could not imagine. She felt much disturbed at being told, because she felt as though she had promised not to tell. To know these things as facts, however, seemed terrible to her" (DA).

80. "I had to pacify her somewhat, however, and she promised to come back Friday" (DA).

81. Preceded by, "The telling of her trouble did not have the desired result" (DA).

82. "I know now that we had not got to the bottom of her trouble" (DA).

83. The published account of the assault breaks off here.

84. "The telling of this, however, did not relieve her" (DA).

85. "She wanted me to let her go home, but I felt that if she did, it would only be to have more convulsions and that it would be better to get to the bottom of the thing at once, if possible, and have it over with. So I held my hands over her eyes and insisted that she tell me what she saw. She resisted strongly, twisting, turning and writhing about in her chair. She seemed about to have an attack, but I persisted and suddenly it passed" (DA).

86. "At the recommendation of Dr. Lee" (DA). Roger I. Lee (1881–1965), M.D. Harvard 1905; Physician to Out-Patient Department, M.G.H.

87. "It is interesting to note this transformation of the symptoms. During the interview the patient had every appearance of being about to have a convulsion, but instead of that she became paralysed. It was as if something were trying to come to her mind but could not get in, and was crowded instead into her legs and hand. Whatever happened, it carried with it a complete loss of voluntary control. The hand was clenched, about the thumb, and could not be opened; the legs hung limp, flexible, and utterly powerless; she could no more stand on them than if they had been tape. *What* it was, however, that flew from her head, and took refuge in her limbs, she did not know. Her nearest description of it was that it was a 'cloud.' "

"What that 'cloud' concealed was now the object of our quest." . . .

"Here is a reason for the recurrent 'old dream,' in which she ran and stumbled and picked herself up and ran on stumbling. Here is one reason for feeling that 'something awful' had happened to her. Here is a reason for dreaming she was in the woods running away from something. Here is a reason for feeling she had hidden something. She had hidden this thing. She had never told anybody. And here is an adequate reason for the so-called St. Vitus Dance, which followed in a few months. Here, too, we may see the origin of the patient's strong feeling against sex. But the release of whatever repression that had resulted in the crowding out of consciousness of the memory of this early event, was not sufficient to afford any apparent relief. Much still remained to be done" (Emerson 1912–13, 393–94).

88. "At my insistence, she remembered and reproduced many scenes with him. But she could remember none of especial significance. I put my hands over her eyes" (ibid.).

89. "I got her to tell me all she could about Jack. The most significant thing that she remembered was this: She was at his house once with a party and just as she entered the room where he was she overheard him say to another girl" the remark that follows (DA).

90. "This troubled her a good deal and she wondered what he meant" (DA).

91. "I told her to be brave and look things in the face no matter what they were" (DA).

92. Emerson noted that he was discouraged at the slowness of his progress at this point (DA).

93. "I questioned her about the assault in the woods" (DA).

94. "She knows her mother was unlikely to have believed her if she had told" (DA).

95. Emerson had "asked her about the time at school when the girl told the smutty story" (DA).

96. "I asked her whether she ever thought about the assault" by the neighbor (DA). Emerson omitted this from the published version.

97. "And told her to tell me what she saw or thought of" (DA).

98. "Then her mind turned to the woods; then she saw the neighbor; then back to her mother and to Dick [i.e., Jack]" (Emerson 1912–13, 395).

99. In ibid., "that" is substituted for "as."

100. "Mother always said she'd come back" (DA).

101. Where the attack took place.

102. This sentence is omitted from the published version.

103. This "startles" Emerson. "I now thought I knew why her attacks had not stopped with the former revelations. She had not told all. It seemed probable that Jack had tempted her and she had fallen. Whatever the truth might turn out to be, however, her hand would not relax, neither would she regain the use of her legs, until she had remembered all there was to remember and faced it bravely, bad as it might be." (DA). Of the following two sessions, Emerson wrote: "The next two days yielded little in the way of tangible results" (Emerson 1912–13, 395).

104. In the dream, Emerson wrote, "We see the conflict set up by her own cravings clashing with her mother's emotional training" (DA).

105. Emerson noted that "the above shows the progress of the Übertragung, or transference of her affections to me. On this I had to depend, for her willingness to tell me further details of her past experiences, distressing as these might seem" (DA).

106. "In view of these facts," Emerson found this "not surprising" (DA).

107. "In her silent, probably more or less sullen set against the author of her being, she was but unconsciously imitating her mother in the most despicable of her moods" (DA).

108. In October 1909, Rachel was admitted to the Massachusetts General Hospital, where Putnam (and possibly others) treated her with hypnosis and psychoanalysis, unsuccessfully, Emerson would later note. It is likely Rachel first met Putnam when she was hospitalized, in May 1908, at the New England Hospital for Women and Children, at which time he was serving as consulting neurologist to the hospital.

109. "Another boy," according to Emerson (i.e., not Henry S.). Rachel reported to Emerson that "she woke up hearing herself holler, 'Let me tell it.'" She began talking about Harry as soon as she saw Emerson, telling him that "Harry was distinctly a bad boy." (DA).

110. I.e., streetcars.

111. I.e., bicycle.

112. "But she said she never had anything whatever to do with Harry. She hated him" (DA).

113. Leslie H. Spooner (1881–1925), M.D. Harvard 1907; Assistant Physician to the Out-Patient Department, M.G.H. Salvarsan, or 606, was the trade name of an arsenic compound, rather toxic, discovered by Paul Ehrlich in 1909, and used to treat syphilis.

114. Edith Burleigh, social worker at M.G.H., active in the treatment milieu, and Superintendent of the Girls' Parole Department, Boston; see Lunbeck 1994.

115. George Cheever Shattuck (1879–1972), M.D. Harvard 1905; Assistant Physician to the Out-Patient Department, M.G.H.

116. Possibly James Lander Gamble (1883–1959), M.D. Harvard 1910; House Officer, M.G.H.

117. Richard Clarke Cabot (1868–1939), M.D. Harvard 1892; Professor at Harvard Medical School, physician and founder of the Social Service Department at M.G.H.

118. Zander treatment, after Dr. Gustaf Zander, a method of medical gymnastics employing a mechanical apparatus, based on the principle of "movement as a therapeutic agent." Groups of muscles were exercised sequentially, and the extent of movement and the energy expended were carefully measured. The operator moved his own muscles and the machine caused the patient's corresponding muscle groups to move—an interesting metaphor for the mutual engagement in psychoanalysis. Levertin (1893) contains many illustrations (quotation, 9). Fifty-four Zander machines were installed in the M.G.H. in 1904, and were in use until 1917 (Washburn 1939, 329). On hydrotherapy, see Hinsdale 1910.

119. "Then I asked her what she herself now thought was the real trouble." Her answer follows (DA).

120. "'Would you not be willing to look and see if it is so?' I asked" (Emerson 1912–13, 395).

121. "(To escape the consequences of adultery)" (DA).

122. I.e., the stumbling dream.

123. A 1912 report from the Department of Neurology, M.G.H., noted that massage was "being given in systematic fashion, without compensation, by three persons" (Washburn 1939, 319).

124. New England Hospital for Women and Children, Roxbury, founded in 1862 to give women "medical aid of competent physicians of their own sex." See Drachman 1984.

125. Emma V. Culbertson (1854–1920), M.D. Women's Medical College of Pennsylvania 1881; 1913–14, Attending Surgeon, New England Hospital for Women and Children. See below, sessions 244–257, and accompanying notes. Culbertson operated on Rachel in 1908, most likely performing an abortion.

126. "I told her she was dreaming most of the time, and that her dreams were so real to her that they had an effect equal to actuality. Thus her convulsions were really intensified orgasms, symbolizing an imagined coitus with Jack" (DA).

127. "But was absolutely helpless. Her hand remained contracted" (Emerson 1912–13, 396).

128. "'Try to look and know,' I urged" (ibid.).

129. Emerson asked her, "Why are you so afraid to look?" (DA).

130. "You must look . . . and tell me what you see," Emerson said (DA).

131. "This is further evidence of the 'Übertragung' or transference" (DA). See Chapter 3 on *Eagle Blood*, involving hypnotism and marriage.

132. Presumably to keep her hand open.

133. "When I held my hands over her eyes, she had a very significant series of visions" (Emerson 1912–13, 396).

134. I.e., the secret.

135. Ella R., a friend.

136. Mr. A., who boarded with her step-grandmother, or "aunt," in Beverly, a town on the North Shore of Boston, approximately seven miles north of the city.

137. A beach resort north of Boston.

138. "She comes every morning to the 'Nerve Room' in a wheel chair, which has a back that can be let down. When I tilt it back she lied on this as on a stretcher" (DA).

139. "(She had had hard work to decide to do so.)" (Emerson 1912–13, 397).

140. "This man from Beverly looks so much like him," meaning Jack (session 29).

141. Barclay 1910, pp. 50 ff., a popular novel. The heroine, a plain woman with a beautiful soul, volunteers to sing at an aristocratic gathering, and becomes transfigured as she sings a reverential love song, "The Rosary." The hero falls in love with her as she sings, and he declares his love; she blindly rejects him, and then deeply regrets it, and has a change of heart. Meanwhile, he has become blinded by an accident and has hardened his heart against her, and she disguises herself as a nurse to care for him. He falls in love with her, as nurse, and through a complicated plot she woos him successfully and they happily wed. The verses of the song contain phrases such as "The hours I spent with you are as pearls on a string and the memories of you become as beads on a rosary." There are clearly powerful transference feelings encoded in these words, as indeed in the plot as a whole, where the heroine wins the heart of the hero by becoming his caretaker. The theme of blindness is suggestive in light of Rachel's inability to see clearly.

142. "Suddenly she started violently, and I asked her what happened" (Emerson 1912–13, 397).

143. "She then went on to tell how badly she felt whenever she saw this neighbor" (ibid.).

144. The neighbor, who at this point lived in Beverly.

145. "The man comes occasionally to visit her father" (Emerson 1912–13, 397).

146. "Yet at the same time she was not conscious of any reason for her feeling. Here then is a striking amnesia. Such an exciting experience for a sensitive girl of thirteen, as being thrown to the floor, by a neighbor, whom she disliked, to whom she had been sent by her mother, probably on some trivial errand, would not normally be easily forgotten. She would naturally remember how she picked herself up afterwards and got home. Here, then, is a problem" (ibid.).

147. Emerson left this sentence out of the published version of the case. It is unclear whether Rachel said this or whether it is his speculation.

148. "I had her lie back in her chair and close her eyes. She reproduces the scene of the attack" (Emerson 1912–13, 398).

149. Menstrual flow.

150. Possibly a Dr. Johnson (not identified), mentioned at the end of the dream. Several Johnsons practice medicined in Boston at this time, but we could not determine if any were black; there was no Dr. Johnson on the M.G.H. staff. It is not clear whether Rachel's Dr. Johnson was a real figure.

151. Not identified; one of several Dr. Smiths on the M.G.H. staff in 1912.

152. "Then, as nothing further seemed to come, I put. . . ." (Emerson 1912–13, 398).

153. " 'Was it really so?' I asked. 'Is it not all imagination?' " (ibid.).

154. Prefaced by, "This morning I tried to speak lightly and said," (DA).

155. "I asked" (Emerson 1912–13, 399).

156. Her grandfather's people wanted to invite him to tea (DA).

157. I.e., Adams Nervine Asylum.

158. "And when after a morning of fruitless effort I asked her if she didn't feel sorry at our lack of success, she replied" (Emerson 1912–13, 398).

159. "I adopted a rather stern attitude towards her, and scolded her for not trying as hard as she might" (DA).

160. "She reproduces the same scene as before, but this time added more details. He struggles with her and finally does get on the bed but she slips off and lies on the floor" (DA).

161. I.e., drawers down.

162. "I assured her that she must not only 'know' it, in an intellectual sense, but she must actually realize it, and get rid of her pent-up emotion. She must cry" (DA).

163. "And she ended piteously" (DA).

164. "Friday and Saturday brought little advance" (Emerson 1912–13, 399).

165. "This rather long series of free associations I got this morning seemed significant. I will give most of them here" (DA).

166. "At this point I really scolded her for not being braver, for not trying harder to look and see the whole thing through" (DA).

167. Rachel had perhaps internalized Emerson's technique here, involuntarily reproducing the writing exercise performed in several sessions.

168. Presumably as an aid to free association.

169. "She said, 'I was thinking of the woods' " (Emerson 1912–13, 399).

170. Emerson thought these words were especially significant, in light of revelations that were yet to come (Emerson 1912–13, 400).

171. I.e., Rachel's father.

172. Hermann C. Bucholz, M.D. Leipzig, Germany, 1901; Assistant in Orthopedic and Physical Therapy, Harvard Medical School; Orthopedic Surgeon and Surgeon in Charge of Medico-Mechanical Department, M.G.H.

173. "She again reproduced the scenes in the woods and in the room, but this time separate and distinct. The only thing she added to the previous accounts was the assurance that in the assault in the woods she knew only one man tried coitus-like movements with her" (DA).

174. From this point until "I know I am keeping something back," does not appear in Emerson 1912–13, 400.

175. Emerson left the following eight sessions out of the published account, writing, "the next week showed no apparent advance" (ibid.).

176. "She gave a lot of free associations, but nothing of significance" (DA).

177. Perhaps in reference to the scene in session 10, in which she overheard Baldwin "throw a girl . . . into a hypnotic convulsion," which Emerson likened to an orgasm, thus belying his contention that her complete self-absorption protected her from the effects of such intrusions (1913–14c, 290; see chapter 3, n. 43). Baldwin had, by this point in the case, been involved in the exhaustive efforts to force open her hand.

178. Emerson's entire entry in DA for this session reads, "Nothing of significance was either learned or done to-day."

179. Emerson's own notes show he had seen her 47 times.

180. "The patient was unable to come to the out patient clinic owing to a slight indisposition. Tuesday was the same" (DA).

181. Richard S. Eustis, M.D. Harvard 1911; House Officer, M.G.H.

182. "She told me the name of one of the two men who assaulted her in the woods. The other man she never knew, she said, except by sight" (DA).

183. "I told her to lie down, when she got back to the ward, and consciously try to identify this feeling" (DA). "The next two days showed little advance" (Emerson 1912–13, 400).

184. "To get this feeling she had to lie flat on her back" (DA).

185. "She got her hand part way open last night. She was lying on her back and for a moment knew the end. Her hand partly opened with this knowledge, and then her mind came back to the hand itself, and it closed again. She ended piteously, 'I don't know it now at all.' 'Afterwards,' she added, 'it seemed as if I knew it and yet I did not know it; just as when you know a person's name and have it right on the end of your tongue and can't say it.'" Emerson gave her another association test and found that her association time had been reduced, which he attributed to "the release of many unconscious inhibitions and . . . the progress of the psycho analysis" (DA).

186. "She said, despairingly" (Emerson 1912–13, 400).

187. An "occupational therapy" class, led by a trained teacher, paid for by Putnam. "The class included psycho-neurotic out-patients" (Washburn 1939, 475).

188. The phrase "the whole list" was inserted above the line of type between "those" and "words."

189. William James.

190. "Here we can see an almost complete Übertragung or transference of her affections from her mother to me. As dreams are symbolical fulfillment of wishes, her second dream of this same night [follows in text] is also significant" (DA).

191. Probably for a clinical demonstration before a group of medical students; see dream in session 59.

192. "But when I was that age my parents said I couldn't" (Emerson 1912-13, 401).

193. "The following Monday, April 15, our persistent efforts were rewarded" (ibid.).

194. "I then had her lie down, on her wheel chair, and questioned her, using these phrases, adding some phrases and words I knew myself. . . . It is evident that the resistances

are gradually breaking down. Having recently read the paper on obscene words by Ferenczi, in the *Zentralblatt für Psychoanalyse* [Ferenczi 1911], I determined to try if I could not overcome her resistance to realizing the end of the assault in the room by using some such words. As many of the patient's resistances against speaking of such things had already been overcome, I got from her, with no great difficulty, the slang phrases used by the girl who told the 'smutty' story that so upset her when she was fifteen" (DA). The translated paper (Ferenczi 1916) opens noting that "in all analyses one is sooner or later faced with the question of whether one should mention in front of the patient the popular (obscene) designations of the sexual and excremental organs, functions, and material, and get him to utter in an unvarnished, unaltered way the obscene words, phrases, curses, etc., that occur to his mind." Several pages later, Ferenczi writes, "I came to the conclusion that the popular (obscene) designations for sexuality and excretion, the only ones known to the child, are in the most intimate manner associated with the deeply repressed nuclear complex of the neurotic as well as of the healthy" (ibid., 112, 115).

195. "The questioning made her sick to her stomach; she thought of the woods, then of the room" (DA).

196. I.e., what had happened. "While lying back in her chair, with her eyes closed, she said, '*yes, I know it*,' and as she said this, her hand opened, and she put it to her head in most dramatic fashion" (Emerson 1912–13, 401).

197. Although her hand had opened, Rachel was still paralyzed, "having no control whatever over either leg" (DA).

198. In this class she used the hand that had been clenched for so long (DA).

199. Emerson deemed these dreams significant (DA).

200. I.e., she remembered the assault more clearly, "but the last thing she can remember is just lying exhausted on the floor" (DA).

201. Emerson did not comment on this in DA.

202. "I asked her why she had not had a convulsion instead of being paralyzed. She answered, first, because she didn't want to have one before me; and second, because she was so afraid if she did have one, the doctors would stick pins in her, to test her, as they did before" (Emerson 1912–13, 402).

203. "But still her legs remained powerless, so we turned our attention to clearing up completely her stubborn amnesia for the final details, the finale" (DA).

204. "Trying more drastic means of overcoming this resistance, I had the patient lie on the floor and left her there, alone in the room, telling her she could get up herself if she remembered the rest of the events occurring after the assault, such as, how she got up, how she got home, what her mother said, etc. After ten or fifteen minutes wait I went back, only to find, however, that my efforts, if of any effectiveness at all, were not immediately so. She remembered nothing more than what she had already revealed; and her legs remained useless. She was still paralyzed" (DA).

205. "When the girl told her about sexual matters, when she was about fifteen, she almost lost the use of her legs and they thought she was going to have 'St. Vitus Dance' again. Thursday and Friday we got nowhere" (Emerson 1912–13, 403).

206. "Last night the patient showed the effect of my experiment" (DA).

207. "This dramatic struggle of two opposing influences for supremacy, in the theater of the brain, during a dream, is highly significant of mental processes in general" (DA).

208. Since the previous Wednesday night (DA).

209. "Today, for the first time, she had a somatic feeling in her genitals, showing that the abnormal anesthesia there is passing away" (DA).

210. "To-day the patient told me the name of the neighbor who assaulted her" (DA).

211. "To-day I tried another device for helping her to get at her unconscious memories. I had her write a list of any words that come to her mind" (DA).

212. I.e., of the list of words she had written out. After she wrote "times I was with him [Jack]," she "threw down the pencil and refused to go on." Ten words later she wrote "you and here and everything I've told you." Emerson commented, "slow, feeling ought not to have told so much." He did not reproduce the list in the typed daily case notes (DA).

213. Because she was "so upset" by the fear that Jack may have done something to her. She finally consented to come, Emerson wrote (DA).

214. "Wednesday, Thursday and Friday showed no advance" (Emerson 1912–13, 403).

215. "I had her write another list of words, but got nothing of sufficient importance to record here" (DA).

216. "It has seemed for some time that probably the slowness with which the patient overcomes her amnesia is due in part to the fact that she almost never cries, or releases her pent-up emotion in any other adequate way. Whenever she starts to cry in the ward, the nurses pet her and tell her not to cry and so she shuts right up. To-day I saw Dr. Shattuck, and after telling him in outline the patient's story, and her need for emotional release, he gave orders that the nurses were to be told to let her cry, whenever she started to do so. I told her too, that she should cry whenever she could." Emerson thought that her "self-control" over her crying was significantly implicated in her "repressions" (DA).

217. In DA, Emerson changed this to "couldn't tell."

218. "The prescription worked" (DA).

219. "The gradual softening of her feelings is shown by the following dream" (DA).

220. "The man who raped her" (DA).

221. I.e., for his release (DA).

222. A leather band for sharpening a razor.

223. ". . . how it all ended" (DA).

224. "Tuesday showed no gain" (Emerson 1912–13, 404).

225. Emerson noted of this session, "Nothing of importance psychologically was discovered" (DA). "Thrills" is colloquial for orgasm, circa 1910 (Eric Partridge, *A Dictionary of Slang and Unconventional English*. 2 vols. London, 1961). "Notebook" refers to his "secret" notebook, discussed in chapter 3.

226. Emerson wrote that he asked her to "try to remember what happened between the time when her assailant left her in the room and the time when she remembered being at home and in bed" (DA).

227. "After relating a few more or less irrelevant things," the patient suddenly revealed what appears in the next paragraph (DA). "While lying back with her eyes closed, she suddenly said, 'I know.' When she had told this she moved her legs slightly" (Emerson 1912–13, 404).

228. "She said she remembered now why her mother sent her over to this neighbor's" (DA).

229. I.e., the wife of Richard T., the neighbor who raped her.

230. "While waiting for her to tell anything further that came to her mind, the door of the consulting-room suddenly opened and one of the doctors looked in to see if it were occupied. The patient started and shuddered violently" (DA). Walter E. Paul, M.D. Harvard 1887; neurologist, M.G.H.

231. "Going through the terrible experience, and when the door opened she thought the man had returned" (DA).

232. "She pooh-poohed it" (DA).

233. Weld Ward, primarily for dermatology cases, with two beds assigned to neurology; patients were in single rooms (Washburn 1939, 301).

234. "Improvement during the next few days was rapid" (Emerson 1912–13, 405).

235. "After telling me a few things, more or less irrelevant, I bade her lie down" (DA).

236. "The most important thing she told me was her feeling toward her mother." She was crying while talking about her. "Here is evident one of her motives for repression. If she knew what had happened, she could not reconcile that with respect for a mother who would make her associate with such a man. One of the motives for concealment, therefore, was the desire to keep her respect for her mother" (DA).

237. In his write-up of the following day's session, Emerson noted that "the assault took place in the spring, just before school ended. The 'St. Vitus Dance' began at the beginning of the Fall term. She was then ten years old" (DA).

238. "From what she told me to-day it must have taken her three months to put the episode in the room entirely out of her mind" (DA).

239. "Gradually her amnesia is passing away" (DA).

240. Emerson saw this statement illustrative of "how she achieved her *first* repression" (DA).

241. "Both dreams were undoubtedly concerned with the 'Übertragung,' or her affection for me, and her regret at leaving the hospital" (DA).

242. "The patient walked back from the nerve room to the ward, going up and down four flights of stairs" (DA).

243. "The pictures, she said, were of the two assaults and other allied types. The baleful influence of her mother's memory stands out here as a terrible commentary on her cowardly counsels of the past" (DA).

244. "Luckily, for the success of this treatment, her mother had been dead several years" (DA).

245. At some point, Rachel met Mrs. Emerson and, it is likely, the children (see Rachel's letter to Mrs. Emerson, 6 August 1921 [following session 292], "Give my love to the children"). See Rachel's dream of being at Emerson's home, with his daughter; the next night, she dreamed of creating a mother, modeled on Mrs. Emerson, for herself (see Patients' Dreams, sessions 135 and 136).

CHAPTER 5

1. Emerson 1913–14e, 180.
2. DA.
3. He saw her briefly on June 10, and possibly met with the father.
4. Emerson, 1914–15, 333.
5. Ibid., 339.
6. On endogamous family constellations, see Forrester 1990, 51–52, and Rieff 1963.
7. Emerson learned from Rachel that the father was "ugly about her going to Waltham Training School for Nurses," presumably because he wanted her home to care for him (Notes, following session 80).
8. Emerson 1913–14e, 192.
9. Emerson 1913–14d, 46.
10. Ibid., 50.
11. Emerson 1913–14c, 286–87. It is doubtful that the fever could have been of hysterical origin; some undetected source of infection was likely present. There was no question the fever was feigned or factitious, as daily readings were taken by hospital staff. A chart of the fever's course is reproduced in Emerson 1913–14d, 50.
12. Emerson 1913–14d, 51.
13. Ibid.
14. Emerson apparently felt this exclusion, for on one occasion he refused to read what she had written, demanding instead that she tell him herself.
15. Emerson 1913–14d, 53.
16. Ibid., 54.
17. Ibid., 56. Emerson mentioned snakes but once in the published account, writing there of her dream (session 181), in which a snake jumped into her mouth. "Clearly the snake in her mouth was symbolical of her thumb," he wrote, "for she was sucking her thumb just before, or at that time" (Emerson 1913-14e, 194). This constituted a remarkable instance of self-censorship, for, throughout this part of the treatment, and especially in sessions 145 through 164, Rachel struggled mightily with the question of whether the sexual referents of her many dreams of playing with snakes were in fact "real" (session 162), linking the persistent dreams to masturbation. Emerson's interpretation that the snake was symbolic of the penis was not particularly daring, as there were any number of contemporaneous papers in the psychoanalytic literature in which snakes were cast as symbolic of the penis. He did, however, note that he analyzed this dream "by Socratic method," likely, then, sharing his interpretation with her. Emerson was clearly unsettled about going public with the talk of snakes and masturbation, telling his Psychopathic Hospital colleagues only that "she has told things almost incredible in regard to snakes," which, he continued, "may or may not be true" (Staff Meeting, following session 175). Rachel's dream snakes—snakes being for her at once harmless pets, of which, Emerson noted, she was "very fond" (1913–14d, 194) and "loathsome" creatures from which her girlfriends recoiled (session 146)—served as a vehicle through which her intense conflicts about sexuality found expression. She struggled first with memories of masturbating, and then linked the snakes to the sexually aggressive penises in her life, in

session 162 thinking of the snake turning "into brother then thought of Jack, T., men in woods etc." The next day she thought she was vomiting snakes, reporting that "her mind went from vomiting snakes to intercourse with brother" (session 163).

18. Emerson 1913–14d, 46.
19. Emerson 1915b, 425.
20. Abraham Myerson (Staff Meeting, following session 175).
21. Father to Emerson, 28 April [1912], citing what Rachel reported Dr. Smith said to her.
22. Session 178; echoed in the father's prediction that "in another year she would be crazy" (session 103).
23. Emerson 1913–14c, 292.
24. Neither she nor Emerson was yet considering, at this point in the analysis, whether Jack's "diagnosis" of pregnancy may indeed have been correct. Emerson interpreted her daydreams (among "her most insistent," he wrote [Emerson 1913–14e, 195]) and night dreams of pregnancy along Freudian lines, as expressive of wishes and hopes, and it is possible that Rachel picked up on this as a way, for the moment, to avoid delving deeper (following her statement, quoted in the text, of how the pregnancy seemed a wish and a dream, she said, "It seems foolish if I've been dreaming that and a thought could make me sick"). But in her dream life the issue of the pregnancy would not be so easily stilled. Within two weeks (session 184) of first reporting the pregnancy dream, she was dreaming of cutting herself up, cutting "off her hand, leg, etc. 'It seemed as if I was two people,' she said, 'and I was lying on the table, yet I was standing then cutting myself up.'" She woke as she was "chopping her body up." Dreams of destroying herself followed, and of drowning and burying her dead body (sessions 184–185), all of which is suggestive in light of the conflict broached in session 229, six months later, over whether the surgery she'd undergone in 1908 was in fact an abortion.
25. On the staff meeting, see Lunbeck 1994, 133–43.
26. Southard to Emerson, 15 February 1913, Emerson Papers.
27. Southard to Emerson, 20 March 1913, Emerson Papers.

CHAPTER 6

1. Waltham Training School for Nurses.
2. "At the first interview, the patient told me her nausea had started a week before, just after dinner, at night. No adequate cause could be found" (Emerson 1913–14d, 44).
3. Waltham Baby Hospital, founded 1902, for the care of sick babies, or those whose parents were sick, dead, or otherwise incapacitated.
4. "As before, she blamed it all on her father. She said he was very nice to her now, but he seemed to be doing it on purpose, to 'get around' her, in some way" (Emerson 1913–14d, 45).
5. "There is something troubling her" (ibid.).
6. "During the next three interviews the resistances developed were tremendous. The net result was a further suspicion against Dick" (ibid.).
7. Emerson wrote this line up the right side of the paper.
8. Churchgoing had apparently been part of Rachel's life, but following this cri de coeur, her references to church and God were either negative or absent.

9. Parentheses empty in original.

10. "The next day while trying to look she said plaintively, . . ." (Emerson 1913–14d, 45).

11. "Finally she remembered Dick, her lover, had assaulted her in her own house" (ibid.).

12. "At the next interview, Monday, nothing more was remembered" (ibid.).

13. I.e., where she was currently living.

14. Emerson left the room at this point.

15. Another patient, also diagnosed as a hysteric.

16. "Tuesday she remembered that it was the candy which had started the vomiting again this fall. The assault, too, took place a week or so before Thanksgiving. She remembered that she had been eating candy on the day of the assault and felt queer, not faint or dizzy exactly, and Dick had helped her to the couch. Wednesday and Thursday she remembered further details and Friday she remembered all" (Emerson 1913–14d, 45–46).

17. Massachusetts General Hospital (M.G.H.).

18. Likely Mark Homer Rogers, M.D. Harvard 1904; Assistant Orthopaedic Surgeon, Out-Patient Department, M.G.H.

19. Probably amyl-nitrate, a "smelling salt."

20. "Again assuming that the past repressed memory, or psycho-pathogenic nucleus, had been found and released, the patient was discharged from the hospital, where she had stayed two days, and allowed to work" (Emerson 1913–14d, 46).

21. Most likely a member of the nursing school staff.

22. "Still clinging to the theory of repression, another siege was begun to overcome what turned out to be the greatest resistance of all so far met. Of course the first suspicion turned again toward Dick. I questioned her. 'Did Dick do anything more?'" (ibid., 46–47).

23. "In light of what was later learned the following description of her feelings is especially significant" (ibid., 47).

24. The presence of these chemicals in the urine signals the equivalent of starvation, whether caused by fasting, vomiting, or uncontrolled diabetes. She may well have lost 15 percent or so of her weight (on admission examination at Boston Psychopathic Hospital, 27 February 1913, her weight was 147 pounds, her height, 5 feet 8 1/2 inches).

25. She "repeatedly brought forth all the reasons she had against looking, already fully reported." Emerson had told her "to look backward mentally and tell whatever she found" (Emerson 1913–14d, 47).

26. "She lost her voice the day before about 2 P.M. It was an almost perfect aphonia. She could speak only in the faintest whisper" (ibid.).

27. "Many times I urged, 'What do you see now?'" (ibid.).

28. "The next day the patient said that everything she had remembered seemed more remote and unreal" (ibid., 48).

29. "During the interview, she suddenly became completely paraplegic and was again admitted to the hospital. I was unable to see the patient for a week" (ibid.).

30. George Clymer, M.D. Harvard 1911; Assistant Neurologist, M.G.H.

31. I.e., she was still paralyzed.

32. "She remembered and told me of one final distressing meeting with Dick, though it appeared to be of no especial significance" (Emerson 1913–14d, 48).

33. "She described a real attack of psychic blindness or hysterical amaurosis. She said she seemed blind, in a dream, the night before, and woke up actually blind, remaining so for a short time. She had another attack of blindness later, lasting about two minutes. Then she confessed that she had been having such attacks for nearly two weeks. She said she didn't tell of it hoping it would pass off" (ibid., 49).

34. "Twice, during our interview, the patient went suddenly blind, once for nine minutes, another time for three minutes. What caused it I could not determine then" (ibid.).

35. "The next day she was blind for half an hour during our interview and although she could see a little when she went back to the ward, her sight almost completely left her as soon as she returned and she was practically blind all the afternoon, her sight going completely before she went to sleep" (ibid.).

36. "At the next interview I got hold of a thread that led us into still deeper recesses of the patient's subconsciousness, where she kept her repressed complexes" (ibid.).

37. "It was kept up until she was eighteen or nineteen and her brother fourteen or fifteen" (ibid.).

38. "This brought the patient to a sort of self-consciousness and from that time she discouraged her brother's coming, though it was not absolutely stopped" (ibid., 50).

39. The preceding day.

40. The man who boarded with her "aunt" in Beverly, who looked like Jack.

41. "This is perfectly intelligible from the point of view of her repressions and my urging her, against her resistances, to tell all" (Emerson 1913–14d, 51).

42. I.e., having to do with her menstrual periods.

43. S[ocial?] S[ervice?] Sup[intenden?]t? Possibly a reference to Cabot, Chief of West Medical Service, to which she had been admitted, and founder of the Social Service; Chief of the Social Service was Ida M. Cannon, whom she may have assumed was Cabot's wife.

44. Dates do not agree with Emerson's.

45. "I could get nothing further at this interview" (Emerson 1913–14d, 52).

46. "And so it went for the next two weeks, no definite advance apparently being made" (ibid.). Rachel was still in the hospital at this point.

47. Possibly, Out-Patient Department, where he practiced.

48. "The patient got a clear memory image of this fourth psychic trauma, but no further details"(Emerson 1913–14d, 52).

49. "On this date, too, another symptom showed itself. The patient said she heard music. She had complained previously that music made her sick. When I questioned her she had said, 'Oh! I hate music . . . When I hear it, it makes me think of what I've been through.' " (ellipses in original; ibid.).

50. ". . . in a deep hole. Just as she was about to bury the last I came along and asked her what she was doing. She would not tell but I found out" (ibid., 53).

51. "In the second dream she dreamed 'it' was not so" (ibid.).

52. Added by Emerson.

53. "The next few days showed nothing gained" (Emerson 1913–14d, 53).

54. I.e., below.

55. Emerson was teaching medical students at this point, and apparently took his class to the hospital to see Rachel. Karl Menninger wrote that as a medical student, he and his

classmates had a three-hour session with Emerson at the M.G.H., in which they were exposed to psychoanalysis (Menninger 1961, 137).

56. Accepted?

57. "A week after being discharged the patient returned saying she still vomited" (Emerson 1913–14d, 53).

58. "Nothing was learned during the interview" (ibid.).

59. Emerson recording what Smith said to him.

60. Emerson received a "telephone call saying the patient had had a convulsion. From the description it is clear she had had a 'grande attaque' and lest she have another she was taken the next day to the hospital" (Emerson 1913–14d, 53).

61. D. Dennett, M.D. Maine 1891.

62. In notes—"Grand hy. attack." Her brother, it appears, accompanied her to the hospital, telling the admitting physician she had been "of a jolly, sociable nature," but that she'd become disobedient three years previously—"she wanted her own way," he said—and had become sick "after a love affair about a year ago." He described her fits: "She never fell on floor but would sit down and stiffen out—she would scream on entering into a 'fit' or on coming out of it—this would last one or two hours—would try to bite tongue and would put spoon in mouth to prevent it—she would then bang her head on floor." On admission, her condition was noted as agitated; a neurological examination found her "body in continuous motion. Jerky movement, irregular, involving mostly the extensor muscles of the neck, arms, legs, elevator of shoulders, flexors of fingers and plantar flexors of foot. The most common movements are those of the shoulders and arms—elevation of shoulders, extension of forearms. Flexion of fingers common." It was noted that she was able to walk to the ward. The report of the "psychological examination" performed on her found her intelligence normal: "Patient passed satisfactorily the Binet test. Shows good judgement and foresight. Attention good. . . . Lacks self-confidence. Not suggestible. . . . Very nervous and shaky. No evidence of mental aberration. Not defective." Patient file, Boston Psychopathic Hospital.

63. Emerson had recently been appointed to the hospital staff.

64. "The analysis of this dream developed enormous resistances, which, on being overcome, revealed the fact that the patient had masturbated as a child. Even as the patient told this she opened her hand and there has been no return of this symptom" (Emerson 1913–14d, 54).

65. Ward III, "female observation ward," was for disturbed and agitated patients in need of close supervision; Ward V was an open ward, on which patients were subjected to fewer restrictions and less oversight.

66. ". . . just before the convulsion" (Emerson 1913–14d, 55).

67. Ward V.

68. "During the analysis, the patient suddenly started up and said, 'I know why I hear music. Mother was playing that morning.' (i.e. the morning her brother and she were together)" (Emerson 1913–14d, 55).

69. A nurse.

70. "Some of the significance of this is at once obvious" (Emerson 1913–14d, 55).

71. Herman Adler (1876–1935), M.D. Columbia 1901; Instructor, then Assistant Professor of Psychiatry, Harvard Medical School, 1911–16.

72. "Patient remarked this A.M. [before seeing Emerson] that she would not care to go to Dr. Emerson's office if it wasn't for her own good" (ward notes, in patient file, Boston Psychopathic Hospital).

73. Emerson wrote in the published account that the father had "touched" her, "and after that she did it herself more than she remembered, and that she had been with her brother, 'right along'" (Emerson 1913–14d, 56). Subsequently, in the final installment of the published account, Emerson would write that the father had "masturbated" her, and relate the story of his solicitation of her (Emerson 1913-14e, 180–81). In the Staff Meeting, he said "it was learned that her father had merely handled her perhaps improperly at the age of 7."

74. Of this revelation, Emerson wrote, "the analysis only showed further detail and did not reach a deeper level" (Emerson 1913–14d, 56).

75. A religious movement, with great appeal across class and racial lines, whose adherents attempted to make "contact with the spirits of the dead." See Braude 1989 (quotation 3). See session 9, in which Rachel reported on her reading in *Eagle Blood* of a scene of a séance.

76. Or diethyl barbiturate; on other nights she had been given cocoa or "pleicibo pill."

77. Later, Rachel would tell Emerson that "Dr Putnam wanted someone in the Social Service to explain things [i.e., regarding sex] to me and I wouldn't listen" (session 199); Burleigh was apparently delegated to do so. Emerson wrote "Mrs. C." in his notes; he may have meant to write "Miss C.," to refer to Rachel, or it may be that the mother was also talked to about Rachel and her lack of sexual knowledge.

78. "This aphonia lasted a day" (Emerson 1913–14e, 181).

79. The note that she gave to Emerson, which he told her he would not read (session 171). In the published account, Emerson, in the wake of these revelations, characterized the mother as having been "sexually abused" by the father, a term he had not yet used with respect to the father's relations with Rachel (Emerson 1913–14d, 56).

80. I.e., the mother.

81. Around the time she had St. Vitus Dance.

82. Written on 7 April; Emerson noted the date incorrectly.

83. See session 21: Emerson had forced a pencil into her hand and covered her eyes with his hands; an hour later she had written something that looked to him like the word "Adultery."

84. "The patient came to me with her right arm bandaged. . . . This suggested a trait of character which had previously not been suspected. A little questioning revealed considerable capacity for revenge and cruelty, though here, of course, directed against herself. The masochistic significance of this will be much clearer later"(Emerson 1913–14e, 182).

85. "Her sexual sins"(ibid., 182).

86. The Psychopathic Hospital roof garden.

87. The staff meeting is from the patient's file, Boston Psychopathic Hospital. Admitted 27 February 1913; discharged 2 May 1913. On Boston Psychopathic Hospital personnel, see Lunbeck 1994.

88. Dr. Dennett of Winchester.
89. Referring to her desire to leave the hospital, which she entered as a "voluntary" patient. On statutes and procedures governing admission and discharge, see Lunbeck 1994, 81–113.
90. I.e., the voluntary admission paper.
91. A. Warren Stearns (1885–1959), M.D. Tufts 1910; Dean of Tufts Medical School 1927–45.
92. A remarkable statement on Emerson's part, as he knew she became ill in the summer of 1911. He started treating her in January 1912.
93. Reference to the transcript of the staff meeting, above. She had submitted a three-day notice of intention to leave the hospital, part of the procedure for a voluntary admission. The hospital could request a court hearing to oppose the discharge.
94. A fellow patient.
95. Nurse referred to in session 155.
96. A fellow patient.
97. "It seemed as if I came out of myself and tried in a number of ways to get rid of my old self" (Emerson 1913–14e, 184).
98. I.e., herself.
99. "On the body" (Emerson 1913–14e, 184).
100. Possibly lye (sodium hydroxide).
101. Corrosive sublimate, mercury bichloride. In different preparations, it was used as a tonic, as an antisyphilitic, or as an antiseptic.
102. "A few days later, the vomiting being much improved, and no other new symptoms manifesting themselves, the patient was discharged" (Emerson 1913–14e, 185).

CHAPTER 7

1. It appears that she entered the M.G.H. on 18 January 1917 and left it, to enter the Adams Nervine Asylum, on 6 March 1917. There is a reference to her leaving "the clinic" on 14 February (session 284), but it is clear that following that she was still under nurses' supervision, still a patient.
2. Emerson found it increasingly difficult, in this phase of the case, to distinguish actuality from fantasy and to sort out the veracity of Rachel's memories. In the first year and one half of the treatment, he had an ally in these tasks in Rachel's own attempts to establish veracity, in her attempts to distinguish among incidents she fully remembered; things she could envision had happened, but did not remember; and things she neither remembered nor imagined might have happened. The increased appearance of dissociation in this final segment of the case, perhaps augmented by her drug use, meant that making distinctions among grades of memory was much more problematic than it had been earlier on.
3. Emerson, reflecting on the limitations of the traumatic model in treating hysteria, wrote that psychoanalysis was moving toward considering the "the conception of character, and thus the whole problem of personality" (Emerson 1915b, 422).
4. Ibid.

5. Emerson 1913–14e, 204.

6. Emerson 1913–14c, 290.

7. Emerson 1913–14e, 206.

8. Cf. Commentary, Part I. On the evolution of the fundamental rule, see Laplanche and Pontalis 1988, s.v. "fundamental rule."

9. Freud 1914a. Emerson's paper (1916–17b) was originally presented at the eighth annual meeting of the American Psychopathological Association, May 1916. Although the title is intriguingly close to Freud's trilogy of papers, "Some Character-Types Met with in Psycho-Analytic Work," it is unlikely Emerson had read them by the time he published his article; Freud's papers were published in 1916 in the last issue of *Imago* (Freud 1916). Freud first used the term narcissism in 1910 (Laplanche and Pontalis 1988, s.v. "narcissism").

10. Emerson 1916–17b, quotation 267.

11. Emerson 1918–19, quotation 23.

12. Emerson 1919c, 63.

13. Emerson 1913–14c, 290.

14. Ibid., 291.

15. Emerson 1919a, 344–46, 346. Emerson's abstract of Freud's paper "Triebe und Triebschicksale," which was later translated into English in 1925 under the title "Instincts and Their Vicissitudes" (Freud 1915), was titled "Impulses and Their Mutations."

16. Emerson 1916b, 459. Consider also: "Psychoanalysts have said that with such questions [re ethics] they had no business" (Emerson 1915b, 425).

17. Emerson 1919c, 60. See Laplanche and Pontalis 1988, s.v. "subconscious." See also Burnham 1967, 58–60, on American psychiatrists' and psychologists' understanding of the subconscious.

18. Emerson 1913–14e, 201.

19. See Lunbeck 1994, 223–25, for a discussion of Emerson's pedagogical project.

20. Emerson 1913–14e, 206.

21. We are indebted in this discussion to the arguments of Forrester 1990, 30–47.

22. Freud 1905 [1904], quotation, 260. The paper was delivered as a lecture in 1904, and first published in 1905. It appeared, in translation, in Brill 1909, which Emerson cited repeatedly.

23. Forrester 1990, 38. Note also that Rachel's father referred to the treatment as "hypnotism" (session 180).

24. Emerson 1917. Emerson's "Further Advice on the Technique of Psychoanalysis. (III). Remarks on the Transference," was an abstract of Freud's "Weitere Ratschläge zur Technik der Psychoanalyse (III): Bemerkungen über die Übertragungsliebe." Emerson's abstract opens with: "While the beginner in psychoanalysis may tremble at the difficulties in front of him, by far the hardest situation to handle is the transference (Übertragung). This is the situation where a female patient falls violently in love with the physician." Emerson's first sentence summarizes the first paragraph of the German text; the second sentence condenses and alters the meaning of the second paragraph of the German text. The *SE* renders the German literally, the sentence in question reading: "What I have in mind is the case in which a woman patient shows by unmistakable indications, or

openly declares, that she has fallen in love, as any other mortal woman might, with the doctor who is analysing her" (Freud 1915 [1914], 159). For the original German, with the shortened title used after 1924, see Freud 1946.

25. Freud 1915 [1914].
26. Emerson 1915b.
27. Forrester 1990, 84, citing Freud 1916–17, *SE* 16, 443.
28. Freud 1905 [1904], 261.
29. Emerson 1913–14e, 204.
30. Freud 1914b, 154. See also Laplanche and Pontalis 1988, s.v. "transference neurosis."
31. Emerson 1930, citing Freud 1921.
32. Explaining the dissociative process, Emerson wrote that "what at first was, perhaps, only partially successful, *i.e.*, the repression of an unbearable idea, may become finally so completely successful that the mind becomes actually separated into independent parts. . . . As Freud says, the patient does not intend to split his consciousness[,] he intends only to rid himself of distress, but what he actually accomplishes is dissociation. In our patient the various symptoms are interpreted as the end products of such split-off psychic groups. From this point of view, the 'St. Vitus Dance' is quite intelligible, when the patient tells us that it was started by her running around and around the supper-table, falling down, and getting up; it is but the reproduction of the run in the woods when chased and assaulted" (Emerson 1913–14e, 189).
33. Stearns was particularly interested in diagnosis (see, for example, Southard and Stearns 1914, a careful review of how diagnoses are changed as patients are transferred from one hospital to another, one of numerous such articles in *The Boston Medical and Surgical Journal* by Southard and Stearns), perhaps one to be consulted for his opinion and reassurance in matters of diagnosis.
34. Edward Wyllys Taylor (1866–1932), M.D. Harvard 1891; Chief of Neurology Service, M.G.H., James Jackson Putnam Professor of Neurology, Harvard University, 1905–1926.
35. Freud 1915 [1914], 166.
36. Emerson 1913–14e, 205–6.
37. Emerson had earlier explained to Rachel that a pistol was a symbolic penis (session 87).
38. On the erotic possibilities opened up by the automobile (and on the role of psychoanalysis in documenting such), consider Emerson's relating case of a married Mr. X., who was in the habit of jumping into his car, picking up "some pretty girl," and taking "her for a tearing ride to some country inn where they would have dinner together." Drink would lower his inhibitions, "and the ride home was accompanied by fondling and caressing, even masturbating his fair companion." He would then go home and masturbate, not altogether satisfactorily. Emerson wrote that the images of his mother and of his wife prevented him from having intercourse with his pretty companions (Emerson 1916–17b, 266–67).
39. Emerson 1913–14b, 51. Emerson treated Miss A. intensively for the month of August 1912, during which she was a patient at the Boston Psychopathic Hospital, and intermittently through 1916.

40. Emerson 1913–14b, 51, 53, citing Brill 1910, 24–25, Brill's translation of Freud 1905. Although Emerson used the translation, he altered one of Brill's pronouns, suggesting he was also working with the German text.

41. Boston.

42. Tansy, a plant, *Tanacetum vulgare,* also known as "buttons," an aromatic but bitter tasting herb whose leaves had many medicinal uses; known as a safe emmenagogue and considered useful in the treatment of hysteria.

43. Like Rachel, we are not entirely certain either that she had been pregnant—though the weight of the evidence would support her suspicion that she was—or that the surgical procedure she underwent was an abortion; she may have had a spontaneous abortion prior to the surgery, in which pregnancy-related tissue may have been removed. The brief notation, next to her name, in a fortuitously surviving casebook of the hospital's surgical pathology records reads, under the heading "Specimen," "cervical polyp. uterine scrapings," and, under the heading "Diagnosis," "cervical polyp. decidua." It is very likely that the term "decidua" referred to pregnancy-related tissue (though it may also have referred to menstrually related tissue; Stedman's *Medical Dictionary* [*A Practical Medical Dictionary,* 9th ed., Baltimore, 1926], s.v. "decidua," gives only one usage, decidua menstrualis, that does not refer to a pregnant uterus). The casebook contains detailed clinical records for 120 "classified" cases (Rachel's fell into a large "unclassified" group, for which clinical records are missing); in every case in which the notation "decidua" appears, it refers to a pregnancy. It appears that the hospital did not use the term abortion with reference to unmarried women. The few times the term is used in the casebook, it is used in cases of married women who presented with pain and/or hemorrhage; operations in those cases appear to have been to remove remains of an already failed pregnancy or a tubal pregnancy (New England Hospital for Women and Children 1908b). The terminology of gynecological surgery and pathology was in flux in the early years of the twentieth century (Dorothy Lansing, personal communication), which makes interpreting this group of medical records all the more difficult. Rachel had last been with Jack in December 1907, she told Emerson (though the dates both he and she gave regarding her relationship with him varied; in the DA, Emerson gave her age, for the duration of the six months, as nineteen, while elsewhere he gave it as eighteen). As Rachel remembered it, she had first consulted Dr. Stevens "because of trouble with hands"; she was also, however, nervous and not menstruating. Stevens, examining her, found a "structure," and arranged for surgery to remove it. While being operated on, Rachel began hemorrhaging; Stevens, frightened, sent for the mother (session 252). It is possible, if she was pregnant, that it was an incestuous pregnancy; it is also possible that she had miscarried prior to the operation; finally, it is also possible, given the limited data base in these records, that they were not using the microscopic diagnosis of decidua" as indicating pregnancy, but rather as menstrual decidua. See Drachman 1984,85–87, on the surgeries performed at the hospital. The hospital's annual report for the year 1908 classifies 111 surgical operations performed in that year under the heading "curettage," 10 of them "for incomplete abortion," 6 for "miscarriages." It also lists 1 operation to remove a "cervical polyp" (New England Hospital for Women and Children 1908a).

44. Woodside Cottage, Framingham, established 1900. Twenty-five beds. Frank W. Patch, M.D. Boston 1888.

45. Railway spine was a mid-nineteenth-century diagnosis for cases of persistent psychological symptomology following railway accidents, often, it was charged, in cases in which compensation was at issue. Physical treatments were at first deemed appropriate for what later clinicians, among them Charcot, would consider to be the effects of psychic trauma, not organic damage.

CHAPTER 8

1. A severe infectious sore throat.

2. Dates added by Emerson.

3. Helen G. F. Mack, M.D. Boston 1895; gynecologist.

4. Or, differently? Original reads "diff."

5. I.e., the mother (may have) sent Henry to get and care for Rachel after she confessed her sexual misdeeds.

6. Correct spelling is "strychnine"—an alkaloid with numerous medicinal uses in small doses, but usable as a poison.

7. Emerson drew a line connecting "Jack" and "Mother's seducer," and "Jack" and "Henry." It is possible Jack was the name of her mother's seducer, but it is also possible he was registering that she had merged her mother's seducer and her own lover Jack.

8. Not identified; possibly another social worker at the meeting where Putnam and Burleigh spoke to her about sex.

9. A well-known Boston department store.

10. Another friend, not the same as Gertrude C.

11. Emerson drew a line from "pregnant" to "father" in his notes.

12. Postcard with photograph of the Massachusetts Homeopathic Hospital, sent to Emerson in Ontario, Canada, where he was vacationing.

13. Enclosed was a postcard picturing a quiet, idyllic scene—trees in the foreground, a waterfall behind—on which Rachel had written, "Good girl's work."

14. Not identified. Rachel may have been disguising his name here.

15. A generic term for a variety of acute and chronic kidney diseases.

16. She was working to pay his anesthesiology bill.

17. Emerson inferred that she had experienced a severe dissociative episode.

18. See chapter 7, n. 43.

19. Sara E. Stevens, M.D. Tufts 1896; physician, New England Hospital Dispensary.

20. Frederick B. M. Cady, M.D. Harvard 1907; Assistant Neurologist, M.G.H.

21. Elizabeth Taylor Gray, M.D. Women's Medical College of New York Infirmary for Women and Children 1895; Assistant Surgeon, New England Hospital for Women and Children.

22. The hospital chauffeur, "last summer's follower," possibly the "engineer" mentioned above.

23. Abortion was illegal in Massachusetts in this period.

24. Cf. session 1: "didn't know mother was sick till told of her death."

25. Ella R.'s mother.

26. Aphasia is a generic term for certain speech disorders brought on by organic brain disease, usually strokes. Emerson was probably using it to describe her trouble with speaking, rather than assuming an organic cause.

27. Talitha Cumi Maternity Home, established 1836, "to provide a home for the shelter and salvation of erring girls who are facing maternity." Maurice Gerstein, *Medical Directory of Greater Boston,* 4th ed., Boston, 1913–14.

28. Working as a nurse; discharged seven to twelve months later (session 271).

29. No record of an admission to the Psychopathic Hospital was found.

30. Myrton Berry Raynes, M.D. Baltimore 1896.

31. A nurse.

32. Trianol is a powerful hypnotic, which was used in cases of nervous insomnia. Veronal is a tradename for barbital.

33. A classic hysterical symptom, an arching of the back while supine, which likely would have been construed to symbolically represent some sexual scene and/or childbirth.

34. Rachel had been working for the military as a "tent nurse"; from the time of the Civil War, tents had been used in the treatment of battlefield infections, the ventilation being conducive to healing.

35. Rachel told Emerson his surname was R., not T. She apparently wrote and told this; Emerson drew a line through "and told" and added "no."

36. I.e., to Dr. Patch's sanitarium.

37. A phrase strikingly similar to that used by Breuer's patient Anna O.—"chimney sweeping"—to describe what she termed the "talking cure." It is possible Emerson told Rachel of Anna O.'s metaphor; he would have known of it, as Freud referred to it in his Clark Lectures (Freud 1910 [1909], 13; originally in Breuer and Freud 1893–95, 30). It is also possible Rachel's resort to domestic imagery was unprompted.

38. House of the Good Samaritan Hospital, Brookline; 43 beds. Roger I. Lee, M.D., was on the attending staff.

CHAPTER 9

1. Boston Psychopathic Hospital psychiatrists were nearly unanimous in the opinion that this was a case of hysteria. Were a comparable meeting to be held today, a number of other diagnostic possibilities would likely be raised. Hysteria is no longer part of the psychiatrist's diagnostic repertoire; borderline personality disorder, a diagnosis with pejorative overtones largely used in cases of young women, occupies a cultural niche similar to that hysteria once did. Indeed, a number of clinicians have attempted to "rediagnose" Breuer and Freud's hysterics (Breuer and Freud 1893–95; see, for example, Meissner 1979) as borderlines. While the phenomena associated with the classic usage of hysteria still exist, they have been reallocated to a number of other categories, such as somatoform disorder (emphasizing somatic symptoms and including conversion disorder) and histrionic character (emphasizing the dramatizing aspects of the character). Micale (1995) discusses hysteria's twentieth-century fate.

Among other current diagnoses that might be considered in this case are the following. (1) *Dissociative identity disorder (multiple personality)*. Although in the later phases of the treatment the patient suffered a marked increase in the intensity and frequency of dissociative symptoms, there is little evidence to support a diagnosis of multiple personality disorder, the most extreme form of dissociation. (2) *Conversion disorder plus post-traumatic stress disorder.* A number of symptoms that, until the past several decades, were considered indicative of hysteria are now thought to be part of the post-traumatic stress disorder spectrum. Some of the patient's startle responses, or ease of her regression into hallucinatory states, might now be thought attributable to the disorder; in this case, clearly the "traumatic stress disorder" was not merely "post," but ongoing. (3) *Temporal lobe epilepsy.* The patient's physicians ruled out epilepsy of organic origin, but with their limited diagnostic tools they would not have been in a position to rule out more subtle forms of epilepsy, especially temporal lobe epilepsy, which can present as a confusing mixture of disturbed mental states (with amnesias, confusion, hallucinations) and physical symptoms, such as falling or fainting. The condition is now treatable (not always successfully) with antiseizure medications and, in severe cases, neurosurgery. (4) *Sleep paralysis.* This is especially relevant to the later stages of her treatment; the diagnosis, with its accompanying nightmares, may well fit with some of the patient's hallucinatory experiences, especially those involving snakes. There is now thought to be some relationship between sleep paralysis and dissociative disorders, with some overlap with the traumatic stress syndromes (Powell and Nielson 1998). Sleep paralysis might be pharmacologically treatable, but the diagnosis would only account for a fraction of Rachel's symptoms.

Even with the help of contemporary treatment methods, these disorders are by no means easy to treat, and clinicians could easily envision an outcome such as Rachel's in patients carrying one of those diagnoses. In short, modern psychiatric understanding of Rachel's case may or may not have made a dramatic difference in the outcome, though there would have been more careful attention paid to why treatment was not succeeding. Emerson's stance on diagnosis can be glimpsed in his statement, in the context of weighing differently inflected hysteria diagnoses in the case of Miss A., that "*classification* is less important here than *causation*" (1913–14b, 48; emphasis in original).

2. See Freud 1904 [1903].
3. See Blass and Simon 1992; Blass and Simon 1994; Simon and Bullock 1994; and Simon 1994.
4. Emerson lauded Freud's change of heart, writing he thereby evidenced "that flexibility which goes with a great mind" (Clinical Society of the University of Michigan 1911, 235).
5. Emerson 1913–14b, 48.
6. Coriat 1945, 4. Freud discussed Oedipus Rex and the child's "relation to his parents owing to the first stirrings of sexuality" in *The Interpretation of Dreams, SE* 4, pp. 260 ff. (Freud 1900), which Emerson almost certainly read.
7. Emerson 1913–14e, 181, 205.
8. Ibid., 205.
9. Emerson 1913–14b.
10. Emerson 1918; see also Emerson 1926. It is clear from Emerson's correspondence with patients and others that his practice continued, at least through the 1920s, if not be-

yond, but his case notes for these years have apparently not survived. Emerson was secretary of the American Psychopathological Association in 1913 for three years and again in the 1930s (Taylor 1982), and he was a member of the American Psychoanalytic Association, through the 1920s at least, and on the organization's council in 1923. At a meeting of the latter in 1925, he delivered a paper, "Illusions and Ideals in Psychoanalysis"; in 1929, he delivered Emerson 1930. In 1925, he established the Care of the Patient lectures at Harvard Medical School, funded by a gift from one of his patients; the series—known as the "Emerson Lectures"—lasted sixteen years. Emerson's lectures appeared as Emerson 1929 (Taylor 1982).

11. See, for example, Emerson 1930 and 1933.

12. Burnham 1978, 199; Gifford refers to the period from 1918 to 1930 as the "dark ages of Boston analysis" (1978a, 332).

13. Among them Mr. Erik Homberger (Erikson), in 1934 approving his transfer of membership from the Viennese society.

14. Gifford 1978a, 333, 345. See Hale 1995 on the professionalization of psychoanalysis in the United States, and Cameron and Forrester 2000, 248–52, esp., on consequences of the same in Britain.

15. Taylor 1982, 47–48. Gifford 1978a, 332, wrote that Putnam's death left Coriat "as our sole Freudian analyst," a judgment with which Coriat concurred (1945). Cameron and Forrester 2000, 251–52, write that "professionalization may have been intended to create Freudians, but its effect may also have been to unmake them—or at least to make them disappear from the view."

CHAPTER 10

1. Undated manuscript, probably 1913, Emerson papers.

2. I.e., piano.

3. Both brother and father underscored twice in original.

Bibliography

SE   Freud, Sigmund. 1953–74. *The Standard Edition of the Complete Psychological Works of Sigmund Freud,* translated by James Strachey in collaboration with Anna Freud, assisted by Alix Strachey and Alan Tyson. 24 vols. London.

DA   Emerson, Eugene Louville. 1912. Detailed account of a psychoanalytic study and treatment of hysteria. Emerson Papers, Box 16b.

Emerson Papers Emerson, Louville Eugene. Papers. Countway Library of Medicine. Boston.

Abraham, Karl. 1922. Manifestations of the female castration complex. *Int. J. Psycho-Anal.* 3: 1–29.

Barclay, Florence. 1910. *The Rosary.* New York.

Blass, Rachel B., and Bennett Simon. 1992. The development and vicissitudes of Freud's ideas on the Oedipus complex. In Jerome Neu, ed., *The Cambridge Companion to Freud.* Cambridge.

———. 1994. The value of the historical perspective to contemporary psychoanalysis: Freud's 'seduction hypothesis'. *Int. J. Psycho-Anal.* 75: 677–94.

Braude, Ann. 1989. *Radical Spirits: Spiritualism and Women's Rights in Nineteenth Century America.* Boston.

Breuer, Josef, and Sigmund Freud. 1893–95. *Studies on Hysteria. SE* 2.

Brill, A. A. 1909. Translation of Freud, *Selected Papers on Hysteria and Other Psychoneuroses.* New York.

———. 1910. Translation of Freud, *Three Contributions to the Sexual Theory.* New York.

———. 1913. Translation of Freud, *The Interpretation of Dreams.* New York.

Burnham, John Chynoweth. 1967. *Psychoanalysis and American Medicine: 1894–1918. Medicine, Science, and Culture.* New York.

———. 1978. Boston psychiatry in the 1920s: Looking forward. In *Psychoanalysis, Psychotherapy and the New England Medical Scene, 1894–1944,* edited by George E. Gifford Jr., 196–205. New York.

Campbell, Robert J. 1981. *Psychiatric Dictionary.* New York.

Cameron, Laura, and John Forrester. 2000. Tansley's psychoanalytic network: An episode out of the early history of psychoanalysis in England. *Psychoanalysis and History* 2: 189–256.

Caplan, Eric. 1998. *Mind Games: American Culture and the Birth of Psychotherapy.* Berkeley.

Clinical Society of the University of Michigan. 1911. Discussion. *Physician and Surgeon* 33: 233–36.

Coriat, Isador H. 1917. Some statistical results of the psycho-analytic treatment of the psychoneuroses. *Psychoanalytic Rev.* 4: 209–16.

———. 1945. Some personal reminiscences of psychoanalysis in Boston: An autobiographical note. *Psychoanal. Rev.* 32: 1–8.

Creelman, James. 1902. *Eagle Blood.* Boston.

Drachman, Virginia A. 1984. *Hospital with a Heart: Women Doctors and the Paradox of Separatism at the New England Hospital, 1862–1969.* Ithaca.

Duberman, Martin B. 1977. The therapy of C. M. Otis: 1911. *Christopher Street* 2 (5): 33–37.

———. 1980. "I am not contented": Female masochism and lesbianism in early twentieth-century New England. *Signs* 5:825–41.

Ellenberger, Henri. 1970. *The Discovery of the Unconscious: The History and Evolution of Dynamic Psychiatry.* New York.

Emerson, Louville Eugene. Papers. Countway Library of Medicine. Boston.

———. 1907. An investigation in the simultaneous stimulation of adjacent touch spots on the skin: The physiology of nerves with particular reference to the theoretical problem of inhibition. Unpublished Ph.D. dissertation, Harvard University.

———. 1911. Psychoanalysis and social service. *Physician and Surgeon* 33: 209–19.

———. 1912. Detailed account of a psychoanalytic study and treatment of hysteria. Emerson Papers.

———. 1912–13. A psychoanalytic study of a severe case of hysteria. *J. Ab. Psychol.* 7: 385–406.

———. 1913–14a. Abstracts from Internationale Zeitschrift für Ärtzliche Psychoanalyse. *Psychoanalytic Rev.* 1: 108–12.

———. 1913–14b. The case of Miss A: A preliminary report of a psychoanalytic study and treatment of a case of self-mutilation. *Psychoanalytic Rev.* 1: 41–54.

———. 1913–14c. Psychoanalysis and hospitals. *Psychoanalytic Rev.* 1: 285–94.

———. 1913–14d. A psychoanalytic study of a severe case of hysteria. *J. Ab. Psychol.* 8: 44–56.

———. 1913–14e. A psychoanalytic study of a severe case of hysteria. *J. Ab. Psychol.* 8: 180–207.

————. 1914–15. Psychopathology of the family. *J. Ab. Psychol.* 9: 333–40.

————. 1915a. Abstracts from Internationale Zeitschrift für Ärtzliche Psychoanalyse. *Psychoanalytic Rev.* 2: 106–13.

————. 1915b. A philosophy for psychoanalysts. *Psychoanalytic Rev.* 2: 422–27.

————. 1915–16. The psychoanalytic treatment of hystero-epilepsy. *J. Ab. Psychol.* 10: 315–28.

————. 1916a. Abstracts from Internationale Zeitschrift für Ärtzliche Psychoanalyse. *Psychoanalytic Rev.* 3: 218–23.

————. 1916b. Concerning Freud's principle of reality. *Psychoanalytic Rev.* 3: 459–60.

————. 1916c. Review of *The Freudian Wish and Its Place in Ethics,* by E. B. Holt. *Harvard Graduate's Magazine,* August/September, 143–44.

————. 1916–17a. Discussion. *J. Ab. Psychol.* 11: 415, 417.

————. 1916–17b. Some psychoanalytic studies of character. *J. Ab. Psychol.* 11: 265–74.

————. 1917. Abstracts from Internationale Zeitschrift für Ärtzliche Psychoanalyse. *Psychoanalytic Rev.* 4: 451–54.

————. 1918. *Nervousness: Its Causes, Treatment, and Prevention.* Boston.

————. 1918–19. A clinical study of the origin, development and disappearance of a system of delusions. *J. Ab. Psychol.* 13: 23–28.

————. 1919a. Abstracts from Internationale Zeitschrift für Ärtzliche Psychoanalyse. *Psychoanalytic Rev.* 6: 343–46.

————. 1919b. Dr. James Jackson Putnam. Obituary. *J. Nervous and Mental Disease,* March, 268–71.

————. 1919c. The subconscious in its relation to the conscious, preconscious, and unconscious. *Psychoanalytic Rev.* 6: 59–64.

————. 1926. "If you are given to nerves, forget it and get busy." *The Boston Globe,* 9 May. Editorial Feature section.

————. 1929. *Patient and Physician: Personal Care.* Cambridge, Mass.

————. 1930. Some remarks on transference. *Psychoanalytic Rev.* 17: 360–61.

————. 1933. Emerson and Freud: A study in contrasts. *Psychoanalytic Rev.* 20: 208–14.

Falzeder, Ernst, and Eva Brabant, eds. 2000. *The Correspondence of Sigmund Freud and Sándor Ferenczi. Volume 3, 1920–1933,* translated by Peter T. Hoffer. Cambridge, Mass.

Faust, Drew Gilpin, ed. 1992. *Macaria, or, Altars of Sacrifice,* by Augusta Jane Evans. Baton Rouge. Originally published in 1864.

Fenichel, Otto. 1945. *The Psychoanalytic Theory of Neurosis.* New York.

Ferenczi, Sándor. 1911. Über obszöne Worte. *Zentralblatt für Psychoanalyse* 1: 390–99.

————. 1916. On obscene words. In *Contributions to Psycho-Analysis,* translated by Ernest Jones, 112–30. Boston.

————. 1927. Technical difficulties in the analysis of a case of hysteria (1919). In *Further Contributions to the Theory and Technique of Psycho-Analysis,* translated by Jane Isabel Suttie, 189–97. New York.

Forrester, John. 1990. *The Seductions of Psychoanalysis: Freud, Lacan and Derrida.* Cambridge.

Fox-Genovese, Elizabeth, ed. 1992. *Beulah,* by Augusta Jane Evans. Baton Rouge. Originally published in 1859.

Freud, Sigmund. 1900. *The Interpretation of Dreams. SE* 4, 5.

————. 1904 [1903]. Freud's psycho-analytic procedure. *SE* 7: 249–54.

———. 1905 [1901]. Fragment of an analysis of a case of hysteria. *SE* 7: 7–122.

———. 1905 [1904]. On psychotherapy. *SE* 7: 257–68.

———. 1905. *Three Essays on the Theory of Sexuality. SE* 7: 130–245.

———. 1908. 'Civilized' sexual morality and modern nervous illness. *SE* 9: 181–204.

———. 1909. Notes upon a case of obsessional neurosis. *SE* 10: 158–320.

———. 1910 [1909]. Five lectures on psycho-analysis. *SE* 11: 9–56.

———. 1910a. A special type of choice of object made by men (contributions to the psychology of love I). *SE* 11: 165–75.

———. 1910b. 'Wild' psycho-analysis. *SE* 11: 221–27.

———. 1912a. The dynamics of transference. *SE* 12: 99–108.

———. 1912b. Recommendations to physicians practising psycho-analysis. *SE* 12: 111–20.

———. 1913. On beginning the treatment (further recommendations on the technique of psycho-analysis I). *SE* 12: 123–44.

———. 1914a. On narcissism: An introduction. *SE* 14: 73–102.

———. 1914b. Remembering, repeating and working-through (further recommendations on the techniques of psycho-analysis II). *SE* 12:147–56.

———. 1915. Instincts and their vicissitudes. *SE* 14: 117–40.

———. 1915 [1914]. Observations on transference-love (further recommendations on the technique of psycho-analysis III). *SE* 12: 159–71.

———. 1916. Some character-types met with in psycho-analytic work. *SE* 14: 311–33.

———. 1916–1917 [1915–17]. Introductory lectures on psycho-analysis. *SE* 15, 16.

———. 1921. *Group Psychology and the Analysis of the Ego. SE* 18: 69–143.

———. 1946. Bemerkungen über die Übertragungsliebe. In *Gesammelte Werke,* Volume 10, 306–21. edited by Anna Freud. London and Frankfurt am Main.

———. 1953–74. *The Standard Edition of the Complete Psychological Works of Sigmund Freud,* translated by James Strachey in collaboration with Anna Freud, assisted by Alix Strachey and Alan Tyson. 24 vols. London.

Friedman, Lawrence. 1991. A reading of Freud's *Papers on Technique. Psychoanalytic Quarterly* 60: 564–95.

Gifford, George E., Jr., ed. 1978a. *Psychoanalysis, Psychotherapy, and the New England Medical Scene, 1894–1944.* New York.

———. 1978b. George Arthur Waterman, 1872–1960, and office psychiatry. In *Psychoanalysis, Psychotherapy, and the New England Medical Scene, 1894–1944,* 227–41. New York.

Gordon, Linda. 1988. *Heroes of Their Own Lives: The Politics and History of Family Violence.* New York.

Greenacre, Phyllis. 1975. On reconstruction. *J. Amer. Psychoanal. Assn.* 23: 693–712.

Hale, Nathan G., Jr. 1971a. *Freud and the Americans: The Beginnings of Psychoanalysis in the United States, 1876–1917.* New York.

———, ed. 1971b. *James Jackson Putnam and Psychoanalysis: Letters between Putnam and Sigmund Freud, Ernest Jones, William James, Sandor Ferenczi, and Morton Prince, 1877–1917.* Cambridge, Mass.

———. 1995. *The Rise and Crisis of Psychoanalysis in the United States: Freud and the Americans, 1917–1985.* New York.

Hinsdale, Guy. 1910. *Hydrotherapy.* Philadelphia.

Jeliffe, Smith Ely. 1916. Technique of psychoanalysis. *Psychoanalytic Rev.* 3: 26–42, 161–75, 254–71, 394–405.

Jones, Ernest. 1945. Reminiscent notes on the early history of psycho-analysis in English-speaking countries. *Int. J. Psycho-Anal.* 26: 8–10.

———. 1959. *Free Associations: Memories of a Psycho-Analyst.* New York.

Jung, C. G. 1909. The association method. In *Experimental Researches,* vol. 2 of *The Collected Works of C. G. Jung,* edited by Sir Herbert Read, Michael Fordham, and Gerhard Adler; translated by R. F. C. Hull; executive editor, William McGuire. Princeton, 1981.

Kaplan, Louise J. 1991. *Female Perversions: The Temptations of Emma Bovary.* New York.

Kiceluk, Stephanie. 1992. The patient as sign and story: Disease pictures, life histories, and the first psychoanalytic case history. *J. Clin. Psychoanal.* 1: 333–68.

———. 1996. The disenchantment of Freud: Erasure and the problem of narrative construction in the case of Emmy von N. In *Proof and Persuasion: Essays on Authority, Objectivity, and Evidence,* edited by Suzanne Marchand and Elizabeth Lunbeck. Turnhout, Belgium.

Lacan, Jacques. 1985. Intervention on transference. In *Feminine Sexuality: Jacques Lacan and the école freudienne,* edited by Juliet Mitchell and Jacqueline Rose, translated by Jacqueline Rose. New York.

Laplanche, J., and J.-B. Pontalis. 1988. *The Language of Psychoanalysis.* Translated by Donald Nicholson-Smith. London.

Levertin, Alfred. 1893. *Dr. G. Zander's Medico-Mechanical Gymnastics: Its Method, Importance and Application.* Stockholm.

Lunbeck, Elizabeth. 1994. *The Psychiatric Persuasion: Knowledge, Gender, and Power in Modern America.* Princeton.

Mahony, Patrick J. 1986. *Freud and the Ratman.* New Haven.

Managers of the Adams Nervine Asylum. 1910. *Thirty-third Annual Report.* Boston.

———. 1917. *Fortieth Annual Report.* Boston.

Marx, Otto. 1978. Morton Prince and psychopathology. In *Psychoanalysis, Psychotherapy and the New England Medical Scene, 1894–1944,* edited by George E. Gifford, Jr., 155–62. New York.

Meissner, William W. 1979. A study on hysteria: Anna O. rediviva. *Annual of Psychoanalysis* 7: 17–52.

Menninger, Karl. 1961. Footprints. In *The Birth of an Institute: Twenty-Fifth Anniversary. The Boston Psychoanalytic Institute,* edited by Ives Hendrick, 127–51. Freeport, Maine.

Meyer, Adolf. 1905a. Normal and abnormal association. *Psychological Bull.* 2: 242–50.

———. 1905b. Abstract and review of Franz Riklin, "Analytische Untersuchungen der Symptome und Associationen eines Falles von Hysteria (Lina H.)" *Psychological Bull.* 2: 253–59.

———. 1906. Interpretation of obsessions. *Psychological Bull.* 3: 280–83.

Micale, Mark. 1995. *Approaching Hysteria: Disease and Its Interpretations.* Princeton.

Michaels, Robert. 2000. The case history. *J. Amer. Psychoanal. Assn.* 48: 355–75.

New England Hospital for Women and Children. 1908a. *Forty-sixth Annual Report.* Boston.

———. 1908b. Records of Surgical Specimens, 3 January–28 December 1908. Rare Books and Special Collections, Countway Library of Medicine.

Paskauskas, R. Andrew, ed. 1995. *The Complete Correspondence of Sigmund Freud and Ernest Jones, 1908–1939*. Cambridge, Mass.

Powell, Russell A., and Tore A. Nielson. 1998. Was Anna O.'s black snake hallucination a sleep paralysis nightmare? *Psychiatry* 61: 239–48.

Putnam, James Jackson. Papers. Courtway Library of Medicine. Boston.

———. 1906. Recent experiences in the treatment and study of hysteria at the Massachusetts General Hospital; with remarks on Freud's method of treatment by "Psycho-Analysis." *J. Ab. Psychol.* 1: 26–41.

Read, Stanford. 1920. Review of the recent psycho-analytical literature in English. *Int. J. Psycho-Anal.* 1: 68–85.

Rieff, Philip. 1963. Introduction to *Dora: An Analysis of a Case of Hysteria,* by Sigmund Freud. New York.

Sicherman, Barbara. 1978. Isador H. Coriat: The making of an American psychoanalyst. In *Psychoanalysis, Psychotherapy and the New England Medical Scene, 1894–1944,* edited by George E. Gifford, Jr., 163–80. New York.

Simon, Bennett. 1994. Fact and fantasy in the history of Freud's views on incest and seduction. *Psychiatric Clinics of North America* 17: 571–81.

Simon, Bennett, and Christopher Bullock. 1994. Incest and psychoanalysis: Are we ready to fully acknowledge, bear, and understand? *J. Amer. Psychoanal. Assn.* 42: 1261–82.

Southard, E. E., and Stearns, A. Warren. 1914. The margin of error in Psychopathic Hospital diagnoses. *Boston Medical and Surgical Journal* 171: 895–900.

Stern, Adolph. 1921. The American Psychoanalytical Association. *Int. J. Psycho-Anal.* 2: 251–53.

Strachey, James. 1958. Editorial introduction to papers on technique, by Sigmund Freud. *SE* 12: 85–88.

Taylor, Eugene. 1982. Louville Eugene Emerson: Psychotherapy, Harvard, and the early Boston scene. *Harvard Medical School Alumni Bull.* 56: 42–48.

Washburn, Frederic A. 1939. *The Massachusetts General Hospital: Its Development, 1900–1939.* Boston.

Wyman, Herbert M., and Stephen Rittenberg. 1992. Reflections on the written presentation of psychoanalytic clinical data: Necessary source and perennial problem. *J. Clin. Psychoanal.* 1: 323–32.

Index

MAR 1 7 2004